SAUL, BENJAMIN, AND THE EMERGENCE OF MONARCHY IN ISRAEL

ANCIENT ISRAEL AND ITS LITERATURE

Thomas C. Römer, General Editor

Editorial Board:
Susan Ackerman
Thomas B. Dozeman
Alphonso Groenewald
Shuichi Hasegawa
Konrad Schmid
Naomi A. Steinberg

Number 40

SAUL, BENJAMIN, AND THE EMERGENCE OF MONARCHY IN ISRAEL

Biblical and Archaeological Perspectives

Edited by

Joachim J. Krause, Omer Sergi, and Kristin Weingart

SBL PRESS

SBL PRESS
Atlanta

Copyright © 2020 by SBL Press

All rights reserved. No part of this work may be reproduced or transmitted in any form or by any means, electronic or mechanical, including photocopying and recording, or by means of any information storage or retrieval system, except as may be expressly permitted by the 1976 Copyright Act or in writing from the publisher. Requests for permission should be addressed in writing to the Rights and Permissions Office, SBL Press, 825 Houston Mill Road, Atlanta, GA 30329 USA.

Library of Congress Cataloging-in-Publication Data

Names: Krause, Joachim J., editor. | Sergi, Omer, 1977– editor. | Weingart, Kristin, 1974– editor.
Other titles: Ancient Israel and its literature ; no. 40.
Title: Saul, Benjamin and the emergence of monarchy in Israel : biblical and archaeological perspectives / edited by Joachim J. Krause, Omer Sergi, and Kristin Weingart.
Description: Atlanta : SBL Press, 2020. | Series: Ancient Israel and its literature ; 40 | Includes bibliographical references and index.
Identifiers: LCCN 2020012825 (print) | LCCN 2020012826 (ebook) | ISBN 9781628372816 (paperback) | ISBN 9780884144502 (hardback) | ISBN 9780884144519 (ebook)
Subjects: LCSH: Saul, King of Israel. | Benjamin (Biblical figure) | Bible. Samuel. | Bible. Kings. | Jews—Kings and rulers. | Monarchy—Palestine—History. | Excavations (Archaeology)—Palestine. | Palestine—Antiquities.
Classification: LCC BS579.K5 S38 2020 (print) | LCC BS579.K5 (ebook) | DDC 222/.4095—dc23
LC record available at https://lccn.loc.gov/2020012825
LC ebook record available at https://lccn.loc.gov/2020012826

Contents

Preface vii
Abbreviations ix

Saul, Benjamin, and the Emergence of Monarchy in Israel:
    Problems and Perspectives
    Joachim J. Krause, Omer Sergi, and Kristin Weingart 1

On Philistines and Early Israelite Kings: Memories and Perceptions
    Ido Koch 7

Saul and Highlands of Benjamin Update: The Role of Jerusalem
    Israel Finkelstein..33

Saul, David, and the Formation of the Israelite Monarchy:
    Revisiting the Historical and Literary Context of 1 Samuel 9–
    2 Samuel 5
    Omer Sergi 57

Possible Historical Settings of the Saul-David Narrative
    Wolfgang Oswald 93

The Land of Benjamin between the Emerging Kingdoms of
    Israel and Judah: A Historical Hypothesis on the Reign
    of Rehoboam
    Joachim J. Krause 111

Jeroboam and Benjamin: Pragmatics and Date of 1 Kings 11:26–40;
    12:1–20
    Kristin Weingart...133

Benjamin in Retrospective: Stages in the Creation of the Territory
   of the Benjamin Tribe
   Oded Lipschits 161

The Israelite Tribal System: Literary Fiction or Social Reality?
   Erhard Blum 201

Contributors 223
Ancient Sources Index 225
Place Names Index 232

Preface

The papers published in this volume were presented at the second Tübingen-Tel Aviv Research Colloquium held in Tübingen, 16–18 June 2017, under the title "Saul and Benjamin in Biblical and Archaeological Perspective." Established by the editors of the present volume in 2015, the Tübingen-Tel Aviv Research Colloquium series brings together the faculty of both universities in the fields of Hebrew Bible, archaeology, and history of ancient Israel. The colloquia set themselves to foster research on the history of ancient Israel.

Our heartfelt thanks are due to Deutsche Forschungsgemeinschaft (DFG) for a major grant in support of the 2017 colloquium; to the Tübingen staff, most notably to Sabine Rumpel, who made the conference run so smoothly; and to the editorial board directed by Thomas Römer, general editor, for accepting this volume into the Ancient Israel and Its Literature series.

Tübingen and Tel Aviv
March 2019
Joachim J. Krause
Omer Sergi
Kristin Weingart

Abbreviations

AASOR	Annual of the American Schools of Oriental Research
ÄAT	Ägypten und Altes Testament
AB	Anchor (Yale) Bible Commentary
ABS	Archaeology and Biblical Studies
ADPV	Abhandlungen des Deutschen Palästina-Vereins
AeL	*Egypt and the Levant*
AGAJU	Arbeiten zur Geschichte des antiken Judentums und des Urchristentums
AIL	Ancient Israel and Its Literature
AJA	*American Journal of Archaeology*
ANEM	Ancient Near Eastern Monographs
ANESSup	Ancient Near Eastern Studies Supplement
AOAT	Alter Orient und Altes Testament
AoF	*Altorientalische Forschungen*
ARC	*Archaeological Review From Cambridge*
ASORAR	American Schools of Oriental Research Archaeological Reports
ATANT	Abhandlungen zur Theologie des Alten und Neuen Testaments
ATD	Alte Testament Deutsch
BA	*Biblical Archaeologist*
BARIS	British Archaeological Review International Series
BASOR	*Bulletin of the American Schools of Oriental Research*
BES	*Bulletin of the Egyptological Seminar*
BETL	Bibliotheca Ephemerides Theologicae Lovanienses
BHS	Biblia Hebraica Stuttgartensia
Bib	*Biblica*
BibEnc	Biblical Encyclopedia
BibInt	*Biblical Interpretation*
BibInt	Biblical Interpretation Series

BJS	Brown Judaic Studies
BKAT	Biblischer Kommentar, Altes Testament
BWANT	Beiträge zur Wissenschaft vom Alten Testament
BZAW	Beihefte zur Zeitschrift für die alttestamentliche Wissenschaft
BO	*Bibliotheca Orientalis*, new series
CBC	Cambridge Bible Commentary
CBQ	*Catholic Biblical Quarterly*
CHANE	Culture and History of the Ancient Near East
CREJ	Collection de la Revue des Études juives
DSB	Daily Study Bible
EdF	Erträge der Forschung
EncBib	Cassuto, Umberto, et al., ed. *Encyclopedia Biblica*. Jerusalem: Bialik, 1965–1988.
ErIsr	*Eretz Israel*
FAT	Forschungen zum Alten Testament
FOTL	Forms of Old Testament Literature
FRLANT	Forschungen zur Religion und Literatur des Alten und Neuen Testaments
GAT	Grundrisse zum Alten Testament
HAT	Handbuch zum Alten Testament
HBAI	*Hebrew Bible and Ancient Israel*
HdO	Handbuch der Orientalistik
HSS	Harvard Semitic Studies
HThKAT	Herders theologischer Kommentar zum Alten Testament
IBC	Interpretation: A Bible Commentary for Teaching and Preaching
ICC	International Critical Commentary
IEJ	*Israel Exploration Journal*
JAEI	*Journal of Ancient Egyptian Interconnections*
JANES	*Journal of the Ancient Near Eastern Society*
JAOS	*Journal of the American Oriental Society*
JAR	*Journal of Anthropological Research*
JBL	*Journal of Biblical Literature*
JBS	Jerusalem Biblical Studies
JHS	*Journal of Hebrew Studies*
JNES	*Journal of Near Eastern Studies*
JNSL	*Journal of Northwest Semitic Languages*
JPOS	*Journal of the Palestine Oriental Society*

JSJ	*Journal for the Study of Judaism*
JSOT	*Journal for the Study of the Old Testament*
JSOTSup	Journal for the Study of the Old Testament Supplement
KAI	Donner, Herbert, and Wolfgang Röllig. *Kanaanäische und aramäische Inschriften*. 2nd ed. Wiesbaden: Harrassowitz, 1966–1969.
KAT	Kommentar zum Alten Testament
LB(A)	Late Bronze Age
LHBOTS	Library of Hebrew Bible/Old Testament Studies
MB	Middle Bronze Age
NEA	*Near Eastern Archaeology*
NEchtB	Neu Echter Bibel
OBO	Orbis Biblicus et Orientalis
ÖBS	*Österreichische Biblische Studien*
OJA	*Oxford Journal of Archaeology*
OIS	Oriental Institute Seminar
OLA	Orientalia Lovaniensia Analecta
OLZ	*Orientalistische Literaturzeitung*
ORA	Oriental Religions in Antiquity
OTL	Old Testament Library
OTS	Old Testament Studies
PAe	Probleme der Ägyptologie
PEQ	*Palestine Exploration Quarterly*
PJb	*Palästina-Jahrbuch*
RB	*Revue biblique*
RGTC	Répertoire Géographique des Textes Cunéiformes
SAOC	Studies in Ancient Oriental Civilizations
SBLMS	Society of Biblical Literature Monograph Series
SBLStBL	Society of Biblical Literature Studies in Biblical Literature
SBTS	Sources for Biblical and Theological Study
Sem	*Semitica*
SHCANE	Studies in the History and Culture of the Ancient Near East
SJOT	*Scandinavian Journal of the Old Testament*
SMNIA	Tel Aviv University Sonia and Marco Nadler Institute of Archaeology Monograph Series
StBoT	Studien zu den Boğazköy-Texten
SubBi	Subsidia Biblica
SymS	Symposium Series
TA	*Tel Aviv*

TAVO	Tübinger Atlas des Vorderen Orients
TQ	*Theologische Quartalschrift*
TRu	*Theologische Rundschau*, new series
Transeu	*Transeuphratène*
TynBul	*Tyndale Bulletin*
TZ	*Theologische Zeitschrift*
UF	*Ugarit-Forschungen*
UTB	Uni-Taschenbücher
VT	*Vetus Testamentum*
VTSup	Supplements to Vetus Testamentum
WMANT	Wissenschaftliche Monographien zum Alten und Neuen Testament
YNER	Yale Near Eastern Researches
ZABR	*Zeitschrift für altorientalische und biblische Rechtsgeschichte*
ZAH	*Zeitschrift für Althebräistik*
ZÄS	*Zeitschrift für ägyptische Sprache und Altertumskunde*
ZAW	*Zeitschrift für die alttestamentliche Wissenschaft*
ZBK	Zürcher Bibelkommentare
ZDPV	*Zeitschrift des deutschen Palästina-Vereins*

Saul, Benjamin, and the Emergence of Monarchy in Israel: Problems and Perspectives

Joachim J. Krause, Omer Sergi, and Kristin Weingart

The formation of the Israelite monarchy lies at the heart of ancient Israel studies from its early beginnings and involves historical, archaeological, and biblical studies. From a historical point of view, the formation of the Israelite monarchy should be seen in the context of the transitional period between the Late Bronze and the Iron Ages, a period that saw the formation of local territorial polities throughout the Levant. From an archaeological point of view, the debate relates to the archaeological research of the southern Levant in general and the central Canaanite hill country in particular, with a special emphasis on Jerusalem and its environs. Last but certainly not least, the issue requires the study of biblical traditions regarding the early monarchy that are embedded in the books of Samuel and Kings.

Recent historical and archaeological studies cast doubt on much of the historicity of the Saul and David traditions in Samuel–Kings, especially with regard to the reconstruction of a great united monarchy under the rule of David from Jerusalem. The main gap contemporaneous scholarship faces is between the biblical narrative—according to which the monarchy emerged first in Jerusalem and only later in Israel (Shechem, Tirzah, and Samaria)—and between historically and archaeologically based reconstructions, which tend to demonstrate the exact opposite: Israel and Judah developed separately, side by side during the Iron IIA, and it was Israel that grew up to be a territorial monarchy before Judah, which only flourished in its shadow.

Such a historical reconstruction calls for fresh exegetical approaches to the biblical traditions about Saul, David, and the early monarchy in Jerusalem. A most interesting focal point is the place of Benjamin within the biblical traditions about the early monarchy, for according to the biblical narrative this region, situated north of Jerusalem, was the home of the early Israelite monarchy under the reign of Saul (1 Sam 9–14). It is a matter of lasting dispute, however, whether Benjamin and Saul were affiliated with Israel or with Judah. Yet it is exactly this dispute that is embedded in the question of the early formation of the Israelite monarchy and that can bridge the gap between the biblical narrative and the archaeologically based historical reconstruction.

To this matter the following papers are devoted. As for archaeology, they present the most recent evidence pertaining to the emergence of state and regional power structures and propose historical reconstructions based on that evidence. Exegetically, the date, textual pragmatics, and historical value of biblical texts dealing with the emergence of monarchy in Israel and Judah and the allocation of the Benjaminite territory come under discussion. This integration of approaches allows for a nuanced and differentiated picture of one of the most crucial periods in the history of ancient Israel. Methodologically, it bridges a gap often felt between studies approaching the emergence of monarchy in Israel predominantly or exclusively from one of the two angles. Rather than attempting to harmonize archaeological data and biblical texts or to supplement each respective approach by integrating only a fitting portion of data stemming from the other, both perspectives come into their own. The result is a nuanced picture of diverging results as well as surprising overlaps.

All in all, the essays collected in this volume reflect on many aspects of the early Israelite monarchy: state formation, local and collective identities, southern Canaan in the Iron I–IIA, the composition and redaction of the literary traditions about Saul and David, and the historical value of these traditions. Eventually, though using different methods and highlighting different aspects of the subject at hand, they all aim to ponder the question of the united monarchy under Saul and David in light of current historical and archaeological discourse.

Commencing the discussion, Ido Koch details "On Philistines and the Early Israelite Kings: Memory and Perceptions." The Philistines are the leitmotif in the stories of the early monarchy. Their aggressive and foreign character plays a crucial role in the cohesion of the Israelites and the establishment of the monarchy, that is, the rise and fall of Saul and the rise of David. This literary image is at the heart of the common scholarly assumption that the struggle with the Philistines was a landmark in the creation of a highlander social identity. This assumption has been further expanded in recent archaeological discourse to explain the distribution of various material remains as reflecting either the Philistine incursion or the highlander resistance. However, Koch questions both assumptions by tracing and dating the old memories of the Philistines in the stories of the early monarchy, especially those of Saul.

In "Saul and Highlands of Benjamin Update: The Role of Jerusalem," Israel Finkelstein revisits his hypothesis of a tenth-century BCE north Israelite territorial entity centered in the Benjamin plateau hinted at in pre-Deuteronomistic biblical material on the house of Saul. Following an archaeological reconstruction of the highland polities in the Iron IIA, he suggests that Saul's kingdom encompassed the entire central hill country between Jerusalem and Shechem. Finkelstein views this polity as the forerunner of the kingdom of Israel, where, based on the Saul memories, the concept of the united monarchy came into being in the days of Jeroboam II.

Picking up the thread, Omer Sergi's "Saul, David, and the Formation of the Israelite Monarchy: Revisiting the Historical and Literary Context of 1 Samuel 9–2 Samuel 5" contests one of the most accepted hypotheses in biblical scholarship, namely, that the biblical traditions about Saul originated in the kingdom of Israel and that they arrived in Judah only after the fall of Samaria (720 BCE) and stimulated the composition of the stories about David's rise, which are dated, accordingly, to the seventh century BCE. It is therefore assumed that the connection between David and Saul is only literary. Examining nuanced archaeological data from the central Canaanite hill country in the Iron IIA, Sergi argues for the formation of a polity that encompassed both Benjamin and Jerusalem as early as the tenth century BCE. On this basis he sets out to analyze the biblical traditions about Saul and David in 1 Sam 9–2 Sam 5, arguing that they should not be read as an allegory but rather as a story about the formation of the Israelite monarchy in Jerusalem. Bringing the kinship identity of Israel to the fore, he argues that in these stories *Israel* does not refer to the northern kingdom but rather to the kinship identity of the inhabitants of Benjamin and Jerusalem.

In this line, Wolfgang Oswald explores "Possible Historical Settings of the Saul-David Narrative." The Saul-David narrative (*1 Sam 9–2 Sam 8) deals with the legitimacy of the rule of King David and at the same time with the legitimacy of the Davidic dynasty. The legitimacy of the Judahite dynasty is obviously contested by Benjaminite elites, and the purpose of the narrative is to defend it vis-à-vis these Benjaminites. While the point of dispute is kingship over Israel, the parties of the dispute are Benjamin and Judah. As is evident in 1 Chr 10, this dispute was an enduring issue in the history of Judah. Oswald's assumption is that periods of change and uncertainty in the relation between Judah and Benjamin were the occasions in which the problem of the legitimacy of the Davidic dynasty became virulent. He identifies and describes four such historical settings for the successive development, first of the Saul-David tradition, then the Saul-David narrative, and eventually the reworking of the narrative.

Joachim J. Krause focuses on the early phase of the kingdom of Judah in "The Land of Benjamin between the Emerging Kingdoms of Israel and Judah: A Historical Hypothesis on the Reign of Rehoboam." In the context of a rather controversial debate concerning the great united monarchy as depicted in the biblical accounts of David and Solomon, doubting the very existence of Solomon's son and successor Rehoboam currently is at one end of the spectrum; at the other end are mere paraphrases of the biblical record. Working toward a balanced picture between these polar positions, Krause seeks to put a piece of the puzzle dubbed "the trouble with Benjamin" in its proper place. To this end, in a first step the textual material on Rehoboam is reevaluated as to its varying degrees of value as a source. This discrimination allows Krause to correlate, in a second step, the external data available, namely, the Egyptian evidence for the campaign of Shoshenq I to Palestine. This campaign must have had considerable implications for the rival kingdoms' struggle for Benjamin, as was shown cogently in an analysis by Israel Finkelstein. Against Finkelstein, however, the combined interpretation of textual material, both from the Bible and the Karnak inscription, and archaeological data points to Rehoboam's reign as the historical context of this development. In light of these considerations, Krause sketches a historical hypothesis: given the vital necessity for small Judah to define and defend the border vis-à-vis its stronger neighbor to the north, especially in view of the vulnerable position of Jerusalem and taking into account that Judah's chances to succeed in an escalation of the latent conflict were rather scant, the intervention of a foreign power pursuing its own goals in the region could have opened a window of opportunity for Rehoboam in his struggle for Benjamin.

Turning to the Northern Kingdom in the same phase, Kristin Weingart writes on "Jeroboam and Benjamin: Pragmatics and Date of 1 Kings 11:26–40; 12:1–20." The biblical accounts in 1 Kgs 11:26–40 and 12:1–20 are, in all likelihood, not a historical portrayal of the foundation of the kingdom of Israel. But when and to what end were the kingdom's origins presented this way? Based on the reconstruction of a pre-Deuteronomistic base layer, Weingart focuses on the textual pragmatics and historical settings of 1 Kgs 11–12. She is able to show that, not only was Jeroboam originally introduced in a favorable light, but the separation of the Israelite tribes from Judah was also presented as a justified and consequent step prompted by Rehoboam's pretension and bad governance. At the same time, the depiction of Jeroboam that models him as a second David reveals a high degree of veneration for David. The latter is in keeping with the manner in which the origins of the Northern Kingdom are described: not as a glorious founding myth but rather with a legitimatory and almost apologetic tone. The narrative profile, literary stratigraphy, and textual pragmatics of the texts point to a northern Israelite setting and a date before the end of the Northern Kingdom in 720 BCE. Insights into the pragmatics and literary history of the texts also shed light on the development of the peculiar addition within 1 Kgs 11:26–40 that implies that ten tribes for Jeroboam and one tribe for Rehoboam resemble twelve pieces of Ahijah's garment.

The last two essays deal with the question of the tribal identity of Israel, especially in regard to Benjamin. "Benjamin in Retrospective: Stages in the Creation of the Territory of the Benjamin Tribe," by Oded Lipschits, suggests that the biblical territory of the tribe of Benjamin is a late artificial aggregation of two distinct historical and geopolitical units that were never part of the same geopolitical region: Benjamin (= "the son of the south") was a small tribe around Bethel, the southern Ephraim hills and Jericho, connected to the northern hill country, whereas the Gibeon plateau was part of the agricultural hinterland of Jerusalem. The destruction of the kingdom of Israel was the point of departure for a new period in the hill country, when for the first time the small, hilly southern entity did not have a larger and stronger northern neighbor. It was only in the days of Josiah that Judah could conquer the area of Bethel and Jericho and extend its border up to this line. After the 586 BCE destruction of Jerusalem, the city was severed from its agricultural hinterland, and the Babylonians created the district of Mizpah to the north of Jerusalem. Greater Benjamin became a unified administrative region, with Jerusalem as a marginal component at its southern border. However, soon after, already in the early Persian period, when the returnees from Babylon renewed the status of Jerusalem, the counterpolemic claims against Benjamin and Mizpah and in favor of Jerusalem and Judah could be written, especially in texts dealing with the premonarchic period. Based on these observations, Lipschits analyzes the traditions about Saul and David and the role of Benjamin in the formation of the Jerusalemite monarchy. He concludes that the first monarch of the kingdom of Jerusalem, who came from the agricultural hinterland to the north of the city, was killed and that his kingdom was taken by David, originally from the agricultural hinterland to the south of Jerusalem. David succeeded in conquering Jerusalem and uniting it with the Judahite territory in the southern Judean hills around Hebron. In the Jerusalemite historiography, Saul was connected with the non-Israelite city of Gibeon and pushed to the north. The late use of the label *Benjaminite* also had deceptive intentions: it was aimed at distancing Saul from Jerusalem, labeling him as *Israelite* and setting him apart from the *Judahite* house of David.

Concluding the volume, in "The Israelite Tribal System: Literary Fiction or Social Reality?," Erhard Blum examines the antiquity of the Israelite tribal system in view of current hypotheses that propose to understand it as a late literary construction. He refers to fundamental insights of social anthropology and discusses the epigraphic attestation of kinship-based social entities, which are also mentioned in the biblical texts: Manassite clans referred to in the Samaria ostraca and the tribe of Gad mentioned in the Mesha Stela. In the light of this evidence, a late invention of the tribal system after 587 or 720 BCE proves untenable from a historical point of view. Israel's kinship identity is rather to be understood as an old and important factor in the social reality of ancient Israelites. In addition, the roles of Benjamin and Judah in the tribal system have interesting implications for the understanding and the much-debated issue of the existence of a united kingdom of David.

In sum, by presenting different approaches regarding the role of Saul and Benjamin in the foundation of the Israelite monarchy, the present volume aims to contribute to a more nuanced discussion of these matters and to shed some new light on the early Israelite monarchy in history and historiography.

On Philistines and Early Israelite Kings: Memories and Perceptions

Ido Koch

1. Introduction

The Philistines serve as an important literary device in the tales of the emergence of monarchy in Israel: they are the Other against whom the plot is constructed. According to the grand narrative in 1 Sam 4–2 Sam 8, the Philistines are the fierce warriors who threatened the highland tribes who, in response, united and established kingship. Decades of struggle culminated in the coronation of Saul, his heroic deeds, his downfall, and the rise of David, who ultimately vanquished the Philistines. From the moment of their defeat onward, this Other appears only sporadically in the stories of the monarchy in Israel (e.g., 1 Kgs 15:15, 27) and Judah (e.g., 2 Kgs 18:8).

For many years this sequence of the formative days of the emergence of monarchy in Israel dominated historical reconstructions and was synchronized with ancient written sources and material remains. But the assumingly perfect accord of biblical texts, Egyptology, and archaeology suffers from major flaws that preclude accepting the historicity of the grand narrative. Instead, an alternative interpretation of the material remains involved is presented and a framework for reconstructing several genuine memories of the Philistines in the stories of the early monarchy is proposed.

2. The Early Iron Age Philistine Problem

Western European literature and art has preserved the cultural memory of the Philistine association with the Other. One major reason has been the decision of Greek translators to use the Greek word ἀλλοφύλων ("foreigners") for most occurrences of the name Philistine (not including translations of the Pentateuch, Joshua, and the B text of Judges), a term that was used in other Hellenistic period writings such as the book of Maccabees.¹ Embraced as a prime character in Christian theology, David and his deeds influenced Western European literature and art and, alongside the stories of Samson and Saul, constantly created a contemporary depiction of the Philistines.² A famous anecdote is the naming of seventeenth-century CE uneducated townspeople of Jena by the students of the local university as *Philister* after a violent clash that ensued following a sermon delivered by their pastor who preached of the heroic death of Samson.³ During the following centuries the renewed application of the term Philistine proliferated in European literature as best seen in *Culture and Anarchy* by Matthew Arnold (1865), where it is used to describe uncultured and uneducated individuals, mostly of low class.⁴

Inevitably, this was the setting of the early academic study of the Philistines. Equipped with a thorough knowledge of the biblical, Greek, and Latin literary corpora, scholars synchronized the biblical history with other sources to create a coherent historical narrative. Beginning as early as Stephanus of Byzantium, scholars combined biblical references of the Philistine origins from Crete with Homeric literature. By the seventeenth century, linguistic analyses paralleled various terms attested in the Hebrew

---

1. Rodrigo de Sousa, "The Land Is Full of Foreign Children: Language and Ideology in LXX Isa. 2.6," in *Studies on the Text and Versions of the Hebrew Bible in Honour of Robert Gordon*, ed. Geoffrey Kahn and Diana Lipton, VTSup 149 (Leiden: Brill, 2011), 188–89, with earlier literature. Cf. the more nuanced vocabulary used by Josephus when dealing with the Philistines in his *Jewish Antiquities*; see Michael Avioz, "The Philistines in Josephus' Writings," *TZ* 71 (2015): 144–55.

2. Raymond-Jean Frontain and Jan Wojcik, eds., *The David Myth in Western Literature* (West Lafayette: Purdue University Press, 1980); Colum Hourihane, ed., *King David in the Index of Christian Art* (Princeton: Princeton University Press, 2002); Nevada Levi DeLapp, *The Reformed David(s) and the Question of Resistance to Tyranny: Reading the Bible in the Sixteenth and Seventeenth Centuries*, LHBOTS, Scriptural Traces 601 (London: Bloomsbury, 2014).

3. Dieter Arendt, "Brentanos Philister—Rede am Ende des romantischen Jahrhunderts oder Der Philister—Krieg und seine unrühmliche Kapitulation," *Orbis Litterarum* 55 (2000): 84.

4. Robert Henry Super, ed., *Culture and Anarchy: With Friendship's Garland and Some Literary Essays* (Ann Arbor: University of Michigan Press, 1965).

Bible with Greek counterparts, arguing, for example, that the Philistines once belonged to Greece's pre-Hellenic society, the πελασγοί, the Pelasgians, who, according to this scenario, migrated to the southern Levant.[5] Another angle was added to the Philistine story with the commencement of the study of Egyptology and the decipherment of hieroglyphs, which supplied written and pictorial sources that commemorated the victories of Ramesses III (early twelfth century BCE) against the Philistines and other warrior groups. Special attention was given to a specific scene in the relief depicting a land battle. There, Philistine warriors are seen accompanied by women and children on carts. This was interpreted as depicting the migration of the Philistines from the Aegean. In light of the biblical references to the Philistine struggle with the Israelites in the days of the Judges (Judg 3:31; 13–16), it was concluded that following their battles with Ramesses III the Philistines settled in their new homeland: Philistia.[6]

This synchronized framework of the arrival of the Philistines and their struggle with the Israelites has been the dominant paradigm in the archaeology of Palestine since the late nineteenth century CE.[7] Archaeologists working in Ottoman- and British-ruled Palestine identified these events in the material remains unearthed in their large-scale excavations: The destruction of the Late Bronze settlements was associated either with the Israelites—who were supposedly documented in the Merenptah Stele as present in the country—or with the newly arrived Philistines.[8] Moreover, it led to the abandonment of the traditional image of the Philistine as a savage and was replaced with a definition of "Philistine material culture" as a sophisticated, technologically advanced urban society, which was

---

5. Ilan Sharon, "Philistine Bichrome Painted Pottery: Scholarly Ideology and Ceramic Typology," in *Studies in the Archaeology of Israel and Neighboring Lands in Memory of Douglas L. Esse*, ed. Samuel R. Wolf, SAOC 59 (Chicago: Oriental Institute of the University of Chicago, 2001), 558–59.

6. Probably the most influential was the historical reconstruction presented by Gaston Maspero, *Histoire ancienne des peuples de l'Orient classique* (Paris: Hachette & Cie, 1875).

7. R. A. Stewart Macalister, *The Philistines: Their History and Civilization*, Schweich Lecture 1911 (London: Oxford University Press, 1914).

8. See, e.g., the reconstruction of the settlement history of Tell Beit-Mirsim during the Iron I by William F. Albright, *The Excavation of Tell Beit Mirsim III: The Iron Age*, AASOR 21–22 (New Haven: American Schools of Oriental Research, 1943), 36–37. For a revised perspective see Raphael Greenberg, "New Light on the Early Iron Age at Tell Beit Mirsim," *BASOR* 265 (1987): 55–80.

compared to its counterpart, the rural "Israelite material culture."[9] Prime attention was given to pottery forms and styles, cultic objects, architectural concepts, and dietary practices. The presence, absence, and disappearance of these material remains were interpreted as reflecting the Philistine-Israelite struggle described in the stories of the early monarchy.

But as time passed each of the disciplines involved in the Philistine paradigm developed an inner discourse on the various elements constituting the grand narrative of the Philistine migration from the Aegean, settlement in the Levant, and struggle with the Israelites. From the archaeological perspective, Philistine archaeology, that is, the subdiscipline studying the material remains of southwest Israel/Palestine during the Iron I, is flourishing. The reaction to a growing criticism regarding old paradigms of mass migration and complete population turnover and the growing influence of social archaeology brought about a decade of theory-based scholarship that underlines complexity and multivocality, characterized by a nuanced study of the remains from sites identified with the Philistine prime cities.[10] One specific hypothesis continues the

---

9. For the Philistine material culture, see Trude Dothan, *The Philistines and Their Material Culture* (New Haven: Yale University Press, 1982); Amihai Mazar, "The Emergence of the Philistine Material Culture," *IEJ* 35 (1985): 95–107; Trude Dothan and Moshe Dothan, *People of the Sea: The Search for the Philistines* (New York: Macmillan 1992); Lawrence E. Stager, "The Impact of the Sea Peoples in Canaan (1185–1050 BCE)," in *The Archaeology of Society in the Holy Land*, ed. Thomas E. Levy (London: Leicester University Press, 1995), 332–48; Tristan J. Barako, "The Philistine Settlement as Mercantile Phenomenon?," *AJA* 104 (2000): 513–30. For Israelite material culture, see, e.g., William G. Dever, "Ceramics, Ethnicity, and the Question of Israel's Origins," *BA* 58 (1995): 200–213; but see the critique and revision already in Israel Finkelstein, "Ethnicity and Origin of the Iron I Settlers in the Highlands of Canaan: Can the Real Israel Stand Up?" *BA* 59 (1996): 198–212.

10. David Ben-Shlomo et al., "Cooking Identities: Aegean-style Cooking Jugs and Cultural Interaction in Iron Age Philistia and Neighboring Regions," *AJA* 112 (2008): 225–46; Assaf Yasur-Landau, "The Role of the Canaanite Population in the Aegean Migration to the Southern Levant in the Late Second Millennium BCE," in *Materiality and Social Practice: Transformative Capacities of Intercultural Encounters*, ed. Joseph Maran and Philipp W. Stockhammer (Oxford: Oxbow, 2012), 191–97; Louise A. Hitchcock and Aren M. Maeir, "Beyond Creolization and Hybridity: Entangled and Transcultural Identities in Philistia," *ARC* 28 (2013): 51–74; Aren M. Maeir, Louise A. Hitchcock, and Liora Kolska Horwitz, "On the Constitution and Transformation of Philistine Identity," *OJA* 32 (2013): 1–38; Avraham Faust, "The 'Philistine Tomb' at Tel 'Eton: Culture Contact, Colonialism, and Local Responses

biblically derived line of thought that the unification of the highland tribes occurred due to the Philistine threat: the resistance to the Philistines led to the rejection of the practices associated with the aggressors and thus, eventually, to the Israelite ethnogenesis.[11] Soon after that, a similar model was projected over several settlements in the lowlands that were described as populated by the remnant of the Canaanites who had survived the Philistine conquest: trapped between the Philistines and the emerging Israelites, the inhabitants of these communities were credited with their own social self-definition, adopting or rejecting practices associated with either of their neighbors.[12]

Yet from the point of view of Egyptology and biblical studies, the picture is far different. For the former, there is one major obstacle: the localization of Ramesses III's terrestrial battle against the Philistines in the southern Levant was driven by historical preconceptions. The texts and the iconography point to a northern Levantine location, in the land of Amurru; not a single toponym from the southern Levant is mentioned.[13]

---

in Iron Age Shephelah, Israel," *JAR* 71 (2015): 195–230; Shirly Ben-Dor Evian, "Ramesses III and the 'Sea-Peoples': Towards a New Philistine Paradigm," *OJA* 36 (2017): 267–85; Maeir and Hitchcock, "The Appearance, Formation and Transformation of Philistine Culture: New Perspectives and New Finds," in *"Sea Peoples" Up-to-Date: New Research on Transformation in the Eastern Mediterranean in the Thirteenth–Eleventh Centuries BCE*, ed. Peter M. Fischer and Teresa Bürge, Contributions to the Chronology of Eastern Mediterranean 35 (Vienna: Österreichischen Akademie der Wissenschaften, 2017), 149–62; Maeir and Hitchcock, "Rethinking the Philistines: A 2017 Perspective," in *Rethinking Israel: Studies in the History and Archaeology of Ancient Israel in Honor of Israel Finkelstein*, ed. Oded Lipschits, Yuval Gadot, and Matthew J. Adams (Winona Lake, IN: Eisenbrauns, 2017), 247–66.

11. Avraham Faust, *Israel's Ethnogenesis: Settlement, Interaction, Expansion and Resistance* (London: Equinox, 2006).

12. Shlomo Bunimovitz and Zvi Lederman, "The Archaeology of Border Communities: Renewed Excavations at Tel Beth-Shemesh, Part 1: The Iron Age," *NEA* 72 (2009): 114–42; Bunimovitz and Lederman, "Canaanite Resistance: The Philistines and Beth-Shemesh—A Case Study from Iron Age I," *BASOR* 364 (2011): 37–51; Avraham Faust and Hayah Katz, "Philistines, Israelites and Canaanites in the Southern Trough Valley during the Iron Age I," *AeL* 21 (2011): 231–47.

13. Itamar Singer, "Egyptians, Canaanites, and Philistines in the Period of the Emergence of Israel," in *From Nomadism To Monarchy: Archaeological and Historical Aspects of Early Israel*, ed. Israel Finkelstein and Nadav Na'aman (Jerusalem: Yad Ben-Zvi, 1994), 291 n. 52 with earlier literature; Dan'el Kahn, "The Campaign of Ramesses III against Philistia," *JAEI* 3.4 (2011): 3; Shirly Ben-Dor Evian, "The Battles between

The twelfth-century BCE date for the settlement of the Philistines—a major pin for the Philistine synchronism—must be excluded from consideration. From the biblical perspective, the early date of composition of the stories on pre- and early-monarchic Israel was questioned long ago and their historical value have been the subject of debate since the 1990s.[14] In sum, there are no anchors to identify the Philistines with the inhabitants of southwestern Israel/Palestine during the Iron I. From that point until a reference to Philistia is made in inscriptions of Adad-Nirrari III (811–783 BCE),[15] nothing is known about their history during these three centuries: Were they unified or divided? Did they settle in the northern Levant before they arrived in the southern Levant? When did they arrive?

Lastly, clustering various material remains together and labeling them Philistine (or any other) material culture (even for a period when their presence in the region is beyond question) is highly problematic.[16] First, these ethnonyms reflect the ancient writers' perceptions of social structures rather than the historical groups they refer to; they are literary constructs, used by the writers for their own agenda in any given period and in various roles. Second, modern scholars' comprehension of ethnonyms is complicated even further, since each is influenced by the historical narratives in their subconscious, and their own perception of contemporaneous ethnicities. Assembling all attestations of an ethnonym as reflecting the same group over centuries ignores the flexibility of their components, which includes and excludes potential members. Their projection over material remains is therefore an interpretation of an interpretation, one that does

---

Ramesses III and the Sea-Peoples: When, Where and Who? An Iconic Analysis of the Egyptian Reliefs," *ZÄS* 143 (2016): 151–68.

14. There is an enormous amount of scholarship dealing with the Philistine narratives in the Hebrew Bible. For the Samson stories, see summaries in Philippe Guillaume, *Waiting for Josiah: The Judges*, JSOTSup 385 (London: T&T Clark, 2004), 155–59 with earlier bibliography. For the stories in the book of Samuel, see the scholarly opinions in this volume.

15. Ariel M. Bagg, *Die Orts-und Gewässernamen der neuassyrischen Zeit: Die Levante*, RGTC 7.1 (Wiesbaden: Reichert, 2007), 189–91.

16. Susan E. Sherratt, "'Ethnicities,' 'Ethnonyms,' and Archaeological Labels: Whose Ideologies and Whose Identities?," in *Archaeological Perspectives on the Transition and Transformation of Culture in the Eastern Mediterranean*, ed. Joanne Clarke, Levant Supplementary Series 2 (Oxford: Oxbow, 2005), 25–38; Raz Kletter, "In the Footsteps of Bagira: Ethnicity, Archaeology, and 'Iron Age I Ethnic Israel,'" *Approaching Religion* 4.2 (2014): 2–15.

not leave space for additional social identities that were not commemorated in the rather limited textual evidence.

3. Southwest Israel/Palestine during the Iron I: An Alternative View

The pots-and-people paradigm of Philistine material culture has been probed repeatedly. In response, various explanations have been suggested regarding the changes observed in the material remains of the Iron I in southwest Israel/Palestine.[17] One line of reasoning argues that the Iron I remains must be considered in light of the previous period, reflecting the societal regeneration and reorientation following the collapse of the Egyptian Empire.[18] In short, a social order based on interaction with the Egyptian court and its agents had been established during the long period of Egyptian hegemony in the southern Levant (sixteenth to twelfth centuries BCE), which is best seen through the many innovations in the practices of the local elite, as it affected cult, iconography, diet, architecture, and

---

17. John F. Brug, *A Literary and Archaeological Study of the Philistines*, BARIS 265 (Oxford: BAR, 1985); Susan E. Sherratt, "'Sea Peoples' and the Economic Structure of the Late Second Millennium in the Eastern Mediterranean," in *Mediterranean Peoples in Transition: Thirteenth to Early Tenth Centuries BCE, in Honor of Trude Dothan*, ed. Seymour Gitin, Amihai Mazar, and Ephraim Stern (Jerusalem: Israel Exploration Society, 1998), 292–313; Sherratt, "The Mediterranean Economy: 'Globalization' at the End of the Second Millennium B.C.E.," in *Symbiosis, Symbolism, and the Power of the Past: Canaan, Ancient Israel, and Their Neighbors from the Late Bronze Age through Roman Palaestina*, ed. William G. Dever and Seymour Gitin (Winona Lake, IN: Eisenbrauns, 2003), 37–62; Robert Drews, "Canaanites and Philistines," *JSOT* 81 (1998): 39–61; Drews, "Medinet Habu: Oxcarts, Ships, and Migration Theories," *JNES* 59 (2000): 161–90; Alexander A. Bauer, "Cities of the Sea: Maritime Trade and the Origin of Philistine Settlement in the Early Iron Age Southern Levant," *OJA* 17 (1998): 149–68; Bauer, "The Sea Peoples as an Emergent Phenomenon," in *ΑΘΥΡΜΑΤΑ: Critical Essays on the Archaeology of the Eastern Mediterranean in Honour of E. Susan Sherratt*, ed. Yoannis Galanakis, Toby C. Wilkinson, and John Bennet (Oxford: Archaeopress, 2014), 32–40.

18. Sharon, "Philistine Bichrome," 600–601; Ido Koch, *The Shadow of Egypt: Colonial Encounters in Southwest Canaan during the Late Bronze Age and Early Iron Age* [Hebrew] (Jerusalem: Yad Ben-Zvi, 2018), 91–98; Koch, "Collapse and Regeneration in Southwest Canaan during the Late Second Millennium BCE," in *From Nomadism to Monarchy? Thirty Year Update*, ed. Ido Koch, Omer Sergi, and Oded Lipschits (University Park: Penn State University Press, forthcoming).

burial practices.[19] By the late thirteenth and early twelfth centuries BCE all seats of this elite had been destroyed. Ashkelon, Gezer, and Yenoam were captured by Merenptah following revolts; the consequences leading to the destruction of the other sites are still shrouded in mystery.[20]

From the debris emerged a new and fragmented social order. Some of the old centers of power, such as Megiddo, were renewed and may have hosted the successors of the previous elite. In other regions new centers were established, reflecting fluctuation in the distribution of power that shifted from the old centers that flourished during the Late Bronze II to new centers that emerged during the Iron I.[21] The prime example is the decline in the status of Gezer and Gath and the rise of Tel Miqne/Ekron as the large urban center of the region. Luxuriating in the withdrawal of the Egyptian suzerain coupled with major developments in local nonfood agriculture, predominantly specialized animal exploitation and large-scale textile production, the society based at Ekron and neighboring sites had greater wealth in its hands than ever before.[22]

The residents of Iron I Ekron had a sturdier economic and social base than their predecessors and were able to reinforce their trade relations with other regions, exchanging concepts and technologies. Egypt at the time had lost much of its strength, internally as well as externally; the possibility also existed that the weakness of Egypt led the regenerated society in southwest Canaan to reject part of its heritage, which led to localization of non-Egyptian practices mostly from Cyprus: pottery production (mostly Cypriot and Anatolian background), textile production (unknown origin), figurines (Aegean-style), construction of hearths (Cypriot-style), burial customs (North Levantine, but also Egyptian),

---

19. Koch, *Shadow of Egypt*, 81–87, 101–12; Koch, "The Egyptian-Canaanite Interface as Colonial Encounter: A View from Southwest Canaan," *JAEI* 18 (2018): 24–39; Ido Koch et al., "Amulets in Context: A View from Late Bronze Age Tel Azekah," *JAEI* 16 (2017): 9–24.

20. Jesse M. Millek, "Sea Peoples, Philistines, and the Destruction of Cities: A Critical Examination of Destruction Layers 'Caused' by the 'Sea Peoples,'" in Fischer and Bürge, *"Sea Peoples" Up-to-Date*, 113–40.

21. Ido Koch, "Settlements and Interactions in the Shephelah during the Late Second through Early First Millennia BCE," in *The Shephelah during the Iron Age: Recent Archaeological Studies*, ed. Oded Lipschits and Aren M. Maeir (Winona Lake, IN: Eisenbrauns, 2017), 183–86.

22. Ido Koch, "Early Philistia Revisited and Revised," in Lipschits, *Rethinking Israel*, 196–98 with literature.

and cooking traditions (Aegean-style).²³ Several of these practices, mostly those on the household level, were probably brought by newcomers; based on Late Bronze Age written sources, these might have included skilled workers, sailors, and merchants seeking new markets alongside others looking for new opportunities.²⁴ As time passed, these innovations were abandoned or further developed, a process in the making that was shared by several communities, and mainly Tel Miqne, which selectively adopted and adapted practices and concepts that were usable in the local context.

In sum, the transformations observed in the archaeological record of Iron I southwest Canaan should be understood in light of the context of the period: The character of the local society's integration with Egypt that greatly affected the trajectories of their disintegration and the consequent regionalization and societal reorientations. It presented an opportunity for individuals and groups to forge new alliances and to acquire wealth and influence, leading to reconfiguration of regional societal complexity and to the emergence of new social structures and new modes of interaction.

4. Musing on the Philistines in the Stories of the Early Monarchy

Our knowledge of the Philistines is largely based on non-Philistine written sources. Besides a seventh-century BCE royal inscription from Ekron all other sources are Egyptian, Assyrian, Babylonian, and biblical.²⁵ We are therefore relying on external views.

---

23. Laura B. Mazow, "Competing Material Culture: Philistine Settlement at Tel Miqne-Ekron in the Early Iron Age," in *Material Culture Matters: Essays on the Archaeology of the Southern Levant in Honor of Seymour Gitin*, ed. John R. Spencer, Robert A. Mullins, and Aaron J. Brody (Winona Lake, IN: Eisenbrauns, 2014), 131–63; Ben Shlomo et al., "Cooking Identities"; Hitchcock and Maeir, "Beyond Creolization"; Maeir et al., "On the Constitution"; Yasur-Landau, "Role of the Canaanite Population."

24. For commercial diasporas during the Late Bronze Age, see, e.g., Marie-Henriette Gates, "Maritime Business in the Bronze Age Eastern Mediterranean: The View from Its Ports," in *Intercultural Contacts in the Ancient Mediterranean: Proceedings of the International Conference at the Netherlands-Flemish Institute in Cairo, 25th to 29th October 2008*, ed. Kim Duistermaat and Ilona Regulski, OLA 202 (Leuven: Peeters, 2011), 388 with further literature.

25. For the Ekron inscription, see Seymour Gitin, Trude Dothan, and Joseph Naveh, "A Royal Dedicatory Inscription from Ekron," *IEJ* 47 (1997): 1–16.

Glimpses of the early Philistines can be found in the Egyptian sources, embedded in the multilayered literary and pictorial language of royal ideology.[26] The Philistines probably originated from the Aegean, as attested by their name and their spikey headgear, and were equipped with Anatolian/Aegean weaponry, Aegean-style boats, and Anatolian ox-driven carts.[27] Another detail is their description as *ṯhr*, a designation for well-trained, paid-men in the service of the courts of Hatti and Egypt.[28] The Philistines can therefore be described as belonging to a transregional phenomenon of vigorous warrior bands with an Aegean and Anatolian background, active throughout the eastern Mediterranean during the final centuries of the second millennium BCE that either raided coastal regions or fought in their service throughout the Late Bronze Age.[29] Some of the

---

26. Donald B. Redford, "Egypt and Western Asia in the Late New Kingdom: An Overview," in *The Sea Peoples and Their World: A Reassessment*, ed. Eliezer D. Oren, University Museum Monograph 108 (Philadelphia: University Museum, University of Pennsylvania, 2000), 1–20; Gareth R. Roberts, "Identity, Choice, and the Year 8 Reliefs of Ramesses III at Medinet Habu," in *Forces of Transformation: The End of the Bronze Age in the Mediterranean; Proceedings of an International Symposium Held at St. John's College, University of Oxford 25–26th March 2006*, ed. Christoph Bachhuber and R. Gareth Roberts, Themes from the Ancient Near East BANEA Publication Series 1 (Oxford: Oxbow, 2009), 60–68; Ben-Dor Evian, "Battles between Ramesses III."

27. For the etymology of the ethnonym Philistine, see Thomas Schneider, "The Philistine Language: New Etymologies and the Name David," *UF* 43 (2011): 570. For their headgear and its Aegean parallels, see Assaf Yasur-Landau, "The 'Feathered Helmets' of the Sea Peoples: Joining the Iconographic and Archaeological Evidence," *Talanta* 44 (2013): 27–40. For the Aegean background of the Philistine (and other related warriors') boats and the Anatolian background of their ox-driven carts depicted in the Egyptian reliefs, see Yasur-Landau, "On Birds and Dragons: A Note on the Sea Peoples and Mycenaean Ships," in *Pax Hethitica: Studies on the Hittites and Their Neighbours in Honor of Itamar Singer*, ed. Yorem Cohen, Amir Gilan, and Jared L. Miller, StBoT 51 (Wiesbaden: Harrassowitz, 2010), 399–410; Yasur-Landau, "Chariots, Spears and Wagons: Anatolian and Aegean Elements in the Medinet Habu Land Battle Relief," in *The Ancient Near East in the Twelfth–Tenth Centuries BCE Culture and History: Proceedings of the International Conference Held at the University of Haifa, 2–5 May, 2010*, ed. Gershon Galil et al., AOAT 392 (Münster: Ugarit-Verlag, 2012), 549–67.

28. Shirly Ben-Dor Evian, "'They Were *ṯhr* on Land, Others at Sea...': The Etymology of the Egyptian Term for 'Sea-Peoples,'" *Sem* 57 (2015): 57–75.

29. Amir Gilan, "Pirates in the Mediterranean—A View from the Bronze Age," *Mittelmeerstudien* 3 (2013): 49–66; Jeffrey P. Emanuel, "'Sherden from the Sea': The Arrival, Integration, and Acculturation of a 'Sea People,'" *JAEI* 5 (2013): 14–16.

Philistines were pirates, as described in the Naval Battle of Ramesses III, and some were mercenaries, as depicted in additional battle scenes of Ramesses III where warriors with similar headgear are seen fighting in the service of the king.[30] Some of these individuals even became propertied and achieved high social status. The collapse of the palatial system during the late thirteenth–twelfth century BCE, the turmoil in some parts of the eastern Mediterranean, and the consequent political fragmentation could have been exploited by such bands and their leaders.

The Philistines are described in the stories of the early monarchy as well-trained, fierce warriors. There is hardly any other information about them. They are depicted as raiding villages in the highland (e.g., 1 Sam 13:17–18) and the lowland (1 Sam 23:1–5), as occupying several strongholds across the highland—at Geba (1 Sam 13:3) and Bethlehem (2 Sam 23:14)—and as hiring *'brym*, Hebrews (1 Sam 14:21–22 with LXX), groups of warriors similar to the Habiru mentioned in Late Bronze sources. Naturally, a special place is kept for the heroic victories of Saul and Jonathan (1 Sam 13–14*), David in the service of Saul (1 Sam 18:14–30*), and David's heroes (2 Sam 21:15–22; 23:9–17), who were transformed in the grand episode of David and Goliath (1 Sam 17). Finally, the Philistines are pejoratively described as uncircumcised (1 Sam 14:6; 18:25, 27; 31:4; 2 Sam 1:20; 3:14; see also Judg 14:3; 15:18), a literary means denoting the ultimate Other.[31]

No doubt, the stories of the early monarchy were recounted for generations before they were written, rewritten, and overwritten in multiple phases by many generations of scribes, and much ink has been spilled over the reconstruction of its literary history. Both the compilation of the complex text and its interpretation have been shaped by the ideology, personal knowledge, and perception of the past by everyone involved. Yet there are several elements that provide clues to the historical Philistines as kept through genuine memories of the rise of the Israelite monarchy.

---

30. For their depiction as pirates, see Louise A. Hitchcock and Aren M. Maeir, "A Pirate's Life for Me: The Maritime Culture of the Sea Peoples," *PEQ* 148 (2016): 245–64.

31. Itzhaq Shai, "Philistia and the Philistines in the Iron Age IIA," *ZDPV* 127 (2011): 123–24; see also Avraham Faust, "The Bible, Archaeology, and the Practice of Circumcision in Israelite and Philistine Societies," *JBL* 134 (2015): 274–80; Maeir and Hitchcock, "Rethinking the Philistines," 258–59.

A prime anchor of the old memories is the toponymy of the Philistines or, rather, its limited scope. The knowledge of Philistine geography in the stories of Saul is limited to the fact that they arrived from the lowland; unless one reads previous episodes in the Joshua–Samuel sequence no coherent information on the Philistine geography is provided until the appearance of David. Only then does the reader receive a vivid description of the lowland west of Judah that is sometimes called by an ethnonym construct: The "land [*'rṣ*] of the Philistines" (1 Sam 27:1, 3; 29:11; 30:16; 31:9; see also 1 Kgs 5:1; 2 Kgs 8:2–3), and "the field [*śdh*] of the Philistines" (e.g., 1 Sam 6:1; 27:7, 11). One component in these stories is especially important: the prominence of Gath, which Nadav Na'aman associated with a memory of the greatness of Gath prior to its destruction by Hazael during the second half of the ninth century BCE (2 Kgs 12:18; Amos 6:2).[32] The ongoing excavations at Tell eṣ-Ṣafi, the site of ancient Gath, provide ample evidence of the prosperity of the city throughout the Iron IIA before its destruction in the second half of the ninth century BCE, thus providing a framework for arguing for a historical nucleus embedded in the stories about the early days of David.[33] It can be further argued that these stories conceal a rich memory of Gath, especially compared to the anecdotal reference to the city's greatness in Amos 6:2, the only other source that preserved its greatness.

Not one of the centers that Judah founded during the late Iron IIA in the Shephelah or the Beer-sheba–Arad Valley is mentioned in the stories of the early monarchy.[34] Furthermore, the social conditions described in several episodes seem to predate this period of consolidation of the Jerusalemite regional hegemony. These are mainly episodes in the complex narrative of David leading his band of warriors in the Keilah and Ziklag episodes (1 Sam 23:1–5; 27; 30), and the anecdotes of the heroic deeds

---

32. Nadav Na'aman, "Sources and Composition in the History of David," in *The Origin of the Ancient Israelite States*, ed. Volkmar Fritz and Philip R. Davies, JSOTSup 228 (Sheffield: Sheffield Academic, 1996), 176–78; Na'aman, "In Search of Reality behind the Account of David's Wars with Israel's Neighbours," *IEJ* 52 (2002): 210–12.

33. Aren M. Maeir, "The Historical Background and Dating of Amos-VI,2: An Archaeological Perspective from Tell-es-Safi/Gath," *VT* 54 (2004): 319–34; Maeir, *Tell es-Safi/Gath 1: The 1996–2005 Seasons* (ÄAT 69; Wiesbaden: Harrassowitz, 2012); Maeir, "Philistine Gath after Twenty Years: Regional Perspectives on the Iron Age at Tell eṣ-Ṣafi/Gath," in Lipschits and Maeir, *Shephelah during the Iron Age*, 133–54.

34. Na'aman, "In Search of Reality," 202–3; Israel Finkelstein, "Geographical and Historical Realities behind the Earliest Layer in the David Story," *SJOT* 27 (2013): 137.

of his men (2 Sam 21:15–22; 23:8–39).[35] A prime example related to the Philistines is the rescue of Keilah (1 Sam 23:1–5). Na'aman pointed out the remarkable accord between this episode and the Qiltu affair described in the Amarna correspondence (EA 279, 280, 287, 289) in place and in social condition.[36] As described in their letters sent to the Egyptian king, the rulers of fourteenth-century BCE Gath and Jerusalem struggled over the town of Qiltu (biblical Keilah, modern al-Qila) and complained that the town had been seized by a band of Habiru. This resemblance is hardly a coincidence and may show that in the *longue durée* the region of the eastern lowland was a no man's land, with bands of outlaws dominating the territory as early as the fourteenth century BCE and as late as the time reflected in the David story.

The anchoring of the stories to specific places is illuminating. Recent studies have explored the subject of the endurance and literary growth of memories, and there is a growing interest in the study of memories and their role in the writing, rewriting, and overwriting of biblical texts.[37] A major focus of this interest has been in those memories anchored in locations—a region or a city, existing or in ruins—and specific landmarks, both natural and made by man.[38] A place might be remembered as the setting of an episode, and then become the stage for the characters of a different narrative act. Places also have the capacity to become symbols: The importance of a character or even of an event has the potential to impart either a positive or negative symbolic role that could trigger a literary manipulation of a memory. Writers continuously add details anchored to their daily lives and *Zeitgeist* to their work, detaching a place from its contemporary setting and supplementing fabricated elements. They also at times even totally obliterate a place from the collective memory.

The detailed narrative on the service of David and his warriors under the auspices of Achish son of Maoch the king of Gath preserved another

---

35. Stanley Isser, *The Sword of Goliath: David in Heroic Literature*, SBLStBL 6 (Atlanta: Society of Biblical Literature, 2003); Omer Sergi, "State Formation, Religion and 'Collective Identity' in the Southern Levant," *HBAI* 4 (2015): 64–70; Finkelstein, "Geographical and Historical Realities," 137–49.

36. Nadav Na'aman, "David's Sojourn in Keilah in Light of the Amarna Letters," *VT* 60 (2010): 87–97.

37. Daniel Pioske, "Retracing a Remembered Past: Methodological Remarks on Memory, History, and the Hebrew Bible," *BibInt* 23 (2015): 291–315.

38. Diana V. Edelman and Ehud Ben Zvi, eds., *Memory and the City in Ancient Israel* (Winona Lake, IN, Eisenbrauns, 2014).

clue for the early setting of the memory. Scholars have long observed that Achish, ruler of Gath in the stories of David, is titled *mlk*, king, in contrast to *srn*, the more common title for a high-ranking Philistine in Joshua–Samuel. A literary reading of the Conquest–Judges–Monarchy sequence, they suggest, indicates that *srny plštym* were the rulers of the Philistines and that Achish was the first among equals.[39] A common argument in support of this interpretation has been the suggested etymological association of the term *srnym* (always in the plural) with Greek τύραννος ("a ruler") and with its predecessor, Luwian *tarwanis*, although the suggested etymology is not flawless and other options have been considered.[40]

A closer look at these titles reveals a more complex situation: Achish is named *king* of Gath in the short anecdote of David's first attempt to escape from Saul (1 Sam 21:11–16), in the series of episodes related to David's service under his auspice (1 Sam 27:2–28:2; 29:1–11), and in the story of the rise of Solomon (1 Kgs 2:39–40). It is only in the episode describing the preparations for the battle of the Gilboa (1 Sam 29) that additional high-ranking Philistines are mentioned alongside Achish: *srnym* and *śrym*.

The traditional interpretation of *srny plštym* as the rulers of the Philistines can be gleaned only from a very specific reading.[41] Five Philistine *srnym* of Gaza, Ashdod, Ashkelon, Gath, and Ekron are specifically referred to only in the conquest summary formula in Josh 13:3. The parallel in Judg 3:3 refers more generally to five Philistine *srnym* with no specific localization. A complex picture emerges from the Ark Narrative. The episodes take place in Philistine cities and feature "all the *srnym* of

---

39. Anson F. Rainey, "Syntax, Hermeneutics and History," *IEJ* 48 (1998): 243; Peter B. Machinist, "Biblical Traditions: The Philistines and Israelite History," in *The Sea Peoples and Their World: A Reassessment*, ed. Eliezer D. Oren, University Museum Monograph 108 (Philadelphia: University Museum, University of Pennsylvania, 2000), 58.

40. For the etymological associations, see Federico Giusfredi, "The Problem of the Luwian Title Tarwanis," *AoF* 36 (2009): 140–45. For the problems and other options, see Itamar Singer, "The Philistines in the Bible: A Short Rejoinder to a New Perspective," in *The Philistines and Other "Sea Peoples" in Text and Archaeology*, ed. Ann E. Killebrew and Gunnar Lehmann, ABS 15 (Atlanta: Society of Biblical Literature, 2013), 20–21 with earlier literature; Schneider, "Philistine Language," 572.

41. Volker Wagner, "Die סרנים der Philister und die Ältesten Israels," *ZABR* 14 (2008): 408–33; Alexander Zukerman, "Titles of Seventh Century BCE Philistine Rulers and Their Historical-Cultural Background," *BO* 68 (2011): 467.

the Philistines" (1 Sam 5:8, 11) but with neither number nor localization. In the episode in which the ark is sent off the five *srnym* are referred to but with no clear localization (1 Sam 6:4, 12, 16). It is only in a single verse (1 Sam 6:17) that reference is made to the construct of the five cities—but the *srnym* themselves are not mentioned. Antithetically, the story of Samson and Delilah refers to the *srnym* as high-ranking Philistines, but mentions neither number nor localization (Judg 16:5, 8, 18, 23, 27, 30); the same can be said regarding mention of the *srnym* in the episode of Samuel's victory in the battle of Mizpah (1 Sam 7:7), and in the preparations for the battle of Gilboa (1 Sam 29:2, 6, 7). It is in the later episode that the *srnym* are equated with *śry plštym* (1 Sam 29:9), a term that appears only once beyond this chapter, in a short anecdote describing the success of David in defeating *śry plštym* (1 Sam 18:30) thus denoting their military character.[42]

The association of the *srnym* with territorial domain is thus absent in the stories on David, where rulership is associated solely with Achish. Had the *srnym* originally been high-ranking individuals, most probably of military significance, and only in a later historical stage gained territorial domain? The absence of the term in extrabiblical sources and the reference to kings of the Philistines (e.g., Jer 25:20) suggests otherwise: the transformation of the *srnym* into a domain-related term took place in a later *literary* stage, when it gained its other meaning of rulership, referring to the Philistine leaders before the emergence of the monarchy in Israel.

In sum, the memories of the Philistines in the stories of the early monarchy are about skilled warriors who were based in the lowland south of the Yarkon Basin and raided the rural settlements to their east.[43] They were headed by warlords (*srnym* and *śrym*) and served a king, who is never, interestingly, designated as a Philistine. The accord between these memories of the Philistine warriors and the image of the *prst* warriors as commemorated by the much earlier Egyptian sources, despite the gap of several centuries, is illuminating and thus opens the floor to new questions

---

42. On the selection of the title *śr* in the Ekron inscription as the title of the local ruler, see Gitin, Dothan, and Naveh, "Royal Dedicatory Inscription," 11; Ryan Byrne, "Philistine Semitics and Dynastic History at Ekron," *UF* 34 (2002): 13; Zukerman, "Titles of Seventh Century," 168–69.

43. See also Omer Sergi, " Saul, David, and the Formation of the Israelite Monarchy: Revisiting the Historical and Literary Context of 1 Samuel 9–2 Samuel 5," in the present volume.

about the circumstances that brought them to the region and led, in due course, to their hegemony over the local society.

5. Concluding Remarks

Aside from biblical memory, the main Philistine heritage in the southern Levant is the transformation of its ethnonym, *plšt*, to a toponym—mentioned in Neo-Assyrian sources as early as the days of Adad-nirari III (above) and in a few biblical verses (Exod 15:14; Isa 14:29, 31; Joel 4:4; Pss 60:10; 83:8; 87:4; 108:10). Fundamental as naming the region as Philistia was—eventually to be projected over the entire country—it was not accompanied by additional marked changes in the regional toponomy, which kept its autochthonous onomasticon for centuries.[44] Continuation can also be observed in the use of the Canaanite script, as seen in several epigraphic finds from Tell *eṣ-Ṣafi*/Gath and satellite settlements, among them a short late-Iron I–early Iron IIA inscription referring to names with possible Anatolian etymology. The prestigious status of the local dialect is best seen in the latest, longest, and most famous among the epigraphic finds from Philistia: the Ekron royal inscription from the Iron IIC, in which the local name of the city it mentioned alongside the nonlocal name of the ruler, and the local names of his ancestors.[45] Such a process might reflect the arrival(s) of small groups of newcomers during the early Iron Age, who interacted with locals, gradually adopted the local language (and probably local practices) and eventually granted their own collective identity to the local society.

Hypothetically, the Philistines could have arrived in the region during the days of Egyptian hegemony or after its collapse. Opting for the former choice, they could have served in an Egyptian garrison in Gaza and remained after the demise of the empire to become the lords of the new,

---

44. Itzhaq Shai, "Understanding Philistine Migration: City Names and Their Implications," *BASOR* 354 (2009): 15–27.

45. On the use of Canaanite script in Gath and its neighbors during the early Iron Age, the sporadic attestations to Indo-European terms and names, and the development of a local dialect in Iron II Philistia, see Ryan Byrne, "The Refuge of Scribalism in Iron I Palestine," *BASOR* 345 (2007): 3, 17–23; Brent Davis, Aren M. Maeir, and Louise A. Hitchcock, "Disentangling Entangled Objects: Iron Age Inscriptions from Philistia as a Reflection of Cultural Processes," *IEJ* 65 (2015): 140–66; Shai, "Philistia and the Philistines," 125–26.

postcollapse society. A fascinating illumination of such a scenario might be seen decorating a scarab embedded in a gold ring found in an affluent Late Bronze III tomb at Tell el-Farʾah (S), depicting a figure similar to the Philistines in the reliefs of Ramesses III receiving a large ankh from Amun-Re in a setting otherwise reserved for royal figures.[46] Alternatively, the Philistines might be associated with the destruction of the postcollapse society during the late Iron I, a chaotic period that concluded with the emergence of Gath as the regional hegemon during the Iron IIA. Any combination of these scenarios is possible as well; the absence of written sources precludes any coherent reconstruction.

It was a period of connectivity,[47] including firm connections between the region that would become Philistia and the highland as reflected in the settlement pattern. The large urban centers of the lowland, Ekron and Gath, were connected to the rural highlands (a few towns and many villages) through topographic corridors: particularly the Beth-horon ascent (between the al-Jib plateau and the Valley of Ajalon) and the numerous intermittent streams (Hebrew: *naḥal*) that drain the highland from south of Bethlehem to Hebron and lead to the Shephelah.[48] This is especially clear to the east of the Elah Valley, where the Arqob—a rugged, stony terrain that is lower than the highland yet higher than the Shephelah hills—serves as a natural topographical stairway. The interactions through these short, few-hour walk treks are reflected in the exchange of pottery vessels, forms, and styles, and several pictorial conventions seen on locally produced seals.[49] These were the same topographic corridors that were

---

46. Othmar Keel and Christoph Uehlinger, *Gods, Goddesses, and Images of God in Ancient Israel*, trans. Thomas H. Trapp (Minneapolis: Fortress, 1998), 110.

47. Yuval Gadot, "The Iron I in the Samaria Highland: A Nomad Settlement Wave or Urban Expansion?," in Lipschits, *Rethinking Israel*, 103–14; Koch, "Settlements and Interactions," 186–89, 191–93.

48. Koch, "Settlements and Interactions," 181.

49. On coastal pottery in the highland, both vessels and influence on local production, and on highland-produced pottery in the lowland, see Anat Cohen-Weinberger, Nahshon Szanton, and Joe Uziel, "Ethnofabrics: Petrographic Analysis as a Tool for Illuminating Cultural Interactions and Trade Relations between Judah and Philistia during the Iron Age II," *BASOR* 377 (2017): 1–20; Koch, "Settlements and Interactions," 189–91 with earlier literature. On the distribution of limestone seals with iconography shared by the highland and lowland of the southern part of the country see Koch, "Stamp-Amulets from Iron IIA Shephelah: Preliminary Conclusions Regarding Production and Distribution, Pictorial Assemblage, and Function" [Hebrew with English

eventually used by the Philistine bands to raid the highlands: the Bethhoron ascent leading to the homeland of Saul and the intermittent streams east of the Elah Valley that lead to the homeland of David, the two regions where the encounters took place and the memories of the early Philistines were retained through the stories of the rise of the monarchy in Israel.

Bibliography

Albright, William F. *The Excavation of Tell Beit Mirsim III: The Iron Age.* AASOR 21–22. New Haven: American Schools of Oriental Research, 1943.

Arendt, Dieter. "Brentanos Philister—Rede am Ende des romantischen Jahrhunderts oder Der Philister—Krieg und seine unrühmliche Kapitulation." *Orbis Litterarum* 55 (2000): 81–102.

Avioz, Michael. "The Philistines in Josephus' Writings." *TZ* 71 (2015): 144–55.

Bagg, Ariel M. *Die Orts-und Gewässernamen der neuassyrischen Zeit: Die Levante.* RGTC 7.1. Wiesbaden: Reichert, 2007.

Barako, Tristan J. "The Philistine Settlement as Mercantile Phenomenon?" *AJA* 104 (2000): 513–30.

Bauer, Alexander A. "Cities of the Sea: Maritime Trade and the Origin of Philistine Settlement in the Early Iron Age Southern Levant." *OJA* 17 (1998): 149–68.

Bauer, Alexander A. "The Sea Peoples as an Emergent Phenomenon." Pages 32–40 in *ΑΘΥΡΜΑΤΑ: Critical Essays on the Archaeology of the Eastern Mediterranean in Honour of E. Susan Sherratt*. Edited by Yoannis Galanakis, Toby C. Wilkinson, and John Bennet. Oxford: Archaeopress, 2014.

Ben-Dor Evian, Shirly. "The Battles between Ramesses III and the Sea-Peoples: When, Where and Who? An Iconic Analysis of the Egyptian Reliefs." *ZÄS* 143 (2016): 151–68.

———. "Ramesses III and the 'Sea-Peoples': Towards a New Philistine Paradigm." *OJA* 36 (2017): 267–85.

———. " 'They Were *ṯhr* on Land, Others at Sea…': The Etymology of the Egyptian Term for 'Sea-Peoples.' " *Sem* 57 (2015): 57–75.

---

summary], in *New Studies on Jerusalem 22*, ed. Avraham Faust and Eyal Baruch (Ramat Gan: Rennert Center for Jerusalem Studies, 2017), 75–93, 10*.

Ben-Shlomo, David, Itzhaq Shai, Alexander Zukerman, and Aren M. Maeir. "Cooking Identities: Aegean-Style Cooking Jugs and Cultural Interaction in Iron Age Philistia and Neighboring Regions." *AJA* 112 (2008): 225–46.

Brug, John F. *A Literary and Archaeological Study of the Philistines*. BARIS 265. Oxford: BAR, 1985.

Bunimovitz, Shlomo, and Zvi Lederman. "The Archaeology of Border Communities: Renewed Excavations at Tel Beth-Shemesh, Part 1: The Iron Age." *NEA* 72 (2009): 114–42.

———. "Canaanite Resistance: The Philistines and Beth-Shemesh—A Case Study from Iron Age I." *BASOR* 364 (2011): 37–51.

Byrne, Ryan. "Philistine Semitics and Dynastic History at Ekron." *UF* 34 (2002): 1–23.

———. "The Refuge of Scribalism in Iron I Palestine." *BASOR* 345 (2007): 1–31.

Cohen-Weinberger, Anat, Nahshon Szanton, and Joe Uziel. "Ethnofabrics: Petrographic Analysis as a Tool for Illuminating Cultural Interactions and Trade Relations between Judah and Philistia during the Iron Age II." *BASOR* 377 (2017): 1–20.

Davis, Brent, Aren Maeir, and Louise Hitchcock. "Disentangling Entangled Objects: Iron Age Inscriptions from Philistia as a Reflection of Cultural Processes." *IEJ* 65 (2015): 140–66.

DeLapp, Nevada Levi. *The Reformed David(s) and the Question of Resistance to Tyranny: Reading the Bible in the Sixteenth and Seventeenth Centuries*. LHBOTS. Scriptural Traces 601. London: Bloomsbury, 2014.

Dever, William G. "Ceramics, Ethnicity, and the Question of Israel's Origins." *BA* 58 (1995): 200–213.

Dothan, Trude. *The Philistines and Their Material Culture*. New Haven: Yale University Press, 1982.

Dothan, Trude, and Moshe Dothan. *People of the Sea: The Search for the Philistines*. New York: Macmillan 1992.

Drews, Robert. "Canaanites and Philistines." *JSOT* 81 (1998): 39–61.

———. "Medinet Habu: Oxcarts, Ships, and Migration Theories." *JNES* 59 (2000): 161–90.

Edelman, Diana V., and Ehud Ben Zvi, eds. *Memory and the City in Ancient Israel*. Winona Lake, IN: Eisenbrauns, 2014.

Emanuel, Jeffrey P. "'Sherden from the Sea': The Arrival, Integration, and Acculturation of a 'Sea People.'" *JAEI* 5 (2013): 14–27.

Faust, Avraham. "The Bible, Archaeology, and the Practice of Circumcision in Israelite and Philistine Societies." *JBL* 134 (2015): 273–90.

———. *Israel's Ethnogenesis: Settlement, Interaction, Expansion and Resistance*. London: Equinox, 2006.

———. "The 'Philistine Tomb' at Tel 'Eton: Culture Contact, Colonialism, and Local Responses in Iron Age Shephelah, Israel." *JAR* 71 (2015): 195–230.

Faust, Avraham, and Hayah Katz. "Philistines, Israelites and Canaanites in the Southern Trough Valley during the Iron Age I." *AeL* 21 (2011): 231–47.

Finkelstein, Israel. "Ethnicity and Origin of the Iron I Settlers in the Highlands of Canaan: Can the Real Israel Stand Up?" *BA* 59 (1996): 198–212.

———. "Geographical and Historical Realities behind the Earliest Layer in the David Story." *SJOT* 27 (2013): 131–50.

Frontain, Raymond-Jean, and Jan Wojcik, eds. *The David Myth in Western Literature*. West Lafayette: Purdue University Press, 1980.

Gadot, Yuval. "The Iron I in the Samaria Highland: A Nomad Settlement Wave or Urban Expansion?" Pages 103–14 in *Rethinking Israel: Studies in the History and Archaeology of Ancient Israel in Honor of Israel Finkelstein*. Edited by Oded Lipschits, Yuval Gadot, and Matthew J. Adams. Winona Lake, IN: Eisenbrauns, 2017.

Gates, Marie-Henriette. "Maritime Business in the Bronze Age Eastern Mediterranean: The View from Its Ports." Pages 381–94 in *Intercultural Contacts in the Ancient Mediterranean: Proceedings of the International Conference at the Netherlands-Flemish Institute in Cairo, 25th to 29th October 2008*. Edited by Kim Duistermaat and Ilona Regulski. OLA 202. Leuven: Peeters, 2011.

Gilan, Amir. "Pirates in the Mediterranean—A View from the Bronze Age." *Mittelmeerstudien* 3 (2013): 49–66.

Gitin, Seymour, Trude Dothan, and Joseph Naveh, "A Royal Dedicatory Inscription from Ekron." *IEJ* 47 (1997): 1–16.

Giusfredi, Federico. "The Problem of the Luwian Title Tarwanis." *AoF* 36 (2009): 140–45.

Greenberg, Raphael. "New Light on the Early Iron Age at Tell Beit Mirsim." *BASOR* 265 (1987): 55–80.

Guillaume, Philippe. *Waiting for Josiah: The Judges*. JSOTSup 385. London: T&T Clark, 2004.

Hitchcock, Louise A., and Aren M. Maeir. "Beyond Creolization and Hybridity: Entangled and Transcultural Identities in Philistia." *ARC* 28 (2013): 51–74.

———. "A Pirate's Life for Me: The Maritime Culture of the Sea Peoples." *PEQ* 148 (2016): 245–64.

Hourihane, Colum, ed. *King David in the Index of Christian Art*. Princeton: Princeton University Press, 2002.

Isser, Stanley. *The Sword of Goliath: David in Heroic Literature*. SBLStBL 6. Atlanta: Society of Biblical Literature, 2003.

Kahn, Dan'el. "The Campaign of Ramesses III against Philistia." *JAEI* 3.4 (2011): 1–11.

Keel, Othmar, and Christoph Uehlinger. *Gods, Goddesses, and Images of God in Ancient Israel*. Translated by Thomas H. Trapp. Minneapolis: Fortress, 1998.

Kletter, Raz. "In the Footsteps of Bagira: Ethnicity, Archaeology, and 'Iron Age I Ethnic Israel.'" *Approaching Religion* 4.2 (2014): 2–15.

Koch, Ido. "Collapse and Regeneration in Southwest Canaan during the Late Second Millennium BCE." In *From Nomadism to Monarchy: Thirty Years Update*. Edited by Ido Koch, Omer Sergi, and Oded Lipschits. University Park: Penn State University Press, forthcoming.

———. "Early Philistia Revisited and Revised." Pages 189–205 in *Rethinking Israel: Studies in the History and Archaeology of Ancient Israel in Honor of Israel Finkelstein*. Edited by Oded Lipschits, Yuval Gadot, and Matthew J. Adams. Winona Lake, IN: Eisenbrauns, 2017.

———. "The Egyptian-Canaanite Interface as Colonial Encounter: A View from Southwest Canaan." *JAEI* 18 (2018): 24–39.

———. "Settlements and Interactions in the Shephelah during the Late Second through Early First Millennia BCE." Pages 181–207 in *The Shephelah during the Iron Age: Recent Archaeological Studies*. Edited by Oded Lipschits and Aren M. Maeir. Winona Lake, IN: Eisenbrauns, 2017.

———. *The Shadow of Egypt: Colonial Encounters in Southwest Canaan during the Late Bronze Age and Early Iron Age* [Hebrew]. Jerusalem: Yad Ben-Zvi, 2018.

———. "Stamp-Amulets from Iron IIA Shephelah: Preliminary Conclusions Regarding Production and Distribution, Pictorial Assemblage, and Function" [Hebrew, with English summary]. Pages 75–93, 10* in *New Studies on Jerusalem 22*. Edited by Avraham Faust and Eyal Baruch. Ramat Gan: Rennert Center for Jerusalem Studies, 2017.

Koch, Ido, Sabine Kleiman, Manfred Oeming, Yuval Gadot, and Oded Lipschits. "Amulets in Context: A View from Late Bronze Age Tel Azekah." *JAEI* 16 (2017): 9–24.
Macalister, R. A. Stewart. *The Philistines: Their History and Civilization*. Schweich Lectures 1911. London: Oxford University Press, 1914.
Machinist, Peter B. "Biblical Traditions: The Philistines and Israelite History." Pages 53–84 in *The Sea Peoples and Their World: A Reassessment*. Edited by Eliezer D. Oren. University Museum Monograph 108. Philadelphia: University Museum, University of Pennsylvania, 2000.
Maeir, Aren M. "The Historical Background and Dating of Amos-VI,2: An Archaeological Perspective from Tell-es-Safi/Gath." *VT* 54 (2004): 319–34.
———. "Philistine Gath after Twenty Years: Regional Perspectives on the Iron Age at Tell *eṣ- Ṣafi*/Gath." Pages 133–54 in *The Shephelah during the Iron Age: Recent Archaeological Studies*. Edited by Oded Lipschits and Aren M. Maeir. Winona Lake, IN: Eisenbrauns, 2017.
———. *Tell es-Safi/Gath 1: The 1996–2005 Seasons*. ÄAT 69. Wiesbaden: Harrassowitz, 2012.
Maeir, Aren M., and Louise A. Hitchcock. "The Appearance, Formation and Transformation of Philistine Culture: New Perspectives and New Finds." Pages 149–62 in *"Sea Peoples" Up-to-Date: New Research on Transformation in the Eastern Mediterranean in the Thirteenth–Eleventh Centuries BCE*. Edited by Peter M. Fischer and Teresa Bürge. Contributions to the Chronology of Eastern Mediterranean 35. Vienna: Österreichischen Akademie der Wissenschaften, 2017.
———. "Rethinking the Philistines: A 2017 Perspective." Pages 247–66 in *Rethinking Israel: Studies in the History and Archaeology of Ancient Israel in Honor of Israel Finkelstein*. Edited by Oded Lipschits, Yuval Gadot, and Matthew J. Adams. Winona Lake, IN: Eisenbrauns, 2017.
Maeir, Aren M., Louise A. Hitchcock, and Liora Kolska Horwitz. "On the Constitution and Transformation of Philistine Identity." *OJA* 32 (2013): 1–38.
Maspero, Gaston. *Histoire ancienne des peuples de l'Orient classique*. Paris: Hachette & Cie, 1875.
Mazar, Amihai. "The Emergence of the Philistine Material Culture." *IEJ* 35 (1985): 95–107.
Mazow, Laura B. "Competing Material Culture: Philistine Settlement at Tel Miqne-Ekron in the Early Iron Age." Pages 131–63 in *Material Culture Matters: Essays on the Archaeology of the Southern Levant in*

Honor of Seymour Gitin. Edited by John R. Spencer, Robert A. Mullins, and Aaron J. Brody. Winona Lake, IN: Eisenbrauns, 2014.

Millek, Jesse M. "Sea Peoples, Philistines, and the Destruction of Cities: A Critical Examination of Destruction Layers 'Caused' by the 'Sea Peoples.'" Pages 113–40 in *"Sea Peoples" Up-to-Date: New Research on Transformation in the Eastern Mediterranean in the Thirteenth–Eleventh Centuries BCE*. Edited by Peter M. Fischer and Teresa Bürge. Contributions to the Chronology of Eastern Mediterranean 35. Vienna: Österreichischen Akademie der Wissenschaften, 2017.

Na'aman, Nadav. "David's Sojourn in Keilah in Light of the Amarna Letters." *VT* 60 (2010): 87–97.

———. "In Search of Reality behind the Account of David's Wars with Israel's Neighbours." *IEJ* 52 (2002): 200–224.

———. "Sources and Composition in the History of David." Pages 170–86 in *The Origins of the Ancient Israelite States*. Edited by Volkmar Fritz and Philip R. Davies. JSOTSup 228. Sheffield: Sheffield Academic, 1996.

Pioske, Daniel. "Retracing a Remembered Past: Methodological Remarks on Memory, History, and the Hebrew Bible." *BibInt* 23 (2015): 291–315.

Rainey, Anson F. "Syntax, Hermeneutics and History." *IEJ* 48 (1998): 239–51.

Redford, Donald B. "Egypt and Western Asia in the Late New Kingdom: An Overview." Pages 1–20 in *The Sea Peoples and Their World: A Reassessment*. Edited by Eliezer D. Oren. University Museum Monograph 108. Philadelphia: University Museum, University of Pennsylvania, 2000.

Roberts, R. Gareth. "Identity, Choice, and the Year 8 Reliefs of Ramesses III at Medinet Habu," Pages 60–68 in *Forces of Transformation: The End of the Bronze Age in the Mediterranean; Proceedings of an International Symposium Held at St. John's College, University of Oxford 25–26th March 2006*. Edited by Christoph Bachhuber and R. Gareth Roberts. Themes from the Ancient Near East BANEA Publication Series 1. Oxford: Oxbow, 2009.Schneider, Thomas. "The Philistine Language: New Etymologies and the Name David." *UF* 43 (2011): 569–80.

Sergi, Omer. "State Formation, Religion and 'Collective Identity' in the Southern Levant." *HBAI* 4 (2015): 56–77.

Shai, Itzhaq. "Philistia and the Philistines in the Iron Age IIA." *ZDPV* 127 (2011): 119–34.

———. "Understanding Philistine Migration: City Names and Their Implications." *BASOR* 354 (2009): 15–27.

Sharon, Ilan. "Philistine Bichrome Painted Pottery: Scholarly Ideology and Ceramic Typology." Pages 555–609 in *Studies in the Archaeology of Israel and Neighboring Lands in Memory of Douglas L. Esse*. Edited by Samuel R. Wolf. SAOC 59. Chicago: Oriental Institute of the University of Chicago, 2001.

Sherratt, Susan E. "'Ethnicities,' 'Ethnonyms,' and Archaeological Labels: Whose Ideologies and Whose Identities?" Pages 25–38 in *Archaeological Perspectives on the Transition and Transformation of Culture in the Eastern Mediterranean*. Edited by Joanne Clarke. Levant Supplementary Series 2. Oxford: Oxbow, 2005.

———. "The Mediterranean Economy: 'Globalization' at the End of the Second Millennium B.C.E." Pages 37–62 in *Symbiosis, Symbolism, and the Power of the Past: Canaan, Ancient Israel, and Their Neighbors from the Late Bronze Age through Roman Palaestina*. Edited by William G. Dever and Seymour Gitin. Winona Lake, IN: Eisenbrauns, 2003.

———. "'Sea Peoples' and the Economic Structure of the Late Second Millennium in the Eastern Mediterranean." Pages 292–313 in *Mediterranean Peoples in Transition: Thirteenth to Early Tenth Centuries BCE, in Honor of Trude Dothan*. Edited by Seymour Gitin, Amihai Mazar, and Ephraim Stern. Jerusalem: Israel Exploration Society, 1998.

Singer, Itamar. "Egyptians, Canaanites, and Philistines in the Period of the Emergence of Israel." Pages 282–338 in *From Nomadism to Monarchy: Archaeological and Historical Aspects of Early Israel*. Edited by Israel Finkelstein and Nadav Na'aman. Jerusalem: Yad Ben-Zvi, 1994.

———. "The Philistines in the Bible: A Short Rejoinder to a New Perspective." Pages 19–27 in *The Philistines and Other "Sea Peoples" in Text and Archaeology*. Edited by Ann E. Killebrew and Gunnar Lehmann. ABS 15. Atlanta: Society of Biblical Literature, 2013.

Sousa, Rodrigo de. "The Land Is Full of Foreign Children: Language and Ideology in LXX Isa. 2.6." Pages 181–96 in *Studies on the Text and Versions of the Hebrew Bible in Honour of Robert Gordon*. Edited by Geoffrey Kahn and Diana Lipton. VTSup 149. Leiden: Brill, 2011.

Stager, Lawrence E. "The Impact of the Sea Peoples in Canaan (1185–1050 BCE)." Pages 332–48 in *The Archaeology of Society in the Holy Land*. Edited by Thomas E. Levy. London: Leicester University Press, 1995.

Super, Robert Henry, ed. *Culture and Anarchy: With Friendship's Garland and Some Literary Essays*. Ann Arbor: University of Michigan Press, 1965.

Wagner, Volker. "Die סרנים der Philister und die Ältesten Israels." *ZABR* 14 (2008): 408–33.

Yasur-Landau, Assaf. "Chariots, Spears and Wagons: Anatolian and Aegean Elements in the Medinet Habu Land Battle Relief." Pages 549–67 in *The Ancient Near East in the Twelfth–Tenth Centuries BCE Culture and History: Proceedings of the International Conference Held at the University of Haifa, 2–5 May, 2010*. Edited by Gershon Galil, Ayelet Gilboa, Aren M. Maeir, and Dan'el Kahn. AOAT 392. Münster: Ugarit-Verlag, 2012.

———. "The 'Feathered Helmets' of the Sea Peoples: Joining the Iconographic and Archaeological Evidence." *Talanta* 44 (2013): 27–40.

———. "On Birds and Dragons: A Note on the Sea Peoples and Mycenaean Ships." Pages 399–410 in *Pax Hethitica: Studies on the Hittites and Their Neighbours in Honor of Itamar Singer*. Edited by Yorem Cohen, Amir Gilan, and Jared L. Miller. StBoT 51. Wiesbaden: Harrassowitz, 2010.

———. "The Role of the Canaanite Population in the Aegean Migration to the Southern Levant in the Late Second Millennium BCE." Pages 191–97 in *Materiality and Social Practice: Transformative Capacities of Intercultural Encounters*. Edited by Joseph Maran and Philipp W. Stockhammer. Oxford: Oxbow, 2012.

Zukerman, Alexander. "Titles of Seventh Century BCE Philistine Rulers and Their Historical-Cultural Background." *BO* 68 (2011): 465–71.

Saul and Highlands of Benjamin Update: The Role of Jerusalem

Israel Finkelstein

1. Introduction

In recent years, I have published a number of works on the highlands of Benjamin.[1] They have dealt with two main issues: the territorio-political affiliation of the highlands of Benjamin with Israel or Judah and the rise of a north Israelite territorial entity in the tenth century BCE, which I associated with the biblical tradition on the house of Saul.[2] These issues are fundamental to understanding the emergence of the two Hebrew kingdoms and the background of several historical descriptions and historiographical concepts in the Bible. The fragmentary nature of the sources of information makes research on these themes difficult. First, in order to reach the old, pre-Deuteronomistic Saul tradition in the book of Samuel one needs to peel off later layers, especially the strong Deuteronomistic one, not to mention that the scope of the old material

---

1. With the phrase *highlands of Benjamin*, I refer to the geographical term (the flat highland plateau between Jerusalem and Bethel), which does not necessarily fully align with the biblical tribal one.

2. For the political affiliations of the highlands of Benjamin, see Israel Finkelstein, "Saul, Benjamin and the Emergence of 'Biblical Israel': An Alternative View," *ZAW* 123 (2011): 348–67; contra Nadav Na'aman, "Saul, Benjamin and the Emergence of 'Biblical Israel,'" *ZAW* 121 (2009): 211–24, 335–49. For the rise of a north Israelite territorial entity, see Israel Finkelstein, "The Last Labayu: King Saul and the Expansion of the First North Israelite Territorial Entity," in *Essays on Ancient Israel in Its Near Eastern Context, A Tribute to Nadav Na'aman*, ed. Yairah Amit et al. (Winona Lake, IN: Eisenbrauns, 2006), 171–78; Finkelstein, *The Forgotten Kingdom: The Archaeology and History of Northern Israel*, ANEM 5 (Atlanta: Society of Biblical Literature, 2013), 37–61.

is debatable.³ Second, there is only one extrabiblical source, the Egyptian account of the Shoshenq I campaign to Canaan. Being a list, rather than annals, it gives a somewhat vague testimony; also, the exact date of Shoshenq's reign and the date of the campaign (or campaigns) during his reign are disputed (more below). Third, much of the archaeology of the highlands of Benjamin in the period under discussion—the late Iron I and early Iron IIA—leaves much to be desired from the perspectives of both chronology and interpretation of the nature of the remains.

The invitation to the second Tübingen–Tel Aviv research colloquium, which is summarized in this book, prompted me to take a fresh look at both issues: the geographical and historical background to the Saul narrative and the question of territorial affiliation of the highlands of Benjamin. The discussion below leads me to comment on other themes: the circumstances of the contemporaneous rise of the two Hebrew kingdoms and the origin of the united monarchy concept in the Bible. Let me say in advance that the missing parts in the puzzle are far more considerable than those that exist. Hence, I offer my observations as a platform for discussion—a background stage-setting for what may be cached behind the biblical text, the Shoshenq list, and the fragmentary archaeological data.

2. My Former Reconstruction

I start with a short summary of my views prior to the Tübingen–Tel Aviv Colloquium on the subject of Saul, Benjamin, and the early monarchy.

(1) I have argued that Israel and Judah were in dispute over the land of Benjamin. Until the decline of the Omride dynasty, it was part of the north. Then, in a period when Israel was weakened as a result of the pressure of Hazael, it was taken over by Judah in the time of King Jehoash, who seems to have acted under Damascene auspices. The area was probably

---

3. E.g., Otto Kaiser, "Der historische und der biblische König Saul (Teil I)," *ZAW* 122 (2010): 520–45; Kaiser, "Der historische und der biblische König Saul (Teil II)," *ZAW* 123 (2011): 1–14; Diana Edelman, *King Saul in the Historiography of Judah*, JSOTSup 121 (Sheffield: JSOT Press, 1991); Eben Scheffler, "Saving Saul from the Deuteronomist," in *Past, Present, Future: The Deuteronomistic History and the Prophets*, ed. Johannes C. de Moor and H. F. van Rooy, OTS 44 (Leiden: Brill, 2000), 214–57; Christophe Nihan, "Saul Among the Prophets (1 Sam 10:10–12 and 19:18–24): The Reworking of Saul's Figure in the Context of the Debate on Charismatic Prophecy in the Persian Era," in *Saul in Story and Tradition*, ed. Carl S. Ehrlich and Marsha C. White, FAT 47 (Tübingen: Mohr Siebeck, 2006), 88–118.

controlled again by Israel in the days of Joash and Jeroboam II. Renewed Judahite domination of the region is clearly attested starting in the late eighth century, as a result of the fall of the north and of Judah becoming an Assyrian vassal.

(2) I have proposed the existence—in the tenth century BCE—of a north Israelite polity, which was centered in the plateau of Gibeon–Bethel. This entity is hinted at by shreds of pre-Deuteronomistic Saul royal traditions in the book of Samuel and by the list of towns taken over during the campaign of Shoshenq I to Canaan. These sources refer to the same territories in the highlands and the Gilead around the outlet of the Jabbok River, in approximately the same period (the tenth century BCE). A late Iron I/early Iron IIA (in terms of absolute chronology, this also translates to the tenth century BCE) polity in this region is also insinuated by the unique concentration of fortified sites; together with Khirbet Qeiyafa (more below) these are the only contemporary fortifications known in the sedentary areas west of the Jordan River.[4]

(3) Scholars are in dispute regarding the seat of Saul. This stems from the Geba/Gibeah confusion in the biblical texts.[5] There are two possibilities here: According to the first, Geba/Gibeah of Saul/Gibeah of Benjamin refers to the same place, which should be identified with the village of Jaba on the desert fringe. Contra many scholars, Tell el-Ful is not an option, as the archaeological evidence for activity there in the period under discussion is meager at best.[6] Another option is to locate the seat of Saul more centrally, at Gibeon.[7]

---

4. For the absolute chronology, see Israel Finkelstein and Eli Piasetzky, "Radiocarbon Dating the Iron Age in the Levant: A Bayesian Model for Six Ceramic Phases and Six Transitions," *Antiquity* 84 (2010): 374–85.

5. For the possibility that the confusion stems from Israelite and Judahite pronunciation/spelling, see Patrick M. Arnold, *Gibeah: The Search for a Biblical City*, JSOTSup 79 (Sheffield: Sheffield Academic, 1990), 37–38, 42.

6. For Tell el-Ful as an option, see recently Nadav Na'aman, "Jebusites and Jabeshites in the Saul and David Story-Cycles," *Bib* 95 (2014): 489–92. Against Tell el-Full, see Israel Finkelstein, "Tell el-Ful Revisited: The Assyrian and Hellenistic Periods (with a New Identification)," *PEQ* 143 (2011): 106–18.

7. Joseph Blenkinsopp, "Did Saul Make Gibeon His Capital?," *VT* 24 (1974): 1–7; Gösta W. Ahlström, *The History of Ancient Palestine from the Palaeolithic Period to Alexander's Conquest*, JSOTSup 146 (Sheffield: Sheffield Academic, 1993), 436; Diana Edelman, "Saul ben Kish in History and Tradition," in *The Origins of the Ancient Israelite States*, ed. Volkmar Fritz and Philip R. Davies, JSOTSup 228 (Sheffield: Sheffield

(4) I argued (in a recent article more than in the original ones) that the pre-Deuteronomistic Saul story includes parts of the following materials:[8] (a) Saul's search for his father's mules;[9] (b) his coronation in an unnamed place by an unnamed man of God; (c) the kernel of the story on the rescue of Jabesh from the city-state of Ammon; (d) the battle of Geba and Michmash; (e) seemingly the opening of the narrative on the battle in the Valley of Elah; (f) additional clues in the early layer of the David story;[10] and (g) the kernel of the story on the battle of Gilboa; the geography and the link with the former Egyptian center of Beth-shean are too specific to be invented by later authors.

(5) I assumed that the territory of the Saul polity included the highlands north of Jerusalem and the western slopes of the Gilead, with possible extension to the northeastern Shephelah in the Valley of Elah.[11] At least part of this territory may be echoed in the summary of the regions ruled by Ishbaal in 2 Sam 2:9.[12] This seems to be a northern-derived text used by a Deuteronomistic author, who may have added the term "all Israel."

(6) The penetration of Shoshenq I into the highlands is an exception in the history of Egyptian campaigns to Canaan. There is hardly a way to

---

Academic, 1996), 155–56; Karl van der Toorn, "Saul and the Rise of the Israelite State Religion," *VT* 43 (1993): 520–23; Ernst A. Knauf, "Saul, David, and the Philistines: From Geography to History," *BN* 109 (2001): 17.

8. The most recent article is Israel Finkelstein, "A Corpus of North Israelite Texts in the Days of Jeroboam II?," *HBAI* 6 (2017): 262–89. For the matter of the pre-Deuteronomistic Saul story, see different views in, e.g., Nadav Na'aman, "The Pre-Deuteronomistic Story of King Saul and Its Historical Significance," *CBQ* 54 (1990): 638–58; Edelman, "Saul ben Kish," 151–56; Walter Dietrich, *The Early Monarchy in Israel: The Tenth Century B.C.E.*, BibEnc 3 (Atlanta: Society of Biblical Literature, 2007), 155–57; Marsha C. White, "The History of Saul's Rise: Saulide State Propaganda in 1 Samuel 1–14," in *"A Wise and Discerning Mind": Essays in Honor of Bourke O. Long*, ed. Saul M. Olyan and Robert C. Culley, BJS 325 (Providence, RI: Brown Judaic Studies, 2000), 271–92.

9. On this, see, Diana Edelman, "Saul's Journey through Mt. Ephraim and Samuel's Ramah (1 Sam. 9:4–5, 10:2–5)," *ZDPV* 104 (1988): 44–58; more below.

10. Israel Finkelstein, "The Geographical and Historical Realities behind the Earliest Layer in the David Story," *SJOT* 27 (2013): 131–50.

11. Israel Finkelstein and Alexander Fantalkin, "Khirbet Qeiyafa: An Unsensational Archaeological and Historical Interpretation," *TA* 39 (2012): 38–63.

12. On the list see Diana Edelman, "The 'Ashurites' of Eshbaal's State (2 Sam. 2.9)," *PEQ* 117 (1985): 85–91; Nadav Na'aman, "The Kingdom of Ishbaal," *BN* 54 (1990): 33–37; more below.

explain this risky maneuver other than as a reaction to the menace posed to renewed Egyptian interests in Canaan by a highlands polity. I would refer mainly to expansion attempts of such highlands entity to the lowlands in the west and north (compare the case of Labayu of Shechem in the Amarna period).[13] With no historical great united monarchy, a contemporary *northern* polity in the central highlands is the only option for such a threatening entity. Shoshenq I took over the heartland of the Saulide territory in the plateau of Gibeon and its extension in the area of the Jabbok in the Gilead.

(7) This issue is related to the territorial affiliation of the much discussed site of Khirbet Qeiyafa. The layout of the site hints at a highlands origin of the builders. Alexander Fantalkin and I proposed that the site belonged to the north Israelite Saulide polity and that it was destroyed/abandoned as a result of the Shoshenq I campaign.[14] A north Israelite affiliation of the site fits the references to the (otherwise geographically odd) presence of Saul in the Valley of Elah and the area of Adullam. In an article published recently, Fantalkin and I show that material culture characteristics of the site are better understood as representing a northern (rather than Judahite) association.[15]

(8) A Saul royal tradition—the source of the pre-Deuteronomistic Saul material—was composed in Israel in the days of Jeroboam II, that is, in the first half of the eighth century BCE—just slightly more than a century and a half after the events.[16]

(9) The written royal Saul tradition was brought to Jerusalem by Israelites who moved to the south after 720 BCE. The archaeological evidence is unmistakable: a dramatic demographic transformation in Jerusalem in particular and Judah in general in the Iron IIB.[17] This transformation can in no way be explained as the result of natural population growth, economic prosperity, or intra-Judahite movement of people. Appearance of

---

13. Israel Finkelstein and Nadav Na'aman, "Shechem of the Amarna Period and the Rise of the Northern Kingdom of Israel," *IEJ* 55 (2005): 172–93.

14. Finkelstein and Fantalkin, "Khirbet Qeiyafa," 38–63.

15. Alexander Fantalkin and Israel Finkelstein, "The Date of Abandonment and Territorial Affiliation of Khirbet Qeiyafa: An Update," *TA* 44 (2017): 53–60.

16. Finkelstein, "Corpus of North Israelite Texts."

17. Israel Finkelstein and Neil A. Silberman, "Temple and Dynasty: Hezekiah, the Remaking of Judah and the Rise of the Pan-Israelite Ideology," *JSOT* 30 (2006): 259–85.

Israelite material culture in Judah starting in the late eighth century supports this historical reconstruction.[18] The Israelite Saul tradition was later incorporated into Deuteronomistic writings. The ratio of northerners in the population of Judah prevented the authors from dismissing it; rather, it was contained and put to the service of Judahite royal ideology.[19]

3. Difficulties in My Former Historical Reconstruction

This reconstruction was not free of difficulties.

(1) The central highlands were traditionally divided between two territorial entities, one located at Shechem or its vicinity and the other in Jerusalem. Ostensibly, a territorial formation with its hub in the Gibeon plateau is an exception in this long-term situation.[20]

(2) One should ask: At the time of the Gibeon plateau polity, who ruled in the nearby, traditional southern hub of Jerusalem? The biblical answer—using the term Jebus/Jebusite—is an enigma; it resonates as stemming from a late polemic or a pun more than depicting a memory of a historical situation.

3. A pre-Deuteronomistic layer in Samuel contains stories about David as a leader of an Apiru band, which was active on the southern fringe of the highlands of Judah. A pivotal part of the story deals with his maneuvers between the rulers of the highlands (Saul) and the Shephelah (the king of Gath).[21] Saul is referred to as acting in the area of the Valley of Elah, and probably also the southern Hebron hills (e.g., 1 Sam 23:19; 24:1–2; it is difficult to separate Saul from the David story here). Was this possible without control over Jerusalem?

---

18. Israel Finkelstein, "Migration of Israelites into Judah after 720 BCE: An Answer and an Update," *ZAW* 127 (2015): 188–206; contra Nadav Na'aman, "Dismissing the Myth of a Flood of Israelite Refugees in the Late Eighth Century BCE," *ZAW* 126 (2014): 1–14.

19. For the containment of the Saul traditions, see P. Kyle McCarter, "The Apology of David," *JBL* 99 (1980): 489–504; Baruch Halpern, *David's Secret Demons: Messiah, Murderer, Traitor, King* (Grand Rapids: Eerdmans, 2001), 73–103. For the Saul traditions being put to the service of Judahite ideology, see Finkelstein and Silberman, "Temple and Dynasty," 259–85.

20. "Ostensibly," because et-Tell ("Ai") of the Early Bronze (together with Tell el-Far'ah North) is a similar case.

21. Nadav Na'aman, "David's Sojourn in Keilah in Light of the Amarna Letters," *VT* 60 (2010): 87–97; Finkelstein, "Geographical and Historical Realities," 131–50.

(4) Related to the question of Jerusalem, two pre-Deuteronomistic references in Samuel mention Philistine garrisons stationed in the highlands—in Geba or Gibeon (1 Sam 10:5; 13:3) and in Bethlehem (2 Sam 23:14, one of the heroic stories that appear in two groups in 2 Sam 21:15–22 and 23:8–21).[22] This raises a number of questions: There was no Philistine united military force in the tenth century; the main Philistine city-states that bordered on the highlands were Gath (though we know relatively little about its archaeology in this phase) and Ekron (until the end of Stratum IV there). Were they strong enough to put garrisons in the highlands? If not, are the references to Philistine garrisons ahistorical, or does Philistine stand for Egypt? Obviously, the two garrisons were established to the north and south of Jerusalem; if they were meant to control it, the questions are, when were they founded and who ruled in Jerusalem at that time?

Below I will try to deal with these difficulties and offer a reasonable reconstruction of the history of the region in the tenth century BCE.

Excursus: Was the Benjamin Plateau Ruled by Jerusalem?

Omer Sergi has recently proposed that Jerusalem emerged as a dominant highlands stronghold as early as the late eleventh/early tenth century BCE and that already in this early phase it ruled over the Benjamin plateau.[23] Sergi's theory is based on two foundations:

The Dating of the Stepped Stone Structure on the Eastern Slope of the City of David Ridge

Sergi dates this structure, which he describes as monumental architecture, to the late eleventh/early tenth century BCE and interprets it as evidence for the existence of a centralized rule in Jerusalem of that time. Under the title "Stepped Stone Structure" Sergi lists several components of construc-

---

22. Deciding about the location of the highland garrison depends on resolving the confusion Geba/Gibeah/Gibeon. For the heroic stories, see Stanley Isser, *The Sword of Goliath: David in Heroic Literature*, SBLStBL 6 (Atlanta: Society of Biblical Literature, 2003).

23. Omer Sergi, "The Emergence of Judah as a Political Entity between Jerusalem and Benjamin," *ZDPV* 133 (2017): 1–23; dressing Na'aman, "Saul, Benjamin," 211–24, 335–49, with ostensible archaeological considerations.

tion on the slope above the Gihon Spring. This listing confuses a rather simple situation. There are basically two elements of construction here: stone terraces and/or support walls on the slope, which were covered in one place by a stone mantle (below I use the better description "stone coating"). These elements drew more attention from scholars than they deserved because they are the only structures in Jerusalem that date to pre-eighth-century BCE phases of the Iron Age and can ostensibly be used to illuminate the nature of the city in the tenth century BCE. Their dating is disputed; the task of the researcher is to sort out facts from arguments meant to keep the glass half full, that is, confirm the biblical description of a glamorous Solomonic Jerusalem.[24] The facts are as follows:

1. In one place (Kenyon's Square A/I), the terraces were built over fills dating to the transitional period between the Late Bronze Age and the Iron I; the pottery drawing looks to me more Late Bronze than Iron I.[25]
2. The fill in the terrace system (Kenyon's Squares A/I–III and Trench I) yielded mainly Late Bronze and possibly also Iron I pottery.[26]
3. In Shiloh's Area G, Iron IIC buildings were constructed over the stone coating, which covers the terraces.[27] Jane Cahill's early so-called floors in one of these building, which she dates to the Iron IIA are no more than construction fills.[28]

---

24. Jane M. Cahill, "Jerusalem at the Time of the United Monarchy: The Archaeological Evidence," in *Jerusalem in Bible and Archaeology: The First Temple Period*, ed. Andrew G. Vaughn and Ann E. Killebrew, SymS 18 (Atlanta: Society of Biblical Literature, 2003), 13–80; Amihai Mazar, "Jerusalem in the Tenth Century B.C.E.: The Glass Half Full," in Amit, *Essays on Ancient Israel*, 255–72; Avraham Faust, "The Large Stone Structure in the City of David: A Reexamination," *ZDPV* 126 (2010): 116–30.

25. Margreet L. Steiner, *The Settlement in the Bronze and Iron Ages*, vol. 3 of *Excavations by Kathleen M. Kenyon in Jerusalem 1961–1967*, Copenhagen International Seminar 9 (London: Sheffield Academic, 2001), 24, description in 24–28; pottery drawing in fig. 4.5.

26. Steiner, *Settlement in the Bronze and Iron Ages*, fig. 4.16.

27. Yigal Shiloh, *Excavations at the City of David I: 1978–1982, Interim Report of the First Five Seasons*, Qedem 19 (Jerusalem: Hebrew University of Jerusalem, 1984), 29; Steiner, *Settlement in the Bronze and Iron Ages*, 58–77.

28. Cahill, "Jerusalem at the Time of the United Monarchy," 56–66. For the "floors" as fill, see Israel Finkelstein et al., "Has the Palace of King David in Jerusalem Been Found?" *TA* 34 (2007): 154.

4. There is more than one phase of construction in the stone coating.[29]
5. The latest sherds retrieved from between the stones in the massive terraces (part of the Stepped Stone Structure) were described as possibly dating to the tenth century BCE—in terms of the time meaning the Iron IIA. Indeed, a few items published by Steiner seem to date to that period (a few items described as originating from under the massive terraces may even date slightly later).[30]

We face two possible chronological scenarios.

Scenario A

All components of the Stepped Stone Structure terraces and stone coating (except renovation of the latter) are contemporaneous. In this case the structure is indeed impressive and should be dated to an advanced phase in the Iron IIA, if not slightly later (contemporaneous or later than the latest sherds in no. 5 above). The broader logic—the possible relation with the early phase of construction in the Large Stone Structure immediately above the slope and appearance of monumental architecture in other places in Judah—points to the later phase of the late Iron IIA in the late ninth century BCE.[31]

A new, important piece of information regarding activity on the eastern slope has recently been added—radiocarbon dates of short-lived samples extracted from below the eastern face of the Gihon Spring Tower.[32] The

---

29. Finkelstein et al., " Palace of King David," 151–154.

30. See Steiner, *Settlement in the Bronze and Iron Ages*, fig. 5.11, left column; for items dating slightly later, see middle column, items 16, 56.

31. Eilat Mazar, *Preliminary Report on the City of David Excavations 2005 at the Visitors Center Area* (Jerusalem: Shalem, 2007); E. Mazar, *The Palace of King David: Excavations at the Summit of the City of David, Preliminary Report of Seasons 2005–2007* (Jerusalem: Shoham Academic Research and Publication, 2009); for the architectural elements belonging to it and the question of dating see Finkelstein et al., "Palace of King David," 142–64. Date for the Iron IIA according to radiocarbon measurements: Finkelstein and Piasetzky, "Radiocarbon Dating," 374–85; Michael B. Toffolo et al., "Absolute Chronology of Megiddo, Israel in the Late Bronze and Iron Ages: High Resolution Radiocarbon Dating," *Radiocarbon* 56 (2014): 221–44.

32. Johanah Regev et al., "Absolute Dating of the Gihon Spring Fortifications, Jerusalem," *Radiocarbon* 59 (2017): 1171–93.

results clearly show that we are dealing with an accumulation, as the dates range between the early second millennium and the ninth century BCE. The drawing published by the authors seems to show that this section of the eastern wall of the Spring Tower is a renovation of the original Middle Bronze tower, possibly after it had collapsed.[33] If so, the latest radiocarbon date puts the renovation in the late ninth century. It is possible, then, that the entire treatment of the slope, including the construction of the Stepped Stone Structure, dates to the late ninth century BCE. The goal was to prevent collapse and damage to the area of the spring.

Scenario B
The Stepped Stone Structure is part of a support system that functioned for many centuries in a spot where the slope is especially steep and collapse may risk the area of the spring. In this case one would assume beginning of operations in the Middle Bronze Age, with the construction of the fortifications around the spring, and continuous activity until the Iron Age if not later. Dating one spot of the terracing according to pottery below or within the fill is meaningless, because the situation may change a short distance away. In any event, in this scenario too, the combination of the radiocarbon dates from below the Spring Tower and the latest pottery in the fills on the slope point to the late Iron IIA, in the (late?) ninth century BCE. Considering all pieces of information from the slope and the area of the spring, this scenario is the more reasonable.

In both Scenarios A and B there is no validity to Sergi's dating of a single monumental structure in the late eleventh/early tenth century BCE.

Analysis of Settlement Patterns in the Central Highlands

Sergi asserts that the area between Bethlehem and Bethel was densely settled in the Iron I–IIA, while the hill country to its north remained uninhabited or thinly settled; hence he associates the sites between Jerusalem and Bethel with Jerusalem. This idea does not conform to the data. The area south of Shechem was densely settled in the Iron I.[34] The absence of sites in the few kilometers between et-Taiyiba and the valley of Shiloh

---

33. For the drawing, see Regev et al., "Absolute Dating," fig. 4.
34. Israel Finkelstein and Zvi Lederman, *Highlands of Many Cultures: The Southern Samaria Survey, the Sites*, SMNIA 14 (Tel Aviv: Institute of Archaeology, 1997), 894–96, 949.

is meaningless. Due to environmental factors, this area was not settled even in the peak periods of activity in the highlands, and in any event, there is no such void immediately to its west.[35] As for the Iron IIA, for two reasons, identification of habitation in this period was complicated: First, diagnostic sherds for subdivision within the Iron II are not easy to come by in the case of sites that yielded just a few Iron Age items. Second, in the early 1990s, when the results of the survey were prepared for publication, identification of such sherds had not yet been well established. Still, if one looks at the list of pottery types, the map of the Iron Age I–II represents, in fact, the Iron IIA.[36] Clearly, the area between Bethel and Shechem was densely settled. Hence there is no reason for Sergi to question the ability of Shechem to rule 30 to 40 kilometers to its south. The settlement patterns are therefore mute on the question of the northern border of Jerusalem's rule.

With these two pillars removed, Sergi's theory remains a theory—with no solid foundation.

4. An Updated Reconstruction

Here I wish to propose a more elaborate, three-stage scenario for the history of the Saulide territorial entity.[37]

Stage I: The Beginning

Saul came from a well-to-do rural family, in or near the town of Geba/Gibeah, identified in the present-day village of Jaba on the eastern fringe of the Gibeon-Bethel plateau, or from Gibeon, which features a (late?) Iron I fortification system (for reasons to prefer this or that site, see below).[38]

---

35. Cf. the lack of settlement, e.g., to the Iron II; Finkelstein and Lederman, *Highlands of Many Cultures*, 951.

36. Finkelstein and Lederman, *Highlands of Many Cultures*, 29, 950.

37. For the immense literature on Saul, see Dietrich, *Early Monarchy*, 162–64 (as of 2007); different studies with bibliographies in Ehrlich and White, *Saul in Story and Tradition*; more recently, Hannes Bezzel, *Saul: Israels König in Tradition, Redaktion und früher Rezeption*, FAT 97 (Tübingen: Mohr Siebeck, 2015). I will concentrate on questions of territorial expansion and historical background.

38. For survey results from Jaba, see Amir Feldstein et al., "Southern Part of the Maps of Ramallah and el-Bireh and Northern Part of the Map of 'Ein Kerem,"

The *core* territory of his rule is probably referred to in the story about the search for his father's asses (1 Sam 9:4–5): the lands of Shalishah, Shaʿalim, Zuph, and Yemini.[39] That Yemini equals Benjamin is obvious. For the land of Shaʿalim/land of Shual, see 1 Sam 13:17, associated with Ophrah, northeast of Bethel. Zuph may be related to Ramathaim (1 Sam 1:1), seemingly Ramathaim of 1 Macc 11:34 and Arimathea of Matt 27:57; John 19:38. If so, better than Ramah, it should probably be identified in or near Rantis in the western sector of the biblical land of Ephraim.[40] These toponyms seem to cover the areas of Benjamin and southern Ephraim. Their ancient origin is implied by their absence from Deuteronomistic writings. Indeed, the reference to the hill country of Ephraim (הר אפרים) in verse 4a is a Deuteronomistic addition. However, the author did not fully understand the term *hill country of Ephraim* any longer, because Deuteronomistic authors use it to delineate the *entire* central highlands area of the Northern Kingdom (Josh 19:50; 21:21; Judg 4:5; 10:1; 1 Kgs 12:25).

In his early days, Saul's seat of power must have been his hometown. This is the straightforward meaning of the text, which refers to Gibeah of Saul.[41] With no firm rule in the highlands, a strongman could have wrested a small territory for himself between the two traditional hubs of Shechem and Jerusalem. Somewhat comparable situations could be Jeroboam I in Zeredah, in the southwest of the biblically described inheritance of Ephraim, and the family that ruled in the village of Ras Karkar, which dominated the same area in the late Ottoman period.[42] An early hub on the desert fringe—rather than Gibeon—would be more logical and less threatening to nearby Jerusalem.

I have already mentioned that sites in the heartland of the Saulide territory feature casemate fortifications. I refer to Tell en-Nasbeh, et-Tell (Ai), Gibeon, and Khirbet ed-Dawwara; the fortifications in these places date

---

in *Archaeological Survey of the Hill Country of Benjamin*, ed. Israel Finkelstein and Yitzhak Magen (Jerusalem: Israel Antiquities Authority, 1993), 177–79. For Gibeon, see Finkelstein, *Forgotten Kingdom*, 40.

39. See also Knauf, "Saul, David, and the Philistines," 15–18.
40. Zechariah Kallai, "Ramah, 4" [Hebrew], *EncBib* 7:375.
41. Contra Na'aman, "Jebusites and Jabeshites," 481–97.
42. For Jeroboam I, see Moshe Kochavi, "The Identification of Zeredah, Home of Jeroboam Son of Nebat, King of Israel" [Hebrew], *ErIsr* 20 (1989): 198–201. For the Ottoman period, see Yehoshua Ben Arieh, "The Sanjak of Jerusalem in the 1870s" [Hebrew], *Cathedra* 36 (1985): 96.

to the late Iron I and/or early Iron IIA, in the tenth century.[43] Casemate-fortified sites seem to hint at the rise of territorial entities in other parts of the southern Levant as well, that is, Moab near the Arnon and Ammon.[44]

Stage II: Expansion to the South

Nadav Na'aman has recently suggested that Jerusalem was "one of Saul's power bases."[45] I likewise think that at a certain stage Saul became strong enough to take control of Jerusalem, the center of power near him. In the later phases of the Late Bronze Age and the early Iron I, the city-state of Jerusalem must have continued to rule over the southern part of the central highlands, similar to the situation in the Amarna period. The takeover of a seat of power by a neighboring strongman is not unfamiliar in these periods, as seen, for instance, in the rise to power of Aziru in Amurru of the fourteenth century BCE.[46] Parallels from other periods are Dahr el-Omar in Acco and Fahr ed-Din in Lebanon in the Ottoman period.

The takeover of Jerusalem (impossible to know from whom) enabled Saul to expand to the south as far as the Hebron hills and to the border with Gath, the major city-state of the Shephelah. At a certain stage, he seems to have managed to extend his activity to the upper Shephelah. Khirbet Qeiyafa could have been built as a stronghold facing Gath.[47] This transitional Iron I/early Iron IIA site shows affiliation with material culture characteristics of sites in the northern part of the central highlands

---

43. Finkelstein, *Forgotten Kingdom*, 38–40.

44. For Arnon, see Israel Finkelstein and Oded Lipschits, "The Genesis of Moab: A Proposal," *Levant* 43 (2011): 139–52. Ammon is manifested in the casemate-like fortification at Tell el-Umeiry: Israel Finkelstein, "Tell el-Umeiri in the Iron I: Facts and Fiction," in *The Fire Signals of Lachish: Studies in the Archaeology and History of Israel in the Late Bronze Age, Iron Age, and Persian Period in Honor of David Ussishkin*, ed. Israel Finkelstein and Nadav Na'aman (Winona Lake, IN: Eisenbrauns, 2011), 113–28.

45. Na'aman, "Jebusites and Jabeshites," 495, 497.

46. Itamar Singer, "A Concise History of Amurru," in *Amurru Akkadian: A Linguistic Study*, ed. Shlomo Izre'el, HSS 41 (Atlanta: Scholars Press, 1991) 2:134–95; Yuval Goren, Israel Finkelstein, and Nadav Na'aman, "The Expansion of the Kingdom of Amurru according to the Petrographic Investigation of the Amarna Tablets," *BASOR* 329 (2003): 2–11.

47. Finkelstein and Fantalkin, "Khirbet Qeiyafa," 38–63.

and the northern valleys rather than nearby sites in Judah.⁴⁸ The building of Khirbet Qeiyafa could have led to confrontation with Gath, vaguely memorialized in the old tradition on the battle in the Valley of Elah (I refer mainly to 1 Sam 17:1–3). Originally (before the account was usurped by the Deuteronomistic David story and authored in Greek ambiance) it commemorated the hero Elhanan (2 Sam 21:19).⁴⁹

The expansion to the south must have put Saul in conflict with another contender to the regional seat of power, David of Bethlehem, who was pushed to the southern fringe, to maneuver between Saul's Jerusalem, Philistine Gath, and the southern "copper chiefdom" of Tel Masos.⁵⁰ The story of the conquest of Jebus by David is etiological, based on the phenomenon of rock-cut tunnels near the Gihon Spring known to the late-monarchic inhabitants of Jerusalem. Whether it is based on an old conquest tradition, and who was the conqueror, is difficult to say. The Deuteronomistic reference to pre-Davidic Jerusalem as Jebus possibly refers to a group settled there and at the same time mocks its ancient inhabitants.⁵¹

Once conquered, Jerusalem could have been fortified like the sites in the Gibeon plateau. The ancient mound is located on the Temple Mount, so this issue cannot be investigated.⁵²

Stage III: Expansion to the North

At a certain point, Saul may have taken advantage of a decline of Shechem and expanded to the north as well.⁵³ This is evident from the Gilboa tradition (why would a later author invent this?), from the reference to Bezek

---

48. Fantalkin and Finkelstein, "Date of Abandonment," 53–60.
49. Isser, *Sword of Goliath*, 34–7.
50. Finkelstein, "Geographical and Historical Realities," 131–50.
51. Na'aman, "Jebusites and Jabeshites," 481–97.
52. Israel Finkelstein, Ido Koch, and Oded Lipschits, "The Mound on the Mount: A Solution to the Problem with Jerusalem?," *JHS* 11 (2011): art. 12; https://tinyurl.com/SBL2636a.
53. The destruction of Stratum XI there was probably contemporaneous to the devastation of Shiloh in the second half of the eleventh century BCE. For Shechem see Israel Finkelstein, "Shechem in the Late Bronze Age," in *Timelines: Studies in Honour of Manfred Bietak*, ed. Ernst Czerny et al., OLA 149 (Leuven: Peeters, 2006) 2:349–56; for Shiloh, see Israel Finkelstein and Eliazer Piasetzky, "The Iron I–IIA in the Highlands and Beyond: ^{14}C Anchors, Pottery Phases and the Shoshenq I Campaign," *Levant* 38 (2006): 45–61.

in 1 Sam 11:8 (here probably only the toponym is old; why would a later author invent a link to a place not important in his time?) and to Jabesh, and from 2 Sam 2:9, which was discussed above. This means that the area ruled by Saul in his peak prosperity stretched over the entire central highlands all the way north to the border of the Jezreel Valley, if not into the valley itself, covering the territories of the two traditional city-states of the highlands: Jerusalem and Shechem combined.

Saul's expansion to the margins of the Jezreel Valley and the coastal plain, that is, close to the strategic international road to the north, brought about his demise, as it collided with renewed ambitions of Egypt of the late Twenty-First and early Twenty-Second Dynasties regarding Canaan. Once again, this situation was not new, being comparable to the confrontation between Labayu of Shechem with Egypt of the Eighteenth Dynasty in the Amarna period and, if one looks for more recent history, to the clash of Dhahr el-Omar with the Ottomans following his takeover of Acco.

5. A United Monarchy of Saul?

The Saul polity created a peculiar situation of a leader considered to be northern ruling from a southern hub. An oral memory of this situation could have been committed to writing in the north in the time of Jeroboam II, when scribal infrastructure for such an endeavor already existed. Other northern royal foundation and heroic traditions (in the latter I refer to the savior stories in the book of Judges) could also have been assembled and put in writing at that time.[54] Domination of Judah by Israel in the days of Joash and Jeroboam II is evidenced from the chronistic part of 2 Kgs 14:11b–13a and is hinted at by the finds at Kuntillet ʿAjrud.[55] Hence the Saul story could have been considered in the north as a forerunner of the idea of a great united monarchy that is ruled by a northern king. The written Saul royal tradition—of a northern king ruling over a united monarchy from Jerusalem—reached Judah with Israelites after 720 BCE and could have served as a model for the idea of a united monarchy ruled by Davidic kings from Jerusalem.[56]

---

54. Finkelstein, "Corpus of North Israelite Texts."

55. E.g., Shmuel Aḥituv, Esther Eshel, and Zeʾev Meshel, "The Inscriptions," in *Kuntillet ʿAjrud (Horvat Teman): An Iron Age II Religious Site on the Judah-Sinai Border*, ed. Zeʾev Meshel (Jerusalem: Israel Exploration Society, 2012), 126.

56. On northern texts arriving in Judah after 720 BCE and incorporated into the

6. Egypt and the Highlands

Shoshenq I, the founder of the Twenty-Second Dynasty and seemingly the more assertive of the Egyptian rulers of the time, reacted to the north Israelite challenge. He campaigned into the highlands and took over the Saulide power bases in the Gibeon plateau and the area of the Jabbok River in the western Gilead. The fortified sites of Khirbet Qeiyafa, Khirbet Dawwara, et-Tell, and Gibeon were destroyed or abandoned. Shoshenq reorganized the territory of the highlands—back to the traditional situation of two city-states under his domination.[57] He may have chosen adversaries of the house of Saul to rule over these polities: David in Jerusalem and Jeroboam I in Shechem (on chronology see below). For the latter, the possible reference to association with Egypt in the Jeroboam I Masoretic Text and in the alternative history in the Septuagint (if the latter includes pre-Deuteronomistic materials) may mean that Jeroboam's rise to power could have been associated with these events—as a vassal of Egypt.[58] Jeroboam—a local (perhaps Apiru) strongman from the highland northwest of modern Ramallah—may have opposed Saul's expansion to the north, fled to Egypt as a result, and returned in coordination with Shoshenq I.

To pacify the highlands and prevent future trouble, Shoshenq I could have established garrisons in certain key places. This may be the background to the references of Philistine garrisons on both sides of

---

Bible, see, e.g., William M. Schniedewind, *How the Bible Became a Book: The Textualization of Ancient Israel* (Cambridge: Cambridge University Press, 2004); Wolfgang Schütte, *Israels Exil in Juda: Untersuchungen zur Entstehung der Schriftprophetie*, OBO 279 (Fribourg: Academic Press; Göttingen: Vandenhoeck & Ruprecht, 2016); references to additional studies in Cynthia Edenburg and Reinhard Müller, "A Northern Provenance for Deuteronomy? A Critical Review," *HBAI* 4 (2015): 148–61.

57. They became territorial kingdoms later, Israel in the first half of the ninth century BCE and Judah in its second half.

58. For a positive answer see Adrian Schenker, "Jeroboam and the Division of the Kingdom in the Ancient Septuagint: LXX 3 Kingdoms 12.24 A–Z, MT 1 Kings 11–12; 14 and the Deuteronomistic History," in *Israel Constructs Its History: Deuteronomistic History in Recent Research*, ed. Albert de Pury, Thomas Römer, and Jean-Daniel Macchi, JSOTSup 306 (Sheffield: Sheffield Academic, 2000), 214–57; Schenker, "Jeroboam's Rise and Fall in the Hebrew and Greek Bible," *JSJ* 39 (2008): 367–73. For a different view, seeing the Septuagint addition as a midrash, see Ziporah Talshir, *The Alternative Story of the Division of the Kingdom*, JBS 6 (Jerusalem: Simor, 1993); Marvin A. Sweeney, "A Reassessment of the Masoretic and Septuagint Versions of the Jeroboam Narratives in 1 Kings/3 Kingdoms 11–14," *JSJ* 38 (2007): 165–95.

Jerusalem: Bethlehem, hometown of David (2 Sam 23:14), and Geba or Gibeon, hometown of Saul (1 Sam 13:3; on this the centrally located Gibeon is preferable). Gath, the major city-state of the Shephelah, seems to have associated with the pharaoh: not only was it not damaged by him, following his campaign Gath grew in size and influence. People from Gath could have been in the service of Shoshenq in these strongholds, providing the background for the reference to *matzav* and *netziv Plishtim* (rather than Egypt) in these two places. When the stories were committed to writing, Egypt in the highlands was a fading memory, while the Philistine city-states were still a menace to Judah. We know about the two garrisons near Jerusalem because of the Judahite connection. Obviously, Shoshenq must have put similar garrison forces near Shechem and in the Jezreel Valley (for the latter note the Shoshenq stele at Megiddo).

A major question is whether this reconstruction can work chronologically. The answer is positive. According to the Bible-free chronology for the Third Intermediate Period suggested by Thomas Schneider, the reign of Shoshenq I is dated at 962–941 BCE.[59] The most probable radiocarbon date for the destruction of Khirbet Qeiyafa is 956–942 BCE.[60] Being typological numbers, the forty-year reign of David and the same length for Solomon signify nothing more precise than a long time; the accession of David can fall in the early years of Shoshenq I's reign. Finally, assuming that the information in the book of Kings on the length of reign of the northern monarchs is based on a north Israelite text, which was composed in the early eighth century, calculating back from the secure date of the death of Joram in 841 puts the accession of Jeroboam I around 940 BCE.[61] All this should be evaluated with two additional notes: (1) the traditional date given by Kenneth Kitchen to Shoshenq I (945–924 BCE) can also work, especially noting that Ishbaal ruled for a number of years after Saul;[62] (2) Shoshenq may have undertaken more than one campaign

---

59. Thomas Schneider, "Contributions to the Chronology of the New Kingdom and the Third Intermediate Period," *AeL* 20 (2010): 373–403.

60. Fantalkin and Finkelstein, "Date of Abandonment," 53–60.

61. For the date of composition for the text, see Jonathan M. Robker, *The Jehu Revolution: A Royal Tradition of the Northern Kingdom and Its Ramifications*, BZAW 435 (Berlin: de Gruyter, 2012); Finkelstein "Corpus of North Israelite Texts."

62. Kenneth A. Kitchen, *The Third Intermediate Period in Egypt (1100–650 BC)*, 2nd ed. (Warminster: Aris & Phillips, 1986).

to Canaan, starting early in his reign.⁶³ A final note: zooming out from details, to consider all these events and processes that apparently took place during the period and in the same geographical arena separately seems illogical historically.

Since I am reconstructing history from just a few vague sources, it should not come as a surprise that my updated scenario still faces at least two difficulties: (1) If Jerusalem had been the seat of Saul, why does it not appear in the Shoshenq I list? Was the name mentioned in a blurred part of the relief?⁶⁴ Or, perhaps following the campaign and the placing of David there, Jerusalem could have been considered a vassal rather than adversary of Egypt; note that there is no reference to Shechem (the seat of Jeroboam I) either. (2) If 2 Sam 2:9 is considered an authentic pre-Deuteronomistic source, why is Judah not mentioned? But this source could have been reshaped by a Deuteronomistic author.

7. Conclusions

In this article I offered a more nuanced, three-stage process for the geographical expansion of the Saulide entity in the tenth century BCE. In the peak of its rule, the house of Saul could have ruled from Jerusalem over the entire central highlands, that is, over the territories of the two traditional Bronze Age city-states of Shechem and Jerusalem. The memory of this early united monarchy, which was ruled by a northern king (at least from the perspective of the later Israel) from the southern hub, may have served as a model for the idea of a great united monarchy ruled by a northern king in the time of Jeroboam II, and no less important, for the Deuterono-

---

63. For the idea of more than one campaign, see Donald B. Redford, "Studies in Relations between Palestine and Egypt during the First Millennium BC," *JAOS* 93 (1973): 10; Redford, *Egypt, Canaan and Israel in Ancient Times* (Princeton: Princeton University, 1992), 312; Aidan Dodson, "Towards a Minimum Chronology of the New Kingdom and Third Intermediate Period," *BES* 14 (2000): 8. For dating it early in his reign, see Redford, *Egypt, Canaan and Israel*, 312; Shirly Ben-Dor Evian, "Shishak's Karnak Relief—More than Just Name Rings," in *Egypt, Canaan and Israel: History, Imperialism, Ideology and Literature; Proceedings of a Conference at the University of Haifa, 3–7 May 2009*, ed. Shay Bar, Dan'el Kahn and J. J. Shirley, CHANE 52 (Leiden: Brill, 2011), 11–22.

64. Hermann Michael Niemann, "The Socio-Political Shadow Cast by the Biblical Solomon," in *The Age of Solomon: Scholarship at the Turn of the Millennium*, ed. Lowell K. Handy, SHCANE 11 (Leiden: Brill, 1997), 297.

mistic concept of a united monarchy ruled from Jerusalem by a Davidide. Though admittedly hypothetical, this reconstruction is in line with the few fragmentary sources of information on the highlands in the tenth century BCE. It also provides a reasonable scenario for the otherwise rather enigmatic contemporaneous rise of Israel and Judah.

Bibliography

Aḥituv, Shmuel, Esther Eshel, and Zeʾev Meshel. "The Inscriptions." Pages 73–142 in *Kuntillet ʿAjrud (Horvat Teman): An Iron Age II Religious Site on the Judah-Sinai Border*. Edited by Zeʾev Meshel. Jerusalem: Israel Exploration Society, 2012.

Ahlström, Gösta W. *The History of Ancient Palestine from the Palaeolithic Period to Alexander's Conquest*. JSOTSup 146. Sheffield: Sheffield Academic, 1993.

Arnold, Patrick M. *Gibeah: The Search for a Biblical City*. JSOTSup 79. Sheffield: Sheffield Academic, 1990.

Ben Arieh, Yehoshua. "The Sanjak of Jerusalem in the 1870s" [Hebrew]. *Cathedra* 36 (1985): 73–122.

Ben-Dor Evian, Shirly. "Shishak's Karnak Relief—More than Just Name Rings." Pages 11–22 in *Egypt, Canaan and Israel: History, Imperialism, Ideology and Literature; Proceedings of a Conference at the University of Haifa, 3–7 May 2009*. Edited by Shay Bar, Danʾel Kahn, and J. J. Shirley. CHANE 52. Leiden: Brill, 2011.

Bezzel, Hannes. *Saul: Israels König in Tradition, Redaktion und früher Rezeption*. FAT 97. Tübingen: Mohr Siebeck, 2015.

Blenkinsopp, Joseph. "Did Saul Make Gibeon His Capital?" *VT* 24 (1974): 1–7.

Cahill, Jane. "Jerusalem at the Time of the United Monarchy: The Archaeological Evidence." Pages 13–80 in *Jerusalem in Bible and Archaeology: The First Temple Period*. Edited by Andrew G. Vaughn and Ann E. Killbrew. SymS 18. Atlanta: Society of Biblical Literature, 2003.

Dietrich, Walter. *The Early Monarchy in Israel: The Tenth Century B.C.E.* BibEnc 3. Atlanta: Society of Biblical Literature, 2007.

Dodson, Aidan. "Towards a Minimum Chronology of the New Kingdom and Third Intermediate Period." *BES* 14 (2000): 7–18.

Edelman, Diana. "The 'Ashurites' of Eshbaal's State (2 Sam. 2.9)." *PEQ* 117 (1985): 85–91.

———. *King Saul in the Historiography of Judah.* JSOTSup 121. Sheffield: JSOT Press, 1991.

———. "Saul ben Kish in History and Tradition." Pages 142–59 in *The Origins of the Ancient Israelite States.* Edited by Volkmar Fritz and Philip R. Davies. JSOTSup 228. Sheffield: Sheffield Academic, 1996.

———. "Saul's Journey through Mt. Ephraim and Samuel's Ramah (1 Sam 9:4–5, 10:2–5)." *ZDPV* 104 (1988): 44–58.

Edenburg, Cynthia, and Reinhard Müller. "A Northern Provenance for Deuteronomy? A Critical Review." *HBAI* 4 (2015): 148–61.

Ehrlich, Carl S., and Marsha C. White. *Saul in Story and Tradition.* FAT 47. Tübingen: Mohr Siebeck, 2006.

Fantalkin, Alexander, and Israel Finkelstein. "The Date of Abandonment and Territorial Affiliation of Khirbet Qeiyafa: An Update." *TA* 44 (2017): 53–60.

Faust, Avraham. "The Large Stone Structure in the City of David: A Reexamination." *ZDPV* 126 (2010): 116–30.

Feldstein, Amir, Giora Kidron, Nizan Hanin, Yair Kamaisky, and David Eitam. "Southern Part of the Maps of Ramallah and el-Bireh and Northern Part of the Map of 'Ein Kerem." Pages 163–234 in *Archaeological Survey of the Hill Country of Benjamin.* Edited by Israel Finkelstein and Yitzhak Magen. Jerusalem: Israel Antiquities Authority, 1993.

Finkelstein, Israel. "A Corpus of North Israelite Texts in the Days of Jeroboam II?" *HBAI* 6 (2017): 262–89.

———. *The Forgotten Kingdom: The Archaeology and History of Northern Israel.* ANEM 5. Atlanta: Society of Biblical Literature, 2013.

———. "The Geographical and Historical Realities behind the Earliest Layer in the David Story." *SJOT* 27 (2013): 131–50.

———. "The Last Labayu: King Saul and the Expansion of the First North Israelite Territorial Entity." Pages 171–88 in *Essays on Ancient Israel in Its Near Eastern Context: A Tribute to Nadav Na'aman.* Edited by Yairah Amit, Ehud Ben Zvi, Israel Finkelstein, and Oded Lipschits. Winona Lake, IN: Eisenbrauns, 2006.

———. "Migration of Israelites into Judah after 720 BCE: An Answer and an Update." *ZAW* 127 (2015): 188–206.

———. "Shechem in the Late Bronze and the Iron I." Pages 349–56 in vol. 2 of *Timelines: Studies in Honor of Manfred Bietak.* Edited by Ernst Czerny, Irmgard Hein, Hermann Hunger, Dagmar Melman, and Angela Schwab. 3 vols. OLA 149. Leuven: Peeters, 2006.

———. "Saul, Benjamin and the Emergence of 'Biblical Israel': An Alternative View." *ZAW* 123 (2011): 348–67.

———. "Tell el-Ful Revisited: The Assyrian and Hellenistic Periods (with a New Identification)." *PEQ* 143 (2011): 106–18.

———. "Tell el-Umeiri in the Iron I: Facts and Fiction, with a History of the Collared Rim Pithoi." Pages 113–28 in *The Fire Signals of Lachish: Studies in the Archaeology and History of Israel in the Late Bronze Age, Iron Age, and Persian Period in Honor of David Ussishkin*. Edited by Israel Finkelstein and Nadav Na'aman. Winona Lake, IN: Eisenbrauns, 2011.

Finkelstein, Israel, and Alexander Fantalkin, "Khirbet Qeiyafa: An Unsensational Archaeological and Historical Interpretation." *TA* 39 (2012): 38–63.

Finkelstein, Israel, and Eliazer Piasetzky. "The Iron I–IIA in the Highlands and Beyond: ^{14}C Anchors, Pottery Phases and the Shoshenq I Campaign." *Levant* 38 (2006): 45–61.

———. "Radiocarbon Dating the Iron Age in the Levant: A Bayesian Model for Six Ceramic Phases and Six Transitions." *Antiquity* 84 (2010): 374–85.

Finkelstein, Israel, Ido Koch, and Oded Lipschits. "The Mound on the Mount: A Solution to the Problem with Jerusalem?" *JHS* 11 (2011): article 12. https://tinyurl.com/SBL2636a.

Finkelstein, Israel, and Nadav Na'aman. "Shechem of the Amarna Period and the Rise of the Northern Kingdom of Israel." *IEJ* 55 (2005): 172–93.

Finkelstein, Israel, and Neil A. Silberman. "Temple and Dynasty: Hezekiah, the Remaking of Judah and the Rise of the Pan-Israelite Ideology." *JSOT* 30 (2006): 259–85.

Finkelstein, Israel, and Oded Lipschits. "The Genesis of Moab: A Proposal." *Levant* 43 (2011): 139–52.

Finkelstein, Israel, Ze'ev Herzog, Lily Singer-Avitz, and David Ussishkin. "Has the Palace of King David in Jerusalem Been Found?" *TA* 34 (2007): 142–64.

Finkelstein, Israel, and Zvi Lederman. *Highlands of Many Cultures: The Southern Samaria Survey, the Sites*. SMNIA 14. Tel Aviv: Institute of Archaeology, 1997.

Goren, Yuval, Israel Finkelstein, and Nadav Na'aman. "The Expansion of the Kingdom of Amurru according to the Petrographic Investigation of the Amarna Tablets." *BASOR* 329 (2003): 1–11.

Halpern, Baruch. *David's Secret Demons: Messiah, Murderer, Traitor, King*. Grand Rapids: Eerdmans, 2001.
Isser, Stanley. *The Sword of Goliath: David in Heroic Literature*. SBLStBL 6. Atlanta: Society of Biblical Literature, 2003.
Kaiser, Otto. "Der historische und biblische König Saul (Teil I)." *ZAW* 122 (2010): 520–45.
———. "Der historische und der biblische König Saul (Teil II)." *ZAW* 123 (2011): 1–14.
Kallai, Zechariah. "Ramah, 4" [Hebrew]. *EncBib* 7:375.
Kitchen, Kenneth A. *The Third Intermediate Period in Egypt (1100–650 BC)*. 2nd ed. Warminster: Aris & Phillips, 1986.
Knauf, Ernst A. "Saul, David, and the Philistines: From Geography to History." *BN* 109 (2001): 15–18.
Kochavi, Moshe. "The Identification of Zeredah, Home of Jeroboam Son of Nebat, King of Israel" [Hebrew]. *ErIsr* 20 (1989): 198–201.
Mazar, Amihai. "Jerusalem in the Tenth Century B.C.E.: The Glass Half Full." Pages 255–72 in *Essays on Ancient Israel in Its Near Eastern Context: A Tribute to Nadav Na'aman*. Edited by Yairah Amit, Ehud Ben Zvi, Israel Finkelstein, and Oded Lipschits. Winona Lake, IN: Eisenbrauns, 2006.
Mazar, Eilat. *The Palace of King David: Excavations at the Summit of the City of David, Preliminary Report of Seasons 2005–2007*. Jerusalem: Shoham Academic Research and Publication, 2009.
———. *Preliminary Report on the City of David Excavations 2005 at the Visitors Center Area*. Jerusalem: Shalem, 2007.
McCarter, P. Kyle. "The Apology of David." *JBL* 99 (1980): 489–504.
Na'aman, Nadav. "David's Sojourn in Keilah in Light of the Amarna Letters." *VT* 60 (2010): 87–97.
———. "Dismissing the Myth of a Flood of Israelite Refugees in the Late Eighth Century BCE." *ZAW* 126 (2014): 1–14.
———. "Jebusites and Jabeshites in the Saul and David Story-Cycles." *Bib* 95 (2014): 481–97.
———. "The Kingdom of Ishbaal." *BN* 54 (1990): 33–37.
———. "The Pre-Deuteronomistic Story of King Saul and Its Historical Significance." *CBQ* 54 (1990): 638–58.
———. "Saul, Benjamin and the Emergence of 'Biblical Israel.'" *ZAW* 121 (2009): 211–24, 335–49.
Niemann, Hermann Michael. "The Socio-Political Shadow Cast by the Biblical Solomon." Pages 252–99 in *The Age of Solomon: Scholarship at*

the Turn of the Millennium. Edited by Lowell K. Handy. SHCANE 11. Leiden: Brill, 1997.

Nihan, Christophe. "Saul among the Prophets (1 Sam. 10:10–12 and 19:18–24): The Reworking of Saul's Figure in the Context of the Debate on Charismatic Prophecy in the Persian Era." Pages 88–118 in *Saul in Story and Tradition.* Edited by Carl S. Ehrlich and Marsha C. White. FAT 47. Tübingen: Mohr Siebeck, 2006.

Redford, Donald B. *Egypt, Canaan and Israel in Ancient Times.* Princeton: Princeton University, 1992.

———. "Studies in Relations between Palestine and Egypt during the First Millennium BC." *JAOS* 93 (1973): 3–17.

Regev, Johanna, Joe Uziel, Nahshon Szanton, and Elisabetta Boaretto. "Absolute Dating of the Gihon Spring Fortifications, Jerusalem." *Radiocarbon* 59 (2017): 1171–93.

Robker, Jonathan M. *The Jehu Revolution: A Royal Tradition of the Northern Kingdom and Its Ramifications.* BZAW 435. Berlin: de Gruyter, 2012.

Scheffler, Eben. "Saving Saul from the Deuteronomist." Pages 263–71 in *Past, Present, Future: The Deuteronomistic History and the Prophets.* Edited by Johannes C. de Moor and H. F. van Rooy. OTS 44. Leiden: Brill, 2000.

Schenker, Adrian. "Jeroboam and the Division of the Kingdom in the Ancient Septuagint: LXX 3 Kingdoms 12.24 A–Z, MT 1 Kings 11–12; 14 and the Deuteronomistic History." Pages 214–57 in *Israel Constructs Its History: Deuteronomistic History in Recent Research.* Edited by Albert de Pury, Thomas Römer, and Jean Daniel Maacchi. JSOTSup 306. Sheffield: Sheffield Academic, 2000.

———. "Jeroboam's Rise and Fall in the Hebrew and Greek Bible." *JSJ* 39 (2008): 367–73.

Schneider, Thomas. "Contributions to the Chronology of the New Kingdom and the Third Intermediate Period." *AeL* 20 (2010): 373–403.

Schniedewind, William M. *How the Bible Became a Book: The Textualization of Ancient Israel.* Cambridge: Cambridge University Press, 2004.

Schütte, Wolfgang. *Israels Exil in Juda: Untersuchungen zur Entstehung der Schriftprophetie.* OBO 279. Fribourg: Academic Press; Göttingen: Vandenhoeck & Ruprecht, 2016.

Sergi, Omer. "The Emergence of Judah as a Political Entity between Jerusalem and Benjamin." *ZDPV* 133 (2017): 1–23.

Shiloh, Yigal. *Excavations at the City of David I: 1978–1982, Interim Report of the First Five Seasons.* Qedem 19. Jerusalem: Hebrew University of Jerusalem, 1984.

Singer, Itamar. "A Concise History of Amurru." Pages 134–95 in vol. 2 of *Amurru Akkadian: A Linguistic Study.* Edited by Shlomo Izre'el. HSS 41. Atlanta: Scholars Press, 1991.

Steiner, Margreet, L. *The Settlement in the Bronze and Iron Ages.* Vol. 3 of *Excavations by Kathleen M. Kenyon in Jerusalem 1961–1967.* Copenhagen International Seminar 9. London: Sheffield Academic, 2001.

Sweeney, Marvin A. "A Reassessment of the Masoretic and Septuagint Versions of the Jeroboam Narratives in 1 Kings/3 Kingdoms 11–14." *JSJ* 38 (2007): 165–95.

Talshir, Ziporah. *The Alternative Story of the Division of the Kingdom.* JBS 6. Jerusalem: Simor, 1993.

Toffolo, Michael B., Eran Arie, Mario A. S. Martin, Elisabetta Boaretto, and Israel Finkelstein. "Absolute Chronology of Megiddo, Israel in the Late Bronze and Iron Ages: High Resolution Radiocarbon Dating." *Radiocarbon* 56 (2014): 221–44.

Toorn, Karel van der. "Saul and the Rise of the Israelite State Religion." *VT* 43 (1993): 519–42.

White, Marsha C. "The History of Saul's Rise: Saulide State Propaganda in 1 Samuel 1–14." Pages 271–92 in *"A Wise Discerning Mind": Essays in Honor of Burke O. Long.* Edited by Saul M. Olyan and Robert C. Culley. BJS 325. Providence, RI: Brown Judaic Studies, 2000.

Saul, David, and the Formation of the Israelite Monarchy: Revisiting the Historical and Literary Context of 1 Samuel 9–2 Samuel 5

Omer Sergi

1. Introduction

The traditions about the formation of the Israelite monarchy that are embedded within 1 Sam 9–2 Sam 5 tell about Saul, the first king of the Israelites, who failed to establish a dynastic monarchy; he was succeeded by his rival, David, who succeeded exactly where Saul failed: David established a long-lasting dynastic monarchy and brought the Israelites and the Judahites under his rule. In spite of the fact that the storyline in 1 Sam 9– 2 Sam 5 is characterized by a rather coherent narrative (at least in its theme and plot), with many links tying together the different accounts embedded in it, the conventional wisdom that rules contemporary scholarship on the matter is that these traditions stem from two distinct sources, each of different origin: north Israelite traditions about Saul (usually identified in 1 Sam 9–14), which tell about the rise and fall of the first Israelite king; and a Judahite collection of stories about David's rise, which presents David as Saul's legitimate successor (1 Sam 16–2 Sam 5).[1] It is assumed that the north Israelite Saul traditions arrived in Judah only after the fall of Samaria (720 BCE) and stimulated the composition of the stories about David's rise, which are dated, accordingly, to the seventh century BCE. It is further assumed that the stories about David's rise create the first literary

---

1. For the coherence of the narrative, see Walter Dietrich and Thomas Naumann, "The David–Saul Narrative," in *Reconsidering Israel and Judah: Recent Studies on the Deuteronomistic History*, ed. Gary N. Knoppers and J. Gordon McConville (Winona Lake, IN: Eisenbrauns, 1995), 276–318.

link between Saul the Israelite and David the Judahite in order to present Judah as the political and cultural successor of the former kingdom of Israel.[2] In other words, it is argued that the stories about David's rise connect two formerly unrelated literary protagonists—the first king of Israel (Saul) and the first king of Judah (David)—in order to present the house of David (Judah) as the rightful successor to the house of Saul (Israel).

At the heart of this hypothesis lies the assumption that the stories about David's rise in 1 Sam 16–2 Sam 5 are actually an allegory to the histories of Israel and Judah. This assumption, however, is the result of historical, not literary, observation: historically, it is quite clear that the kingdoms of Israel and Judah were never united within one political entity under the rule of the house of David from Jerusalem.[3] It is therefore assumed that any portrayal of the first king of Judah (David) as the heir of the first king of Israel (Saul) could only reflect a Judahite wishful thinking and not an accurate political reality. The main problem with this assumption, however, is the fact that both the early Saul traditions and the stories about

---

2. E.g., Walter Dieterich and Stefan Münger, "Die Herrschaft Sauls und der Norden Israels," in *Saxa Loquentur: Studien zu Archäologie Palästinas/Israels; Festschrift für Volkmar Fritz zum 65. Geburtstag*, ed. Cornelius G. den Hertog, Ulrich Hübner, and Stefan Münger, AOAT 302 (Münster: Ugarit-Verlag, 2003), 39–54; Reinhard G. Kratz, *The Composition of the Narrative Books of the Old Testament* (London: T&T Clark, 2005), 181–82; Israel Finkelstein, "The Last Labayu: King Saul and the Expansion of the First North Israelite Territorial Entity," in *Essays on Ancient Israel in Its Near Eastern Context: A Tribute to Nadav Na'aman*, ed. Yairah Amit et al. (Winona Lake, IN: Eisenbrauns, 2006), 171–88; Finkelstein, "Saul, Benjamin and the Emergence of 'Biblical Israel': An Alternative View," *ZAW* 123 (2011): 348–67; Walter Dietrich, *The Early Monarchy in Israel: The Tenth Century B.C.E.*, BibEnc 3 (Atlanta: Society of Biblical Literature, 2007), 247–48, 304–8; Otto Kaiser, "Der historische und biblische König Saul (Teil I)," *ZAW* 122 (2010): 524–26; Jacob L. Wright, *David, King of Israel and Caleb in Biblical Memory* (Cambridge: Cambridge University Press, 2014), 39–50, 141–46; Hannes Bezzel, *Saul: Israels König in Tradition, Redaktion und früher Rezeption*, FAT 97 (Tübingen: Mohr Siebeck, 2015), 228–34; but see Nadav Na'aman, "Saul, Benjamin and the Emergence of 'Biblical Israel,'" *ZAW* 121 (2009): 211–24, 335–49, who already challenged this perception.

3. E.g., Israel Finkelstein, "A Great United Monarchy? Archaeological and Historical Perspectives," in *One God—One Cult—One Nation: Archaeological and Biblical Perspectives*, ed. Reinhard G. Kratz and Hermann Spieckermann, BZAW 405 (Berlin: de Gruyter, 2010), 3–28. For state formation in Judah, see Omer Sergi, "Judah's Expansion in Historical Context," *TA* 40 (2013): 226–46; Sergi, "The Emergence of Judah as a Political Entity between Jerusalem and Benjamin," *ZDPV* 133 (2017): 1–23; and further below.

David's rise are well embedded in the social and political realia of southern Canaan in the early Iron Age (below), and therefore there is no real reason to read them as allegories. Rather, we should at least try to read them for what they are—an attempt to portray the rise of the Israelite monarchy.

The following study aims to do exactly that: to read the biblical traditions embedded within 1 Sam 9–2 Sam 5 in light of the historical context (i.e., the sociopolitical realia) they reflect and consequently to discuss their origins and historical significance. In order to do so, I shall begin with a brief review of the archaeological and historical data shedding light on the formation of Israel and Judah as south Levantine territorial polities.

2. The Formation of Israel and Judah in the Central Canaanite Hill Country: Archaeological and Historical Perspectives

Massive sedentarization characterizes the central Canaanite highlands during the Iron I (late twelfth to early tenth centuries BCE), when local mobile-pastoral groups shifted from subsistence economy based mainly on animal husbandry to an agropastoral mode of life.[4] The Iron I settlers in the hill country were, accordingly, the indigenous mobile-pastoral population of the Samaria and Judean hills, and, if so, they were not only well acquainted with the regions in which they chose to settle but they were also an integral part of the highlands' social structure.[5] Most of the newly

---

4. For the current state of research regarding the absolute chronology of the early Iron Age (based on a large body of radiocarbon measurements), see Sharen Lee, Christopher Bronk Ramsey, and Amihai Mazar, "Iron Age Chronology in Israel: Results from Modeling with a Trapezoidal Bayesian Framework," *Radiocarbon* 55 (2013): 731–40; Michael B. Toffolo et al., "Absolute Chronology of Megiddo, Israel in the Late Bronze and Iron Ages: High Resolution Radiocarbon Dating," *Radiocarbon* 56 (2014): 221–44.

5. E.g., Israel Finkelstein, *The Archaeology of the Israelite Settlement* (Jerusalem: Israel Exploration Society, 1988); Finkelstein, "The Great Transformation: The 'Conquest' of the Highlands Frontiers and the Rise of the Territorial States," in *The Archaeology of Society in the Holy Land*, ed. Thomas Levy (London: Leicester University Press, 1995), 349–65; Finkelstein, "Ethnicity and the Origin of the Iron I Settlers in the Highlands of Canaan: Can the Real Israel Stand Up?," *BA* 59 (1996): 198–212; Baruch Rosen, "Economy and Subsistence," in *Shiloh: The Archaeology of a Biblical Site*, ed. Israel Finkelstein, SMNIA 10 (Tel Aviv: Institute of Archaeology, 1993), 362–67; and for Transjordan, see Eveline J. van der Steen, *Tribes and Territories in Transition: The Central East Jordan Valley in the Late Bronze Age and Early Iron Ages, A Study of the Sources*, OLA 130 (Leuven: Peeters, 2004); Benjamin Porter, *Complex Communities:*

founded settlements clustered in the Samaria hills, between the Jezreel Valley and Shiloh.[6] The hilly terrain south of Shiloh, all the way to Bethel (some 20 kilometers south of Shiloh), was only sparsely settled during the Iron I and even more so in the Iron IIA. The next cluster of settlements concentrated in the Benjamin plateau, between Bethel in the north and Jerusalem in the south.[7] Noteworthy is the fact that settlement expansion into the hilly terrain of the Shechem and Shiloh regions demonstrates clear spatial continuity between the northern and southern Samaria hills, while no such clear continuity exists south of Shiloh or south of Jerusalem. This leaves the southern cluster of settlements (in the Benjamin plateau) relatively isolated.

Shechem (Tell Balâṭah) was the most important political and economic center in the Samaria hills throughout the second millennium BCE, as is demonstrated by both textual sources (Egyptian Execration Texts, el-Amarna archive) and archaeological remains. Since the MB II–III and to the Iron I (with a short hiatus in the LB I) Shechem was a well-fortified highland stronghold with sanctuaries built on its summit.[8] Shechem demonstrates clear and organic continuity in the transition from the Late Bronze Age to the Iron I, but it was utterly destroyed at the end of that

---

The Archaeology of Early Iron Age West-Central Jordan (Tucson: University of Arizona Press, 2013).

6. Finkelstein, "Great Transformation," 349–65; Adam Zertal, *The Shechem Syncline*, vol. 1 of *The Manasseh Hill Country Survey*, CHANE 21.1 (Leiden: Brill, 2004); Zertal, *The Eastern Valleys and the Fringe of the Desert*, vol. 2 of *The Manasseh Hill Country Survey*, CHANE 21.2 (Leiden: Brill, 2008); Adam Zertal and Nivi Mirkam, *From Nahal 'Iron to Nahal Shechem*, vol. 3 of *The Manasseh Hill Country Survey*, CHANE 21.3 (Leiden: Brill, 2016); Yuval Gadot, "The Iron I in the Samaria Highlands: A Nomad Settlement Wave or Urban Expansion?," in *Rethinking Israel: Studies in the History and Archaeology of Ancient Israel in Honor of Israel Finkelstein*, ed. Oded Lipschits, Yuval Gadot, and Matthew J. Adams (Winona Lake, IN: Eisenbrauns, 2017), 103–14.

7. Finkelstein, *Archaeology of the Israelite Settlement*, 188–92, 198–99, 201–2; Finkelstein and Zvi Lederman, *Highlands of Many Cultures: The Southern Samaria Survey, the Sites*, SMNIA 14 (Tel Aviv: Institute of Archaeology, 1997), 949–51; Sergi, "Emergence of Judah," 5–12.

8. Edward F. Campbell, *Text*, vol. 1 of *Shechem III: The Stratigraphy and Architecture of Shechem/Tell Balâṭah*, ASORAR 6 (Boston: American Schools of Oriental Research, 2002); Israel Finkelstein, "Shechem in the Late Bronze and the Iron I," in *Timelines: Studies in Honor of Manfred Bietak*, ed. Ernst Czerny et al., OLA 149 (Leuven: Peeters, 2006) 2:349–56.

period, namely, in the early tenth century BCE.[9] Throughout most of the Iron IIA (tenth–ninth centuries BCE) Shechem was only sparsely settled, and during that period the political and economic weight shifted first to Tell el-Farʿah north, identified with biblical Tirzah, and later to Samaria.[10]

Sometime during the end of the tenth or the early ninth century BCE, Tirzah rapidly developed from a rather poor settlement (Stratum VIIa) to a rich urban center exhibiting social hierarchy, cultic activity, and long distance trade (Stratum VIIb). It was utterly destroyed shortly after, probably still within the first half of the ninth century BCE, and was abandoned throughout the ninth century BCE.[11] Following the destruction of Tirzah in the early ninth century, power balance shifted back to the heartland of Samaria, where a palatial compound was lavishly built on what was previously an agricultural estate that had no preceding urban or monumental tradition.[12] It manifested the accumulation of wealth and consequently also political power in the hands of a newly emerged elite, the Omride dynasty, with which the palace on the Samaria hilltop is exclusively identified (1 Kgs 16:24).[13] Assuming that the rich agricultural estate preceding

---

9. For the continuity, see Campbell, *Text*, 210–33; Finkelstein, "Shechem in the Late Bronze," 352. The excavators dated the destruction to the twelfth century BCE (Campbell, *Text*, 230–33), but the small Iron I assemblage published contains vessels representing the end of the Iron I (Finkelstein, "Shechem in the Late Bronze," 352).

10. The published data (Campbell, *Text*, 235–70) do not allow one to conclude when exactly in the Iron Age Shechem flourished again, whether in the late Iron IIA or later, in the early Iron IIB. In either case, it seems that throughout most of the tenth century and probably some parts of the ninth century Shechem was not a major player in the region. For the identification of Tirzah, see William F. Albright, "The Site of Tirzah and the Topography of Western Manasseh," *JPOS* 11 (1931): 241–51.

11. For a recent evaluation of stratigraphic and chronological sequence in Tell el-Farʿah, see Assaf Kleiman, "Comments on the Archaeology and History of Tell el-Farʿah North (Biblical Tirzah) in the Iron IIA," *Sem* 60 (2018): 85–104.

12. For a recent discussion of the stratigraphy of the palatial compound in Samaria, see Omer Sergi and Yuval Gadot, "Omride Palatial Architecture as Symbol in Action: Between State Formation, Obliteration and Heritage," *JNES* 76 (2017): 105–6, with further literature.

13. E.g., Israel Finkelstein, "Omride Architecture," *ZDPV* 116 (2000): 114–38; Finkelstein, *The Forgotten Kingdom: The Archaeology and History of Northern Israel*, ANEM 5 (Atlanta: Society of Biblical Literature, 2013), 85–94; Hermann Michael Niemann, "Core Israel in the Highlands and Its Periphery: Megiddo, the Jezreel Valley and the Galilee in the Eleventh–Eighth Century BCE," in *Megiddo IV: The 1998–2002 Seasons*, ed. Israel Finkelstein, David Ussishkin, and Baruch Halpern, SMNIA 24 (Tel

the erection of the Omride palace in Samaria was the family's estate, it reflects the wealth accumulated in the hands of the Omrides prior to their rise to power.[14]

By the early ninth century BCE, from their seat in the heartland of Samaria, the Omrides extended their political hegemony over vast territories that inhabited different social groups, as is also clear from biblical and extrabiblical sources.[15] The extension of Omride political hegemony was marked in the landscape by the erection of royal compounds on the western (Megiddo VA–IVB) and eastern (Jezreel) edges of the Jezreel Valley. A new fortified town was erected in the Hulah Valley (Hazor X–IX), on the ruins of what was once the royal capital of one of the strongest polities in second millennium BCE Canaan. All these buildings manifested the power and wealth of the highland dynasty, and served as the locale for integrating local elites into the web of the newly established Omride hegemony.[16] The Omrides extended their political hegemony also to the more arid and less sedentary regions of the plains of Moab by establishing patronage relationship with local leaders of mobile-pastoral groups (see 2 Kgs 3:4) and by erecting forts on the main trade routes crossing the region.[17]

The dramatic shifts in power balance characterizing the Iron I–IIA in the Samaria hills (from Shechem to Tirzah and to Samaria) had little or no effect on the political formation in the south, around Jerusalem. Jerusalem was the seat of local ruling elite as early as the second millennium BCE,

---

Aviv: Institute of Archaeology, 2006), 821–42; Niemann, "Royal Samaria, Capital or Residence? Or: The Foundation of the City of Samaria by Sargon II," in *Ahab Agonistes: The Rise and Fall of the Omri Dynasty*, ed. Lester L. Grabbe, LHBOTS 421 (London: T&T Clark, 2007), 184–207.

14. For the archaeological remains of the agricultural estate that precedes the building of the palace in Samaria (Building Period 0), see Lawrence E. Stager, "Shemer's Estate," *BASOR* 277/278 (1990): 93–107; Norma Franklin, "Samaria: From the Bedrock to the Omride Palace," *Levant* 36 (2004): 190–94. For their wealth before the rise to power, see Sergi and Gadot, "Omride Palatial," 109.

15. Niemann, "Core Israel," 821–42; Nadav Na'aman, "The Northern Kingdom in the Late Tenth–Ninth Centuries BCE," in *Understanding the History of Ancient Israel*, ed. H. G. M. Williamson, Proceedings of the British Academy 143 (Oxford: Oxford University Press, 2007), 399–418; Israel Finkelstein, "Stages in the Territorial Expansion of the Northern Kingdom," *VT* 61 (2011): 227–42; Finkelstein, *Forgotten Kingdom*, 83–112.

16. Niemann, "Core Israel," 821–42; Sergi and Gadot, "Omride Palatial," 108–10.

17. Israel Finkelstein and Oded Lipschits, "Omride Architecture in Moab: Jahatz and Atharot," *ZDPV* 126 (2010): 29–42.

and yet, monumental architecture in the City of David appeared—for the first time since the Middle Bronze Age—only in the early Iron Age, with the erection of the Stepped Stone Structure on the eastern slopes of the city of David.[18] It is almost unanimously agreed that the foundations of this structure were laid no earlier than the mid-late Iron I, that is, in the late eleventh or early tenth century BCE.[19] The Stepped Stone Structure, which stood out in the rural landscape surrounding Jerusalem, marked it as a highland stronghold, the seat of a local ruling elite. It seems, therefore, that by the end of the eleventh/early tenth century BCE, a centralized political rule was established in Jerusalem, with a developing hierarchical social structure. In order to explain this social change, one must shift the view from Jerusalem to its surroundings.

Throughout the fourteenth through twelfth centuries BCE, Jerusalem ruled over a rather barren land inhabited mainly by mobile-pastoralists, while to its south there were some sedentary settlements.[20] Massive sed-

---

18. For Jerusalem as a seat for a local ruling elite in the second millennium, see Nadav Na'aman, "Canaanite Jerusalem and Its Central Hill Country Neighbors in the Second Millennium B.C.E.," *UF* 24 (1992): 257–91.

19. A collared-rim jar found in situ on a floor of a structure buried immediately below the stone terrace of the Stepped Stone Structure, together with pottery sherds retrieved from within the stone terraces, date its construction to the late Iron I, or the very early Iron IIA, and see Margreet L. Steiner, *The Settlement in the Bronze and Iron Ages*, vol. 3 of *Excavations by Kathleen M. Kenyon in Jerusalem 1961–1967*, Copenhagen International Series 9 (London: Sheffield Academic, 2001), 24–28, figs. 4.3–4.6, 29–36; fig. 4.16; Jane Cahill, "Jerusalem at the Time of the United Monarchy: The Archaeological Evidence," in *Jerusalem in Bible and Archaeology: The First Temple Period*, ed. Andrew G. Vaughn and Ann E. Killebrew, SymS 18 (Atlanta: Society of Biblical Literature, 2003), 13–80, esp. 46–51; Amihai Mazar, "Jerusalem in the Tenth Century B.C.E.: The Glass Half Full," in Yairah, *Essays on Ancient Israel*, 255–72; Mazar, "Archaeology and the Biblical Narrative: The Case of the United Monarchy," in Kratz and Spieckermann, *One God—One Cult—One Nation*, 29–58, for Jerusalem see 34–49. In his recent discussion, Finkelstein completely ignored the collared rim jar found on a floor immediately below the stone terraces, as well as from the Iron I sherds in the terraces themselves (Israel Finkelstein, "Jerusalem and the Benjamin Plateau in the Early Phases of the Iron Age: A Different Scenario," *ZDPV* 134 [2018]: 190–95). For a recent and updated discussion of the Stepped Stone Structure, its construction, and date, see Sergi, "Emergence of Judah," 2–5.

20. For the region north of Jerusalem, see Israel Finkelstein, "The Sociopolitical Organization of the Central Hill Country in the Second Millennium B.C.E.," in *Biblical Archaeology Today, 1990: Proceedings of the Second International Congress on Biblical Archaeology; Supplement; Pre-Congress Symposium; Population, Production and

entarization characterizes the eleventh century BCE, when for the first time since the Middle Bronze Age settlements were founded north of Jerusalem, in the Benjamin plateau, while to its south their number did not increase critically.[21] Hence, if the Stepped Stone Structure reflects the establishment of political power, it was mainly in order to impose political authority over the settlers north of Jerusalem; they were the only inhabitants who could provide the kings of Jerusalem with the required (human and financial) resources, as well as the political motivation, to erect it.

As was demonstrated above, the cluster of settlements north of Jerusalem was relatively isolated, while the regions north of Bethel and south of Jerusalem were less settled in the Iron I–IIA. Jerusalem—at the southern end of this cluster—was the seat of local rulers since the second millennium BCE, and by the late eleventh/early tenth century BCE the Stepped Stone Structure differentiated it from the rural settlements in its vicinity. Thus, in the absence of territorial continuity and vis-à-vis the long-standing political status of Jerusalem, it is difficult to believe that Shechem could have established its political hegemony over rural settlements located some 30 to 40 kilometers to its south (as suggested by Israel Finkelstein), especially when Jerusalem's political status was reaffirmed with the erection of the Stepped Stone Structure.[22] Moreover, during the early Iron IIA and following the destruction of Shiloh and Shechem, there was no urban center in the central Canaanite hill country north of Jerusalem. As demonstrated above, even when new urban centers emerged in Tirzah and Samaria (only in the late Iron IIA) they were much more related to activity in the north—in northern Samaria and in the Jezreel/Beth-Shean Valleys. There should be little doubt that the settlements in Benjamin where much more related to the emerging center in their vicinity, Jerusalem, than they were to those in the north.

It should be concluded, therefore, that by the early tenth century BCE, the Benjamin plateau was politically affiliated with Jerusalem, whose political hegemony probably extended between Bethlehem/Beth-zur in the

---

Power, Jerusalem, June 1990, ed. Avraham Biran and Joseph Aviram (Jerusalem: Israel Exploration Society, 1993), 116–23. For the region south of Jerusalem, see the summary in Sergi, "Emergence of Judah," 5–8, with further literature.

21. For recent discussion of the archaeological evidence from Benjamin in the Iron I–IIA, based on both excavations and surveys, see Sergi, "Emergence of Judah," 8–12, with further literature.

22. Finkelstein, "Last Labayu," 171–88; Finkelstein, "Saul, Benjamin," 348–67.

south and Bethel in the north. The erection of the Stepped Stone Structure marks, therefore, the early emergence of a polity ruled from Jerusalem and evidently Benjamin was part of this polity from its early beginnings. Consequently, throughout the Iron IIA the power and strength of Jerusalem grew steadily, reflecting the accumulaton of economic and consequently also political wealth in the hands of its ruling dynasty: the house of David.[23] It will not be before the fall of the Omride dynasty in the second half of the ninth century that the Davidic kings will extend their hegemony from the Judean hills to the Judahite lowlands in the west and to the Beersheba and Arad Valleys in the south.[24]

Lastly, it is important to note the difference between the political formations in the Samaria hills vis-à-vis those characterizing the Jerusalem–Benjamin region: while power balance in the north shifted, culminating in territorial expansion and the formation of the polity ruled by the Omrides—the kingdom of Israel—the south experienced what seems to be a rather organic process of centralization of power in the hands of the ruling elite in Jerusalem, culminating in the formation of the territorial polity ruled by the house of David, the kingdom of Judah. Throughout this time the highlands between Bethel (and later Mizpah) in the south and Shiloh (and even Shechem) in the north were devoid of any political center, and thus it is hard to imagine that the political developments in the north had any influence on the centralization of power in the south.[25] It is evident, therefore, that Israel and Judah developed separately, side by side, throughout the tenth to ninth centuries BCE, and while the

---

23. For the steady growth of Jerusalem during Iron IIA, see Joe Uziel and Nahshon Szanton, "Recent Excavations near the Gihon Spring and Their Reflection on the Character of Iron II Jerusalem," *TA* 42 (2015): 233–50; Uziel and Szanton, "New Evidence of Jerusalem's Urban Development in the Ninth Century BCE," in Lipschits, *Rethinking Israel*, 429–39; Joe Uziel and Yuval Gadot, "The Monumentality of Iron Age Jerusalem prior to the Eighth Century BCE," *TA* 44 (2017): 123–40.

24. E.g., Aren Maeir, Louise Hitchcock, and Liora Kolska Horwitz, "On the Constitution and Transformation of Philistine Identity," *OJA* 32 (2013): 26–38; Sergi, "Judah's Expansion," 226–46; Gunnar Lehmann and Hermann Michael Niemann, "When Did the Shephelah Became Judahite?," *TA* 41 (2014): 77–94.

25. Shiloh, which during the Iron I was a highland stronghold, probably the regional center of southern Samaria, was destroyed by the mid-eleventh century BCE (Israel Finkelstein, "The History and Archaeology of Shiloh from the Middle Bronze Age II to Iron Age II," in *Shiloh: The Archaeology of a Biblical Site*, ed. Israel Finkelstein, SMNIA 10 [Tel Aviv: Institute of Archaeology, 1993], 371–93).

political formation of Israel is marked with struggles and shifting political alliances, that of Judah is marked by centralization of power in the hands of the Davidic ruling family, residing in Jerusalem. With this in mind, I shall now examine the biblical traditions embedded in the book of Samuel regarding the formation of the early Israelite monarchy.

3. The Early Saul Traditions in 1 Samuel 9–14; 31

The earliest traditions about Saul are usually identified within the bulk of material embedded in 1 Sam 9:1–10:16; 11; 13–14; 31. Many of the models suggested for the origin and literary growth of this material are based on the assumption of a long process of writing and editing that involves the reconstruction of several hypothetical stages of composition.[26] The problem is that all these multistage reconstructions are highly uncertain, and, consequently, there is hardly any agreement among scholars about the extent and literary growth of the Saul traditions.[27] On the other hand, the importance of such models is that they all demonstrate, with a rather high degree of certainty, that the material embedded in 1 Sam 9–14 is based on early and pre-Deuteronomistic traditions. Hence, as it seems to be impossible to reconstruct it word for word, it may be more expedient to examine the points of agreement regarding its content.

It is almost unanimously agreed that the beginning of the Saul story may be found in 1 Sam 9:1–10:16, in the legendary tale about the young Benjaminite, the son of a wealthy patriarchal and rural elite, who went to look for his father's asses. On his way he met the man of God, who told him that he is about to perform a great deed.[28] Since Julius Wellhausen, it

---

26. Many of these works are referred to throughout the essay. Among the extensive literature on the subject, it is important to note the following recent studies of Kratz, *Composition of the Narrative Books*, 171–74; Dietrich, *Early Monarchy*, 268–91; Kaiser, "Der historische I," 520–45; Kaiser, "Der historische und biblische König Saul (Teil II)," *ZAW* 123 (2011): 1–14; Bezzel, *Saul*.

27. Nadav Na'aman, "The Pre-Deuteronomistic Story of King Saul and Its Historical Significance," *CBQ* 54 (1990): 640–45; Christophe Nihan, "Saul among the Prophets (1 Sam. 10:10–12 and 19:18–24): The Reworking of Saul's Figure in the Context of the Debate on 'Charismatic Prophecy' in the Persian Era," in *Saul in Story and Tradition*, ed. Carl S. Ehrlich and Marsha C. White, FAT 47 (Tübingen: Mohr Siebeck, 2006), 92–95.

28. The reconstructions of the original core and literary growth of the story in 1 Sam 9:1–10:16 are mostly based on the work of Ludwig Schmidt, *Menschlicher Erfolg und Jahwes Initiative: Studien zu Tradition, Interpretation und Historie in Überliefe-*

has been accepted that this story continues in 1 Sam 11:1–15 (excluding 1 Sam 10:17–27 as a secondary, exilic or even postexilic, expansion), where the words of the man of God are realized: Saul led a successful military campaign to Jabesh-gilead and liberated the Jabeshites from Ammonite subjugation.[29] One point of dispute is whether the successful battle against the Ammonites led to Saul's coronation in the Gilgal in 1 Sam 11:15 or whether the note about the coronation was only later added to the original narrative.[30] I opt for the former, not only because it makes the perfect conclusion to the heroic tale of the young Benjaminite, but also because Saul's kingship is anticipated already in the story of his meeting with the man of God: as argued by Diana Edelman, asses were conceived as a royal animal (cf. 1 Kgs 1:33, 39), and Saul's search for them implies his search for kingship.[31]

---

rungen von Gideon, Saul und David, WMANT 38 (Neukirchen-Vluyn: Neukirchener Verlag, 1970), 58–102. See also, e.g., Fritz Stolz, *Das erste und zweite Buch Samuel*, ZBK 9 (Zurich: TVZ, 1981), 62–70; Anthony F. Campbell, *1 Samuel*, FOTL 8 (Grand Rapids: Eerdmans, 2003), 106–8; Walter Dietrich, *Samuel*, BKAT 8/1.5 (Neukirchen-Vluyn: Neukirchener Verlag, 2008), 288–400; Bezzel, *Saul*, 149–79. For other reconstructions, assuming a more unified narrative with only minor redactional interventions, see, e.g., P. Kyle McCarter, *I Samuel: A New Translation with Introduction, Notes and Commentary*, AB 8 (New York: Doubleday, 1980), 166–88; Na'aman, "Pre-Deuteronomistic Story," 638–58; A. Graeme Auld, *I and II Samuel: A Commentary*, OTL (Louisville: Westminster John Knox, 2011), 98–111.

29. Julius Wellhausen, *Die Composition des Hexateuchs und der historischen Bücher des Alten Testament* (Berlin: de Gruyter, 1889), 240–43. For the general acceptance, see, e.g., Schmidt, *Menschlicher Erfolg*, 79–80; McCarter, *I Samuel*, 26–27, 184–88, 194–96, 205–7; Stolz, *Das erste*, 19–20, 73–77; Na'aman, "Pre Deuteronomistic Story," 644; Campbell, *1 Samuel*, 88–89, 115–16, 128–29; Kratz, *Composition of the Narrative Books*, 171–72; Kaiser, "Der historische I," 533–38; Bezzel, *Saul*, 151–79, 196–204. Yet, some scholars argue that the original continuation of the story in 1 Sam 9:1–10:16 was in the stories about the wars of Saul and Jonathan with the Philistines in 1 Sam 13–14 (e.g., Hans J. Stoebe, *Das Erste Buch Samuelis*, KAT 8/2 [Gütersloh: Gütersloher Verlagshaus, 1973], 64–66; Dietrich, *Early Monarchy*, 268–69; Auld, *I and II Samuel*, 126.) Indeed, the story of Saul's meeting with the man of God anticipates the wars with the Philistines (1 Sam 10:5a). However, 1 Sam 13–14 already presupposes the kingship of Saul, who is enthroned over Israel only as a result of his victory over the Ammonites (1 Sam 11:15, and see below).

30. For 1 Sam 11:15 being early, see, e.g., Schmidt, *Menschlicher Erfolg*, 79–80; Na'aman, "Pre Deuteronomistic Story," 642–43; Kaiser, "Der historische I," 538–40. For it being a later addition, see, e.g., Bezzel, *Saul*, 196–97, 200–201.

31. Diana Edelman, "The Deuteronomist's Story of King Saul: Narrative Art or Editorial Product?," in *Pentateuchal and Deuteronomistic Studies: Papers Read at the*

The coronation in Gilgal places Saul in the geographical and political point of departure for the stories about his wars with the Philistines in 1 Sam 13–14. These stories presuppose Saul's kingship and should be regarded as the direct continuation of 1 Sam 11:1–15.[32] They form a collection of anecdotes and heroic tales that were weaved together because they share the theme of war with the Philistines, but it is mostly agreed that they belong to the early layer of the Saul traditions.[33]

Eventually, it is in the battle with the Philistines on Mount Gilboa that Saul and his sons found their deaths: according to the account in 1 Sam 31:1–13, the victorious Philistines pinned the bodies of Saul and his sons to the walls of Beth-shean, but the Jabeshites, in a bold action, rescued the bodies, brought them to Jabesh-gilead, burned them, buried the bones, and mourned seven days. The question is, of course, whether the report about Saul's death in Gilboa was part of the early Saul traditions. Indeed,

---

XIIIth IOSOT Congress Leuven 1989, ed. Christianus Brekelmans and Johann Lust, BETL 94 (Leuven: Peeters, 1990), 208–14; Edelman, "Saul Ben Kish, King of Israel, as a 'Young Hero'?," in *Le jeune héros: Recherche sur la formation et la diffusion d'un thème littéraire au Proche-Orient ancien*, ed. Jean-Marie Durand, Thomas Römer, and Michael Langlois, OBO 250 (Fribourg: Academic Press; Göttingen: Vandenhoeck & Ruprecht, 2011), 161–83.

32. Na'aman, "Pre-Deuteronomistic Story," 645–49.

33. For the theme of war with the Philistines being the core, see, e.g., Stoebe, *Das Erste Buch*, 63–64, 240–62; McCarter, *I Samuel*, 26–27; Stolz, *Das erste*, 82–83. For different reconstructions of the literary growth of these stories, see David Jobling, "Saul's Fall and Jonathan's Rise: Tradition and Redaction in 1 Sam 14:1–46," *JBL* 95 (1976): 367–76; Stolz, *Das erste*, 87–96; Kaiser, "Der historische II," 1–6; Campbell, *1 Samuel*, 134–50; Bezzel, *Saul*, 208–28. For an approach viewing the stories in 1 Sam 13–14 as a more unified literary work, see McCarter, *I Samuel*, 224–52; Na'aman, "Pre-Deuteronomistic Story," 645–47. There is a scholarly consensus, however, that the rejection of Saul in 1 Sam 13:7b–15 and the story of the altar in 1 Sam 14:32–35 are secondary expansions, e.g., Wellhausen, *Die Composition*, 240–46; McCarter, *I Samuel*, 230; Stolz, *Das erste*, 82; Campbell, *1 Samuel*, 110–15; Auld, *I and II Samuel*, 115–16; Kaiser, "Der historische II," 1–6, 9–11; Bezzel, *Saul*, 214. For the stories belonging to the early layer, see, e.g., Stoebe, *Das Erste Buch*, 64–66; McCarter, *I Samuel*, 26–27; Na'aman, "Pre-Deuteronomistic Story," 645–47; Marsha C. White, "The History of Saul's Rise: Saulide State Propaganda in 1 Samuel 1–14," in *"A Wise Discerning Mind": Essays in Honor of Burke O. Long*, ed. Saul M. Olyan and Robert C. Culley, BJS 325 (Providence, RI: Brown Judaic Studies, 2000), 271–92; White, "Saul and Jonathan in 1 Samuel 1 and 14," in Ehrlich and White, *Saul in Story and Tradition*, 119–38; Kratz, *Composition of the Narrative Books*, 171–74; Dietrich, *Early Monarchy*, 268–69; Auld, *I and II Samuel*, 126.

some scholars have excluded it, arguing that the bulk of the early Saul traditions are embedded only within 1 Sam 1–14, probably with an ending in 1 Sam 14:46–52.[34] However, the war with the Philistines, the basic theme in 1 Sam 13–14, is also the basic theme of 1 Sam 31. Neither narrative mentions David, but both focus on Saul and his sons. Furthermore, this report brings the early Saul traditions to their perfect literary conclusion: Saul came to the throne by rescuing the people of Jabesh-gilead, and when he died, they repaid him by salvaging his body.[35] Hence, there is no reason to assume that the report about the death and burial of Saul and his sons in 1 Sam 31:1–13 was somehow distinct from the stories about the wars of Saul and Jonathan with the Philistines in 1 Sam 13–14.[36] What we have here, therefore, is a collection of an early narrative embedded within 1 Sam 9–14; 31, telling the story of the rise and fall of a heroic king.[37]

It is almost taken for granted that the early Saul traditions as sketched above are of north Israelite origin and that they could not have arrived in Judah prior to the fall of Samaria.[38] However, these traditions hardly reflect any of the geographical or political reality of the kingdom of Israel. Their geographical scope is restricted to the area north of Jerusalem, in the Benjamin region and the southernmost parts of the Ephraim hill country, with only one excursion to the Gilead. The entire hill country north of Bethel, which was the heart of the kingdom of Israel, is completely absent. Nothing in these stories even implies a north Israelite perspective: the main political centers of Israel (Shechem, Tirzah, Samaria); the importance of the cult place in Bethel; the Israelite royal cities in the northern valleys; or the Israelite cult centers in the Gilead, most notably Penuel—are all completely absent from the narrative.[39] Furthermore, there is not even a hint to the Israelite history—its involvement with northern Levantine

---

34. White, "History of Saul's Rise," 271–92; Kratz, *Composition of the Narrative Books*, 171–74, and cf. Bezzel, *Saul*, 115–48.

35. Wright, *David*, 67.

36. Bezzel, *Saul*, 229–34 but see further below.

37. Edelman, "Deuteronomist's Story," 207–20; Edelman, "Saul ben Kish," 161–83.

38. See above, and see also Schmidt, *Menschlicher Erfolg*, 79–80; Jakob H. Grønbæk, *Die Geschichte vom Aufstieg Davids (1 Sam. 15–2 Sam. 5): Tradition und Komposition*, Acta Theologica Danica 10 (Copenhagen: Munksgaard, 1971), 267–69.

39. Mahanaim is mentioned as the capital of Saul's heir, Ishbaal (2 Sam 3:8), but this is not part of the so-called early Saul traditions but rather part of what is assumed to be a Judahite composition; see also Na'aman, "Saul, Benjamin," 346–48.

polities, the fierce relations with Aram-Damascus, or its constant effort (and success) to expand northward.

Saul's military excursion to the Gilead is often viewed as a reflection of Israelite territorial and political interest in the region.[40] Indeed, at least some parts of the Gilead were affiliated with Israel for certain periods during the ninth and eighth centuries BCE.[41] However, as far as we can judge, the Israelite interest in the Gilead was mainly focused on the Jabbok passage (which was on the route leading to Shechem from Transjordan, and see also 1 Kgs 12:25). This region and the sites located along it, Penuel, Mahanaim, and Succoth, play a prominent role in what is often viewed as Israelite literature: the pre-Priestly Jacob cycle, considered by many to be the origin myth of the northern Israelite kingdom, attributes the foundation of these sites to the eponymic ancestor of Israel.[42] They are also important for the story of Gideon's pursuit of the Midianites (Judg 8:4–21), which is considered to be part of an Israelite collection of heroic stories.[43] None of these sites, so prominent in Israelite litera-

---

40. E.g., Dieterich and Münger, "Die Herrschaft Sauls," 41–46; Finkelstein, "Last Labayu," 178–80; Finkelstein, "Saul, Benjamin," 353–55; Wright, *David*, 66–74.

41. For discussions on the political affiliation of the Gilead in the ninth and eighth centuries BCE, see Omer Sergi, "The Gilead between Aram and Israel: Political Borders, Cultural Interaction and the Question of Jacob and the Israelite Identity," in *In Search of Aram and Israel: Politics, Culture and the Question of Identity*, ed. Omer Sergi, Manfred Oeming, and Izaak J. de Hulster, ORA 20 (Tübingen: Mohr Siebeck, 2016), 333–37.

42. For the Jacob cycle as the origin myth of northern Israel, see, e.g., Erhard Blum, *Die Komposition der Vätergeschichte*, WMANT 57 (Neukirchen-Vluyn: Neukirchener Verlag, 1984), 7–186, esp. 175–86; Albert de Pury, "The Jacob Story and the Beginning of the Formation of the Pentateuch," in *A Farewell to the Yahwist? The Composition of the Pentateuch in Recent European Interpretation*, ed. Thomas B. Dozeman and Konrad Schmid, SymS 34 (Atlanta: Society of Biblical Literature, 2006), 51–72; Jeremy M. Hutton, "Mahanaim, Penuel, and Transhumance Routes: Observations on Genesis 32–33 and Judges 8," *JNES* 65 (2006): 161–78; Erhard Blum, "The Jacob Tradition," in *The Book of Genesis: Composition, Reception and Interpretation*, ed. Craig E. Evans, Joel N. Lohr, and David L. Petersen, VTSup 152 (Leiden: Brill, 2012), 181–211; Israel Finkelstein and Thomas Römer, "Comments on the Historical Background of the Jacob Narrative in Genesis," *ZAW* 126 (2014): 317–38; Sergi, "Gilead between Aram and Israel," 333–54.

43. E.g., Walter Gross, *Richter*, HThKAT (Freiburg im Breisgau: Herder, 2009), 367–89, 473–74, with further literature. For discussing the place of the Jabbok outlet in Judg 8:4–21, see Sergi, "Gilead between Aram and Israel," 346–49.

ture, is mentioned in the early Saul traditions. In fact, Saul goes to war in Jabesh-gilead, a toponym mainly referred to in the narratives related to Saul (1 Sam 11:1, 3, 5, 9–11; 31:13; 2 Sam 2:4–5; 21:12, and see also 1 Chr 10:12).[44] Jabesh-gilead is never mentioned in any relation to Israel, not even in the town list of the northern tribes.[45] Furthermore, as correctly observed, cremation is not an Israelite practice and by ascribing it to the people of Jabesh-gilead (1 Sam 31:12) the author probably intended to mark them as non-Israelites.[46] All the above attests to the fact that the role of the Gilead and its residents in the early Saul traditions does not necessarily reflect the Israelite point of view.

Taking a look at the geopolitical picture that arises from the early Saul traditions, they seem to better reflect a Jerusalemite point of view: Saul's sphere of influence is mainly in Benjamin and the southern Ephraim hill country, regions that according to the narrative were transgressed by the Philistines who were the inhabitants of the Judahite Shephelah (1 Sam 13:20; 14:31). The Philistines are depicted as warriors who raided and plundered the rural society in the Benjamin region; they seem to be wealthier (mastering specialized productions; see 1 Sam 13:19–22) and considered the stronger, aggressive side in the conflict (1 Sam 13:5–6, 17–18; 14). The Israelites, on the other hand, are depicted as a rural society, residing in the hill country and its foothills, dependent on Philistine metal production, and in need of defending themselves from Philistine aggressiveness. These characteristics draw the line between the more urban societies of southwestern Canaan and the rural societies of the Benjamin–Jerusalem region prior to the Iron IIB and probably even prior to the fall of Gath in the last third of the ninth century BCE.

The limited geographical scope of these stories is telling: 1 Sam 13–14 contain a detailed topographical description of a small territory north of Jerusalem. Clearly, its authors were well acquainted with the Benjamin region, while the lower regions of Canaan—the northern valleys or the

---

44. Identified as Tell el-Maqlūb, see Martin Noth, "Jabes-Gilead," *ZDPV* 69 (1953): 28–41; Erasmus Gass, *Die Ortsnamen des Richterbuchs in historischer und redaktioneller Perspektive*, ADPV 35 (Wiesbaden: Harrassowitz, 2005), 504–9, with earlier literature. Jabesh-gilead is also mentioned in the story of the outrage at Gibeah (Judg 21), which is dated to the late, postexilic period (Gross, *Richter*, 821–22, with previous literature).

45. Contra Auld, *I and II Samuel*, 121, who calls it an "Israelite city."

46. Wright, *David*, 66–68.

Shephelah (west of Judah)—were less known to them, as may also be deduced from the odd appearance of the Philistines in the Jezreel Valley (1 Sam 31:1, 10). While the archaeological phenomenon of the Philistines is mostly restricted to southwest Canaan in the Iron I, the Jezreel Valley during this period, and before it came under Israelite rule, maintained its former (LBA) social and political structure of city-states and palace economy.[47] There is no reason to assume that the local towns in the Jezreel Valley were somehow affiliated with the Philistines, as suggested by Walter Dietrich and Stefan Münger.[48] Finkelstein's suggestion that the memory of the Philistines in the Jezreel Valley (and especially in Beth-shean) reflects the Egyptian rule during the Late Bronze Age is similarly improbable.[49] As far as we can judge, the pre-Israelite Jezreel Valley was conceived in Israelite historical memory as Canaanite (see Judg 4–5), not as Philistine or Egyptian. Clearly, the author of the Saul story was not well acquainted with the political or social composite of the pre-Israelite Jezreel Valley. The Philistines, on the other hand, were the archenemy of the kingdom of Judah, as is also clear from the important role they play in the stories about the early Davidic monarchy.[50] Indeed, throughout the formative period of the Judahite monarchy, Gath was the strongest polity to its west.[51] Only a narrator from Jerusalem, being remote from the Jezreel Valley, would assume that Saul met in the Jezreel Valley the same enemies he met in Benjamin, namely, the Philistines.

Lastly, from an archaeological point of view the inhabitants of the Benjamin region were affiliated with the Jerusalemite political hegemony as early as the tenth century BCE (above). Thus, if the memory of a Benjaminite hero would have been kept and recorded somewhere, it would have been in the scribal school of Jerusalem. This is also the best explanation for the complete absence of any trace of Israelite geography, politics, or concerns within these early traditions, which rather reflect the political

---

47. For the location of the Philistines, see, e.g., Maeir, Hitchcock, and Horwitz, "Constitution and Transformation," 1–38. For the Jezreel Valley, see Finkelstein, *Forgotten Kingdom*, 27–36.

48. Dietrich and Münger, "Die Herrschaft Sauls," 48.

49. Finkelstein, "Last Labayu," 182–83.

50. Omer Sergi, "State Formation, Religion and 'Collective Identity' in the Southern Levant," *HBAI* 4 (2015): 64–75.

51. Sergi, "Judah's Expansion," 226–46; Lehmann and Niemann, "When Did," 77–94.

realia, problems, and interests of Judah. The question is therefore whether the memory of an Israelite king could have been preserved in Jerusalem. In order to answer that, I shall first discuss the stories about David's rise in their historical and literary context.

4. The Historical and Literary Context of the Stories about David's Rise (1 Samuel 16–2 Samuel 5)

The stories about David's rise in 1 Sam 16–2 Sam 5 include many different narrative strands that were quite loosely put together by a pre-Deuteronomistic scribe. These narratives tell about David's service in Saul's court (1 Sam 16:14–23; 17–19); David's flight from Saul (1 Sam 20–26); his consequent service for the king of Gath (1 Sam 27–2 Sam 1) until the death of Saul (1 Sam 31–2 Sam 1); and David's coronation first over Judah (2 Sam 2:1–4) and later over Israel (2 Sam 5:1–3). Of course, the extent and literary growth of this composition is disputed. However for the purpose of this study suffice it to stress that in spite of its mosaic nature, it is still painted with a unifying royal, pro-Davidic ideology, suggesting that its authors were not mere compilers.[52]

As discussed above, the conventional wisdom that rules contemporary scholarship on the matter regards the stories in 1 Sam 16–2 Sam 5 as the earliest literary link between the Judahite David and the Israelite Saul, which could have only been conceived after the fall of Samaria.[53]

---

52. For further discussion and for different reconstructions of the sources and redactions within this composition see, e.g., Arthur Weiser, "Die Legitimation des Königs Davids: Zur Eigenart und Entstehung der sogen; Geschichte von Davids Aufstieg," VT 16 (1966): 325–54; Grønbæk, *Die Geschichte*; Stolz, *Das erste*, 17–18; Kratz, *Composition of the Narrative Books*, 177–81. Timo Veijola, *Die ewige Dynastie: David und die Entstehung seiner Dynastie nach der deuteronomistischen Darstellung* (Helsinki: Suomalainen Tiedeakatemia, 1975) assigned the composition of the history of David's rise to the Deuteronomistic scribes (and cf. John Van Seters, *The Biblical Saga of King David* [Winona Lake, IN: Eisenbrauns, 2009]), however this view never gained much scholarly consensus (Dietrich, *Early Monarchy*, 245–46). For a critical review of past research, see: Dietrich, *Early Monarchy*, 240–55.

53. Some scholars have gone so far with the assumption that Saul and David were originally unrelated literary figures as to attempt to differentiate clear and distinct narratives within 1 Sam 16–2 Sam 5 (e.g., Wright, *David*, 31–79). These attempts are not based on solid literary criteria, so even adherents of the hypothesis that Saul traditions are of a northern origin still agree that it is impossible to distinguish northern from

This conclusion is based entirely on an allegorical reading of these stories, assuming that the Judahite intellectual elite wished to inherit the former kingdom of Israel. However, it is hard to believe that Israel was some sort of a model to successful monarchy that one would like to identify with shortly after the massive destruction inflicted on it by the Assyrians. On the contrary, the book of Kings, which is often attributed to the same Judahite elite (in the seventh century BCE), explicitly condemns Israel and thus probably reflects much better the view of the Judahite elite regarding Israel in the late monarchic period.

Moreover, this assumption could hardly be supported by the text itself, which like the early Saul traditions, reflects the geopolitical organization of southern Canaan in the early Iron Age, as was demonstrated by Na'aman more than two decades ago:[54] the geographical scope of the stories about David's rise is restricted to the southern Canaanite hill country and its foothills, while the Philistines control the western Shephelah. Accordingly, David is quite independent (as a leader of a warriors' band) whenever he acts in the Judean hill country and its foothills (1 Sam 23–26; 2 Sam 5), but he is at the service of the king of Gath whenever he crosses to the west or the south (cf. 1 Sam 27; 29–30). This geopolitical scenario is further highlighted by the importance of Gath in these stories (1 Sam 17:4, 23, 52; 21:11, 13; 27:2–4, 11). Gath reached its zenith during the tenth through ninth centuries BCE, when it became by far the biggest and the most prosperous city in southern Canaan. However, it was utterly destroyed in the last third of the ninth century and never regained its former power.[55] The stories in 1 Sam 16–2 Sam 5, like those in 1 Sam 9–14 are, therefore, consistent with the social and political reality in south Canaan during the tenth through ninth centuries BCE and prior to the Judahite expansion to the Shephelah, as is also evidenced by the fact that all these traditions fail to mention Lachish, the main royal Judahite town in the Shephelah from

---

southern traditions within 1 Sam 16–2 Sam 5 (Kratz, *Composition of the Narrative Books*, 182; Dietrich, *Early Monarchy*, 298–99; Kaiser, "Der historische II," 6–9).

54. Nadav Na'aman, "Sources and Composition in the History of David," in *The Origins of the Ancient Israelite States*, ed. Volkmar Fritz and Philip R. Davies (Sheffield: Sheffield Academic, 1996), 170–86; Na'aman, "In Search of Reality behind the Account of David's Wars with Israel's Neighbours," *IEJ* 52 (2002): 200–24.

55. Aren M. Maeir, "The Tell es-Safi/Gath Archaeological Project 1996–2010: Introduction, Overview and Synopsis of Results," in *Text*, part 1 of *Tell es-Safi/Gath I: The 1996–2005 Seasons*, ed. Aren M. Maeir, ÄAT 69 (Wiesbaden: Harrassowitz, 2012), 26–49.

the second half of the ninth century BCE.⁵⁶ In light of all the above, the stories of David's rise should not be dated much later then the early eighth century BCE, which means that they were composed much before the fall of Samaria. Since both the early Saul traditions and the stories about David's rise are well acquainted with the geopolitical settings in southern Canaan, they probably reflect a Judahite (or, better, Jerusalemite) and not Israelite point of view. If so, it seems that they were composed adjacent to each other, no later than the early eighth century BCE.⁵⁷

This conclusion may further be supported from a literary point of view. Most scholars agree that the stories of David's rise presuppose the early Saul traditions.⁵⁸ Nonetheless, as they assume that the material in 1 Sam 9–14 predates 1 Sam 16–2 Sam 5, the possibility that the early Saul traditions anticipate the rise of David is often overlooked. The distinct, non-Judahite origin of the Saul traditions is further stressed by emphasizing the fact that the narrative presents Saul in a positive light (compared with the more negative presentation in 1 Sam 16–2 Sam 5) and that David has no role in it. However, that David has no role in the stories of Saul's early career is self-evident, since the stories about David explicitly acknowledge Saul's kingship and even argue that David was his legitimate heir. As for the assertion that Saul is presented in an entirely positive light in 1 Sam 9–14 and 31, it seems to be far too general, and it fails to conceive the nuances of the story.

From the outset, and already in the legendary story of his call (1 Sam 9:1–10:16), the figure of Saul is far from being outlined as specifically heroic or worthy of kingship. The main quality by which Saul is introduced into the narrative refers to his appearance: Saul was a tall person (1 Sam 9:2). Other than that, it is said that he was good, but none of these qualities (tall, good) is particularly necessary for kingship. The entire narrative is driven by the actions of Saul's father (1 Sam 9:3) and Saul's servant (1 Sam

---

56. Sergi, "Judah's Expansion," 226–46; Nadav Na'aman, "The Kingdom of Judah in the Ninth Century BCE: Text Analysis versus Archaeological Research," *TA* 40 (2013): 247–76; Lehmann and Niemann, "When Did," 77–94.

57. Cf. Nadav Na'aman, "The Scope of the Pre-Deuteronomistic Saul-David Story Cycle," in *From Nomadism to Monarchy: Thirty Years Update*, ed. Ido Koch, Omer Sergi, and Oded Lipschits (Tel Aviv: Institute of Archaeology, forthcoming).

58. Stoebe, *Das Erste Buch*, 63–64; Grønbæk, *Die Geschichte*, 262–64; Edelman, "Deuteronomist's Story," 214–20; White, "History of Saul's Rise," 271–84; Dietrich, *Early Monarchy*, 244–45.

9:5–10), while Saul himself remains completely passive: he is the first to give up the search for his father's asses while expressing despair (1 Sam 9:5), and he remains hesitant even when his servant comes up with new solutions to his problems (1 Sam 9:6–8).[59] This portrayal is, indeed, not negative and rather in favor of Saul, however, and especially in light of the heroic portrayal of David's youth (1 Sam 16–19), it does not attribute Saul with any quality that prepares him for his future as a leader.

It is no wonder that the narrative culminates in Saul's death (1 Sam 31:1–13), which like the story of his rise emphasizes his incompetence to lead. According to the narrative, Saul's suicide was not committed in face of his defeat in the battlefield or in light of the death of his sons but because he was "terrified" from the Philistine archers chasing him (31:3–4). This is not a portrayal of heroic death, especially since archers, naturally, do not come in close contact with their enemies and must have kept a certain distance from Saul, who could also escape, hide, or just face his enemies. Moreover, even his suicide was forced on him as his servant disobeyed Saul's direct command to kill him. This short episode makes a perfect end to the story of Saul: Saul's fate from his rise to his fall was in the hand of a servant. More than a representation of a heroic king, it is the characterization of a good man who did not own the qualities that make a good king.

An even less complimentary portrayal of Saul may be found in one of the narrative strands embedded within the stories of Saul and Jonathan's wars with the Philistines (1 Sam 13–14). First Samuel 14:24–30, 36–45 tells about an unnecessary oath taken by Saul that almost brought about the death of the crown prince and the war hero, Jonathan, and that Saul evidently could not keep.[60] This narrative actually anticipates Saul's rejection from the throne, which is rather explicitly announced in direct condemnation made by his son and heir, Jonathan (1 Sam 14:29), and by his "people" (1 Sam 14:45).[61] Jonathan's condemnation is significant, as it prepares the scene for his future betrayal of Saul (1 Sam 19:1–7; 20:30–34) and anticipates his covenant with David (1 Sam 18:1–4; 20:1–17, 35–42;

---

59. Note also the phrasing in 9:8 "and the servant answered Saul *again*," that is, he had to encourage Saul to accomplish his task (finding the asses) and to meet his fate (kingship).

60. Bezzel, *Saul*, 228.

61. McCarter, *I Samuel*, 251–2; Campbell, *1 Samuel*, 150; Steven L. McKenzie, "Saul in the Deuteronomistic History," in Ehrlich and White, *Saul in Story and Tradition*, 60–63; Kaiser, "Der historische II," 4–5.

see also 2 Sam 9). These themes have a significant role in legitimizing the transition of kingship from the house of Saul (through its heir, Jonathan) to the house of David.[62]

In fact, it may be argued that the entire theme of Saul's wars with the Philistines (1 Sam 13–14; 31) anticipates the rise of David. Hannes Bezzel particularly demonstrated the many literary connections binding 1 Sam 13–14 to 1 Sam 31 as a unit meant to prepare the scene for David's rise in 1 Sam 16–2 Sam 5.[63] After all, the theme of Saul's wars with the Philistines ends with the complete demise of the house of Saul (and note that 1 Sam 31:1–13 highlights the death of Saul and *all* [!] his sons), which enables David to rightfully claim his kingship (2 Sam 5:1–3, and esp. v. 2).[64] Moreover, the Philistines, who make their first appearance in the Saul traditions, play a prominent role in the stories of David's rise and in both they serve a very specific literary purpose—whether by bringing the end on Saul's house or by presenting David as a heroic liberator (2 Sam 5:17–25; 8:1), the Philistine advance the narrative toward the inevitable kingship of David.[65] In this sense, the Philistines are the object on which Saul's incompetence is highlighted in contrast to David's success.

---

62. McCarter, *I Samuel*, 252, even argued that the negative presentation of Saul in 1 Sam 13–14 was the reason that a later scribe chose to add an explicit rejection of Saul (1 Sam 13:7b–15) to these stories. On the theme of Jonathan's covenant with David, see Ina Willi-Plein, "I Sam. 18–19 und die Davidshausgeschichte," in *David und Saul im Widerstreit: Diachronie und Synchronie im Wettstreit; Beiträge zur Auslegung des ersten Samuelbuches*, ed. Walter Dietrich, OBO 206 (Fribourg: Academic Press; Göttingen: Vandenhoeck & Ruprecht, 2004), 138–71.

63. Bezzel, *Saul*, 235–37. However, maintaining the presupposition that Saul was Israelite and David was Judahite, Bezzel argued that these narratives were added to the early Saul traditions by a Judahite scribe in order to link them with the stories about David's rise. He dated them accordingly to after the fall of Israel, arguing that the fall of Saul represents the fall of Samaria, and that the role of the Philistines actually reflects the role of the Assyrians in historical reality. This conclusion, however, cannot be maintained. Not only does the story reflect well the social and political realia of the early Iron Age in southern Canaan (and not in Samaria), it is also impossible to maintain that the Philistines in some allegorical way actually represent the historical role of the Assyrians in Israelite history. The Assyrian army (unlike the Philistine) was that of a powerful empire that destroyed many local territorial kingdoms, changing entirely the social and political structure of Canaan. It cannot be equated with the local Philistine garrison trying to control the highland population (1 Sam 10:5; 13:3; 14:1–13).

64. See also Grønbæk, *Die Geschichte*, 262.

65. Sergi, "State Formation," 64–75.

In light of all the above, and while there is no doubt that the traditions in 1 Sam 9–14 and 31 present Saul in a rather favorable light, they still portray him merely as a good person, who almost accidently became a king, while he was lacking the qualities required for successful leadership. The narrative leads therefore to his inevitable tragic end, which allows the rise of the much more skilled leader—David. It is therefore evident that the literary links between the early Saul traditions and the stories about David's rise are not one-sided, as the Saul traditions clearly anticipate and even prepare the scene for the rise of David. Thus, and in light of the fact that both the Saul and the David stories reflect the sociopolitical realia of southern Canaan in the Iron IIA, there should be little doubt that they are the literary product of a Jerusalemite scribal school, meant to portray the formation of the Davidic monarchy. The question is why David, who was the founder of Judah, was conceived in these traditions as the successor of the first king of Israel? The answer for this question lies in the nature of Israelite identity assumed by the narrators of the Saul and the David stories.

5. Israel as a Kinship Identity in the Traditions about the Formation of the Israelite Monarchy

The stories about Saul's wars with the Philistines in 1 Sam 13–14 presuppose his kingship over Israel or, at the least, commemorate him as Israel's military leader and liberator (see 1 Sam 11:15; 14:47). The name *Israel* is mentioned fourteen times in 1 Sam 13–14. In most of these cases the term clearly refers to a group of people; that is, in 1 Sam 13–14 it is a designation for a kinship group and not for a territorial polity. The text identifies the Israelites as a composite of clan/tribal society settled in the Benjamin plateau and in the southern Ephraim hill country (1 Sam 13:4–6, 20; 14:22–24), between Gibeah in the south (or even Bethlehem, see 1 Sam 17:2) and Bethel in the north. It also reflects on the complex nature of Israel as a kinship group, consisting of different clans (like the Benjaminites) that were brought together under a more encompassing kinship identity. Being a Benjaminite (1 Sam 9:1), Saul was also considered an Israelite, and thus the early Saul traditions are telling the story of the rise and fall of a Benjaminite who came to rule his kinsmen, the Israelites. In other words, the story never portrayed Saul as the king of Israel, relating to the northern polity formed by the Omrides far to the north, in the region of Shechem and Samaria. Rather, it tells how Saul came to rule his Israelite kinsmen, residing in the Benjamin plateau.

This calls for a clear distinction between Israel as a political identity, namely, the territorial polity designated by this name from the time of the Omride rule and onward, and Israel as a social identity, the name of a kinship group. The name Israel was used to identify a kinship group (in the Merenptah Stela, late thirteenth century BCE) much before it was utilized to designate the Northern Kingdom, as it is in its other three occurrences outside the Hebrew Bible: in the Mesha Inscription, in the Kurkh Monolith, and in the Dan Inscription (all dated to the mid-second-half of the ninth century BCE).[66] Moreover, in one of these occurrences, in the Assyrian Kurkh Monolith (852 BCE), it is applied to Ahab, who is identified as "Israelite" (KUR.*syrʿalāya*) and not as the king of Israel (as Omri and Joram are identified in the contemporaneous Mesha Stela and Dan Inscription, respectively). It is clear, therefore, that the name Israel had (at least initially) a kinship association, so the question is why the designation of a kinship group was later applied to a political entity. This question is only highlighted by the fact that "Israel" was not the only name of the Northern Kingdom, which was also named (by the Assyrians) "the House of Omri." After all, the occurrences of the name Israel in historical sources are related almost exclusively to the time of the Omride rule, and this fact alone casts doubt on the assumption that Israel was only or mainly a political identity, a name of a territorial polity and nothing more.

Kinship was by essence the most dominant social ideology in ancient Near Eastern societies.[67] Kinship relations were formulated in order to legitimize membership in a group, and they were utilized in order to stretch time and space, and to enable the conception of common identity with unknown others.[68] Kinship relations appear to maintain their essential integrity over long periods of time and even under different political formations. Thus, for instance, the ruling elite in Ebla or Mari could maintain its tribal identity, related to kin, even when residing in a wealthy urban

---

66. For the use of the name *Israel*, see the summary in Michael G. Hasel, *Domination and Resistance: Egyptian Military Activity in the Southern Levant, ca. 1300–1185 BC*, PAe 11 (Leiden: Brill, 1994), 170–204.

67. Ann Porter, *Mobile Pastoralism and the Formation of Near Eastern Civilization: Weaving Together Society* (Cambridge: Cambridge University Press, 2012), 12–37.

68. For kinship relations legitimatizing membership, see Van der Steen, *Tribes and Territories*, 126–32, with further literature. For kinship relations being used to enable common identity, see Porter, *Mobile Pastoralism*, 57–58, 326; Porter, *Complex Communities*, 56–57.

center.[69] Similarly, and closer to the arena of the Saul and David stories, the Mesha Inscription presents Mesha as "king of Moab, the Dibonite." It was already Ernst Knauf who noted that Mesha did not identify himself as a Moabite, namely, with the territorial polity that he formed and ruled, but as a Dibonite, probably his kinship identity, the social group with which he was affiliated.[70] There is, therefore, no real dichotomy between social and political identity, as they both represents identities that are current. That means that Israel was first and foremost a kinship identity, even when the name Israel was given to the polity ruled by the Omrides.[71] Moreover, since extrabiblical sources from the Iron Age identify Israel exclusively with the Omrides, it may be argued that the Omrides were affiliated with a kinship group named Israel, which eventually gave its name to the polity they ruled. That, however, does not mean that all the Israelites lived within the boundaries of the Omride polity and, evidently, at least the early Saul traditions identify Israelites also in the region of Benjamin, far to the south from the Omride's core community in Samaria.

A similar portrayal of Israel as a kinship group residing in the region of Jerusalem and Benjamin also characterizes the stories about David's rise and especially the stories about David's service in Saul's court (1 Sam 18–19; see also 2 Sam 5:1–2). Ina Willi-Plein demonstrated how these stories presuppose an early monarchic political landscape, in which establishing political hegemony was done through marriage and personal

---

69. Daniel Fleming, "Kingship of City and Tribe Conjoined: Zimri-Lim at Mari," in *Nomads, Tribes, and the States in the Ancient Near East: Cross-disciplinary Perspectives*, ed. Jeffrey Szuchman, OIS 5 (Chicago: Oriental Institute of the University of Chicago, 2009), 227–40; Ann Porter, "Beyond Dimorphism: Ideologies and Materialities of Kinship as Time-Space Distanciation," in Szuchman, *Nomads, Tribes and the States*, 201–25; Porter, *Mobile Pastoralism*, 240.

70. Ernst Axel Knauf, "The Cultural Impact of Secondary State Formation: The Cases of Edomites and Moabites," in *Early Edom and Moab: The Beginning of Iron Age in Southern Jordan*, ed. Piotr Bienkowski, Sheffield Archaeological Monographs 7 (Sheffield: Collis, 1992), 47–54. Eveline J. van der Steen and Klaas A. D. Smelik, "King Mesha and the Tribe of Dibon," *JSOT* 32 (2007): 139–62.

71. For recent studies stressing the nature of Israel as a kinship identity within its historical and literary context, see Daniel Fleming, *The Legacy of Israel in Judah's Bible: History, Politics and the Reinscribing of Tradition* (Cambridge: Cambridge University Press, 2012); Kristin Weingart, *Stämmevolk—Staatsvolk—Gottesvolk? Studien zur Verwendung des Israels-Namens im Alten Testament*, FAT 2/68 (Tübingen: Mohr Siebeck, 2014), esp. 171–286, 340–60.

alliances (see 1 Sam 17:58; 18:2, 17).[72] She therefore argued that these stories portray the establishment of kingship over Israel, while Israel refers to a group of people and not to the territorial polity.[73] That means that the story of David's rise, like the traditions about Saul, tells about his rise as the king of the Israelites. It is for this reason that David is presented as the successor of Saul: not as an allegory to hypothetic wishes of late monarchic Judah, but simply because both Saul and David tried to establish their hegemony over the same group of people: the Israelites residing in the Jerusalem–Benjamin highlands.

Of course, the house of David was the ruling dynasty of Judah, whose royal seat was in Jerusalem; this, however, does not mean that David's kinship identity was Judahite (just as Mesha king of Moab was not a Moabite, but a Dibonite). Nowhere in the stories of his rise to kingship is David identified as a Judahite. Quite the contrary, in 1 Sam 17:12 it is stated that his family originated from an Ephrathite clan (thus, Israelite) that settled in Bethlehem, and throughout the stories about his rise David is explicitly identified as Israelite at least three more times (1 Sam 18:18; 27:12; 2 Sam. 5:1).[74] Of specific interest are David's words to Saul in 1 Sam 18:18 ("Who am I? And who are my kindred or my father's clan in Israel that I should become the king's son-in-law?"), which explicitly express the association of Israel with a kinship group consisting of several clans, to which David's family belongs.

This picture, according to which at least some of the inhabitants in the region of Jerusalem were Israelites, concurs with the one portrayed in the early Saul traditions. Furthermore, like the early Saul traditions, the stories about David's rise also attest to the complex nature of Israel as a kinship group consisting of different clans (Saul the Benjaminite, David the Ephrathite). Assuming an Israelite origin for David may also explain why his coronation over the people of Judah (2 Sam 2:1–4) is not taken for granted: not only that David inquired of YHWH before advancing to Hebron (an action he otherwise took only before battles, see 1 Sam 23:2, 4; 30:8; 2 Sam 5:19, 23–24), prior to his arrival he bribed the Judahite leaders, sending them booty he took from the Amalekites (1 Sam 30:26). His coronation over Israel, on the other hand (2 Sam 5:1–3), seems to be much more natu-

---

72. Willi-Plein, "I Sam 18–19," 148–53, 156–59.
73. Willi-Plein, "I Sam. 18–19," 161–68.
74. For the Ephrathites settlements, see Nadav Na'aman, "The Settlements of the Ephrathites in Bethlehem and the Location of Rachel's Tomb," *RB* 121 (2014): 516–29.

ral, as the Israelites themselves declared David their king on account of his being their kinsman and on the account of his previous service in the court of Saul, the former king of the Israelites (2 Sam 5:1–2).

It may, therefore, be concluded, that according to both the early Saul traditions and the stories about David's rise, Saul and David were affiliated with a kinship group named Israel, which consisted of several clans that settled north (Benjaminite clans) and south (Ephrathite clans) of Jerusalem. Besides Israelite clans, this region was also inhabited by Judahite and Jebusite clans (e.g., 2 Sam 2:1–4; 5:6), and eventually, as was demonstrated in the archaeological discussion, all these clans came under the political hegemony of the house of David, whose seat was established in Jerusalem.[75]

6. Summary: The Biblical Traditions about the Formation of the Israelite Monarchy (1 Samuel 9–2 Samuel 5) in Historical Perspective

The stories about the formation of the Israelite monarchy in 1 Sam 9–2 Sam 5 portray the attempt of two local leaders to establish dynastic monarchy over a group of people, identified by the authors as Israelites. Israel in these traditions is a designation for a kinship group, and thus it denoted a social, not a political, identity, one that is ascribed to a group of people, in this case the clans inhabiting the Jerusalem and Benjamin regions. The name Israel in 1 Sam 9–2 Sam 5 does not refer to the territorial polity known by this name from the time of the Omride rule and onward. Moreover, these stories reflect nothing of the formation or the geopolitical configuration of the Northern Kingdom, as they are well embedded in the social and political realia of southern Canaan in the early Iron Age and especially in the core territory of Judah. Hence, the stories about the rise of David in 1 Sam 16–2 Sam 5 should not be read as an allegory for an assumed late monarchic Judahite wish to inherit the Northern Kingdom of Israel. They should be read for what they are: a story about the rise of Israelite monarchy.

In this sense, it is important to remember that these traditions are a literary product of an intellectual elite that should be dated to the period after the formation of the territorial kingdom centered on Jerusalem (second half of the ninth century BCE). The conceptualization of Israel as a kinship group residing north and south of Jerusalem is, therefore, the one ascribed

---

75. See also Nadav Na'aman, "Jebusites and Jabeshites in the Saul and David Story-Cycles," *Bib* 95 (2015): 481–97.

to the population of the region by scribes servicing the ruling dynasty in Jerusalem with its constant need to form a politically and socially unified structure under centralized rule. That said, these traditions concur well with the archaeological picture portrayed above, according to which the Iron IIA saw the growth of Jerusalem as the main political center among the rather isolated cluster of rural settlements between Jerusalem and Bethel. In this state of affairs, it was the ruling dynasty in Jerusalem, the house of David, that reclaimed Israel as its kinship affiliation, and consequently the core community on which they established their rule was seen as Israelite.

What, therefore, may be said regarding the historicity of the traditions about the formation of the Israelite monarchy in the book of Samuel? Indeed, there could be little doubt that these traditions were composed much later than the events they depict, and to a large extent they may even be regarded as legendary. However, as these traditions are well embedded in the political and social realia of southern Canaan in the early Iron Age, they preserve, at least in their essence (but not in their details!) an authentic memory regarding the formation of Judah. Both Saul and David are portrayed as newly formed ruling elites, rising to power among their own kinsmen, the so-called Israelites, by means of agricultural wealth, military skills, and familial relationships. This depiction correlates well with the way we understand the social evolution that generated state formation in the Iron Age Levant.[76] In this regard, the early traditions about Saul and David preserve the memory of a struggle for power in the early monarchic period: the rise of dynastic monarchy in Jerusalem was the result of a struggle between two Israelite ruling families engaged in an attempt to establish their political hegemony over their own Israelite kinsmen settled in the regions north and south of Jerusalem.

---

76. E.g., Glenn M. Schwartz, "The Origins of the Aramaeans in Syria and Northern Mesopotamia: Research Problems and Potential Strategies," in *To the Euphrates and Beyond: Archaeological Studies in Honor of Maurits N. van Loon*, ed. O. M. C. Haex, Hans H. Curvers, and Peter M. M. G. Akkermans (Rotterdam: Balkema, 1989), 275–91; Guy Bunnens, "Syria in the Iron Age: Problems and Definitions," in *Essays on Syria in the Iron Age*, ed. Guy Bunnens, ANESSup 7 (Leuven: Peeters, 2000), 3–19; Stefania Mazzoni, "Syria and the Periodization of the Iron Age: A Cross-Cultural Perspective," in Bunnens, *Essays on Syria in the Iron Age*, 31–59; Trevor R. Bryce, *The World of the Neo-Hittite Kingdoms: A Political and Military History* (Oxford: Oxford University Press, 2012), 163–65, 202–4; Hélène Sader, "History," in *The Aramaeans in Ancient Syria*, ed. Herbert Niehr, HdO 106 (Leiden: Brill, 2014), 11–36.

Bibliography

Albright, William F. "The Site of Tirzah and the Topography of Western Manasseh." *JPOS* 11 (1931): 241–51.

Auld, A. Graeme. *I and II Samuel: A Commentary*. OTL. Louisville: Westminster John Knox, 2011.

Bezzel, Hannes. *Saul: Israels König in Tradition, Redaktion und früher Rezeption*. FAT 97. Tübingen: Mohr Siebeck, 2015.

Blum, Erhard. *Die Komposition der Vätergeschichte*. WMANT 57. Neukirchen-Vluyn: Neukirchener Verlag, 1984.

———. "The Jacob Tradition." Pages 181–211 in *The Book of Genesis: Composition, Reception and Interpretation*. Edited by Craig A. Evans, Joel N. Lohr, and David L. Petersen. VTSup 152. Leiden: Brill, 2012.

Bryce, Trevor R. *The World of the Neo-Hittite Kingdoms: A Political and Military History*. Oxford: Oxford University Press, 2012.

Bunnens, Guy. "Syria in the Iron Age: Problems of Definition." Pages 3–19 in *Essays on Syria in the Iron Age*. Edited by Guy Bunnens. ANESSup 7. Leuven: Peeters, 2000.

Cahill, Jane. "Jerusalem at the Time of the United Monarchy: The Archaeological Evidence." Pages 13–80 in *Jerusalem in Bible and Archaeology: The First Temple Period*. Edited by Andrew G. Vaughn and Ann E. Killebrew. SymS 18. Atlanta: Society of Biblical Literature, 2003.

Campbell, Anthony F. *1 Samuel*. FOTL 7. Grand Rapids: Eerdmans, 2003.

Campbell, Edward F. *Text*. Vol. 1 of *Shechem III: The Stratigraphy and Architecture of Shechem/Tell Balâṭah*. ASORAR 6. Boston: American Schools of Oriental Research, 2002.

Dietrich, Walter. *The Early Monarchy in Israel: The Tenth Century B.C.E.* BibEnc 3. Atlanta: Society of Biblical Literature, 2007.

———. *Samuel*. BKAT 8/1.5. Neukirchen-Vluyn: Neukirchener Verlag, 2008.

Dietrich, Walter, and Stefan Münger. "Die Herrschaft Sauls und der Norden Israels." Pages 39–54 in *Saxa Loquentur: Studien zu Archäologie Palästinas/Israels; Festschrift für Volkmar Fritz zum 65. Geburtstag*. Edited by Cornelis G. den Hertog, Ulrich Hübner, and Stefan Münger. AOAT 302. Münster: Ugarit-Verlag, 2003.

Dietrich, Walter, and Thomas Naumann. "The David–Saul Narrative." Pages 276–318 in *Reconsidering Israel and Judah: Recent Studies on the Deuteronomistic History*. Edited by Gary N. Knoppers and J. Gordon McConville. SBTS 8. Winona Lake, IN: Eisenbrauns, 1995.

Edelman, Diana. "The Deuteronomist's Story of King Saul: Narrative Art or Editorial Product?" Pages 207–20 in *Pentateuchal and Deuteronomistic Studies: Papers Read at the Thirteenth IOSOT Congress Leuven 1989*. Edited by Christianus Brekelmans and Johann Lust. BETL 94. Leuven: Peeters, 1990.

———. "Saul Ben Kish, King of Israel, as a 'Young Hero'?" Pages 161–83 in *Le jeune héros: Recherche sur la formation et la diffusion d'un theme littéraire au Proche-Orient ancien*. Edited by Jean-Marie Durand, Thomas Römer, and Michael Langlois. OBO 250. Fribourg: Academic Press; Göttingen: Vandenhoeck & Ruprecht, 2011.

Finkelstein, Israel. *The Archaeology of the Israelite Settlement*. Jerusalem: Israel Exploration Society, 1988.

———. "Ethnicity and the Origin of the Iron I Settlers in the Highlands of Canaan: Can the Real Israel Stand Up?" *BA* 59 (1996): 198–212.

———. *The Forgotten Kingdom: The Archaeology and History of Northern Israel*. ANEM 5. Atlanta: Society of Biblical Literature, 2013.

———. "The Great Transformation: The 'Conquest' of the Highlands Frontiers and the Rise of the Territorial States." Pages 349–65 in *The Archaeology of Society in the Holy Land*. Edited by Thomas Levy. London: Leicester University Press, 1995.

———. "A Great United Monarchy? Archaeological and Historical Perspectives." Pages 3–28 in *One God—One Cult—One Nation: Archaeological and Biblical Perspectives*. Edited by Reinhard G. Kratz and Hermann Spieckermann. BZAW 405. Berlin: de Gruyter, 2010.

———. "The History and Archaeology of Shiloh from the Middle Bronze Age II to Iron Age II." Pages 371–93 in *Shiloh: The Archaeology of a Biblical Site*. Edited by Israel Finkelstein. SMNIA 10. Tel Aviv: Institute of Archaeology, 1993.

———. "Jerusalem and the Benjamin Plateau in the Early Phases of the Iron Age: A Different Scenario." *ZDPV* 134 (2018): 190–95.

———. "Omride Architecture." *ZDPV* 116 (2000): 114–38.

———. "The Last Labayu: King Saul and the Expansion of the First North Israelite Territorial Entity." Pages 171–88 in *Essays on Ancient Israel in Its Near Eastern Context: A Tribute to Nadav Na'aman*. Edited by Yairah Amit, Ehud Ben Zvi, Israel Finkelstein, and Oded Lipschits. Winona Lake, IN: Eisenbrauns, 2006.

———. "Saul, Benjamin and the Emergence of 'Biblical Israel': An Alternative View." *ZAW* 123 (2011): 348–67.

———. "Shechem in the Late Bronze and the Iron I." Pages 349–56 in vol. 2 of *Timelines: Studies in Honor of Manfred Bietak*. Edited by Ernst Czerny, Irmgard Hein, Hermann Hunger, Dagmar Melman, and Angela Schwab. 3 vols. OLA 149. Leuven: Peeters, 2006.

———. "The Sociopolitical Organization of the Central Hill Country in the Second Millennium B.C.E." Pages 110–31 in *Biblical Archaeology Today, 1990: Proceedings of the Second International Congress on Biblical Archaeology; Supplement; Pre-Congress Symposium; Population, Production and Power, Jerusalem, June 1990*. Edited by Avraham Biran and Joseph Aviram. Jerusalem: Israel Exploration Society, 1993.

———. "Stages in the Territorial Expansion of the Northern Kingdom." *VT* 61 (2011): 227–42.

Finkelstein, Israel, and Oded Lipschits. "Omride Architecture in Moab: Jahatz and Atharot." *ZDPV* 126 (2010): 29–42.

Finkelstein, Israel, and Thomas Römer. "Comments on the Historical Background of the Jacob Narrative in Genesis." *ZAW* 126 (2014): 317–38.

Finkelstein, Israel, and Zvi Lederman. *Highlands of Many Cultures: The Southern Samaria Survey, the Sites*. SMNIA 14. Tel Aviv: Institute of Archaeology, 1997.

Fleming, Daniel. "Kingship of City and Tribe Conjoined: Zimri-Lim at Mari." Pages 227–40 in *Nomads, Tribes, and the States in the Ancient Near East: Cross-disciplinary Perspectives*. Edited by Jeffrey Szuchman. OIS 5. Chicago: Oriental Institute of the University of Chicago, 2009.

———. *The Legacy of Israel in Judah's Bible: History, Politics and the Reinscribing of Tradition*. Cambridge: Cambridge University Press, 2012.

Franklin, Norma. "Samaria: From the Bedrock to the Omride Palace." *Levant* 36 (2004): 189–202.

Gadot, Yuval. "The Iron I in the Samaria Highlands: A Nomad Settlement Wave or Urban Expansion?" Pages 103–14 in *Rethinking Israel: Studies in the History and Archaeology of Ancient Israel in Honor of Israel Finkelstein*. Edited by Oded Lipschits, Yuval Gadot, and Matthew J. Adams. Winona Lake, IN: Eisenbrauns, 2017.

Gass, Erasmus. *Die Ortsnamen des Richterbuchs in historischer und redaktioneller Perspektive*. ADPV 35. Wiesbaden: Harrassowitz, 2005.

Grønbæk, Jakob H. *Die Geschichte vom Aufstieg Davids (1 Sam. 15–2 Sam. 5): Tradition und Komposition*. Acta Theologica Danica 10. Copenhagen: Munksgaard, 1971.

Gross, Walter. *Richter*. HThKAT. Freiburg im Breisgau: Herder, 2009.

Hasel, Michael G. *Domination and Resistance: Egyptian Military Activity in the Southern Levant, ca. 1300–1185 BC.* PAe 11. Leiden: Brill, 1998.

Hutton, Jeremy M. "Mahanaim, Penuel, and Transhumance Routes: Observations on Genesis 32–33 and Judges 8." *JNES* 65 (2006): 161–78.

Jobling, David. "Saul's Fall and Jonathan's Rise: Tradition and Redaction in 1 Sam 14:1–46." *JBL* 95 (1976): 367–76.

Kaiser, Otto. "Der historische und biblische König Saul (Teil I)." *ZAW* 122 (2010): 520–45.

———. "Der historische und biblische König Saul (Teil II)." *ZAW* 123 (2011): 1–14.

Kleiman, Assaf. "Comments on the Archaeology and History of Tell el-Farʿah North (Biblical Tirzah) in the Iron IIA." *Sem* 60 (2018): 85–104.

Knauf, Ernst A. "The Cultural Impact of Secondary State Formation: The Cases of Edomites and Moabites." Pages 47–54 in *Early Edom and Moab: The Beginning of Iron Age in Southern Jordan*. Edited by Piotr Bienkowski. Sheffield Archaeological Monographs 7. Sheffield: Collis, 1992.

Kratz, Reinhard G. *The Composition of the Narrative Books of the Old Testament*. London: T&T Clark, 2005.

Lee, Sharen, Christoph Bronk Ramsey, and Amihai Mazar. "Iron Age Chronology in Israel: Results from Modeling with a Trapezoidal Bayesian Framework." *Radiocarbon* 55 (2013): 731–40.

Lehmann, Gunnar, and Hermann Michael Niemann. "When Did the Shephelah Became Judahite?" *TA* 41 (2014): 77–94.

Maeir, Aren M. "The Tell es-Safi/Gath Archaeological Project 1996–2010: Introduction, Overview and Synopsis of Results." Pages 1–88 in *Text*. Part 1 of *Tell es-Safi/Gath I: The 1996–2005 Seasons*. Edited by Aren M. Maeir. ÄAT 69. Wiesbaden: Harrassowitz, 2012.

Maeir, Aren M., Louise Hitchcock, and Liora Kolska Horwitz. "On the Constitution and Transformation of Philistine Identity." *OJA* 32 (2013): 1–38.

Mazar, Amihai. "Archaeology and the Biblical Narrative: The Case of the United Monarchy." Pages 29–58 in *One God—One Cult—One Nation: Archaeological and Biblical Perspectives*. Edited by Reinhard G. Kratz and Hermann Spieckermann. BZAW 405. Berlin: de Gruyter, 2010.

———. "Jerusalem in the Tenth Century B.C.E.: The Glass Half Full." Pages 255–72 in *Essays on Ancient Israel in Its Near Eastern Context: A Tribute to Nadav Naʾaman*. Edited by Yairah Amit, Ehid Ben Zvi, Israel Finkelstein, and Oded Lipschits. Winona Lake, IN: Eisenbrauns, 2006.

Mazzoni, Stefania. "Syria and the Periodization of the Iron Age: A Cross-Cultural Perspective." Pages 31–59 in *Essays on Syria in the Iron Age*. Edited by Guy Bunnens. ANESSup 7. Leuven: Peeters, 2000.

McCarter, P. Kyle. *I Samuel: A New Translation with Introduction, Notes and Commentary*. AB 8. New York: Doubleday, 1980.

McKenzie, Steven L. "Saul in the Deuteronomistic History." Pages 59–70 in *Saul in Story and Tradition*. Edited by Carl S. Ehrlich and Marsha C. White. FAT 47. Tübingen: Mohr Siebeck, 2006.

Na'aman, Nadav. "Canaanite Jerusalem and Its Central Hill Country Neighbors in the Second Millennium B.C.E." *UF* 24 (1992): 257–91.

———. "In Search of Reality behind the Account of David's Wars with Israel's Neighbours." *IEJ* 52 (2002): 200–24.

———. "Jebusites and Jabeshites in the Saul and David Story-Cycles." *Bib* 95 (2014): 481–97.

———. "The Kingdom of Judah in the Ninth Century BCE: Text Analysis versus Archaeological Research." *TA* 40 (2013): 247–76.

———. "The Northern Kingdom in the Late Tenth–Ninth Centuries BCE." Pages 399–418 in *Understanding the History of Ancient Israel*. Edited by H. G. M. Williamson. Proceedings of the British Academy 143. Oxford: Oxford University Press, 2007.

———. "The Pre-Deuteronomistic Story of King Saul and Its Historical Significance." *CBQ* 54 (1990): 638–58.

———. "Saul, Benjamin and the Emergence of 'Biblical Israel.'" *ZAW* 121 (2009): 211–24, 335–49.

———. "The Scope of the Pre-Deuteronomistic Saul-David Story Cycle." In *From Nomadism to Monarchy: Thirty Years Update*. Edited by Ido Koch, Omer Sergi, and Oded Lipschits. Tel Aviv: Institute of Archaeology, forthcoming.

———. "The Settlement of the Ephrathites in Bethlehem and the Location of Rachel's Tomb." *RB* 121 (2014): 516–29.

———. "Sources and Composition in the History of David." Pages 170–86 in *The Origins of the Ancient Israelite States*. Edited by Volkmar Fritz and Philip R. Davies. Sheffield: Sheffield Academic, 1996.

Niemann, Hermann Michael. "Core Israel in the Highlands and Its Periphery: Megiddo, the Jezreel Valley and the Galilee in the Eleventh–Eighth Century BCE." Pages 821–42 in *Megiddo IV: The 1998–2002 Seasons*. Edited by Israel Finkelstein, David Ussishkin, and Baruch Halpern. SMNIA 24. Tel Aviv: Institute of Archaeology, 2006.

———. "Royal Samaria—Capital or Residence? Or: The Foundation of the City of Samaria by Sargon II." Pages 184–207 in *Ahab Agonistes: The Rise and Fall of the Omri Dynasty*. Edited by Lester L. Grabbe. LHBOTS 421. London: T&T Clark, 2007.

Nihan, Christophe. "Saul among the Prophets (1 Sam. 10:10–12 and 19:18–24): The Reworking of Saul's Figure in the Context of the Debate on Charismatic Prophecy in the Persian Era." Pages 88–118 in *Saul in Story and Tradition*. Edited by Carl S. Ehrlich and Marsha C. White. FAT 47. Tübingen: Mohr Siebeck, 2006.

Noth, Martin. "Jabes-Gilead." *ZDPV* 69 (1953): 28–41.

Porter, Ann. "Beyond Dimorphism: Ideologies and Materialities of Kinship as Time-Space Distanciation." Pages 201–25 in *Nomads, Tribes, and the States in the Ancient Near East: Cross-disciplinary Perspectives*. Edited by Jeffrey Szuchman. OIS 5. Chicago: Oriental Institute of the University of Chicago, 2009.

———. *Mobile Pastoralism and the Formation of Near Eastern Civilization: Weaving Together Society*. Cambridge: Cambridge University Press, 2012.

Porter, Benjamin. *Complex Communities: The Archaeology of Early Iron Age West-Central Jordan*. Tucson: University of Arizona Press, 2013.

Pury, Albert de. "The Jacob Story and the Beginning of the Formation of the Pentateuch." Pages 51–72 in *A Farewell to the Yahwist? The Composition of the Pentateuch in Recent European Interpretation*. Edited by Thomas B. Dozeman and Konrad Schmid. SymS 34. Atlanta: Society of Biblical Literature, 2006.

Rosen, Baruch. "Economy and Subsistence." Pages 362–67 in *Shiloh: The Archaeology of a Biblical Site*. Edited by Israel Finkelstein. SMNIA 10. Tel Aviv: Institute of Archaeology, 1993.

Sader, Hélène. "History." Pages 11–36 in *The Aramaeans in Ancient Syria*. Edited by Herbert Niehr. HdO 106. Leiden: Brill, 2014.

Schmidt, Ludwig. *Menschlicher Erfolg und Jahwes Initiative: Studien zu Tradition, Interpretation und Historie in Überlieferungen von Gideon, Saul und David*. WMANT 38. Neukirchen-Vluyn: Neukirchener Verlag, 1970.

Schwartz, Glenn M. "The Origins of the Aramaeans in Syria and Northern Mesopotamia: Research Problems and Potential Strategies." Pages 275–91 in *To the Euphrates and Beyond: Archaeological Studies in Honor of Maurits N. van Loon*. Edited by O. M. C. Haex, Hans H. Curvers, and Peter M. M. G. Akkermans. Rotterdam: Balkema, 1989.

Sergi, Omer. "The Emergence of Judah as a Political Entity between Jerusalem and Benjamin." *ZDPV* 133 (2017): 1–23.

———. "The Gilead between Aram and Israel: Political Borders, Cultural Interaction and the Question of Jacob and the Israelite Identity." Pages 333–54 in *In Search of Aram and Israel: Politics, Culture, and Identity*. Edited by Omer Sergi, Manfred Oeming, and Izaak J. de Hulster. ORA 20. Tübingen: Mohr Siebeck, 2016.

———. "Judah's Expansion in Historical Context." *TA* 40 (2013): 226–46.

———. "State Formation, Religion and 'Collective Identity' in the Southern Levant." *HBAI* 4 (2015): 56–77.

Sergi, Omer, and Yuval Gadot. "Omride Palatial Architecture as Symbol in Action: Between State Formation, Obliteration, and Heritage." *JNES* 76 (2017): 103–11.

Stager, Lawrence, E. "Shemer's Estate." *BASOR* 277/278 (1990): 93–107.

Steen, Eveline J. van der. *Tribes and Territories in Transition: The Central East Jordan Valley in the Late Bronze Age and Early Iron Ages, A Study of the Sources*. OLA 130. Leuven: Peeters, 2004.

Steen, Eveline J. van der, and Klaas A. D. Smelik. "King Mesha and the Tribe of Dibon." *JSOT* 32 (2007): 139–62.

Steiner, Margreet, L. *The Settlement in the Bronze and Iron Ages*. Vol. 3 of *Excavations by Kathleen M. Kenyon in Jerusalem 1961–1967*. Copenhagen International Series 9. London: Sheffield Academic, 2001.

Stoebe, Hans J. *Das Erste Buch Samuelis*. KAT 8/2. Gütersloh: Gütersloher Verlagshaus, 1973.

Stolz, Fritz. *Das erste und zweite Buch Samuel*. ZBK 9. Zurich: TVZ, 1981.

Toffolo, Michael B., Eran Arie, Mario A.S. Martin, Elisabetta Boaretto, and Israel Finkelstein. "Absolute Chronology of Megiddo, Israel in the Late Bronze and Iron Ages: High Resolution Radiocarbon Dating." *Radiocarbon* 56 (2014): 221–44.

Uziel, Joe, and Nahshon Szanton. "New Evidence of Jerusalem's Urban Development in the Ninth Century BCE." Pages 429–39 in *Rethinking Israel: Studies in the History and Archaeology of Ancient Israel in Honor of Israel Finkelstein*. Edited by Oded Lipschits, Yuval Gadot, and Matthew J. Adams. Winona Lake, IN: Eisenbrauns, 2017.

———. "Recent Excavations near the Gihon Spring and Their Reflection on the Character of Iron II Jerusalem." *TA* 42 (2015): 233–50.

Uziel, Joe, and Yuval Gadot. "The Monumentality of Iron Age Jerusalem prior to the Eighth Century BCE." *TA* 44 (2017): 123–40.

Van Seters, John. *The Biblical Saga of King David*. Winona Lake, IN: Eisenbrauns, 2009.

Veijola, Timo. *Die ewige Dynastie: David und die Entstehung seiner Dynastie nach der deuteronomistischen Darstellung*. Helsinki: Suomalainen Tiedeakatemia, 1975.

Weingart, Kristin. *Stämmevolk—Staatsvolk—Gottesvolk? Studien zur Verwendung des Israels-Namens im Alten Testament*. FAT 2/68. Tübingen: Mohr Siebeck, 2014.

Weiser, Arthur. "Die Legitimation des Königs David: Zur Eigenart und Entstehung der sogen; Geschichte von Davids Aufstieg." *VT* 16 (1966): 325–54.

Wellhausen, Julius. *Die Composition des Hexateuchs und der historischen Bücher des Alten Testament*. Berlin: de Gruyter, 1889.

White, Marsha C. "The History of Saul's Rise: Saulide State Propaganda in 1 Samuel 1–14." Pages 271–92 in *"A Wise Discerning Mind": Essays in Honor of Burke O. Long*. Edited by Saul M. Olyan and Robert C. Culley. BJS 325. Providence, RI: Brown Judaic Studies, 2000.

———. "Saul and Jonathan in 1 Samuel 1 and 14." Pages 119–38 in *Saul in Story and Tradition*. Edited by C. S. Ehrlich and M. C. White. FAT 47. Tübingen: Mohr Siebeck, 2006.

Willi-Plein, Ina. "I Sam. 18–19 und die Davidshausgeschichte." Pages 138–71 in *David und Saul im Widerstreit: Diachronie und Synchronie im Wettstreit; Beiträge zur Auslegung des ersten Samuelbuches*. Edited by Walter Dietrich. OBO 206. Fribourg: Academic Press; Göttingen: Vandenhoeck & Ruprecht, 2004.

Wright, Jacob, L. *David, King of Israel and Caleb in Biblical Memory*. Cambridge: Cambridge University Press, 2014.

Zertal, Adam. *The Eastern Valleys and the Fringe of the Desert*. Vol. 2 of *The Manasseh Hill Country Survey*. CHANE 21.2. Leiden: Brill, 2008.

———. *The Shechem Syncline*. Vol. 1 of *The Manasseh Hill Country Survey*. CHANE 21.1. Leiden: Brill, 2004.

Zertal, Adam, and Nivi Mirkam. *From Nahal 'Iron to Nahal Shechem*. Vol. 3 of *The Manasseh Hill Country Survey*. CHANE 21.3. Leiden: Brill, 2016.

Possible Historical Settings of the Saul-David Narrative

Wolfgang Oswald

1. Introduction

1.1. The Extent of the Saul-David Narrative

The Saul-David narrative covers the major part of the first book of Samuel and the first part of the second book of Samuel. The story of the lost asses in which the encounter between Samuel and Saul is embedded (1 Sam 9:1–10:16) is the narrative beginning of the whole story. The conclusion of the Saul-David narrative is to be found in 2 Sam 8:1–15, the list of the subdued peoples and kings.[1] Besides several small additions, the following sections were *not* part of the original Saul-David narrative: the lot-casting scene (1 Sam 10:17–27), the farewell speech of Samuel (1 Sam 12), the war against the Amalekites (1 Sam 15) and, linked to that story, the anointing of David (1 Sam 16:1–13), the Goliath story (1 Sam 17), the two stories under the title "Is Saul among the Prophets?," the sparing of Saul's life in the night camp (1 Sam 26), Saul's visit to the medium of Endor (1 Sam 28), the scene with the messenger reporting the death of Saul and his sons (2 Sam 1:1–16), and the dynastic promise (2 Sam 7). As I leave aside these texts as later additions, I also do not consider the earlier Benjaminite Saul story. Saul's designation (1 Sam 9.1–10:16), his war against the Ammonites

---

1. This delimitation of the composition deviates from the popular assumption of a story of the rise of David/"Aufstiegsgeschichte" beginning with 1 Sam 16:14. In the present view, the presentation of David's opponent is an integral part of the composition. The conclusion of the composition is marked by the list of officers in 1 Sam 8:16–18 that was attached at the end of the original composition. For an extensive treatment of the delimitation problems in the books of Samuel see Walter Dietrich and Thomas Naumann, *Die Samuelbücher*, EdF 287 (Darmstadt: Wissenschaftliche Buchgesellschaft, 1995), 66–79.

(1 Sam 11:1–13), and the war against the Philistines (1 Sam 13–14) are considered here only as part of the Saul-David narrative.[2]

1.2. The Subject of the Saul-David Narrative

What is the subject of the Saul-David narrative? The first and, in a way, constitutive answer is: the legitimacy of the reign of David. The narrative tells the listeners that the *translatio imperii* from Saul to David was (1) induced by God, (2) due to Saul's failure, and (3) in no way forced by David.[3] But at this point already, one important question arises: is it a story about David and Saul or is it about the house of David and the house of Saul? Is it about David, the Judahite, and Saul, the Benjaminite, or is it about the founder of the house of David from Judah and the founder of the house of Saul from Benjamin?

There are a number of hints in the Saul-David narrative to the subject of the dynasties involved, for example, 1 Sam 20:16: "Thus Jonathan made a covenant with the house of David."[4] In 1 Sam 24:20–21 Saul says to David:

> Now I know that you shall surely be king, and that the kingdom of Israel shall be established in your hand. Swear to me therefore by Yahweh that you will not cut off my descendants after me, and that you will not wipe out my name from my father's house.

The most explicit reference comes from the mouth of Abigail: "For Yahweh will certainly make my lord a steadfast house, because my lord is fighting the battles of Yahweh" (1 Sam 25:28). The two dynasties are explicitly named as rivals in 2 Sam 3:1: "There was a long war between the house of Saul and the house of David. David grew stronger and stronger, while the house of Saul became weaker and weaker."

Besides these scattered references, there is a more important consideration. In the Hebrew Bible, there are several texts about an Israelite or Judahite leader figure gaining an important victory, as for instance, Barak

---

2. For a tradition-historical treatment of the earlier Saul narrative see Daniel Fleming, *The Legacy of Israel in Judah's Bible: History, Politics, and the Reinscribing of Tradition* (Cambridge: Cambridge University Press, 2012), 149–54.

3. See also Walter Dietrich, *Samuel: 1 Sam 1–12*, BKAT 8.1 (Neukirchen-Vluyn: Neukirchener Verlag, 2011), 47*–51*.

4. Unless otherwise noted, all translations are mine.

against Sisera (Judg 4), Ehud against Eglon (Judg 3:12–30), Gideon against Oreb and Zeeb (Judg 7), or Asa against Basha (1 Kgs 15:16–22). All texts mentioned are considerably shorter than the Saul-David narrative. The reason why the latter is so much longer is the importance of the main figures. Their impact on Israel goes beyond a victory in a battle, it also goes beyond the establishment of a state: their legacy is the foundation of the present-day kingdom.

Therefore, the Saul-David narrative deals with the legitimacy not only of David but also of his dynasty. The other side of the coin is the delegitimation of Saul and his sons, that is the house of Saul. One could state the problem this way: where does the legitimate king of Israel come from, from the house of Saul or from the house of David?

But the problem presupposed by the story is even broader. The figures of David and Saul not only stand for their houses but also for their tribes. Saul is a Benjaminite (1 Sam 9:1–2), whereas David is a Judahite (1 Sam 16:1). And the struggle between the two is clearly construed as a struggle between the two tribes. Saul appeals to his tribal kinsmen to take his side against David: "Hear now, you Benjaminites! Will the son of Jesse give every one of you fields and vineyards?" (1 Sam 22:7). Moreover, in the whole story of Ishbaal and Abner, the opponents of David are the Benjaminites (2 Sam 2:15, 25, 31; 3:19; 4:2), whereas the supporters of David are "the house of Judah" (2 Sam 2:10).

This view of the problem is also expressed in the so-called Succession Narrative or Court History (2 Sam 9–20, 1 Kgs 1–2). Shimei ben Gera, for example, accuses David of having murdered the house of Saul (2 Sam 16:7–8). Shimei ben Gera is introduced as a Benjaminite from the clan of Saul (2 Sam 16:5), but in 2 Sam 19:21 he defines himself as "the first of all the house of Joseph." In a similar manner, the Benjaminite Sheba ben Bichri rebels against David, proclaiming: "We have no portion in David, no share in the son of Jesse! Everyone to your tents, Israel!" (2 Sam 20:1), whereas the followers of David are said to be the "men of Judah" (20:2). Both rebels represent Benjamin in a narrow sense and Israel minus Judah in a broader sense. While the tribes of Benjamin and Judah appear as opponents in the Saul-David narrative, in the Court History, two Benjaminites appear as instigators against David.

Thus the story operates on three levels: (1) Saul versus David; (2) the house of Saul versus the house of David; (3) Benjamin versus Judah. The struggle between David and Saul for kingship is a dispute between Benjamin and Judah on the legitimacy of the house of David.

The problem in and behind the Saul-David narrative has even more nuances. The kingship for which the two are competing is, of course, the kingship over Israel (1 Sam 14:47; 24:21), but the kingship over Judah is not a self-evident part of that; it is rather something of its own. This is apparent in the statement on David's reign: "At Hebron he reigned over Judah seven years and six months. And at Jerusalem he reigned over all Israel and Judah thirty-three years" (2 Sam 5:5). Here, Judah is something distinct from "all Israel." Likewise, Abner's intention is "to transfer the kingdom from the house of Saul, and set up the throne of David over Israel and over Judah" (2 Sam 3:10). On the other hand, the kingship of Ishbaal extended over "Gilead, the Ashurites, Jezreel, Ephraim, Benjamin, and over all Israel" (2 Sam 2:9). The first five names designate the territorial extent of the rule, while the latter is not an additional territory but a summary expressing an ideological claim.[5]

All this makes it clear that there can only be one kingship in Israel despite the facts that the actual exercise of power is restricted to a smaller territory and that Judah has a special role. As to the latter, it seems as if the legitimacy of royal rule over Israel and that over Judah were not considered to be identical and therefore had to be stated distinctly. Dominion over Israel did not necessarily include Judah. Moreover, there is another significant asymmetry in the concept of Israelite kingship. Whereas David exerts kingship first over Judah and then over Israel, there is no such dyad in the case of Saul. He was not first king over Benjamin and then over Israel, evidently because there was never a kingdom of Benjamin.

Viewed from the later history as depicted in the book of Kings, these asymmetries are quite logical, since the rule that had to be legitimized for the house of David was twofold: over Judah as a matter of fact and over all Israel as a claim. That is why (1) the inclusion of Judah in the kingship over Israel and (2) the kingship over Judah, respectively, are given special attention in the texts.

Coming back to the issue of Saul and David, it has become clear that the story about these two has a wider scope. All additional aspects mentioned above were always resonating when the story was narrated orally, when the story was written down, and also when the story was reworked. The theme

---

5. See P. Kyle McCarter, *II Samuel: A New Translation with Introduction and Commentary*, AB 9 (Garden City, NY: Doubleday, 1984), 87–88.

of the narrative, the legitimacy of David, unfolds in large sections of the text as a dispute between Judahites and Benjaminites over the controversial issue of the legitimate royal dynasty: is it the Saulides from Benjamin or the Davidides from Judah?

The answer given by the narrative is unequivocal: the legitimate royal dynasty in Israel are the Davidides from Judah. Even more, the narrative defends this claim by showing that the Davidides did not gain their primacy by any illegal or illegitimate means, be it usurpation or any other kind of violence. The story as a whole is narrated from the point of view of Judah, but the addressees of this defense are probably Judahites and Benjaminites. The latter have to accept that it was Saul who acted reprehensibly rather than David. Thus, the story about kingship over Israel is, at the same time, a conflict story between Benjamin and Judah. In sum, the subject of the Saul-David narrative is the legitimacy of the Davidic dynasty, the purpose of the story is to defend its legitimacy and the parties of the dispute are Benjamin and Judah.

But when was the legitimacy of the Davidic dynasty disputed between Benjamin and Judah? It stands to reason that a text like this was produced at a time when this question needed to be settled. Historically, I propose to look for a period of competition, of change or uncertainty in the relations between Benjamin and Judah.

2. Known Situations of Change and Uncertainty between Benjamin and Judah

In the following, I will identify such situations in the course of the history of Benjamin and Judah from the tenth century BCE through the late Persian period in the fourth century BCE.[6]

---

6. In fact, the status of Benjamin during the monarchic period is still under dispute. Nadav Na'aman, "Saul, Benjamin and the Emergence of 'Biblical Israel,'" *ZAW* 121 (2009): 211–24, 335–49, contends that Benjamin was always affiliated with the kingdom of Judah, while Israel Finkelstein, "Saul, Benjamin and the Emergence of 'Biblical Israel': An Alternative View," *ZAW* 123 (2011): 348–67, holds that the affiliation of Benjamin changed at least once.

2.1. The So-Called Gibeon/Gibeah Polity

The first period of interest is that of the so-called Gibeon/Gibeah polity that existed in the eleventh and tenth centuries.[7] In the Gibeon-Bethel region north of Jerusalem, a considerable number of fortified sites existed throughout the Iron I and Early Iron II periods. At this time, Benjamin—or rather the territory of Benjamin—seems to have been the most powerful swathe of land in the region. Some of these sites were abandoned in the second half of the tenth century.[8] These unfavorable changes can be associated with the campaign of Pharaoh Shoshenq in the last quarter of the tenth century. The Shoshenq list from Karnak shows a certain concentration of sites in the very same region north and northwest of Jerusalem.[9] These sites might have been affected by Shoshenq's army, which could explain the decline. One might even ponder if Judah took over parts of Benjamin after the Shoshenq campaign, but that remains uncertain.[10]

2.2. A Dark Period

After this period, the archaeological data does not provide a clear picture as far as the Benjamin-Judah problem is concerned. Benjamin does not seem to have been part of the Tirzah polity that existed prior to the Omride dynasty.[11] If we understand the savior stories of the book of Judges as witnesses to the time around 900 BCE, we may draw some conclusions.[12] Deborah came from the south of the Ephraim mountain ridge, according

---

7. This is the terminology used in Israel Finkelstein, *The Forgotten Kingdom: The Archaeology and History of Northern Israel*, ANEM 5 (Atlanta: Society of Biblical Literature, 2013), 37–61. I roughly follow Finkelstein's account. For a similar assessment see Avraham Faust, "Settlement Patterns and State Formation in Southern Samaria and the Archaeology of (a) Saul," in *Saul in Story and Tradition*, ed. Carl S. Ehrlich and Marsha C. White, FAT 47 (Tübingen: Mohr Siebeck, 2006), 34.

8. See Omer Sergi, "The Emergence of Judah as a Political Entity between Jerusalem and Benjamin," *ZDPV* 133 (2017): 8–12.

9. See Manfred Weippert, *Historisches Textbuch zum Alten Testament*, GAT 10 (Göttingen: Vandenhoeck & Ruprecht, 2010), no. 102, 234–38: Ajalon, Gibeon, Beth-horon, Zemarajim?, Bethel, Gezer.

10. Christian Frevel, *Geschichte Israels*, Studienbücher Theologie 2 (Stuttgart: Kohlhammer, 2015), 171.

11. Again, I follow the presentation in Finkelstein, *Forgotten Kingdom*, 63–82.

12. With regard to the much disputed dating of the savior narratives see Finkel-

to Judg 4:5 from the area between Rama and Bethel, which is Benjaminite territory. Furthermore, we might consider that the second judge, Ehud ben Gera, was from the tribe of Benjamin (Judg 3:15). Both observations suggest that Benjamin, at that time, was oriented toward the north but was most probably not subordinated to the early Israelite rulers residing in Tirzah.

2.3. The Ninth Century BCE

During the ninth century BCE, Benjamin seems to have become part of the emerging kingdom of Judah. Two possible dates are under discussion: the time around 890 BCE and the time around 820 BCE, the former before the rise of the Omride dynasty, the latter after the downfall of the Omrides.

The first date is derived from the biblical account in 1 Kgs 15:16–22, the war between Basha of Israel and Asa of Judah, which concludes, "King Asa built Geba of Benjamin and Mizpah" (more on this in §3.2.2); the second date is based on more general considerations.[13] During the expansion of the Aramaean hegemony in the southern Levant in the last decades of the ninth century BCE, the Northern Kingdom of Israel was very much under pressure and reduced in power and extension. According to 2 Kgs 12:19, king Jehoash of Judah submitted to the Aramean king Hazael and might have profited from it, for example, by gaining dominion over Benjamin.

2.4. The Years between 790 and 780 BCE

In the years between 790 and 780 BCE, the affiliation of Benjamin might have changed again, this time in favor of the Northern Kingdom. According to 2 Kgs 14:11–14, Joash of Israel defeated Amaziah of Judah in a battle near Beth-shemesh and subsequently tore down the walls of Jerusalem. The successor to Joash, Jeroboam II of Israel, is said to have restored the territory of Israel to its full extent, reaching from Lebo-Hamat to the Dead Sea (2 Kgs 14:25). Since the north bank of the Dead

---

stein, *Forgotten Kingdom*, 35; Walter Gross, *Richter*, HThKAT (Freiburg im Breisgau: Herder, 2009), 82–84.

13. For this view see Finkelstein, *Forgotten Kingdom*, 44–7; Finkelstein, "Saul, Benjamin," 361.

Sea is Benjaminite territory (cf. Josh 18:19), one may assume that at least some part of Benjamin was again under Israelite/Samarian control.

2.5. The Aftermath of the Fall of Samaria

The situation changed again in the aftermath of the Assyrian strokes against Samaria in 732 and 722 BCE. It is generally accepted that the Israelite kingdom in its last decade, as well as the later Assyrian province, was reduced to the core territory of Ephraim. When, in 722 BCE the Northern Kingdom ceased to exist, Benjamin did not become a polity of its own. Rather, it came to Judah in this period, or, if had already been a part of the Southern Kingdom before, its affiliation with Judah was strengthened.

2.6. The Aftermath of the Fall of Jerusalem

The next change occurred in the aftermath of the destruction of Judah and Jerusalem in 587 BCE by the Babylonian army. Benjamin was not handed over to Samaria, but the internal relation between Benjamin and Judah changed drastically. While Jerusalem and Judah were a largely devastated area for almost two centuries, Benjamin became the leading region of the province with Mizpah, Motza, and Gibeon as the principal towns.[14] Benjamin and Judah were still together, but now, Benjamin took over the senior role.

2.7. The Fifth and Fourth Centuries

This constellation changed once more during the fifth or fourth century BCE. The first possible date is the decline of Benjamin around 480 BCE, which probably led to the transfer of the capital from Mizpah to the site

---

14. This is the majority opinion, see, e.g., Oded Lipschits, *The Fall and Rise of Jerusalem: Judah under Babylonian Rule* (Winona Lake, IN: Eisenbrauns, 2005), esp. 149–54; Hans M. Barstad, "After the 'Myth of the Empty Land': Major Challenges in the Study of Neo-Babylonian Judah," in *Judah and the Judeans in the Neo-Babylonian Period*, ed. Oded Lipschits and Joseph Blenkinsopp (Winona Lake, IN: Eisenbrauns, 2003), 3–20. This view was partially challenged by Avraham Faust, *Judah in the Neo-Babylonian Period: The Archaeology of Desolation*, ABS 18 (Atlanta: Society of Biblical Literature, 2012), 209–31.

known today as Ramat Raḥel.¹⁵ A second possible date is the progressive recovery of Jerusalem in the early fourth century BCE.¹⁶ From that time on, it seems reasonable to assume that Judah became more influential than Benjamin.

3. Selection of Situations of Higher Historical Probability

One can categorize the historical settings mentioned above into two basic constellations: (1) the affiliation of Benjamin changes from north to south or vice versa; (2) the status of Benjamin changes from independency or domination, respectively, to dependency or vice versa. The Saul-David narrative does not suit all of these possible scenarios. First, the north, whether the Tirzah polity, the kingdom of Israel, or the province of Samaria, does not play any role in the narrative.¹⁷ Second, Benjamin's status at the end of the narrative is clearly dependency from Judah. Thus, of the basic constellations named above, the change from Benjaminite independency or domination to dependency from Judah has the highest probability. This is the constellation in which Benjaminite elites have an interest in contesting the legitimacy of the Davidic dynasty. Conversely, the Judahite elites are challenged to defend their primacy. Out of the seven proposed historical settings, four have a higher probability, those identified above in §§2.1, 2.3, 2.5, and 2.7.

3.1. After the Decline of the Iron I Gibeon/Gibeah Polity

The discussion of the first scenario must necessarily remain somewhat hypothetical; the lack of epigraphical findings makes it hard to establish firmly the correlation between the Saul-David narrative and the archaeological findings. But, as stated above, the Shoshenq list provides some

---

15. Ephraim Stern, *Archaeology of the Land of the Bible: Vol. II; The Assyrian, Babylonian, and Persian Periods 732–332 B.C.E.* (New York: Doubleday, 2001), 322–23, 436–37; Frevel, *Geschichte Israels*, 299.

16. See Oded Lipschits and David Vanderhooft, "Yehud Stamp Impressions in the Fourth Century B.C.E.: A Time of Administrative Consolidation?," in *Judah and the Judeans in the Fourth Century B.C.E.*, ed. Oded Lipschits, Gary N. Knoppers, and Rainer Albertz (Winona Lake, IN: Eisenbrauns, 2007), 75–94.

17. On this subject, see Omer Sergi, "Saul, David, and the Formation of the Israelite Monarchy: Revisiting the Historical and Literary Context of 1 Samuel 9–2 Samuel 5," in this volume.

additional evidence that the Benjamin region in which the Gibeon/Gibeah polity was located had been a strong polity in the second half of the tenth century. One may reasonably assume that the Gibeon/Gibeah polity had a leader (or even more than one leader). To simplify matters, one may call this person "a Saul," as Avraham Faust has suggested.[18] One might further assume that there was a Judahite robber-chief by the name of David who carried out some struggles against this Benjaminite leader by the alias name of Saul. If this hypothesis is right, this antagonism might be considered the source of tradition on which the later authors of the Saul-David narrative drew. But it is very improbable that, already at that early time in the tenth century BCE, the material was put into writing, and it is likewise very improbable that the problem of the dynasty was already at issue. Hence, the decline of the Gibeon/Gibeah polity can provide a possible historical setting for the core of the David-Saul tradition but not for the David-Saul narrative.[19]

3.2. After the Decline of the Tirzah Polity

Let us now examine the ninth century BCE as a possible historical context for the Saul-David narrative. Two scenarios are under discussion: before or after the Omride dynasty. If Benjamin was incorporated into the kingdom of Judah around 830/820, that is, after the Omride dynasty, it would have been a change of belonging from Israel to Judah. This might have happened, but this process, if it took place, was most likely *not* the background for the composition of the Saul-David narrative.

As a matter of fact, we have such texts in the Hebrew Bible taking sides in the controversial issue whether Benjamin belongs to Israel or to Judah. The Jacob story says that Benjamin and Joseph have the same mother (Gen 30:22–24, 35:16–18), which means that the tribe of Benjamin belongs to

---

18. Faust, "Settlement Patterns," 34.

19. Fritz Stolz, *Das erste und zweite Buch Samuel*, ZBK 9 (Zurich: TVZ, 1981), 17, holds that the core of the Saul/David material was a number of "Heldensagen" ("heroic sagas") that came up during or shortly after the lifetime of the protagonists. P. Kyle McCarter, *I Samuel: A New Translation with Introduction and Commentary*, AB 8 (New York: Doubleday, 1980), 29, reconstructs the history of David's rise as a narrative lacking any reference to the theme of the dynasty and considers it probable that this story was composed already at the time of David.

Joseph who stands for the north in this context.[20] The same is true for the Joseph story, in which Benjamin is the beloved brother of Joseph (Gen 43:16, 30, 45:14, 22).[21] On the other hand, the book of Kings, in particular the passage 1 Kgs 12:21–24—the war prevented after the secession—says the opposite. But the Saul-David narrative does not treat this problem.

Thus, the better alternative is the war between King Basha of Israel and King Asa of Judah sometime around 890 BCE, as reported in 1 Kgs 15:16–22. There are two possibilities to handle this section in the book of Kings. First, we might consider the information about the war in 1 Kgs 15:16–22 to stem from the royal annals. Alternatively, we might consider this passage to be a later literary fabric that, nevertheless, contains a piece of older tradition about a temporal expansion of Judah to the north.[22] In the early decades of the two monarchies, neither of them was presumably strong enough to maintain a permanent dominion over Benjamin. Be that as it may, both scenarios provide a possible historical background for the Saul-David narrative. Whether the material had already been written down this early is another question.[23] But contrary to the first scenario in the tenth century BCE, in the present one under king Asa of Judah, the prominent role of the dynasty in the narrative poses no problem. If the succession of kings as laid out in the book of Kings is correct—and there is no strong argument against it—Asa was the fifth Davidic king in Jerusalem. It is very likely that a dynastic identity had evolved by now and that the figure of David had then attained its traditional status as founder of the dynasty and of the kingdom.

At this point, I would like to refer to a specific historical issue: the recurring mention of Moab, Edom, Ammon, Aram, and the rest. In 1 Sam 11:1, we hear of Nahash, the Ammonite, who is called Nahash, king of the Ammonites, in 2 Sam 10:1–2; in addition, in 1 Sam 22:3–4, David seeks help from the king of Moab. This means that in the time of the author of

---

20. See Wolfgang Oswald, *Staatstheorie im Alten Israel: Der politische Diskurs im Pentateuch und in den Geschichtsbüchern des Alten Testaments* (Stuttgart: Kohlhammer, 2009), 145–56.

21. See Oswald, *Staatstheorie im Alten Israel*, 170–84.

22. See Sergi, "Emergence of Judah," 12–16.

23. Dictrich, *1 Sam 1–12*, 57*, thinks of the ninth century as the time of the first collection of the David stories. Stolz, *Das erste*, 19, holds that the first comprehensive narrative, which he calls "the story of the dynasty," was composed two or three generations after David, i.e., in the early ninth century.

these texts, Ammon and Moab were already kingdoms, a scenario that hints to the second third of the ninth century at the earliest.[24] Likewise, interestingly, the Philistines—with the exception of Achish of Gath—are always referred to in a general manner. The opponents of the Israelites are always "the Philistines" as if the Philistine city-states and their rulers had been one heart and one soul all the time. This does not speak for the temporal proximity of the historical events with the literary production. The one exception, Achish of Gath, seems to have its roots in a distinct tradition going back to the third quarter of the ninth century at the latest, that is, before the destruction of Gath by king Hazael of Damascus (1 Kgs 12:17–18). The literary presentation of Achish as a political parodic figure could be a literary fabrication from the seventh century.[25]

3.3. After the Termination of the Northern Monarchy

The next possible historical setting of the Saul-David narrative is the final decades of the eighth century after the conversion of the kingdom of Israel into an Assyrian province. This massive change in status of Ephraim and Samaria may well explain the neglect of any reference to the northern polity in the Saul-David narratives. After 732 BCE the kingdom of Israel was reduced to a rump in the hilly region of Ephraim, and the same is true for the subsequent Assyrian province. Perhaps, Benjamin came to Judah in these years. But even if Benjamin had already been part of the kingdom of Judah, the discontinuation of the once powerful neighbor to the north must have had ramifications for the relation between Benjamin and Judah.[26] In other words, the domination of Jerusalem became stronger and the incorporation of Benjamin into the Judahite kingdom became closer.

In any case, it is easy to imagine what purpose the Saul-David narrative could have fulfilled in this setting. It fosters the primacy of the Judahite kingdom and its dynasty. The narrative asserts that the domination of

---

24. See Frevel, *Geschichte Israels*, 85–86.

25. See Erasmus Gass, "Achisch von Gat als politische Witzfigur," *TQ* 189 (2009): 210–42.

26. According to Dietrich, *1 Sam 1–12*, 47*, the David (and Saul) stories were thoroughly reworked after 722 BCE by a "Höfischer Erzähler" ("courtly novelist"). McCarter, *I Samuel*, holds that the earlier stories, the history of David's rise and the succession story, were reworked and combined into a prophetic history in the years "shortly after the collapse of the northern kingdom" (22).

Judah after the decline of the Northern Kingdom is nothing new, that it has been this way from the beginning. The Davidic dynasty has been holding the kingship not only over Judah but also over all Israel ever since the days of David, so the Benjaminites have to accept the Judahite hegemony. Yet another aspect may be stressed: by the end of the eighth century BCE, the possibility rises that such a voluminous literary work as the Saul-David narrative was put into writing.[27]

3.4. After the Decline of Benjamin in the Fifth Century

After the destruction of Jerusalem, its temple, and large parts of the Judean countryside in 587 BCE, Benjamin took the lead. The Babylonian province of Benjamin-Judah was administered from Benjaminite towns for several decades. In a long and presumably slow process beginning around 480 BCE at the earliest, Judah came back to the foreground and once again assumed the leading role. But as far as we know, the relation between Benjamin and Judah was not the cardinal problem in the early and middle Persian period; rather, the relation between Judah and Samaria was.

This constellation makes it unlikely that the Saul-David narrative was originally written at that time. The various compositions in Ezra-Nehemiah sound different, likewise the Shechem texts in the Hexateuch (e.g., Deut 27; Josh 24). This notwithstanding, one can easily imagine that the Saul-David narrative had been in use and served a purpose in the Persian period. It was certainly able to reinforce the cohesion between the two parts of the province of Yehud.

A late witness to this purpose is the treatment of Benjamin and the house of Saul in Chronicles. The tribe of Benjamin holds a privileged position in the tribal system of Chronicles. It is one of the three important tribes besides Judah and Levi. On the other hand, the Chronicler makes unequivocally clear that the house of Saul is ultimately rejected (1 Chr 10:13–14). This is a good example of the reception and reworking of the Saul-David narrative in the Persian period. The problems treated in this narrative were still relevant in those days. But the Persian period

---

27. See David W. Jamieson-Drake, *Scribes and Schools in Monarchic Judah: A Socio-archeological Approach*, JSOTSup 109 (Sheffield: Almond Press, 1991); Frevel, *Geschichte Israels*, 249–52.

was a time of creative reception, not the time of composition of the Saul-David narrative.[28]

4. Conclusion: A Synthetic View

In the Hebrew Bible, two narratives stress the legitimacy of the Davidic dynasty and their rule over all Israel. The story in the books of Kings defends the Judahite viewpoint against the Northern Kingdom of Israel, or, better, against those elites who stand in the tradition of the Northern Kingdom. The story in the books of Samuel defends the Judahite viewpoint against Benjamin, or, to be more precise, against Benjaminite elites who doubt or even deny Judahite primacy.

Thus, the issue of the legitimacy and the extent of Davidic rule seems to have been an abiding theme in the history of ancient Israel. Were the Davidides entitled to rule over all of Israel? or only over Benjamin and Judah? or only over Judah? These issues were contested, at times between Israel/Ephraim and Judah, at times between Benjamin and Judah. Our concern here is only the latter.

The relation between Benjamin and Judah underwent several changes and periods of instability. It stands to reason that these were the periods in which the legitimacy of the Davidic dynasty was challenged by Benjaminite leaders. The relevant scenario for our purpose is the status change of Benjamin from (relative) independency from Judah or even supremacy over it to dependency on it. As far as we know, this process occurred four times in the course of history. It seems probable that the material of the

---

28. Yairah Amit, "The Saul Polemic in the Persian Period," in *Judah and the Judeans in the Persian Period*, ed. Oded Lipschits and Manfred Oeming (Winona Lake, IN: Eisenbrauns, 2006), 647–61, names three texts from the Persian period treating the figure of Saul and/or treating the relation between Benjamin and Judah: the story of the rape at Gibeah (Judg 19–21), the book of Esther (Est 2:5; 3:1), and Chronicles (1 Chr 10). Apart from these texts, some authors reckon with additions to the Saul-David narrative in the Persian period, see, e.g., Klaus-Peter Adam, "Saul as a Tragic Hero: Greek Drama and Its Influence on Hebrew Scripture in 1 Samuel 14,24–46 (10,8; 13,7–13A; 10,17–27)," in *For and Against David: Story and History in the Books of Samuel*, ed. A. Graeme Auld and Erik Eynikel, BETL 232 (Leuven: Peeters, 2010), 123–83; Adam, "Nocturnal Intrusions and Divine Interventions on Behalf of Judah: David's Wisdom and Saul's Tragedy in 1 Samuel 26," *VT* 59 (2009): 1–33; and the disaffirmation of Adam's late dating by Walter Dietrich, *Samuel: 1 Sam 13–26*, BKAT 8.2 (Neukirchen-Vluyn: Neukirchener Verlag, 2015), 816.

Saul-David narrative was formed, shaped, and reshaped during these transitional phases.

(Stage 1) The traditions behind the Saul-David narrative may have had their origin in the late tenth century when the two eponymous figures supposedly were the heads of the rivaling polities of Gibeon/Gibeah and Jerusalem. (Stage 2) This body of traditions could have attained its first identifiable shape in the early monarchy, in particular during the reign of Asa of Judah in the beginning of the ninth century. From this time on, this subject was part of the dynastic self-conception of Judah (and Benjamin). (Stage 3) This material was probably put into writing after the termination of the Northern Kingdom at the end of the eighth century. Even if one opines that the writing had taken place earlier, one might nevertheless assume that the caesura of 722 BCE left its traces in the material. (Stage 4) From that time on, the Saul-David narrative was the basis for several types of reworking: it was extended by the Succession Narrative, embedded into the Deuteronomistic History, and partially rewritten in Chronicles.

Bibliography

Adam, Klaus-Peter. "Nocturnal Intrusions and Divine Interventions on Behalf of Judah: David's Wisdom and Saul's Tragedy in 1 Samuel 26." *VT* 59 (2009): 1–33.

———. "Saul as a Tragic Hero: Greek Drama and Its Influence on Hebrew Scripture in 1 Samuel 14,24–46 (10,8; 13,7–13A; 10,17–27)." Pages 123–83 in *For and Against David: Story and History in the Books of Samuel*. Edited by A. Graeme Auld and Erik Eynikel. BETL 232. Leuven: Peeters, 2010.

Amit, Yairah. "The Saul Polemic in the Persian Period." Pages 647–61 in *Judah and the Judeans in the Persian Period*. Edited by Oded Lipschits and Manfred Oeming. Winona Lake, IN: Eisenbrauns, 2006.

Barstad, Hans M. "After the 'Myth of the Empty Land': Major Challenges in the Study of Neo-Babylonian Judah." Pages 3–20 in *Judah and the Judeans in the Neo-Babylonian Period*. Edited by Oded Lipschits and Joseph Blenkinsopp. Winona Lake, IN: Eisenbrauns, 2003.

Dietrich, Walter. *Samuel: 1 Sam 1–12*. BKAT 8.1. Neukirchen-Vluyn: Neukirchener Verlag, 2011.

———. *Samuel: 1 Sam 13–26*. BKAT 8.2; Neukirchen-Vluyn: Neukirchener Verlag, 2015.

Dietrich, Walter, and Thomas Naumann. *Die Samuelbücher.* EdF 287. Darmstadt: Wissenschaftliche Buchgesellschaft, 1995.

Faust, Avraham. *Judah in the Neo-Babylonian Period: The Archaeology of Desolation.* ABS 18. Atlanta: Society of Biblical Literature, 2012.

———. "Settlement Patterns and State Formation in Southern Samaria and the Archaeology of (a) Saul." Pages 14–38 in *Saul in Story and Tradition.* Edited by Carl S. Ehrlich and Marsha C. White. FAT 47. Tübingen: Mohr Siebeck, 2006.

Finkelstein, Israel. *The Forgotten Kingdom: The Archaeology and History of Northern Israel.* ANEM 5. Atlanta: Society of Biblical Literature, 2013.

———. "Saul, Benjamin and the Emergence of 'Biblical Israel': An Alternative View." *ZAW* 123 (2011): 348–67.

Fleming, Daniel. *The Legacy of Israel in Judah's Bible: History, Politics, and the Reinscribing of Tradition.* Cambridge: Cambridge University Press, 2012.

Frevel, Christian. *Geschichte Israels.* Studienbücher Theologie 2. Stuttgart: Kohlhammer, 2015.

Gass, Erasmus. "Achisch von Gat als politische Witzfigur." *TQ* 189 (2009): 210–42.

Gross, Walter. *Richter.* HThKAT. Freiburg im Breisgau: Herder, 2009.

Jamieson-Drake, David W. *Scribes and Schools in Monarchic Judah: A Socio-archeological Approach.* JSOTSup 109. Sheffield: Almond Press, 1991.

Lipschits, Oded. *The Fall and Rise of Jerusalem: Judah under Babylonian Rule.* Winona Lake, IN: Eisenbrauns, 2005.

Lipschits, Oded, and David Vanderhooft. "Yehud Stamp Impressions in the Fourth Century B.C.E.: A Time of Administrative Consolidation?" Pages 75–94 in *Judah and the Judeans in the Fourth Century B.C.E.* Edited by Oded Lipschits, Gary N. Knoppers, and Rainer Albertz. Winona Lake, IN: Eisenbrauns, 2007.

McCarter, P. Kyle. *I Samuel: A New Translation with Introduction and Commentary.* AB 8. New York: Doubleday, 1980.

———. *II Samuel: A New Translation with Introduction and Commentary.* AB 9. Garden City, NY: Doubleday, 1984.

Na'aman, Nadav. "Saul, Benjamin and the Emergence of 'Biblical Israel.'" *ZAW* 121 (2009): 211–24, 335–49.

Oswald, Wolfgang. *Staatstheorie im Alten Israel: Der politische Diskurs im Pentateuch und in den Geschichtsbüchern des Alten Testaments.* Stuttgart: Kohlhammer, 2009.

Sergi, Omer. "The Emergence of Judah as a Political Entity between Jerusalem and Benjamin." *ZDPV* 133 (2017): 1–23.

Stern, Ephraim. *The Assyrian, Babylonian, and Persian Periods 732–332 B.C.E.* Vol. 2 of *Archaeology of the Land of the Bible*. New York: Doubleday, 2001.

Stolz, Fritz. *Das erste und zweite Buch Samuel*. ZBK 9. Zurich: TVZ, 1981.

Weippert, Manfred. *Historisches Textbuch zum Alten Testament*. GAT 10. Göttingen: Vandenhoeck & Ruprecht, 2010.

The Land of Benjamin between the Emerging Kingdoms of Israel and Judah: A Historical Hypothesis on the Reign of Rehoboam

Joachim J. Krause

In a recent textbook of the history of Israel, doubts have been raised whether a Judahite king by the name Rehoboam existed at all.[1] According to this view, Rehoboam, translated as "he who makes room for the people" (*Volksweiter*), was a fictitious eponym created as a counterpart to the no less fictitious Jeroboam, or "he who contends against the people" (*Volksstreiter*).[2] In an onomastic seminar, one would of course have to object that the sentence-name Rehoboam should be translated as either "the godhead has made room" or rather "the people has expanded" (or "he—that is, YHWH—has expanded the people," which, however, results in a tripartite syntax hardly attested in Hebrew names), while Jeroboam, being built on the root רבב, not ריב, would in fact come quite close to that meaning, to be translated as something like "may the people become many."[3] Yet, the argument goes, the names have been employed against their more original meaning for an ideological purpose, and in any case

---

1. Christian Frevel, *Geschichte Israels*, Studienbücher Theologie 2 (Stuttgart: Kohlhammer, 2016), 151.

2. Frevel, *Geschichte Israels*, 151.

3. For Rehoboam, see Martin Noth, *Die israelitischen Personennamen im Rahmen der gemeinsemitischen Namengebung*, BWANT 46 (Stuttgart: Kohlhammer, 1928), 193 with n. 4; Johann J. Stamm, "Hebräische Ersatznamen," in *Beiträge zur hebräischen und altorientalischen Namenkunde*, ed. Ernst Jenni and Martin A. Klopfenstein, OBO 30 (Göttingen: Vandenhoeck & Ruprecht; Fribourg: Universitätsverlag, 1980), 69–70; Stamm, "Zwei alttestamentliche Königsnamen," in *Beiträge zur hebräischen und altorientalischen Namenkunde*, 137–43. For Jeroboam, see Noth, *Personennamen*, 206–7; for a different view, see Stamm, "Königsnamen," 143–46.

this presumed purpose is more important than the guess at a pun on the two names. This purpose would be to create a narrative account of the separation of a great united monarchy that historically did not happen, since a united monarchy did not exist.[4] To be sure, the latter contention is a burning issue, but not so much for the present paper.[5] The following discussion presupposes no more and no less than that a "king" (or "chief") called Rehoboam existed, was based in Jerusalem, and for the better part of the last quarter of the tenth century ruled the kingdom of Judah, which later existed alongside the rival kingdom of Israel, ruled by a certain Jeroboam.[6]

While one end of the interpretive spectrum doubts the very existence of Rehoboam, the other end offers mere paraphrases of the biblical record. According to these, King Rehoboam forfeits ten out of twelve tribes destined for him to rule due to his unfathomable folly. Nevertheless, among those who follow "the house of David" is not only Judah (thus 1 Kgs 12:20b) but also the tribe of Benjamin (12:21a). Seemingly on his side right from the beginning, they allow Rehoboam to mobilize a rather formidable number of warriors—180,000 chosen troops—for his attempt to restore his lost reign. In the end, Jeroboam of Israel can count his blessings, for it is only due to a divine intervention at the hands of a certain man of God, Shemaiah, that he is saved from losing his unexpected kingdom just as quickly as he has gained it (12:21–24).

Working toward a balanced picture between these polar positions, I hope to put a piece of the puzzle dubbed "the trouble with Benjamin" in

---

4. Frevel, *Geschichte Israels*, 151.

5. See, e.g., the various contributions collected in Reinhard G. Kratz and Hermann Spieckermann, eds., *One God—One Cult—One Nation: Archaeological and Biblical Perspectives*, BZAW 405 (Berlin: de Gruyter, 2010), esp. Israel Finkelstein, "A Great United Monarchy? Archaeological and Historical Perspectives," 1–28; Amihai Mazar, "Archaeology and the Biblical Narrative: The Case of the United Monarchy," 29–58; and Erhard Blum, "Solomon and the United Monarchy: Some Textual Evidence," 59–78. For a recent restatement of his pointed position as argued in the above and numerous other previous publications, see Israel Finkelstein, *The Forgotten Kingdom: The Archaeology and History of Northern Israel*, ANEM 5 (Atlanta: Society of Biblical Literature, 2013).

6. For the existence of Jeroboam I as a historical figure, see the balanced discussion of evidence in Lester L. Grabbe, "Jeroboam I? Jeroboam II? Or Jeroboam 0? Jeroboam in History and Tradition," in *Rethinking Israel: Studies in the History and Archaeology of Ancient Israel in Honor of Israel Finkelstein*, ed. Oded Lipschits, Yuval Gadot, and Matthew J. Adams (Winona Lake, IN: Eisenbrauns, 2017), 115–23.

its proper place.⁷ In the main, my contribution will be to reevaluate the textual material that we possess on Rehoboam (§1), which is quite diverse not only in what it discloses but also in how reliable a given piece of information is. While some are hardly of any use for a historical reconstruction of Rehoboam's reign and its circumstances, others quite possibly are. In terms of method, it seems crucial to me to evaluate every piece of evidence in its own right and to distinguish between varying degrees of value as a source. Only in doing so will it be possible to correlate, in a second step, the available extrabiblical evidence (§2) before finally sketching a historical hypothesis (§3).

1. Rehoboam of Judah: Evaluating the Biblical Evidence

Sifting through the biblical evidence for Rehoboam of Judah, the following broad survey seeks to evaluate which information commends itself for being used in a historical reconstruction, and in what way. Working backward, I will begin in Chronicles and only from there move on to the book of Kings. In so doing, I will focus on those passages that pertain to the topic at hand, the affiliation of the region of Benjamin.

1.1. The Account in Chronicles

It comes as no surprise that the account in Chronicles (2 Chr 9:31; 10–11) has more to say about Rehoboam than the book of Kings. It has more to say about the man of God Shemaiah as well, the latter playing his role as advisor at critical crossroads not only in the story of Israel's breakaway from the house of David (11:1–4) but also when the pharaoh approaches (12:5–8). We also learn that Rehoboam was an ambitious and strategic builder (11:5–12), a benefactor of the priests and Levites driven away by the infamous Jeroboam (11:13–17), and a father of many sons and

---

7. Philip R. Davies, "The Trouble with Benjamin," in *Reflection and Refraction: Studies in Biblical Historiography in Honour of A. Graeme Auld*, ed. Robert Rezetko, Timothy H. Lim, and W. Brian Aucker, VTSup 113 (Leiden: Brill, 2007), 93–111. See esp. Nadav Na'aman, "Saul, Benjamin and the Emergence of 'Biblical Israel,'" *ZAW* 121 (2009): 211–24, 335–49; and Israel Finkelstein, "Saul, Benjamin and the Emergence of 'Biblical Israel': An Alternative View," *ZAW* 123 (2011): 348–67, each with bibliography.

even more daughters, whom we hear of for the first time in Chronicles (11:18–23).[8]

Within this account, two passages call for a closer look in the present context. The first one is the notice of Rehoboam fortifying a number of cities together with a list of these cities in 2 Chr 11:5–12. Like enumerative genres in general, this list has led historians to hope to gather reliable information from Chronicles.[9] But that hope has been dashed by careful analyses that have adduced strong arguments for understanding the list as reflecting later circumstances. Whether one opts for a Hasmonean reality behind the text or a reflection of the rule of Hezekiah or Josiah, either way the notice of Rehoboam's fortification of Judahite cities has to be excluded from a historical reconstruction of the time it purports to reflect.[10] In any case, it hardly pertains to the question under scrutiny here, for despite the concluding verse giving the impression that fortifying the enumerated cities allowed Rehoboam to hold Judah *and* Benjamin (11:12b; see also 11:10aγ), it is striking that the fortification measures focus on places to the southwest of Jerusalem, while the critical northern border remains broadly out of scope.[11]

The second passage to look at is the Chronicler's version of Pharaoh "Shishak" threatening Jerusalem (12:2–9). To state the obvious at the outset, there are no historical data to be garnered from this account that could not be garnered from the parallel passage in Kings (certainly not the

---

8. For an analysis and interpretation of the Rehoboam account in Chronicles in its own right, see, e.g., Gary N. Knoppers, "Rehoboam in Chronicles: Villain or Victim?," *JBL* 109 (1990): 423–40; Itzhak Amar, "The Characterization of Rehoboam and Jeroboam as a Reflection of the Chronicler's View of the Schism," *JHS* 17 (2017): art. 9, https://tinyurl.com/SBL2636b.

9. See, e.g., the discussion in Peter Welten, *Geschichte und Geschichtsdarstellung in den Chronikbüchern*, WMANT 42 (Neukirchen-Vluyn: Neukirchener Verlag, 1973), 11–15.

10. For a Hasmonean background, see Israel Finkelstein, "Rehoboam's Fortified Cities (II Chr 11,5–12): A Hasmonean Reality?," *ZAW* 123 (2011): 92–107. For the time of Hezekiah or Josiah, see Herbert Donner, *Von der Königszeit bis zu Alexander dem Großen*, vol. 2 of *Geschichte des Volkes Israel und seiner Nachbarn in Grundzügen*, 3rd ed., GAT 4.2 (Göttingen: Vandenhoeck & Ruprecht, 2001), 274, with further references in n. 54.

11. For literary-critical considerations of this section, see Welten, *Geschichte und Geschichtsdarstellung*, 13. The focus on the southwest is observed by Frevel, *Geschichte Israels*, 150.

details regarding the Egyptian army in 12:3). But it will prove illuminating for the subsequent discussion of that *Vorlage* to see how it is embellished by the Chronicler. In fact, the Chronicler employs the Shishak episode for a theological lesson that he carefully prepares for in the preceding context. Thus, he concludes the notice of Rehoboam receiving the priests and Levites ousted by Jeroboam (11:13–17) by stating that "they strengthened the kingdom of Judah, and for three years they made Rehoboam son of Solomon secure," for Rehoboam and his people walked in the way they were supposed to walk in (11:17).[12] This they do for three years. But after that, in the fourth year, Rehoboam "abandoned the torah of YHWH, he and all Israel with him" (12:1). It is against *this* background that the Chronicler invokes the traditional date of the fifth year of Rehoboam (12:2 par. 1 Kgs 14:25) and the corresponding report of Shishak taking away the temple and palace treasures. The significance of this is quite obvious: The Chonicler interprets the event as an act of divine retribution. Indeed, this interpretation not only arises from the contextual position of the episode, but is also spelled out in theologizing additions vis-à-vis the *Vorlage*. This is done succinctly at the beginning, where the Chronicler states his conviction that Shishak came up against Jerusalem "because they had been unfaithful to YHWH" (כי מעלו ביהוה; 2 Chr 12:2b). He elaborates on this by having the prophet Shemaiah appear on the scene for a second time. Shemaiah explains to Rehoboam and the officials of Judah who have gathered at Jerusalem—and at the same time of course to the hearers and readers of Chronicles—the lesson to be learned from this event: "Thus says YHWH: 'You abandoned me, so I have abandoned you to the hand of Shishak'" (12:5). The pharaoh's campaign, directed by YHWH, is the immediate consequence of Rehoboam's transgression. This comment betrays the Chronicler's hand.[13]

1.2. 1 Kings 12:1–24

Turning to 1 Kgs 12, the vivid story of the separation of the united monarchy, I shall limit myself to some brief observations on its aftermath

---

12. Throughout this paper, biblical translations are based on the NRSV, with modifications.

13. See also Manfred Weippert, *Historisches Textbuch zum Alten Testament*, GAT 10 (Göttingen: Vandenhoeck & Ruprecht, 2010), 228 n. 2: "eine theologische Begründung des Feldzugs als Strafaktion Jahwes" (with reference to 12:2b).

as reported in verses 21–24. The story itself distorts Rehoboam beyond recognition. Fool incarnate, pretentious to the bone and utterly resistant to good advice, the break-away of the ten northern tribes is presented as his fault and his fault alone—presumably in an attempt to legitimize his antagonist who, almost without any effort of his own, becomes king of Israel. Thus, even though he hardly appears on the scene at all, 1 Kgs 12 is a chapter about Jeroboam. An in-depth analysis of that chapter and of the antecedents given in 1 Kgs 11:26–39, including the puzzling calculation of twelve minus ten equaling one and the puzzle it indeed provoked in the textual transmission, is beyond the scope of this paper.[14] For the present purpose, it is enough to recall the outcome of the episode: "There was no one who followed the house of David, except the tribe of Judah alone" (לא היה אחרי בית־דוד זולתי שבט־יהודה לבדו; 12:20b). To be sure, the Septuagint makes an addition that appears quite necessary in light of later times: "except the tribe of Judah *and Benjamin* [καὶ Βενιαμιν] alone" (LXX 3 Kgdms 12:20). However, this textual variant is hardly of help for the task at hand.[15]

Yet the prosaic note on Rehoboam's kingdom consisting of Judah alone is not the end of the story as we know it. Its continuation in 1 Kgs 12:21–24 has the new king draft his troops in order to restore the *status quo ante*, which he is prevented from doing only by the word of YHWH. According to this short passage, Benjamin appears to have been part of the southern kingdom right from the start. Here one might gain the impression that

---

14. See, e.g., Martin Noth, *Geschichte Israels*, 7th ed. (Göttingen: Vandenhoeck & Ruprecht, 1969), 214 n. 1; differently Martin Noth, *I Könige 1–16*, vol. 1 of *Könige*, BKAT 9.1 (Neukirchen-Vluyn: Neukirchener Verlag, 1968), 259–60. See further Ernst Würthwein, *Das erste Buch der Könige: Kapitel 1–16*, ATD 11.1 (Göttingen: Vandenhoeck & Ruprecht, 1977), 141–42. See now also Kristin Weingart, "Jeroboam and Benjamin: Pragmatics and Date of 1 Kings 11:26–40; 12:1–20," in the present volume.

15. Beyond this variant, in the Greek we actually possess a self-contained "alternative story of the division of the kingdom" (to use the words of Zipi Talshir) in 3 Kgdms 12:24a–z. While some would look with Adrian Schenker, "Jeroboam and the Division of the Kingdom in the Ancient Septuagint: LXX 3 Kingdoms 12.24 A–Z, MT 1 Kings 11–12; 14 and the Deuteronomistic History," in *Israel Constructs Its History: Deuteronomistic Historiography in Recent Research*, ed. Albert de Pury, Thomas Römer, and Jean-Daniel Macchi, JSOTSup 306 (Sheffield: Sheffield Academic, 2000), 214–57, for earlier material preserved in this text, Zipora Talshir, *The Alternative Story of the Division of the Kingdom*, JBS 6 (Jerusalem: Simor, 1993), has made a strong case for reading it as a midrash of sorts.

the political reality of later monarchic (and postexilic) times is but an extension of a state of affairs established in the very beginning. On closer inspection, however, it seems that this reality of later times is merely retrojected into the foundational phase of the two kingdoms. The reasons for this judgment are well known; suffice it here to repeat them briefly.[16] The edifying tone, together with the appearance of the man of God Shemaiah, better known from Chronicles, clearly makes the passage stand out from its context. Historically, it sounds quite improbable. The number of warriors is, if not "fantastic," certainly too high to be taken at face value (even if we were to lower it with the Greek tradition to 120,000).[17] In addition, the plea for peace between the "brothers" and its documented observance seem to be in latent disaccord with the more matter-of-fact notice of 1 Kgs 14:30 that "there was war between Rehoboam and Jeroboam continually." Most important, the passage clearly betrays a certain interest. From a self-confident southern point of view, it explains why the north was allowed to break away at all, even though frustrating this effort should have been a simple task. It is hard to miss Judaean ideology in this train of thought.

In sum, it does not commend itself to include 1 Kgs 12:21–24 in an attempt to reconstruct the affiliation of Benjamin in the early phase of the kingdom of Judah.[18]

1.3. 1 Kings 14:21–31

Drawing an interim conclusion, apart from the pragmatics of the Jeroboam account in 1 Kgs 11 and 12, which, albeit indirectly, have a bearing on the question of Rehoboam and Benjamin as well, so far we have encountered evidence of rather meager value as a source.[19] Now the actual Rehoboam account in 1 Kgs 14:21–31, picking up the thread where 11:43 has left it,

---

16. See Noth, *I Könige 1–16*, 279–80; Würthwein, *Könige*, 161; Volkmar Fritz, *Das erste Buch der Könige*, ZBK 10.1 (Zurich: TVZ, 1996), 136.

17. Quotation from Würthwein, *Könige*, 161.

18. *Pace* Na'aman, "Saul, Benjamin," 217. Notwithstanding the question of the literary provenience of this passage (which Ernst Axel Knauf, *1 Könige 1–14*, HThKAT [Freiburg im Breisgau: Herder, 2016], 379 recently categorized as "post-chronistisch"), I concur with Finkelstein, "Saul, Benjamin," 349 when he argues that it sets "the 'trap' of Deuteronomistic ideology" the historian ought not to walk into.

19. For Rehoboam and Benjamin, see again Weingart, "Jeroboam and Benjamin," in this volume.

unmistakably betrays its Deuteronomistic provenience. Notwithstanding some peculiar features that are called for by the context, 14:21–24 and 29–31 are textbook examples of the Deuteronomistic framework in the book of Kings.[20] However, it must be mentioned in the same breath—trivial as it might seem—that the Deuteronomistic history of Israel narrative is not freely penned, but based on sources, both oral and written. Notably, this holds for the history of the tenth century no less than for that of, say, the seventh. Against the oft-repeated argument, I fail to see how an alleged lack of *widespread* literacy, even if accurate for a given period, should preclude this assumption.[21] In the case of Rehoboam's reign according to 1 Kgs 14, several aspects point to source material having been used: both Rehoboam's age at accession and the duration of his reign are nonschematic, in marked contrast to the forty years of David and Solomon respectively;[22] the name and origin of Rehoboam's mother (cf. 1 Kgs 11:1, 5) are mentioned; and this fits well with a rather brief but soberingly realistic overall record of Rehoboam's reign.

Two points should be considered in more detail. The first is the notice of continuous conflict or "war" between Rehoboam and Jeroboam (14:30; cf. 1 Kgs 15:6). As we saw, it does not correspond to the ideologically motivated insertion of 1 Kgs 12:21–24, but it is in keeping with an essential imperative faced by any emergent territorial entity, namely, the need to define its borders vis-à-vis neighboring entities. That is to say, the word מלחמה should not be taken to mean full-scale warfare between Israel and Judah but rather a constant struggle over Judah's border to the north—in other words, over Benjamin. The pointed term "border banter"

---

20. For the peculiar features, see Erhard Blum, "Das exilische deuteronomistische Geschichtswerk," in *Das deuteronomistische Geschichtswerk*, ed. Hermann-Josef Stipp, ÖBS 39 (Bern: Lang, 2011), 281–82. For the Deuteronomistic nature, see Noth, *I Könige 1–16*, 325–28.

21. For the oft-repeated argument, see David W. Jamieson-Drake, *Scribes and Schools in Monarchic Judah: A Socio-archaeological Approach*, JSOTSup 109 (Sheffield: Almond Press, 1991), cited by, e.g., Israel Finkelstein, "The Campaign of Shoshenq I to Palestine: A Guide to the Tenth Century BCE Polity," *ZDPV* 118 (2002): 112. But see now Erhard Blum, "Institutionelle und kulturelle Voraussetzungen der israelitischen Traditionsliteratur," in *Tradition(en) im alten Israel: Konstruktion, Transmission und Transformation*, ed. Ruth Ebach and Martin Leuenberger, FAT 127 (Tübingen: Mohr Siebeck, 2019), 3–44.

22. See, however, Knauf, *1 Könige 1–14*, 403, with considerations regarding the variant dates given in the Greek tradition.

A Historical Hypothesis on the Reign of Rehoboam

("Grenzplänkeleien") coined by Martin Noth probably fits the extent of this conflict, but not the vital importance it had for Judah, with Jerusalem being located in a most vulnerable position right on the border.[23] In any case, it should be noted here that the trouble with Benjamin is one of the border and where within the region of Benjamin it is drawn, not so much of Benjamin as a whole. The repeated notice of continued "war" (see also 1 Kgs 15:16) suggests that this border remained neither uncontested nor unchanged over time.[24]

More important still is the second point, the campaign of Pharaoh Shoshenq I to Palestine as reflected in 1 Kgs 14:25–28, including a lengthy elaboration on its consequences for the Judahite protocol:

> In the fifth year of King Rehoboam, King Shishak of Egypt came up against Jerusalem; he took away the treasures of the house of YHWH and the treasures of the king's house; he took everything. He also took away all the shields of gold that Solomon had made; so King Rehoboam made shields of bronze instead and committed them to the hands of the officers of the guard, who kept the door of the king's house. As often as the king went into the house of YHWH, the guard carried them and brought them back to the guardroom.

The opening verses, which pertain to the actual campaign of the pharaoh, have recently been reevaluated by Manfred Weippert.[25] Confirming the possibility that the taking away (לקח) of the treasures need not indicate a violent looting of Jerusalem but may describe the pharaoh receiving tribute, he argues against authors who detach Shoshenq's campaign from the reign of Rehoboam, thus doubting the existence of an archival source behind the notice.[26] To this end, Weippert adduces two solid arguments.

---

23. Quotation from Noth, *I Könige 1–16*, 332, echoed by Fritz, *Könige*, 150.
24. On the latter assumption, see also Finkelstein, "Saul, Benjamin," 348–49; as well as Noth, *Geschichte Israels*, 214; and Klaus-Dietrich Schunck, *Benjamin: Untersuchungen zur Entstehung und Geschichte eines israelitischen Stammes*, BZAW 86 (Berlin: Töpelmann, 1963), 169 and passim.
25. Weippert, *Historisches Textbuch*, 228–30.
26. Among those detaching Shoshenq's campaign from Rehoboam, see now also Frevel, *Geschichte Israels*, 165–71; for reference to 1 Kgs 9:16 and a resulting dating of the campaign to the time Solomon, see Frevel, *Geschichte Israels*, 124. See further Ernst Axel Knauf, "Le roi est mort, vive le roi! A Biblical Argument for the Historicity of Solomon," in *The Age of Solomon: Scholarship at the Turn of the Millennium*, ed. Lowell K. Handy, SHCANE 11 (Leiden: Brill, 1997), 93; and Hermann M. Niemann,

First, the fifth year of Rehoboam is a specific, nonschematic date; second, the tradent who wrote the text that is handed down to us in the book of Kings knew not only the name of the pharaoh but also how to pronounce it correctly (note the *ketiv* form of the name Shushak as opposed to the *qere* Shishak, the latter likely being the result of a scribal error).[27] From where, Weippert asks, has the tradent, working several centuries after the event, taken this information if not from an archival record?

Without even asking this question, some would of course say that he did not take it from anywhere. Rather, the entire passage was contrived and added by the author.[28] Yet what would be the point of such an invention of tradition, a rather inglorious tradition at that? In a short essay, Theodore Mullen proposed the following explanation: "For the deuteronomistic writer, this episode [1 Kgs 14:25–28] provides a comment on the rule of Rehoboam: because he continued in the ways of Solomon, the treasures of the House of Yahweh were carried off by an invading monarch."[29] What is more, Mullen ventures to reconstruct an entire literary genre based on this passage: "The account of the reign of Rehoboam provides a pattern of punishment to be exacted on those kings who fail to lead the people to worship Yahweh in the proper way."[30]

However, this explanation does not fit the specific profile of the passage at hand. Already a cursory glance at the proportions of the text indicates a different interpretation. While the note concerning the actual event in

---

"The Socio-political Shadow Cast by the Biblical Solomon," in Handy, *Age of Solomon*, 296–99. Admitting that there is an intricate problem in the dating of Shoshenq's campaign based on the biblical chronology, Weippert, *Historisches Textbuch*, 228 n. 3 rightly emphasizes that this problem is not solved by freely associating the campaign with Solomon.

27. For details on the second point, see Weippert, *Historisches Textbuch*, 228–29.

28. For a more nuanced discussion, see Finkelstein, "Campaign of Shoshenq," 112–13.

29. E. Theodore Mullen, "Crime and Punishment: The Sins of the King and the Despoliation of the Treasuries," *CBQ* 54 (1992): 237. Prominently adopted by Finkelstein, "Campaign of Shoshenq," 113; Finkelstein, *Forgotten Kingdom*, 41.

30. Mullen, "Crime and Punishment," 237. The problems of this approach could not possibly become more obvious than in Mullen's own attempt to apply the alleged pattern to Hezekiah (2 Kgs 18:13–16) of all kings (Mullen, "Crime and Punishment," 244–47). For 1 Kgs 14:25–28, Mullen in fact acknowledges the possibility of "the use of some type of chronicle or annalistic report" (Mullen, "Crime and Punishment," 237 n. 19).

14:25b–26a could hardly be more taciturn, the author dwells at length on what he presents as its consequence, a rearrangement of ceremony at the Jerusalem court (14:26b–28). Obviously he employs the notice found in the annals merely as an introduction for the matter he wishes to depict.[31] The marked interest in the details of the protocol only confirms this interpretation.[32] As regards our present discussion, the interpretation just proposed is tantamount to the conclusion: 1 Kgs 14:25–28 does not attest to an alleged Deuteronomistic theology of retribution; in fact, it does not attest to theology at all. The "comment on the rule of Rehoboam" Mullen and others have found here is made only by the Chronicler.[33]

2. The Campaign of Shoshenq I to Palestine: Correlating the Extrabiblical Evidence

With this reevaluation of the biblical evidence in hand, we can now go about correlating the extrabiblical evidence to it, in this case coming from Egypt. Fortunately enough, the campaign of Shoshenq I, the founder of the Twenty-Second, or Bubastite, Dynasty, who ruled roughly during the third quarter of the tenth century, is documented not only in the biblical book of Kings but also in a monumental inscription the pharaoh himself has left on a wall in the temple of Amun at Karnak.[34] The inscription provides a list of places covered in the campaign (or rather, series of campaigns), although it does not detail what the pharaoh's troops did in these places (merely passed through? collected tribute? or brought forth captives from?).[35] In any event, Shoshenq apparently sought to establish some sort of Egyptian hegemony in the region.

---

31. Thus with Noth, *I Könige 1–16*, 330–32.

32. Differently Knauf, *1 Könige 1–14*, 405, who explains the *tabula rasa* created by 14:26 (ואת־הכל לקח) as a "Realitätsannäherungs-Notiz, um Salomos phantasierten ungeheuren Reichtum rechtzeitig mit oder vor dem Einsetzen der Annalentradition für Juda zu entsorgen."

33. Quotation from Mullen, "Crime and Punishment," 237.

34. Jan Simons, *Handbook for the Study of Egyptian Topographical Lists Relating to Western Asia* (Leiden: Brill, 1937), 89–102.

35. For it as a series of campaigns, see, e.g., Bernd U. Schipper, *Israel und Ägypten in der Königszeit: Die kulturellen Kontakte von Salomo bis zum Fall Jerusalems*, OBO 170 (Fribourg: Universitätsverlag; Göttingen: Vandenhoeck & Ruprecht, 1999), 127. For an argument that it was captives that were brough forth, see Karl Jansen-Winkeln, "Zur historischen Authentizität ägyptischer und biblischer Quellen: Der

What is there to learn from this source regarding the struggle for Benjamin? Pursuing this question might easily go beyond the constraints of the present context, yet in what follows no attempt is made at a self-contained study of the material. Instead, I merely seek to match some basic results of the scholarly discussion regarding Shoshenq's campaign to Palestine as recorded in the Karnak inscription with the biblical attestation of that same event as reevaluated above.

Before doing so, it is fitting to briefly recall the findings as they pertain to the question at hand. First and foremost, notwithstanding the fact that one line is partly illegible due to physical damage, the inscription offers a rather clear picture regarding the scope of the campaign. While the heartland of Judah as well as Jerusalem remained broadly unimpaired, the Northern Kingdom must have come under great pressure. Judging from the main sites mentioned in the list, including Jeroboam's residence of Penuel, it appears that Shoshenq actually targeted the kingdom of Israel. This operation included several sites in the region of Benjamin that presumably were under Israelite control at that time.[36] Thus, regarding the consequences of the campaign for Judah and Jerusalem, the Karnak inscription actually concurs with 1 Kgs 14.[37] Admittedly, this is a matter

---

Palästinafeldzug Schoschenks I," *OLZ* 103 (2008): 171–72, cited in Weippert, *Historisches Textbuch*, 230 n. 12. With regard to the southern territories mentioned in the list, Alexander Fantalkin and Israel Finkelstein, "The Sheshonq I Campaign and the Eighth-Century-BCE Earthquake—More on the Archaeology and History of the South in the Iron I–IIA," *TA* 33 (2006): 18–42, argue on archaeological grounds that, rather than destroying local structures, the campaign seems to have marked the onset of an intensified involvement in the region. For introduction and further references, see Schipper, *Israel und Ägypten*, 119–32; and Weippert, *Historisches Textbuch*, 228–41. See also Kevin A. Wilson, *The Campaign of Pharaoh Shoshenq I into Palestine*, FAT 2/9 (Tübingen: Mohr Siebeck, 2005), 60–65; Shirly Ben-Dor Evian, "Shishak's Karnak Relief—More than Just Name-Rings," in *Egypt, Canaan and Israel: History, Imperialism, Ideology and Literature*, ed. Shay Bar, Dani'el Kahn, and J. J. Shirley, CHANE 52 (Leiden: Brill, 2011), 11–22.

36. Weippert, *Historisches Textbuch*, 233–38; Schipper, *Israel und Ägypten*, 125–29. By contrast, others hold that Benjamin was Judahite at the time, and that it was there, namely in Gibeon, that Rehoboam met Shoshenq and paid tribute. Most recently, see Omer Sergi, "Rethinking Israel and the Kingdom of Saul," in Lipschits, *Rethinking Israel*, 371–88; see also Nadav Na'aman, "Shishak's Campaign to Palestine as Reflected by the Epigraphic, Biblical and Archaeological Evidence" [Hebrew], *Zion* 63 (1998): 247–76.

37. See, e.g., Donner, *Von der Königszeit bis zu Alexander dem Großen*, 274.

A Historical Hypothesis on the Reign of Rehoboam   123

of considerable dispute.³⁸ The question remains as to *why* Judah was not covered by the campaign. Furthermore, assuming that the reason for this was a tribute paid by the ruler in Jerusalem, one wonders why Jerusalem was not included in the list of subdued places. The latter problem seems both valid and hitherto unresolved.³⁹ Yet it does not undermine the main point in which the Karnak inscription and 1 Kgs 14 agree, *that* Judah and Jerusalem did not suffer from Shoshenq's campaign into Canaan—in stark contrast to the kingdom of Israel.

In order to account for this fact, Israel Finkelstein has outlined an explanatory approach, also integrating the archaeological data available, which I find both persuasive and helpful in its general direction.⁴⁰ Contrary to the impression one might gain from 1 Kgs 14, Shoshenq's campaign was not directed at Jerusalem. (This impression is created solely by the emic perspective prevalent in the biblical depiction according to which any event of world politics is focused directly at the hub of the world.) Rather, Finkelstein argues, the pharaoh targeted a polity to the north, in his words, "an emerging territorio-political formation, which endangered the Egyptian interests in Palestine."⁴¹ In search for a "forgotten kingdom," it is only reasonable *not* to connect this polity with Jeroboam I. Yet Bernd Schipper, Christian Frevel, and others remind us of 1 Kgs 11:40, disclosing as it does an intricate affiliation of Jeroboam with Egypt and indeed with Pharaoh Shoshenq I.⁴² This allows at least for the suspicion that, among pursuing other strategic goals, Shoshenq exacted retribution when visiting this polity to the north, taking "punitive action against a rebellious vassal," to quote Schipper.⁴³ This suspicion might be

---

38. See, e.g., Finkelstein, "Campaign of Shoshenq," 111; Finkelstein, *Forgotten Kingdom*, 43.

39. The problem is pointed out by Knauf, "Le roi est mort," 93. See, however, the fresh approach to solving it by Jansen-Winkeln, "Zur historischen Authentizität," 171–72.

40. Finkelstein, "Campaign of Shoshenq."

41. Finkelstein, "Campaign of Shoshenq," 123; repeated in Finkelstein, *Forgotten Kingdom*, 44.

42. Schipper, *Israel*, 127–28; Frevel, *Geschichte Israels*, 168.

43. As Schipper, *Israel und Ägypten*, 128–29 states in view of Shoshenq's activities in the Negev recorded in the second part of the list, an assumed punitive expedition against Jeroboam would, if accurate, be merely one goal among other, and more important, goals of the campaign. Quotation from Schipper, *Israel und Ägypten*, 128: "eine Strafaktion gegen einen abtrünnigen Vasallen." See also Frevel, *Geschichte Israels*,

further substantiated by the fact that, according to the Karnak inscription, Penuel and other places of official importance in the kingdom of Israel were targeted.

Whatever the case may be, Finkelstein makes a strong point by emphasizing that not only capitals of what we call the kingdom of Israel were covered by the campaign, but also a range of places in Benjamin. As regards the role of the southern entity, or kingdom of Judah, Finkelstein offers two options. Either Shoshenq simply ignored it as irrelevant or "in order to enhance the Egyptian interests in the region Shoshenq sided with the dimorphic chiefdom of the south against the stronger polity which emerged at that time to its north."[44] The latter option is compared to archaeological data for the Philistine cities, which seem to indicate that they "cooperated with Shoshenq and were probably among the main beneficiaries of this campaign."[45] Either way, the Egyptian pressure on the main sites of the Northern Kingdom as well as on its strongholds in Benjamin must have been a major advantage for Rehoboam in the struggle for dominion over the Benjaminite borderland.[46]

Along these general lines, I can only follow the penetrating analysis of Finkelstein, which I find convincing—save for one deviation. This deviation, however, pertains to a point of decisive importance, both here and in the argument as presented by Finkelstein; and in light of the above discussion, it will not come as a surprise that it concerns the biblical evidence of 1 Kgs 14:25–26. Assessing the value of this passage as a source has considerable implications for assessing the historical context of the Shoshenq campaign. Endorsing Mullen's interpretation of that text, Finkelstein argues that "the fifth-year-of-Rehoboam datum may have been schematically arranged to fit the theology of the Deuteronomistic Historian, for instance, his understanding of sin punished by the assault of a foreign power."[47] Hence it is no valid evidence. Without taking into account this

---

168: "eine Strafexpedition gegen den abtrünnigen Vasallen Jerobeam I … oder wie sich der lokale Herrscher auch immer genannt haben mag."

44. Finkelstein, "Campaign of Shoshenq," 112.

45. Finkelstein, "Campaign of Shoshenq," 116.

46. Cf. Donner, *Von der Königszeit bis zu Alexander dem Großen*, 275: "Jerobeam I … muß in arge Bedrängnis geraten sein, über deren Auswirkungen wir leider nichts erfahren."

47. The quotation is from Finkelstein, *Forgotten Kingdom*, 41, but the argument has been developed in Finkelstein, "Campaign of Shoshenq," 110 and passim.

date, however, there is no way to know when exactly the pharaoh appeared in Palestine; "the Shoshenq campaign could have taken place almost any time in the mid- to late tenth century BCE," Finkelstein concludes.[48] As I see it, and hope to have shown, the evidence of 1 Kgs 14 cannot be swept aside quite so easily, and the fact that it is consistent with the picture that emerges from the Karnak inscription, namely, that the Southern Kingdom did not suffer from the campaign in the same way the Northern Kingdom did, only confirms this.

Assuming such a more confident assessment of 1 Kgs 14:25–26, let me add a note in passing on the vexed problem of the dating of Shoshenq's campaign. It is true, and lamentably so, that for an absolute dating of the campaign there is no other basis than the relative date to be gleaned from the biblical record.[49] From a methodological point of view, this is certainly less than one would wish for. However, the deplorable shortage of additional evidence per se is no reason to dismiss the traditional date out of hand. But even if one prefers to refrain from an absolute dating of the campaign of Shoshenq I, the fact remains that according to biblical tradition this pharaoh is associated with both Rehoboam and his contemporary Jeroboam I, whereas 1 Kgs 9:16, the notice of an Egyptian campaign to Palestine during Solomon's reign, does not mention the name of that pharaoh (to say nothing of Saul here).[50] In the end, it should be stated clearly that it remains a task ahead, one for the historian of Egypt in the first place, to put the absolute dating of the campaign of Shoshenq on a more solid footing than that provided by a putative reconstruction of some elusive Judahite annals. Equally clear, however, is the fact that this campaign is explicitly tied to the reign of Rehoboam, which is consistent with the notion of Jeroboam I having maintained a special relationship with Shoshenq I, while any reference whatsoever to another king of either Israel or Judah is not forthcoming.

At this stage, it is possible to summarize my result in three points. First, the campaign of Shoshenq I to Palestine must have had considerable

---

48. Finkelstein, "Campaign of Shoshenq," 110; and Finkelstein, *Forgotten Kingdom*, 41.

49. For helpful references to earlier scholarship, see Finkelstein, "Campaign of Shoshenq," 109–10.

50. For the more recent proposal to date the campaign of Shoshenq I to the time of Solomon, see, e.g., Knauf, "Le roi est mort," 93; Niemann, "Socio-political Shadow," 297.

implications for the rival kingdoms' struggle for Benjamin. This is shown cogently in Finkelstein's analysis. Against Finkelstein, however, I would argue, second, for Rehoboam's reign as the historical context of this development. The burden of proof lies with any alternative view; and sufficient proof has not been presented so far. In particular, the interpretation of 1 Kgs 14:25–26 as an example of Deuteronomistic retribution theology is not fit to bear that burden. Third, if Shoshenq's campaign took place during Rehoboam's reign, the aforementioned implications are relevant to the question at hand, that of *Rehoboam* and Benjamin.

3. Rehoboam and Benjamin: Sketching a Historical Hypothesis

In this final section I shall do no more than retrace the lines just indicated. To do so, however, let me bring in briefly yet another piece of evidence relating to the same situation some twenty to thirty years down the road. Here I refer to 1 Kgs 15:17–22, which reports an alliance between Asa of Judah (Rehoboam's grandson) and Aram-Damascus against Israel. Following the note that "there was war between Asa and King Baasha of Israel all their days" (15:16), we read of Baasha going on the offensive in Benjamin, building Ramah as a border fortification (15:17). In reaction to this, Asa summons up the available treasures of temple and palace in order to win the favor of a certain Ben-Hadad son of Tabrimmon son of Hezion, king of Aram-Damascus (15:18).[51] On the initiative of Asa, the two enter into a ברית, according to which Ben-Hadad shall invalidate his ברית with Baasha (15:19).[52] Following this, as requested by Asa, Ben-Hadad assaults Baasha by invading Israel from the north, thus forcing Baasha to withdraw from the southern front (15:20–21). Asa pushes forward, gains territory in Benjamin, and succeeds in building Geba and Mizpah as border fortifications (15:22; cf. Jer 41:9).

It goes without saying that we cannot take this report at face value either. Just as we did with the notice of "Shishak" coming up "against Jerusalem," we have to take into account the emic perspective here as well. In the case of Asa's coup, it seems hardly credible that the king of marginal

---

51. For the rather dubious identity of this otherwise unattested king, see Omer Sergi, "The Emergence of Judah as a Political Entity between Jerusalem and Benjamin," *ZDPV* 133 (2017): 13.

52. On the diplomatic language used, which gives the impression that this alliance is merely the renewal of an earlier one, see Noth, *I Könige 1–16*, 339–40.

Judah of his own volition prompted a military confrontation between the more powerful neighbors to the north. More probably, Judah as a bystander benefited from such a conflict.[53] Omer Sergi, in his recent piece on "the emergence of Judah as a political entity between Jerusalem and Benjamin," has made a strong case for such a scenario.[54] Thus presupposing a critical reading of 1 Kgs 15, a rather clear picture comes into view. We see Judah being involved in what has been dubbed "border banter" over the strategic Benjaminite territories to the north of Jerusalem. In this struggle, Judah was clearly outgunned by Israel in terms of military strength. But, as Sergi puts it, "Asa gained from the geopolitical circumstances: Israel's struggle over political hegemony in the north Jordan Valley enabled the weaker Judah to strengthen its political authority over the Benjamin Plateau."[55]

Quite comparable to this scenario, I suggest, was the case of the Shoshenq campaign and its implications for the struggle for Benjamin between Rehoboam and Jeroboam. Here, too, there is the vital necessity for small Judah to define and defend the border vis-à-vis its stronger neighbor to the north, especially in view of the vulnerable position of Jerusalem. Here, too, Judah's chances of succeeding in an escalation of the latent conflict would have been rather scant measured against Israel's comparative military strength. And here, too, a window of opportunity was opened by the intervention of a foreign power pursuing its own goals in the region.

Following Finkelstein, there are two options to weigh in this case.[56] One could think of Judah under Rehoboam as a mere profiteer of Shoshenq's campaign against the Northern Kingdom. Alternatively, it seems possible to conceive of Rehoboam and Shoshenq as coalition partners. Either way, the struggle for power among the major geopolitical players in the region had repercussions on marginal Judah.[57] In this case, it presumably allowed Rehoboam to push the border northward and gain control over the better part of the Benjaminite borderland, whether as "vassals under a short-lived Egyptian domination, or after the Egyptian

---

53. For such a reading of 1 Kgs 15:17–22, see Joachim J. Krause, "Asa," *WiBiLex* (2017), https://www.bibelwissenschaft.de/stichwort/13937/; drawing on Sergi, "Emergence of Judah."

54. Sergi, "Emergence of Judah."

55. Sergi, "Emergence of Judah," 15.

56. See Finkelstein, "Campaign of Shoshenq," 112; and §2 above.

57. See Finkelstein, "Saul, Benjamin," 349.

withdrawal from the hill country."[58] A similar suggestion has recently been probed by Frevel: "Perhaps the internationally still uninfluential kingdom (or chiefdom) in Jerusalem profited from the campaign and was able to temporarily gain dominance (with Egyptian approval) over territories in the north."[59]

That this advantage in the struggle for Benjamin hardly lasted long is another story. Indeed, we learn of the volatility of the situation from Asa at the latest who, one generation after Rehoboam, faced exactly the same strategic challenge that his grandfather was confronted with. But that is written as well: "There was war between Rehoboam and Jeroboam continually."

Bibliography

Amar, Itzhak. "The Characterization of Rehoboam and Jeroboam as a Reflection of the Chronicler's View of the Schism." *JHS* 17 (2017): art. 9. https://tinyurl.com/SBL2636b.

Ben-Dor Evian, Shirly. "Shishak's Karnak Relief—More than Just Name-Rings." Pages 11–22 in *Egypt, Canaan and Israel: History, Imperialism, Ideology and Literature; Proceedings of a Conference at the University of Haifa, 3–7 May 2009*. Edited by Shay Bar, Dan'el Kahn, and J. J. Shirley. CHANE 52. Leiden: Brill, 2011.

Blum, Erhard. "Das exilische deuteronomistische Geschichtswerk." Pages 269–95 in *Das deuteronomistische Geschichtswerk*. Edited by Hermann-Josef Stipp. ÖBS 39. Bern: Lang, 2011.

———. "Institutionelle und kulturelle Voraussetzungen der israelitischen Traditionsliteratur." Pages 3–44 in *Tradition(en) im alten Israel: Konstruktion, Transmission und Transformation*. Edited by Ruth Ebach and Martin Leuenberger. FAT 127. Tübingen: Mohr Siebeck, 2019.

———. "Solomon and the United Monarchy: Some Textual Evidence." Pages 59–78 in *One God—One Cult—One Nation: Archaeological*

---

58. Finkelstein, "Campaign of Shoshenq," 128–29. For the first option, see already Knauf, "Le roi est mort," 94.

59. Frevel, *Geschichte Israels*, 171: "Möglicherweise hat die international noch einflussarme Monarchie bzw. das *chiefdom* in Jerusalem von dem Feldzug profitiert und im Anschluss kurzfristig (mit Billigung der Ägypter) Dominanz über Territorien im Norden entfalten können."

and *Biblical Perspectives*. Edited by Reinhard G. Kratz and Hermann Spieckermann. BZAW 405. Berlin: de Gruyter, 2010.

Davies, Philip R. "The Trouble with Benjamin." Pages 93–111 in *Reflection and Refraction: Studies in Biblical Historiography in Honour of A. Graeme Auld*. Edited by Robert Rezetko, Timothy H. Lim, and W. Brian Aucker. VTSup 113. Leiden: Brill, 2007.

Donner, Herbert. *Von der Königszeit bis zu Alexander dem Großen*. Part 2 of *Geschichte des Volkes Israel und seiner Nachbarn in Grundzügen*. 3rd ed. GAT 4.2. Göttingen: Vandenhoeck & Ruprecht, 2001.

Fantalkin, Alexander, and Israel Finkelstein. "The Sheshonq I Campaign and the Eighth-Century-BCE Earthquake—More on the Archaeology and History of the South in the Iron I–IIA." *TA* 33 (2006): 18–42.

Finkelstein, Israel. "The Campaign of Shoshenq I to Palestine: A Guide to the Tenth Century BCE Polity." *ZDPV* 118 (2002): 109–35.

———. *The Forgotten Kingdom: The Archaeology and History of Northern Israel*. ANEM 5. Atlanta: Society of Biblical Literature, 2013.

———. "A Great United Monarchy? Archaeological and Historical Perspectives." Pages 1–28 in *One God—One Cult—One Nation: Archaeological and Biblical Perspectives*. Edited by Reinhard G. Kratz and Hermann Spieckermann. BZAW 405. Berlin: de Gruyter, 2010.

———. "Rehoboam's Fortified Cities (II Chr 11,5–12): A Hasmonean Reality?" *ZAW* 123 (2011): 92–107.

———. "Saul, Benjamin and the Emergence of Biblical Israel: An Alternative View." *ZAW* 123 (2011): 348–67.

Frevel, Christian. *Geschichte Israels*. Studienbücher Theologie 2. Stuttgart: Kohlhammer, 2015.

Fritz, Volkmar. *Das erste Buch der Könige*. ZBK 10.1. Zürich: TVZ, 1996.

Grabbe, Lester L. "Jeroboam I? Jeroboam II? Or Jeroboam 0? Jeroboam in History and Tradition." Pages 115–23 in *Rethinking Israel: Studies in the History and Archaeology of Ancient Israel in Honor of Israel Finkelstein*. Edited by Oded Lipschits, Yuval Gadot, and Matthew J. Adams. Winona Lake, IN: Eisenbrauns, 2017.

Jamieson-Drake, David W. *Scribes and Schools in Monarchic Judah: A Socio-archaeological Approach*. JSOTSup 109. Sheffield: Almond Press, 1991.

Jansen-Winkeln, Karl. "Zur historischen Authentizität ägyptischer und biblischer Quellen: Der Palästinafeldzug Schoschenks I." *OLZ* 103 (2008): 165–73.

Knauf, Ernst Axel. *1 Könige 1–14*. HThKAT. Freiburg im Breisgau: Herder, 2016.

―――. "Le roi est mort, vive le roi! A Biblical Argument for the Historicity of Solomon." Pages 81–95 in *The Age of Solomon: Scholarship at the Turn of the Millennium*. Edited by Lowell K. Handy. SHCANE 11. Leiden: Brill, 1997.

Knoppers, Gary N. "Rehoboam in Chronicles: Villain or Victim?" *JBL* 109 (1990): 423–40.

Kratz, Reinhard G., and Hermann Spieckermann, eds. *One God—One Cult—One Nation: Archaeological and Biblical Perspectives*. BZAW 405. Berlin: de Gruyter, 2010.

Krause, Joachim J. "Asa." *WiBiLex* (2017). https://www.bibelwissenschaft.de/stichwort/13937/.

Mazar, Amihai. "Archaeology and the Biblical Narrative: The Case of the United Monarchy." Pages 29–58 in *One God—One Cult—One Nation: Archaeological and Biblical Perspectives*. Edited by Reinhard G. Kratz and Hermann Spieckermann. BZAW 405. Berlin: de Gruyter, 2010.

Mullen, E. Theodore. "Crime and Punishment: The Sins of the King and the Despoliation of the Treasuries." *CBQ* 54 (1992): 231–48.

Na'aman, Nadav. "Saul, Benjamin and the Emergence of 'Biblical Israel.'" *ZAW* 121 (2009): 211–24, 335–49.

―――. "Shishak's Campaign to Palestine as Reflected by the Epigraphic, Biblical and Archaeological Evidence" [Hebrew]. *Zion* 63 (1998): 247–76.

Niemann, Hermann M. "The Socio-political Shadow Cast by the Biblical Solomon." Pages 252–99 in *The Age of Solomon: Scholarship at the Turn of the Millennium*. Edited by Lowell K. Handy. SHCANE 11. Leiden: Brill, 1997.

Noth, Martin. *Geschichte Israels*. 7th ed. Göttingen: Vandenhoeck & Ruprecht, 1969.

―――. *Die israelitischen Personennamen im Rahmen der gemeinsemitischen Namengebung*. BWANT 46. Stuttgart: Kohlhammer, 1928.

―――. *I Könige 1–16*. Vol. 1 of *Könige*. BKAT 9.1. Neukirchen-Vluyn: Neukirchener Verlag, 1968.

Schenker, Adrian. "Jeroboam and the Division of the Kingdom in the Ancient Septuagint: LXX 3 Kingdoms 12.24 A–Z, MT 1 Kings 11–12; 14 and the Deuteronomistic History." Pages 214–57 in *Israel Constructs Its History: Deuteronomistic Historiography in Recent Research.*

Edited by Albert de Pury, Thomas Römer, and Jean-Daniel Macchi. JSOTSup 306. Sheffield: Sheffield Academic, 2000.

Schipper, Bernd U. *Israel und Ägypten in der Königszeit: Die kulturellen Kontakte von Salomo bis zum Fall Jerusalems*. OBO 170. Fribourg: Universitätsverlag; Göttingen: Vandenhoeck & Ruprecht, 1999.

Schunck, Klaus-Dietrich. *Benjamin: Untersuchungen zur Entstehung und Geschichte eines israelitischen Stammes*. BZAW 86. Berlin: Töpelmann, 1963.

Sergi, Omer. "The Emergence of Judah as a Political Entity between Jerusalem and Benjamin." *ZDPV* 133 (2017): 1–23.

———. "Rethinking Israel and the Kingdom of Saul." Pages 371–88 in *Rethinking Israel: Studies in the History and Archaeology of Ancient Israel in Honor of Israel Finkelstein*. Edited by Oded Lipschits, Yuval Gadot, and Matthew J. Adams. Winona Lake, IN: Eisenbrauns, 2017.

Simons, Jan. *Handbook for the Study of Egyptian Topographical Lists Relating to Western Asia*. Leiden: Brill, 1937.

Stamm, Johann J. "Hebräische Ersatznamen." Pages 59–79 in *Beiträge zur hebräischen und altorientalischen Namenkunde*. Edited by Ernst Jenni and Martin A. Klopfenstein. OBO 30. Göttingen: Vandenhoeck & Ruprecht; Fribourg: Universitätsverlag, 1980.

———. "Zwei alttestamentliche Königsnamen." Pages 137–46 in *Beiträge zur hebräischen und altorientalischen Namenkunde*. Edited by Ernst Jenni and Martin A. Klopfenstein. OBO 30. Göttingen: Vandenhoeck & Ruprecht; Fribourg: Universitätsverlag, 1980.

Talshir, Zipora. *The Alternative Story of the Division of the Kingdom*. JBS 6. Jerusalem: Simor, 1993.

Weippert, Manfred. *Historisches Textbuch zum Alten Testament*. GAT 10. Göttingen: Vandenhoeck & Ruprecht, 2010.

Welten, Peter. *Geschichte und Geschichtsdarstellung in den Chronikbüchern*. WMANT 42. Neukirchen-Vluyn: Neukirchener Verlag, 1973.

Wilson, Kevin A. *The Campaign of Pharaoh Shoshenq I into Palestine*. FAT 2/9. Tübingen: Mohr Siebeck, 2005.

Würthwein, Ernst. *Das erste Buch der Könige: Kapitel 1–16*. ATD 11.1. Göttingen: Vandenhoeck & Ruprecht, 1977.

Jeroboam and Benjamin:
Pragmatics and Date of 1 Kings 11:26–40; 12:1–20

Kristin Weingart

The regnal evaluations within the book of Kings show a notoriously critical stance toward the kings of Israel and Judah. As they are judged solely on the basis of their religious policies and not on other aspects that could have been equally conceivable as characteristics of a good king—such as a proper administration of justice and law, economic progress, successful military pursuits, and the like—only a very few Judahite kings like Hezekiah or Josiah can stand the searching eye of the evaluators.[1] The kings of Israel are presented altogether as a long line of evildoers. Among them, Jeroboam I probably suffered the most at the hands of the Deuteronomistic authors responsible for the evaluations. They saw in his cultic policy the original sin of the Northern Kingdom. As a result, the name Jeroboam became almost inseparably connected with "the sins of Jeroboam" (חטאות ירבעם), which in the Deuteronomistic interpretation of history inevitably led to the ruin of northern Israel.[2] But not everyone shared this critical

---

1. For recent treatments of the judgment formulas within the regnal frame see, e.g., Felipe Blanco Wissmann, *"Er tat das Rechte..."*: *Beurteilungskriterien und Deuteronomismus in 1Kön 12–2Kön 25*, ATANT 93 (Zurich: TVZ, 2008); Benjamin D. Thomas, *Hezekiah and the Compositional History of the Book of Kings*, FAT 2/63 (Tübingen: Mohr Siebeck, 2014); and Sang-Won Lee, "'Den Ort, den JHWH erwählen wird..., sollt ihr aufsuchen' (Dtn 12,5): Die Forderung der Kulteinheit im Deuteronomistischen Geschichtswerk" (PhD diss., Tübingen, 2015), each with an overview of the older discussion.

2. See already Jörg Debus, *Die Sünde Jerobeams: Studien zur Darstellung Jerobeams und der Geschichte des Nordreiches in der deuteronomistischen Geschichtsschreibung*, FRLANT 93 (Göttingen: Vandenhoeck & Ruprecht, 1967), 95; see also Wesley I. Toews, *Monarchy and Religious Institution in Israel under Jeroboam I*, SBLMS 47 (Atlanta: Scholars Press, 1993). Juha Pakkala, "Jeroboam's Sins and Bethel in 1Kgs 12:25–33," *BN* 112 (2002): 86–94, reads 1 Kgs 12:25–33 as a critique of a YHWH cult in Bethel allegedly taking place in exilic times, but so far, there is no archaeological

view of Jeroboam. Samarian coins from the Persian period show that there must have been one or more governors by the name of ירבעם.³ Irrespective of whether it was the given name or an honorary one, its use shows that, within the Samarian community, the name Jeroboam did not have a solely negative reputation; rather, as the name of two great kings of the past, it was held in high esteem.⁴

A look at the portrayal of Jeroboam in the book of Kings outside the regnal frame also reveals a more ambivalent picture. In 1 Kgs 11–14 he is one actor in the unfolding drama of the transition period from the unified kingdom to the establishment of two successor states.⁵ The characterization of the three protagonists Jeroboam, Solomon, and Rehoboam and their respective responsibility for the events has been a matter of ongoing debate that left its traces not only in the biblical presentations of the events in Kings and Chronicles but also in differing accounts in the Masoretic Text and certain strands of the Greek textual tradition.⁶

---

evidence for this, see Israel Finkelstein and Lily Singer-Avitz, "Reevaluating Bethel," *ZDPV* 125 (2009): 33–48. Unless otherwise noted, all translations are mine.

3. The name appears on five different coin types (Yaakov Meshorer and Shraga Qedar, *The Coinage of Samaria in the Fourth Century BCE* [Los Angeles: Numismatic Fine Arts International, 1991], nos. 23–27).

4. For Jeroboam as an honorary name, see Hanan Eshel, "Israelite Names from Samaria in the Persian Period" [Hebrew], in *These Are The Names: Studies in Jewish Onomastics*, ed. Aaron Demsky et al. (Ramat Gan: Bar Ilan University Press, 1997), 24–25; and Gary N. Knoppers, "Revisiting the Samarian Question in the Persian Period," in *Judah and the Judeans in the Persian Period*, ed. Oded Lipschits and Manfred Oeming (Winona Lake, IN: Eisenbrauns, 2006), 277; a different point of view is offered by Israel Eph'al, "Changes in Palestine during the Persian Period in Light of Epigraphic Sources," *IEJ* 49 (1998): 113.

5. There is a wide consensus that 1 Kgs 13 is a late addition to the present context; for differing proposals regarding the interpretation and pragmatics of this somewhat enigmatic episode, see, e.g., Erhard Blum, "Die Lüge des Propheten: Ein Lesevorschlag zu einer befremdlichen Geschichte (I Reg 13)," in *Mincha: Festgabe für Rolf Rendtorff zum 75. Geburtstag*, ed. Erhard Blum (Neukirchen-Vluyn: Neukirchner Verlag, 2000), 27–46; and Frank Ueberschaer, *Vom Gründungsmythos zur Untergangssymphonie: Eine text- und literargeschichtliche Untersuchung zu 1 Kön 11–14*, BZAW 481 (Berlin: de Gruyter, 2015), 202–21 (both with further references).

6. Amos Frisch, "Jeroboam and the Division of the Kingdom: Mapping Contrasting Biblical Accounts," *JANES* 27 (2000): 15–29, shows the general tendency to enhance the criticism of Jeroboam in subsequent accounts of or references to the division of the kingdom like 2 Kgs 17; 2 Chr 11 and 13; and 3 Kgdms 12:24a–z.

The following analysis of 1 Kgs 11:26–40 and 12:1–20 takes the portrayal of Jeroboam in the pre-Deuteronomistic version of the story as its starting point.[7] In recent studies, it has been rightly stressed that 1 Kgs 11–12 are not to be read as a historical report of the division of the kingdom.[8] But if so, what was the purpose of the original account and when was it composed? As will be shown, the pragmatics of the narrative as well as its literary stratigraphy indicate that it originated in the Northern Kingdom of Israel. In addition, tracing the way the text was incorporated into the Deuteronomistic framework of Kings will help to resolve the old *crux*

---

7. Many exegetes agree that there is a pre-Deuteronomistic kernel within the story of Jeroboam and Ahijah in 1 Kgs 11:29–40, even though they differ in the assessment of its retraceability and/or its demarcation (see, e.g., Martin Noth, *Überlieferungsgeschichtliche Studien: Die sammelnden und bearbeitenden Geschichtswerke im Alten Testament* [Darmstadt: Wissenschaftliche Buchgesellschaft, 1957], 72, 79 [11:29aβ.b–31, 36a.α, 37; differing from Noth, *Könige*, BKAT (Neukirchen-Vluyn: Neukirchener Verlag, 1968), 245–46]; Debus, *Die Sünde Jerobeams*, 3–19 [11:29–31]; John Gray, *I and II Kings: A Commentary*, 3rd ed., OTL [London: SCM, 1980], 271, 288 [11:29–32a]; Helga Weippert, "Die Ätiologie des Nordreiches und seines Königshauses [1 Reg 11 29–20]," ZAW 95 [1983]: 346–55 [11:29–31, 37, 38bαβ, 40a.bα]; Mark Leuchter, "Jeroboam the Ephratite," JBL 125 [2006]: 57 [11:29f., 31aα.bα, 35a.bα, 37, 38b]; Ueberschaer, *Gründungsmythos*, 146–60 [11:29–31, 40]). Others take the whole episode as (a) Deuteronomistic creation(s) (e.g., Walter Dietrich, *Prophetie und Geschichte: Eine redaktionsgeschichtliche Untersuchung zum deuteronomistischen Geschichtswerk*, FRLANT 108 [Göttingen: Vandenhoeck & Ruprecht, 1972], 19–20; Ernst Würthwein, *Das erste Buch der Könige. Kapitel 1–16*, ATD [Göttingen: Vandenhoeck & Ruprecht, 1977], 139–44; and Gary N. Knoppers, *The Reign of Solomon and the Rise of Jeroboam*, vol. 1 of *Two Nations under God: The Deuteronomistic History of Solomon and the Dual Monarchies*, HSM 52 [Atlanta: Scholars Press, 1993], 169–71). Ernst Axel Knauf, *1 Könige 1–14*, HThKAT 11 (Freiburg am Breisgau: Herder, 2016), 323, attributes 11:26a, 28a.c, 40 to the oldest layer, which he finds (following Christoph Levin, "Das synchronistische Exzerpt aus den Annalen der Könige von Israel und Juda," VT 61 [2011]: 616–28) in a synchronistic excerpt from older annals of Judah and Israel.

8. See, e.g., Uwe Becker, "Die Reichsteilung nach I Reg 12," ZAW 112 (2000): 210–29; and Ueberschaer, *Gründungsmythos*, 169–70. Older research tended to be more confident in this regard, cf., e.g., Horst Seebass, "Zur Königserhebung Jerobeams I," VT 17 (1967). 325–33; and Noth, *Könige*, 270; and some more recent studies also find echoes of historical developments within the stories—be it tribal rivalries (Leuchter, "Jeroboam the Ephratite") or Jeroboam's connection to Egypt (Pnina Galpaz, "The Reign of Jeroboam and the Extent of Egyptian Influence," BN 60 [1991]: 13–19).

interpretum found in 1 Kgs 11, namely, the mathematical conundrum that ten plus one equals twelve.

1. 1 Kings 11:26–40 and Its Literary Connections

Jeroboam makes his first appearance in 1 Kgs 11:26, and 11:26–28 serve as the exposition of the following account. At the very outset, 1 Kgs 11:26a introduces Jeroboam as a son of Nebat and an Ephrathite of Zeredah. The latter was identified by Moshe Kochavi as a small stronghold in the western flank of the southern Samaria hills.[9] At the same time, the Hebrew designation for Jeroboam's origins (אפרתי) is ambiguous and also reminiscent of David: 1 Sam 17:12 introduces David as בן איש אפרתי (see Ruth 1:2).[10] In addition to the patronym, the name of Jeroboam's mother (צרועה) is given and his social status specified as עבד שלמה.[11] The introduction does not seem to aim at tarnishing his reputation. A comparison to its Septuagintal parallel in 3 Kgdms 11:24b makes this immediately apparent: here Jeroboam is clearly of Ephraimite origin; his father is unknown and his mother a harlot.[12] Not so in the MT. The positive impression is corroborated in 1 Kgs 11:28: Jeroboam is a mighty man (גבור חיל) whom Solomon recognizes as able and fit for a leading position.

The verses 1 Kgs 11:26b and 27a function in a somewhat peculiar way as a heading characterizing the events to be recounted.[13] The heading is

---

9. Moshe Kochavi, "The Identification of Zeredah, Home of Jeroboam Son of Nebat, King of Israel" [Hebrew], *ErIsr* 20 (1989): 198–201.

10. See, e.g., Judg 12:5; 1 Sam 1:1. Leuchter, "Jeroboam the Ephratite," 60–62, even argues that Jeroboam was in fact a Judahite. Regardless of the question whether the text allows any conclusion about a historical Jeroboam I, this proposal is unconvincing. If Kochavi's identification of Zeredah is correct (see above), Jeroboam is connected with the Ephraimite territory. Leuchter's attempt to downplay this connection by asserting that Jeroboam merely served as an administrator in Zeredah is not backed by the text.

11. The name צרועה ("leper") could be a perversion of צרויה, a name attested for the mother of Joab; see 2 Sam 2:18, etc. (see, e.g., Debus, *Die Sünde Jerobeams*, 5; Würthwein, *Könige*, 142; Gray, *Kings*, 290; and Ueberschaer, *Gründungsmythos*, 60).

12. For a comparative analysis of the characterization of Jeroboam in 1 Kings and 3 Kingdoms with similar conclusions see Knoppers, *Two Nations*, 174–79.

13. Barbara Schmitz, *Prophetie und Königtum: Eine narratologisch-historische Methodologie entwickelt an den Königsbüchern*, FAT 60 (Tübingen: Mohr Siebeck, 2008), 121–22.

rather redundant, since it mentions twice that Jeroboam revolted against Solomon (הרים יד במלך). This does not agree with the way Jeroboam's actions are described in the following account (including ch. 12, where he remains remarkably passive). The heading, however, is linked to the greater structure of 1 Kgs 11, which mentions three adversaries of Solomon—Hadad, the Edomite (11:14), Rezon, the son of Eliadah (11:23), and finally Jeroboam—and thus builds up to a climax that culminates in the fulfillment of the threats against Solomon announced in 11:11–13.[14]

The section 1 Kgs 11:29–40 describes the encounter of Jeroboam and Ahijah, the Shilonite, introduced as a prophet (נביא) who performs a symbolic action. This action is obviously aimed at the relation between Solomon and Jeroboam as the wordplay with the name שלמה and the garment שַׂלְמָה implies.[15] Ahijah tears the garment into twelve pieces and gives ten of them to Jeroboam.[16] In a lengthy speech beginning in 11:31,

---

14. This connection is undisputed. The question whether the episodes on Hadad and Rezon are later additions in 1 Kgs 11 (for the discussion see, e.g., Diana Edelman, "Solomon's Adversaries Hadad, Rezon and Jeroboam: A Trio of 'Bad Guy' Characters Illustrating the Theology of Immediate Retribution," in *The Pitcher Is Broken: Memorial Essays for Gösta W. Ahlström*, ed. Steven W. Holloway and Lowell K. Handy, JSOTSup 190 [Sheffield: Sheffield Academic, 1995], 166–91; and Erich Bosshard-Nepustil, "Hadad, der Edomiter: 1 Kön 11,14–22 zwischen literarischem Kontext und Verfassergegenwart," in *Schriftauslegung in der Schrift: Festschrift für Odil Hannes Steck zu seinem 65. Geburtstag*, ed. Reinhard G. Kratz, Thomas Krüger, and Konrad Schmid, BZAW 300 [Berlin: de Gruyter, 2000], 95–109) has no impact on the issue discussed here.

15. See, e.g., Weippert, "Die Ätiologie des Nordreiches," 349; Robert L. Cohn, "Literary Technique in the Jeroboam Narrative," *ZAW* 97 (1985): 27; Leuchter, "Jeroboam the Ephratite," 53.

16. It has been proposed by Heinrich Ewald, *Geschichte Davids und der Königsherrschaft in Israel*, vol. 3 of *Geschichte des Volkes Israel* (Göttingen: Dieterichsche, 1866), 117, and again by S. Min Chun, "Whose Cloak Did Ahijah Seize and Tear? A Note on 1 Kings xi 29–30," *VT* 56 (2006): 268–74, that the garment ripped into pieces belonged to Jeroboam and not Ahijah. As there are two male protagonists, the reference of the suffixes could be equivocal. But the syntactic structure of the verses, especially in 11:30, makes it highly unlikely that a change of reference is intended. Moreover, given that that opinion was correct, Ahijah would probably not ask Jeroboam to "take" (לקח) the pieces allotted to him, but to "keep" them. Many commentators have stressed the affinity between 1 Kgs 11:29–30 and 1 Sam 15:27–28 or even assumed a textual dependency (e.g., Dietrich, *Prophetie und Geschichte*, 16). As Weippert, "Die Ätiologie des Nordreiches," 348–49; and Mordechai Cogan, *1 Kings: A New Translation with Introduction and Commentary*, AB 11 (New York: Doubleday, 2000), 340, correctly note,

he explains his action. The ripping of the garment signifies the removal of kingship from Solomon. The metaphor of tearing the kingdom from one's hands and its scenic realization by Ahijah points back once more to the beginning of chapter 11. In 1 Kgs 11:11–13 we hear repeatedly of YHWH's "tearing of kingship" (קרע את הממלכה) from the hand of Solomon.[17] At the same time, David comes to mind again: according to 1 Sam 15:28 and 28:17, YHWH tears the kingship (קרע את הממלכה) out of the hands of Saul in order to give it to David—a process repeated now between Solomon and Jeroboam.[18]

While the encounter with Ahijah shares a common motif with David and Saul, its connection with 11:11–13 shows a clear relation of announcement and fulfillment that implies a literary dependency. This is especially noticeable in the way the prophetic action and its explanation deviate from each other. According to 11:31, the kingship (ממלכה) will be taken from Solomon, while some of its components, namely, the tribes, will be given to Jeroboam and others to Solomon's son (11:36). In 11:32–34, just as in 11:11–13, Solomon does not lose the kingship, and one tribe remains with him (and not his son) as a part of the kingdom—a shift justified with the perfect conduct of David.[19] Furthermore, the literal correspondences are obvious. All this marks 11:32–34 as a later addition to an older stratum of 1 Kgs 11:26–40.[20] This is further corroborated by the fact that a *Wiederaufnahme* of את עשרה השבטים somewhat clumsily added to the end of 11:35 still betrays its insertion. Without the addition, the speech displays an artful chiastic structure building upon the topics of kingship and tribes.[21]

---

the affinity is limited to the wordplay on קרע, while the context in which the scene is embedded differs considerably. A textual relation is therefore rather improbable.

17. On this motif see also the table provided by Weippert, "Die Ätiologie des Nordreiches," 351.

18. Cf. Schmitz, *Prophetie und Königtum*, 126: "Durch diese Parallelisierung mutiert nicht nur Jeroboam zu David, sondern auch Salomo zu Saul."

19. Weippert, "Die Ätiologie des Nordreiches," 357, correctly stresses the shift from Solomon to Rehoboam when it comes to the actual loss of kingship.

20. Leuchter, "Jeroboam the Ephratite," 54, includes 11:31bβ (and also את עשרת השבטים in 11:35) in the addition and argues that the original story "focuses attention on the king rather than the kingdom." Consequently, he has to exclude the idea that Jeroboam is to receive ten parts of the garment (11:31) from his reconstruction of the original story (57). This, however, turns the ripping of the garment into twelve pieces into a blind motif that has no bearing on the story.

21. Weippert, "Die Ätiologie des Nordreiches," 354, makes similar observations.

verse 31bα	*kingship* ripped from Solomon	A
verse 31bβ	*tribes* given to Jeroboam	B
verse 36a	*tribe* given to Rehoboam	B'
verse 37b, 38	*kingship* given to Jeroboam	A'

We see an additional link to the David narratives in 1 Kgs 11:37. The phrase ומלכת בכל אשר תאוה נפשך repeats verbatim Abner's speech in 2 Sam 3:21 in which he offers David the kingship over the north Israelite tribes.[22]

Verse 36b disturbs the chiastic structure. It establishes another literary link with 1 Kgs 15:4 and 2 Kgs 8:19. These texts, both highly critical evaluations of the Judahite kings Abijah and Jehoram, refer back to the promise of a ניר in Jerusalem in order to explain why YHWH held back from destroying Judah despite the obvious sins of its kings (and people).[23]

We see yet another literary connection in 1 Kgs 11:38–39. The combination of the promise to Jeroboam to be "king over Israel" together with the provision that he shall keep the commandments and follow the shining example of David echoes the promise of an enduring Davidic dynasty in 2 Sam 7 and transfers the latter's promises to Jeroboam while at the same time keeping them open for the Davidic line. As is well known, Jeroboam will forfeit the promises, and his line does not extend beyond his immediate successor. Furthermore, 11:38 has a direct match in 1 Kgs 14:8. Here, we find once again in the mouth of Ahijah the Shilonite the first of the so-called dynastic oracles that structure the Deuteronomistic account of the history of northern Israel. Using the genre of prophetic judgment oracles and being quite formulaic in their phraseology, these oracles announce doom for the successive dynasties of northern Israel. In addition to 1 Kgs 14, they appear in 1 Kgs 16:1–4 against Baasha and 1 Kgs 21:17, 20–22, 24 against Ahab.[24]

---

22. Cf. Weippert, "Die Ätiologie des Nordreiches," 346.

23. The ongoing debate whether the *nîr*-texts belong to the compositional structure of the Deuteronomistic History (see Erhard Blum, "Das exilische deuteronomistische Geschichtswerk," in *Das deuteronomistische Geschichtswerk*, ed. Hermann-Josef Stipp, ÖBS 39 [Bern: Lang, 2011], 282) or constitute secondary additions (so, e.g., Ernst Würthwein, *Die Bücher der Könige: 1. Kön. 17–2. Kön. 25*, ATD [Göttingen: Vandenhoeck & Ruprecht, 1984], 500–501 [DtrN]; and Erik Aurelius, *Zukunft jenseits des Gerichts: Eine redaktionsgeschichtliche Studie zum Enneateuch*, BZAW 319 [Berlin: de Gruyter, 2003], 130) does not need to concern us here.

24. On this group of texts, see, e.g., Blanco Wissmann, *Beurteilungskriterien*, 194–98; Blum, "Geschichtswerk," 278–79; and Sang-Won Lee, "Die Königsbeurteilungen

The literary connections coming into view with these texts (1 Kgs 11:26b–27a, 32–35, 36b, 38–39) are in light of their phraseology and content obviously of Deuteronomistic provenience. They incorporate 1 Kgs 11 into the compositional structures of the book of Kings and the greater Deuteronomistic History—irrespective of whether they belong to one or several redactional strata and also of the different formation models of the greater literary composition.[25] For the present discussion, it may suffice to say that they are all later additions to the text in 1 Kgs 11, whose original structure is still discernable.

The account of 1 Kgs 11:26–40 is continued in 12:1–20. With few exceptions (12:17, 19 and a slight reworking at the beginning, 12:2–3), there is no reason to doubt the unity of this compellingly developed and well composed narrative.[26] The presentation of events is highly critical toward

---

und die Literargeschichte des Deuteronomistischen Geschichtswerks: Anmerkungen zu einer kontroversen Diskussion," *VT* 68 (2018): 581–605.

25. Weippert, "Die Ätiologie des Nordreiches," in her detailed analysis, attributes the additions to the original story to three different layers (see the overview, 374–75).

26. First Kings 12:17 is still lacking in LXX and is best explained as an addition inspired by the Chronistic parallel of the account in Kings, so Alexander Rofé, "Elders or Youngsters? Critical Remarks on 1 Kings 12," in *One God—One Cult—One Nation: Archaeological and Biblical Perspectives*, ed. Reinhard G. Kratz and Hermann Spieckermann, BZAW 405 (Berlin: de Gruyter, 2010), 79–80, cf. Ueberschaer, *Gründungsmythos*, 77, and already Würthwein, *1. Kön. 17–2. Kön. 25*. First Kings 12:19 with its clear verdict on the events and its etiological tendency is widely considered a later addition (see, e.g., Würthwein, *Könige*, 158; Becker, "Reichsteilung," 216; Ueberschaer, *Gründungsmythos*, 168). When it is thought to be original, a Judean setting is usually assumed for the whole episode (see, e.g., Ina Plein, "Erwägungen zur Überlieferung von I Reg 11 26–14 20," *ZAW* 78 [1966]: 10; Noth, *Könige*, 150). There might have been some textual corruption in 1 Kgs 12:2b–3 (on the problems of the MT reading, see, e.g., Steven L. McKenzie, "The Source for Jeroboam's Role at Shechem [1Kgs 11:43–12:3, 12, 20]," *JBL* 106 [1987]: 297–99; for a detailed discussion of the problem, see, e.g., Knoppers, *Two Nations*, 211–14), which caused various attempts to ameliorate the text still discernable in 2 Chr 10:2 as well as in the ancient versions. Becker, "Reichsteilung," 217–20; Rofé, "Elders or Youngsters," 79, and also Ueberschaer, *Gründungsmythos*, 173, all see 12:2–3a as a whole as a secondary addition. Consequently, they argue that Jeroboam is not even seen as taking part in the assembly. This causes some serious problems in the narrative sequence: Not only the announcement in 11:26b, 27a but also the introduction to 12:20 (ויהי כשמע כל ישראל כי שב ירבעם) are turned into loose ends. Ueberschaer, *Gründungsmythos*, 173, sees the problem and argues that an original account of Jeroboam's return was lost in the redaction process of 1 Kgs 11–14, which then prompted a later scribe to add the account in 12:2–3. This

Rehoboam: a weak leader who, unlike David, has to go to the people in order to be appointed and displays an inflated self-esteem combined with a fatal immunity to good advice.²⁷ Jeroboam, on the other hand, remains astoundingly passive, almost disappearing within the larger crowd of "the people" (העם) leading the negotiations.²⁸ The scene itself is reminiscent of 2 Sam 17 featuring Ahithophel and Hushai as antagonistic advisors and displaying a double causality in human misjudgment and divine control in the background (2 Sam 17:14).²⁹ In 1 Kgs 12, the latter is expressed in 12:15, which also connects the two episodes by referring back to Ahijah's speech in 1 Kgs 11. First Kings 12:20 provides a summary and a result— Jeroboam becomes king of Israel, and only one tribe, Judah, remains with the "house of David." The designation בית דוד is brought into the discussion in the final speech of the northern Israelites: מה לנו חלק בדוד ולא נחלה בבן ישי in 12:16, which echoes a very similar speech by Sheba ben Bichri in 2 Sam 20:1 and therefore is once again reminiscent of the David narratives. The closing 1 Kgs 12:20 fits perfectly with the announcement in 1 Kgs 11 and thus rounds off the plot. The story of Jeroboam might have continued with the first building measures of the new king (Pnuel) and his cultic policies, which in retrospect appear so efficacious and fatal from a Deuteronomistic point of view.³⁰

---

argument seems circular. The section's unity has occasionally been called into question, e.g., in recent analyses by Ueberschaer, *Gründungsmythos*, 162–73, who excludes, besides 12:2–3a and 12:17, also 12:15 and 20 from the original account; and Knauf, *Könige*, 368, who identifies three textual layers within 12:1–20.

27. See Burke O. Long, *1 Kings*, FOTL 9 (Grand Rapids: Eerdmans, 1985), 137.

28. Becker, "Reichsteilung," 214, speaks of a "Statistenrolle."

29. For the double causality, see Isac Leo Seeligmann, "Menschliches Heldentum und göttliche Hilfe: Die doppelte Kausalität im alttestamentlichen Geschichtsdenken," in *Gesammelte Studien zur Hebräischen Bibel, mit einem Beitrag von Rudolf Smend*, ed. Erhard Blum, FAT 40 (Tübingen: Mohr Siebeck, 2004), 137–59. For the comparision to Ahitophel and Hushai, see already Leonard Rost, *Die Überlieferung von der Thronnachfolge Davids*, BWANT 42 (Stuttgart: Kohlhammer, 1926), 136–38, noting the correspondence of the two scenes. For Plein, "Erwägungen zur Überlieferung," 11–13, the similarities raise the question whether both episodes could have been written by the same author. Although she eventually argues against that option, she still sees a similar group or school in the background.

30. LXX has in 3 Kgdms 12:24a–z an alternative account of the rise of Jeroboam and the division of the kingdom. The question whether this account represents an older version of the narrative or preserves at least older material than the MT has been the subject of an extensive scholarly debate since the second half of the

2. The Date of 1 Kings 11:*26–40; 12:1–20

According to a taxonomy recently compiled by Erhard Blum, information regarding the original date of a text may belong to one of the following categories: (1) textual features such as genre, language, or content that point to (or exclude) a particular historical period; (2) stratigraphical indications with regard to other texts, discernable via intertextual or intratextual relations and/or typological correlations to other texts; (3) text-pragmatic clues indicating that a text was addressing its audience in a discernable

---

nineteenth century (Debus, *Die Sünde Jerobeams*, 68–80, provides an overview of the older discussion; Thomas, *Hezekiah*, 267–76, does so for the more recent studies). The last comprehensive text-critical treatment was made by Zipora Talshir, *The Alternative Story of the Division of the Kingdom*, JBS 6 (Jerusalem: Simor, 1993), who argued persuasively that 3Kgdms 12:24a–z is a midrashic composition secondary to the standard LXX account in 11:14–12:24. Ueberschaer, *Gründungsmythos*, 186–90, rejects the midrash label but also sees 12:24a–z as a late composition based on and freely using the narrative material present in 1 Kgs 11–14. Building on earlier studies by Julio C. Trebolle-Barrera, *Salomón y Jeroboán: Historia de la recensión de 1 Reyes 2–12;14*, Bibliotheca Salmanticensis, Dissertationes 3 (Salamanca: Universidad Pontificia, 1980), Knoppers, *Two Nations*, and Adrian Schenker, "Jeroboam and the Division of the Kingdom in the Ancient Septuagint: LXX 3 Kingdoms 12.24 A–Z, MT 1 Kings 11–12; 14 and the Deuteronomistic History," in *Israel Constructs Its History: Deuteronomistic Historiography in Recent Research*, ed. Albert de Pury, Thomas Römer, and Jean-Daniel Maacchi, JSOTSup 306 (Sheffield: Sheffield Academic, 2000), 214–57, Thomas recently argued that 3 Kgdms 12:24a–z represents an old pre-Deuteronomistic account of the division of the kingdom that was part of his alleged "Hezekian History" (*Hezekiah*, 280–318). The main thrust of his argument is that 12:24a–z is more coherent and closer to standard patterns discernable in the book of Kings than the MT account. This issue raises a number of questions and would require a more detailed discussion. For the present context, one example must suffice: 3 Kgdms 12:24a has a different evaluation of Rehoboam than 1 Kgs 14:22–24, where, instead of Rehoboam himself, Judah is criticized. In the case at hand, the MT indeed differs from the standard patterns of regnal evaluations, but that does not prove that the MT version of the regnal evaluation is secondary (*pace* Thomas, *Hezekiah*, 286–88). It rather is, in this form, an essential part of the greater system of regnal evaluations in the book of Kings because it introduces the main categories for the subsequent evaluations of the Judean kings (see Lee, "Die Königsbeurteilungen")—a system that probably did not concern the author of 3 Kgdms 12:24a–z when he composed his version of the events.

historical situation or social constellation.³¹ In the case of 1 Kgs 11, these categories are informative to varying degrees.

2.1. Genre, Language, and Content

The language and genre of 1 Kgs 11:*26–40 do not point to any specific date or time span. However, the scholarly discussion shows a different situation with regard to 1 Kgs 12, which is important, if—as proposed above—both chapters originally belonged together. Alexander Rofé argued on mainly linguistic grounds that 12:1–20 is contemporaneous with the book of Chronicles.³² He points to four features: the double relative pronoun in 12:8 (אשר העומדים לפניו), the use of אני and not אנכי, the use of יעץ *niphal*, and the designation ילדים for one group of Rehoboam's advisors.³³ However, none of these features is compelling. The phrase אשר העומדים לפניו is indeed curious, but not typical of any later Hebrew style either; there are numerous examples for the use of אני in preexilic texts; יעץ appears both in the *niphal* in verses 6, 8, 9 and the *qal* in 1 Kgs 12 (vv. 8, 13); and the designation ילדים could well be a sneer at Rehoboam and his peer group.³⁴

---

31. Erhard Blum, "The Linguistic Dating of Biblical Texts—An Approach with Methodological Limitations," in *The Formation of the Pentateuch: Bridging the Academic Cultures of Europe, Israel, and North America*. ed. Jan C. Gertz et al., FAT 111 (Tübingen: Mohr Siebeck, 2016), 303–28.

32. Rofé, "Elders or Youngsters"; see also Melanie Köhlmoos, *Bet-El—Erinnerungen an eine Stadt: Perspektiven der alttestamentlichen Bet-El-Überlieferung*, FAT 49 (Tübingen: Mohr Siebeck, 2006), 158–59.

33. Rofé, "Elders or Youngsters," 82–83.

34. The only parallel to be found for אשר העומדים לפניו is 1 Kgs 21:11, which is also a late text. But since the findings are limited to these two occurrences, this points more to a faulty syntax than to any linguistic development (see Paul Joüon, *A Grammar of Biblical Hebrew*, trans. and rev. T. Muraoka, SubBi 14 [Rome: Pontifical Biblical Institute, 1991], 595.II). A few examples of אני may suffice: Texts like Gen 27 and Hos 5, which in all likelihood originated in preexilic times (see Erhard Blum, "The Jacob Tradition," in *The Book of Genesis: Composition, Reception, and Interpretation*, ed. Craig A. Evans, Joel Lohr, and David L. Peterson, VTSup 152 [Leiden: Brill, 2012], 181–211; Kristin Weingart, *Stämmevolk—Staatsvolk—Gottesvolk? Studien zur Verwendung des Israel-Namens im Alten Testament*, FAT 2/68 [Tübingen: Mohr Siebeck, 2014], 278–82, both with further references), use both אני and אנכי. On the other hand, there are numerous examples for the use of אנכי in later texts, see, e.g., Gen 24, which Alexander Rofé, "An Enquiry into the Betrothal of Rebekah," in *Die hebräische Bibel und ihre zweifache Nachgeschichte: Festschrift für Rolf Rendtorff zum 65. Geburtstag*, ed.

The story itself is rather paradigmatic in nature and reminiscent of wisdom literature.[35] But given the wide distribution and longevity of sapiential thinking and literature in the ancient Near East, the wisdom label is, from a tradition-critical perspective, probably one of the least helpful for dating a specific text.

Does the text's actual content provide better clues? In fact, 1 Kgs 11 does mention extratextual realities such as places and architectural structures that could indicate a certain date.

(1) Besides Zeredah (mentioned above), Shiloh appears as the seat of the prophet Ahijah (11:29).[36] This could indicate that Shiloh is understood as the place of an existing sanctuary. Archaeological finds show that Shiloh might have been a stronghold and the home of a sanctuary in the Iron I, but it was utterly destroyed in the second half of the eleventh century and did not regain its former prominence in later periods.[37] At the same time, Shiloh is an excellent example for extremely long-lasting memories connected to a site and its fate. In much later texts of clearly Judahite origins, Shiloh still features as the site of a former YHWH sanctuary, so, for example, in Jer 7:12, 14; 26:6, 9; or Ps 78:60, probably conceived by later Judahites as the last legitimate YHWH sanctuary in the northern territo-

---

E. Blum, Christian Macholz, and Ekkehard W. Stegemann (Neukirchen-Vluyn: Neukirchner Verlag, 1990), 27–39, himself has convincingly dated to the Persian period. The distinction between אני and אנכי obviously does not provide a decisive clue for the date of a text.

35. See already Alfred Jepsen, *Die Quellen des Königsbuches* (Halle: Niemeyer, 1953), 78–79; also Cogan, *Kings*, 351; Becker, "Reichsteilung," 217. Ueberschaer, *Gründungsmythos*, 169–71, also stresses the sapiential character of 1 Kgs 12. He argues that the text originally reflected general experiences of Judean royal counselors and was secretly transmitted as a kind of informal note ("Schmierzettel") until it became part of the more official historiography at some point. A rather speculative reconstruction like this can neither be proven nor disproven, but it raises some questions: Is it conceivable that a tale referring to known kings like Rehoboam and Jeroboam could have been read just as a fictitious narrative? If not, why should a Judahite tale not only condemn Rehoboam (and criticize Solomon) but also legitimize the separation of the Israelite tribes?

36. According to 1 Sam 14:3, Ahijah is a descendent of Eli who was a priest in Shiloh, but the connection is in all likelihood a result of a later scribal harmonization.

37. Israel Finkelstein, *Shiloh: The Archaeology of a Biblical Site*, SMNIA 10 (Tel Aviv: Institute of Archaeology, 1993); Israel Finkelstein and Eliazer Piasetzky, "The Iron I–IIA in the Highlands and Beyond: ^{14}C Anchors, Pottery Phases and the Shoshenq I Campaign," *Levant* 38 (2006): 45–61.

ry.³⁸ In order for the story to work, one does not need an existing cult in Shiloh; a plausible memory that something similar existed at the time of the story is entirely sufficient.³⁹

(2) Also mentioned is "the Millo" (המלוא) in the City of David (עיר דוד) (11:27). It is usually identified with the so-called Stepped Stone Structure and subject to a controversial debate among notable archaeologists concerning its function and extent.⁴⁰ Interestingly, 1 Kgs 11 simply mentions this architectural feature and presupposes that its addressees were familiar with it.⁴¹ Was the structure widely known or easily to be seen also

---

38. On Ps 78 see Kristin Weingart, "Juda als Sachwalter Israels: Geschichtstheologie nach dem Ende des Nordreiches in Hos 13 und Ps 78," *ZAW* 127 (2015): 440–58.

39. This has been stressed correctly by Israel Finkelstein, *The Forgotten Kingdom: The Archaeology and History of Northern Israel*, ANEM 5 (Atlanta: Society of Biblical Literature, 2013), 49–50. When he brings the following account in 1 Kgs 12:25–33 into the discussion, he concentrates on the issue of Dan. Arguing that Dan did not become Israelite before 800 BCE, Finkelstein (74–75) proposes that the text retrojects circumstances from the time of Jeroboam II into an earlier past (see also Angelika Berlejung, "Twisting Traditions: Programmatic Absence-Theology for the Northern Kingdom in 1 Kgs 12:26–33* [The 'Sin of Jeroboam']," *JNSL* 35 [2009]: 1–42; Christian Frevel, *Geschichte Israels*, Studienbücher Theologie 2 [Stuttgart: Kohlhammer, 2016], 155; for a critical view on the suggestion, see Lester L. Grabbe, "Jeroboam I? Jeroboam II? Or Jeroboam 0? Jeroboam in History and Tradition," in *Rethinking Israel: Studies in the History and Archaeology of Ancient Israel in Honor of Israel Finkelstein*, ed. Oded Lipschits, Yuval Goren, and Matthew J. Adams [Winona Lake, IN: Eisenbrauns, 2017], 115–23). But as the evidence of the Dan inscription and other textual sources show, the case is not so clear; see Erhard Blum, "The Relations between Aram and Israel in the Ninth and Eighth Centuries BCE: The Textual Evidence," in *In Search for Aram and Israel: Politics, Culture, and Identity*, ed. Omer Sergi, Manfred Oeming, and Izak J. de Hulster, ORA 20 (Tübingen: Mohr Siebeck, 2016), 37–56.

40. On the identification see the comprehensive discussion of the matter in Nadav Na'aman, "Biblical and Historical Jerusalem in the Tenth and Fifth–Fourth Centuries, BCE," *Bib* 93 (2012): 28–30 (with further references); see also Na'aman, "Five Notes on Jerusalem in the First and Second Temple Periods," *TA* 39 (2012): 93-103. Regarding the Stepped Stone Structure see also the ongoing debate between Israel Finkelstein et al., "Has the Palace of King David in Jerusalem Been Found?," *TA* 34 (2007): 142–64; Finkelstein, "A Great United Monarchy? Archaeological and Historical Perspectives," in Kratz and Spieckermann, *One God—One Cult—One Nation*, 3–28; and Amihai Mazar, "Archaeology and the Biblical Narrative: The Case of the United Monarchy," in Kratz and Spieckermann, *One God—One Cult—One Nation*, 29–58, both with further references.

41. Na'aman, "Biblical and Historical Jerusalem," 23–30, offers a detailed discussion of the different references to the Millo in the Bible.

in the centuries after its construction or—comparable to Shiloh—part of a collective memory? Without further clues, its mention alone does not point to any specific date.

Thus, with regard to the sites and features mentioned, the archaeological evidence does not seem to provide any clear *terminus ad quem* for 1 Kgs 11.

2.2. Literary Stratigraphy

Assuming the reconstruction above and the suggested literary connections of 1 Kgs 11 are correct, the text clearly predates the Deuteronomistic History—regardless of the question whether the literary connections within the text are to be attributed to different Deuteronomistic layers or compositions or not.[42]

Important clues are found in the manifold connections to the David stories, that is in the so-called Succession Narrative as well as the stories of David's rise, namely, (1) in the plot of the story: for example, the introduction of Jeroboam; the way he rises to kingship (it is ripped from his predecessor by YHWH and offered to him by the tribes of Israel); his flight abroad because the ruling king tries to kill him; (2) in the sapiential character of the presentation: for example, the battle of the advisors in 1 Kgs 12; the dual—divine and human—causality behind the events narrated; and (3) in the introduction of Jeroboam and other literal repetitions such as 11:37 and, most strikingly, 12:16.[43] Given the extent and multitude of connections in so short a text as 1 Kgs 11–12, they do not seem to be accidental, but rather point to a literal dependency and to the aim of casting Jeroboam in a certain light (see below).[44]

---

42. In current scholarship, the extent, literary history, and existence of the (or a) Deuteronomistic History is a hotly debated issue (for an overview see, e.g., Thomas Römer, *The So-Called Deuteronomistic History: A Sociological, Historical and Literary Introduction* [London: T&T Clark, 2005]). For a critical discussion of the recent trend to dismiss Noth's basic ideas, see, e.g., Lee, "Die Königsbeurteilungen."

43. The numerous references to the David narrative have often been noted, see, e.g., Plein, "Erwägungen zur Überlieferung," 11–13; Paul S. Ash, "Jeroboam I and the Deuteronomistic Historian's Ideology of the Founder," *CBQ* 60 (1998): 17–19; Peter J. Leithart, "Counterfeit Davids: Davidic Restoration and the Architecture of 1–2 Kings," *TynBul* 56 (2005): 26–28; Leuchter, "Jeroboam the Ephratite," 60–64. See already Julius Wellhausen, *Die Composition des Hexateuchs und der historischen Bücher des Alten Testaments*, 4th ed. (Berlin: de Gruyter, 1963), 217.

44. Within the Deuteronomistic additions, especially in 1 Kgs 11:38–39, Jeroboam is likened to David even further; he is given a similar promise as David in 2 Sam 7

Unfortunately, the exegetical discussion on the Succession Narrative and the David-Saul narratives may easily be compared to the controversial debates on the Stepped and Large Stone Structures in Jerusalem: a consensus is not in sight. While some see strong indications that at least the Succession Narrative should not be moved too far away from the early years of the kingdom of Judah, many exegetes strongly object to such a proposition.[45] So, given the present state of research, the literary stratigraphy does not allow us to draw a decisive conclusion on the date of 1 Kgs 11:*26–40; 12:1–20.[46]

2.3. The Pragmatics of 1 Kings 11–12

Freed from the Deuteronomist's bias, Jeroboam's introduction in 1 Kgs 11:*26–28 raises the expectation that a positive protagonist is going to enter the stage. His way to kingship is not one of active usurpation; Jeroboam is rather modeled on the young David who became king due to a combination of divine intervention, leadership skills, and personal modesty. In the case of Jeroboam, the pretentious Rehoboam who repeats and aggravates the mistakes of his father Solomon further highlights the former's profile.

(see, e.g., Leuchter, "Jeroboam the Ephratite," 52). But with regard to Jeroboam, the text only paves the way for the total rejection of him and his dynasty that will follow in 1 Kgs 14:7–16. Thus it only draws parallels between Jeroboam and David in order to eventually juxtapose them. First Kings 11:32b, 36b prepare this move on the positive side, i.e., with regard to David and the Davidic dynasty. Ash, "Jeroboam," sees here a Deuteronomistic "ideology of the founder" according to which the behavior of the founder of a dynasty determines its overall fate. While this might be applicable in the case of David and Jeroboam, who according to Ash is presented as an archetypal *Unheilsherrscher* (see also John Holder, "The Presuppositions, Accusations, and Threats of 1 Kings 14:1–18," *JBL* 107 [1998]: 27–38), it is not carried out systematically for all subsequent north Israelite dynasties. See, e.g., the case of Jehu, who is seen rather positively, but whose dynasty nevertheless does not endure.

45. For a short overview of the debate see Weingart, *Stämmevolk*, 170–76.

46. The question of possible connections between the depiction of Jeroboam and Moses and their literary historical implications cannot be examined here; see, e.g., Felipe Blanco Wissmann, "Sargon, Mose und die Gegner Salomos: Zur Frage vor-neuassyrischer Ursprünge der Mose-Erzählung," *BN* 110 (2001): 42–54; Christoph Berner, "The Egyptian Bondage and Solomon's Forced Labor: Literary Connections between Exodus 1–15 and 1 Kings 1–12?," in *Pentateuch, Hexateuch, or Enneateuch? Identifying Literary Works in Genesis through Kings*, ed. Thomas B. Dozeman, Thomas Römer, and Konrad Schmid, AIL 8 (Atlanta: Society of Biblical Literature, 2011), 211–40.

The division of the kingdom is depicted as initiated by YHWH and brought about by the imprudent behavior of Rehoboam. The latter leads to a rejection of Davidic rule over the northern tribes, an outcome that is, from the perspective of the narrator, justified. It is stated most succinctly in 1 Kgs 12:16: מה לנו חלק בבית דוד ולא נחלה בבן ישי ... עתה ראה ביתך דוד.[47] In 2 Sam 20:1, Shebah ben Bichri had used the same call to motivate his revolt against David, which rapidly dwindled down to him alone. Not so in 1 Kgs 12; here, not David himself, but the Davidic dynasty is at stake,[48] and 1 Kgs 12:16 forcefully rejects the claim that David's descendant should rule over more than "his house": "What have we to do with the house of David!" The phrase מה ל introducing a reproach is also found in Josh 22:24; Judg 11:12; 1 Kgs 17:18. The closing sentence עתה ראה ביתך דוד stresses the point once more: It sends Rehoboam back to his clan. Or rather, בית דוד being the name of the Southern Kingdom, back to the kingdom of Judah![49] In the meantime, Jeroboam only reacts and accepts—the pieces of the garment given to him by Ahijah and now the kingship offered to him by the tribes.

What would be the purpose of such an episode dealing after all with the origins of the Northern Kingdom? The story has a clear legitimizing tendency with regard to the establishment of the kingdom of Israel and is an equally distinct justification of Jeroboam's role in the events. At the same time, it does not tell a glorious founding myth of the kingdom; its establishment is rather the result of incompetence and bad decisions on the side of David's successors. Neither does it present Jeroboam as a prominent figure destined to be king from the outset; with regard to him, 1 Kgs 11 has more of an apologetic rather than a venerating tendency.

Nevertheless, the positive view of Jeroboam and the establishment of the Northern Kingdom remain striking. The critical perspective on Solomon (and Rehoboam), the rejection of Davidic rule over more than one

---

47. Ina Willi-Plein, "Nach deinen Zelten, Israel! Grammatik, Pragmatik und eine kritische Episode der Davidshausgeschichte," *ZAH* 17/20 (2004/2007): 218–29, when discussing the phrase לאהליך ישראל, sees "Israel" in 2 Sam 20:1 and 1 Kgs 12:16 as referring to the *Heerbann*, i.e., a military entity and not the people or the tribes. For a critical discussion of this proposal see Weingart, *Stämmevolk*, 185 with n. 72.

48. Cf. Knoppers, *Two Nations*, 221.

49. See the Tel Dan Inscription, *KAI* 310, as well as the Mesha Stela, *KAI* 181. Nevertheless, Leuchter, "Jeroboam the Ephratite," 66, proposes that בית in 12:16 refers to the temple, but this would be a highly unusual usage of בית דוד.

tribe, and its strong theological backing is hardly conceivable in a Judahite composition.[50] It rather points to a north Israelite setting and a date before 720 BCE.[51] One could argue that the apologetic view of Jeroboam would also be feasible after 720 in an attempt to integrate north Israelite traditions into a Judean narrative and thus northern refugees in Judah.[52] But given the blatant denial of Davidic rule over Israelite tribes, it would have quite the opposite effect, namely a destabilizing one. In a north Israelite composition, the legitimizing and apologetic aims are much more plausible pragmatics.

At the same time, the manifold references to David and the modeling of Jeroboam as a *David redivivus* betray a certain appreciation of David that is presupposed and used in order to depict Jeroboam.[53] The account of 1 Kgs 11–12 clearly anticipates in its addressees a familiarity with the traditions now present in the David-Saul story and the Succession Narrative. One can read and understand 1 Kgs 11–12 as it is, but having the David traditions in the background considerably strengthens the narrative profile of the story.

The pragmatics of the narrative presented above strongly suggest that 1 Kgs 11–12 do not provide much historical information on a division of the kingdom or the establishment of the Northern Kingdom of Israel. They rather offer a glimpse into possible discourses on aspects of north Israelite royal ideology and on attempts to determine the relationship to the kingdom of Judah and the Davidic dynasty.[54] As is well known, recent research

---

50. The secondary attempts in 1 Kgs 11:38–39 to add conditions to the promises for Jeroboam clearly highlight the difficulties later Judean scribes faced with the text.

51. Cf. Plein, "Erwägungen zur Überlieferung," 22; Würthwein, *Könige*, 150; Peter Mommer, "Das Verhältnis von Situation, Tradition und Redaktion am Beispiel von 1 Kön 12," in *Altes Testament—Forschung und Wirkung: Festschrift für Henning Graf Reventlow*, ed. Peter Mommer and Winfried Thiel (Frankfurt am Main: Lang, 1994), 56–57; and on his reconstructed base layer J (without 12:1–20) also Ueberschaer, *Gründungsmythos*, 238.

52. Israel Finkelstein, "Saul, Benjamin and the Emergence of 'Biblical Israel': An Alternative View," *ZAW* 123 (2011): 348–67, sees these attempts as the prime motive for the integration of north Israelite materials in the Judean stream of tradition.

53. For Jeroboam as *David redivivus*, see Ash, "Jeroboam," 18. The appreciation of David was also noted by Noth, *Könige*, 271, who detects a basic affirmation of Davidic rule and sees the origin of the story rather in Judean circles.

54. Any attempt to further narrow down the date of these discourses remains inevitably speculative. It has been suggested that the name Jeroboam points to the time

tends to doubt the existence of a unified kingdom as a historical entity and to move the whole idea into the realm of religious ideology.[55] But the conclusion that 1 Kgs 11–12 is more concerned with historical reflection than with the presentation of actual events does not necessarily indicate the improbability or impossibility of a unified kingdom. This is involuntarily shown by the argumentation of Uwe Becker who, while denying any north Israelite influence in 1 Kgs 12, reads the text as justifying the existence of two states ("Ätiologie der Zweistaatlichkeit").[56] If the coexistence of two separate states was a matter that needed an explanation, does this not require at least the concept of a unified state in the background?

3. Jeroboam and Benjamin: Why Does Ten Plus One Equal Twelve?

The suggestion that 1 Kgs 11 rejects Davidic rule over more than one tribe of Israel and that this claim contradicts Judahite royal ideology has caused a problem still to be solved.

Ahijah rips his garment into twelve pieces; therefore 1 Kgs 11 undeniably uses a twelve-tribe concept.[57] The text further insists that only one tribe remains with Rehoboam. This follows from 11:36 and also from 12:20, the concluding verse that summarizes the events: ולא היה אחרי בית דוד זולתי שבט יהודה לבדו.[58] In doing so, 12:20 also makes a solution impossible that has been brought forward now and then in order to solve the mathematical riddle of 1 Kgs 11: that Rehoboam receives one more tribe

---

of Jeroboam II (Frevel, *Geschichte Israels*, 158; see also Blanco Wissmann, "Sargon," 52–54), which would also be an important formative phase in the literary history of the Jacob and Joseph stories, which both deal with the relation between Judah and the Israelite tribes as well (see Weingart, *Stämmevolk*, 236–66).

55. See Finkelstein, "United Monarchy," 3–28 (with references to his earlier works); Frevel, *Geschichte Israels*, 108–19, 164–5, and many more.

56. Becker, "Reichsteilung," 216 (in italics in the original).

57. Leuchter, "Jeroboam the Ephratite," 53, proposes that the division in twelve originally referred to Solomon's twelve administrative districts (see also A. Graeme Auld, *Kings*, DSB [Edinburgh: Saint Andrew Press; Philadelphia: Westminster, 1986], 82). The text, however, clearly speaks of tribes.

58. As in 11:32, 36 (see below), LXX harmonizes in 3 Kgdms 12:20 and reads πάρεξ σκήπτρου Ιουδα καὶ Βενιαμιν μόνοι. The awkward syntax in naming two tribes after the singular σκήπτρον clearly betrays the secondary reworking, all the more so since 3 Kdgms 12:24u shows how the same issue could be expressed in idiomatic Greek.

in addition to Judah, which he already has; rather, 1 Kgs 12:20 emphatically states that it is Judah and Judah alone that follows Rehoboam.[59]

If one tribe remains for Rehoboam and ten for Jeroboam, which tribe is missing?[60] Simeon and Levi have been named as possible candidates: Simeon because of the assumed localization of its territory in the south of Judah and Levi because of its special status among the tribes.[61] But in the tribal lists and the patriarchal stories, both are seen as northern tribes. Simeon belongs to those tribal entities like Reuben that have rather prominent places in the tribal lists, but more or less disappear from view in the history of Israel. Moreover, in the current context, it would be hard to explain why either of them should be missing. As a possible source of the confusion in 1 Kgs 11, Benjamin is a more likely candidate for two reasons.[62]

---

59. Weippert, "Die Ätiologie des Nordreiches," 350, cf. Joseph Robinson, *The First Book of Kings*, CBC (Cambridge: Cambridge University Press, 1972), 139–40, identifying the one additional tribe with Benjamin. Because of 1 Kgs 12:20, attempts to avoid the mathematical dilemma, like the proposals that a correct sum was not intended, either because the numbers refer to administrative districts (Leuchter, "Jeroboam the Ephratite"), or the ten pieces Jeroboam receives are merely symbolical (Richard D. Nelson, *First and Second Kings*, IBC [Atlanta: Westminster John Knox, 1987]) and might refer to "ten times more … power and responsibility" (Auld, *Kings*, 82), do not provide a convincing solution.

60. Würthwein, *Könige*, 141, favors a redaction-critical solution: the original story was only concerned with ten tribes for Jeroboam, while a later redactor introduced Judah and created the problem (see also Dietrich, *Prophetie und Geschichte*, 16–17). Weippert, "Die Ätiologie des Nordreiches," 361, argues for a different model: In the original account, Judah and an additional tribe belong to Rehoboam. After a redactional correction in 12:32a, only one tribe was left. Her further conclusion that Jeroboam now receives only nine tribes remains somewhat enigmatic. LXX avoids the problem: in 11:32 and 36, "two tribes" (δύο σκῆπτρα) are attributed to Rehoboam.

61. For Simeon, see, e.g., Plein, "Erwägungen zur Überlieferung," 19; Martin Rehm, *Das erste Buch der Könige: Ein Kommentar* (Würzburg: Echter, 1982), 126–27; Weippert, "Die Ätiologie des Nordreiches," 356; Georg Hentschel, *1 Könige*, NEchtB (Würzburg: Echter, 1985), 80. For Levi, see, e.g., Marvin A. Sweeney, *I and II Kings: A Commentary*, OTL (Louisville: Westminster John Knox, 2007), 160; see also Noth, *Könige*, 260, who nevertheless remains cautious: "Definitiv wird sich das Problem … nicht klären lassen."

62. See also Jepsen, *Die Quellen*, 43. Knauf, *Könige*, 338–39, reads the Ahijah episode against the background of an alleged conflict of Judean returnees and Benjaminites in postexilic Yehud.

(1) There are indications of redactional activity within 1 Kgs 11–12 concerning the allocation of Benjamin. The most obvious case is 12:21–24:[63] After 12:20 just limited the dominion of Rehoboam to the tribe of Judah (שבט יהודה), 12:21 has him rule over the house of Judah (בית יהודה) and the tribe of Benjamin (שבט בנימין). Moreover, the fact that Rehoboam does not go to war contradicts 1 Kgs 14:30; 15:6, which state that Rehoboam was at war with Jeroboam all his life. The actual aim of the episode related in 12:21–24 seems to lie in the declaration that Rehoboam ruled over Judah *and* Benjamin. This is almost redundantly stressed twice within four verses—in verses 21 and 23—and thus corrects 1 Kgs 12 concerning the allocation of Benjamin. This correction seems to have been necessary, because it is hardly a coincidence that 12:16 echoes the combat call of a Benjaminite. As a result, Benjamin is part and parcel of the north Israelite tribal group that turned its back on Rehoboam. Just as 12:20 confirms, Benjamin did not belong to בית דוד in the original story. Also, in 1 Kgs 11, the transfer of ten tribes to Jeroboam coincides with a redactional juncture: the *Wiederaufnahme* in 11:31b and 35b used to integrate the later addition in 11:32–35a (see above).

(2) This leads to the second point: historical considerations. As is well known, Benjamin was for economic as well as military reasons a much sought after region and a disputed territory between Judah and Israel. While the signs are that at least from the ninth century onward, it belonged to the Judahite sphere of influence, numerous north Israelite texts and traditions, like the Jacob or Joseph story, confirm that northern claims on the area remained strong and vivid.[64] From a northern perspective, twelve minus one is eleven, therefore Benjamin belonged to Joseph.

When it comes to numbers in biblical texts, mathematical correctness might not always be the most important factor. Therefore, the suggestion of the critical apparatus of the BHS to read eleven instead of ten in 1 Kgs 11:31 could be dismissed as an unnecessary attempt at harmonization. Purely mathematical reasons do not suffice.[65] But given the overall profile

---

63. See already Noth, *Könige*, 279; Würthwein, *Könige*, 161, and recently Ueberschaer, *Gründungsmythos*, 174–77; Knauf, *Könige*, 379.

64. For the ninth century, see, e.g., Finkelstein, "Saul, Benjamin," 350–62. For northern claims, see Weingart, *Stämmevolk*, 357–60.

65. For Plein, "Erwägungen zur Überlieferung," 19, esp. the odd arithmetic indicates the old age of the tradition. But did earlier scribes have less mathematical expertise than later ones?

of the text, a plausible motive for a change and the discernable traces of later adjustments in the matter make a good case for the assumption that originally, eleven tribes were given to Jeroboam.

For later Judean tradents—maybe the ones who inserted 11:32–35—Benjamin belonged to Judah. So, with a small change, they kept the issue open. One precious piece of Ahijah's garment remained outside YHWH's allocation to Jeroboam and consequently free for Judah to claim.

In sum, the pragmatics of the reconstructed original layer of 1 Kgs 11:*26–40 (and 12:*1–20) point to an apologetic but, in its core, Jeroboam-friendly account of the events leading to the establishment of the Northern Kingdom, thus indicating a north Israelite setting and a date before 720 BCE for the composition. The literary stratigraphy and textual features like the place names mentioned do not rule out this option. In all likelihood, 1 Kgs 11–12 is not an account of the actual events and circumstances that led to and accompanied the division of the kingdom. It rather is an ideological piece with legitimatory pragmatics with regard to the kingdom of Israel. As such, however, it supports the idea that a division from the בית דוד took place, or was at least kept in the collective memory as a *Ursprungsgeschichte* (story of origin) in northern Israel. In addition, the text reflects traits of a shared identity between Judah and Israel and, with regard to Benjamin, fits with north Israelite hegemonial claims attested elsewhere in northern traditions, like, for example, the patriarchal narratives.

Bibliography

Ash, Paul S. "Jeroboam I and the Deuteronomistic Historian's Ideology of the Founder." *CBQ* 60 (1998): 16–24.

Auld, A. Graeme. *Kings*. DSB. Edinburgh: Saint Andrew Press; Philadelphia: Westminster, 1986.

Aurelius, Erik. *Zukunft jenseits des Gerichts: Eine redaktionsgeschichtliche Studie zum Enneateuch*. BZAW 319. Berlin: de Gruyter, 2003.

Becker, Uwe. "Die Reichsteilung nach I Reg 12." *ZAW* 112 (2000): 210–29.

Berlejung, Angelika. "Twisting Traditions: Programmatic Absence-Theology for the Northern Kingdom in 1 Kgs 12:26–33* (The 'Sin of Jeroboam')." *JNSL* 35 (2009): 1–42.

Berner, Christoph. "The Egyptian Bondage and Solomon's Forced Labor: Literary Connections between Exodus 1–15 and 1 Kings 1–12?" Pages 211–40 in *Pentateuch, Hexateuch, or Enneateuch? Identifying Literary Works in Genesis through Kings*. Edited by Thomas B. Dozeman,

Thomas Römer, and Konrad Schmid. AIL 8. Atlanta: Society of Biblical Literature, 2011.

Blanco Wissmann, Felipe. *"Er tat das Rechte...": Beurteilungskriterien und Deuteronomismus in 1Kön 12–2Kön 25*. ATANT 93. Zurich: TVZ, 2008.

———. "Sargon, Mose und die Gegner Salomos: Zur Frage vor-neuassyrischer Ursprünge der Mose-Erzählung." *BN* 110 (2001): 42–54.

Blum, Erhard. "Das exilische deuteronomistische Geschichtswerk." Pages 269–95 in *Das deuteronomistische Geschichtswerk*. Edited by Hermann-Josef Stipp. ÖBS 39. Bern: Lang, 2011.

———. "The Jacob Tradition." Pages 181–211 in *The Book of Genesis: Composition, Reception, and Interpretation*. Edited by Craig A. Evans, Joel N. Lohr, and David L. Peterson. VTSup 152. Leiden: Brill, 2012.

———. "The Linguistic Dating of Biblical Texts—An Approach with Methodological Limitations." Pages 303–25 in *The Formation of the Pentateuch: Bridging the Academic Cultures of Europe, Israel, and North America*. Edited by Jan C. Gertz, Bernard M. Levinson, Dalit Rom-Shiloni, and Konrad Schmid. FAT 111. Tübingen: Mohr Siebeck, 2016.

———. "Die Lüge des Propheten: Ein Lesevorschlag zu einer befremdlichen Geschichte (I Reg 13)." Pages 27–46 in *Mincha: Festgabe für Rolf Rendtorff zum 75. Geburtstag*. Edited by Erhard Blum. Neukirchen-Vluyn: Neukirchner Verlag, 2000.

———. "The Relations between Aram and Israel in the Ninth and Eighth Centuries BCE: The Textual Evidence." Pages 37–56 in *In Search for Aram and Israel: Politics, Culture, and Identity*. Edited by Omer Sergi, Manfred Oeming, and Izaak J. de Hulster. ORA 20. Tübingen: Mohr Siebeck, 2016.

Bosshard-Nepustil, Erich. "Hadad, der Edomiter: 1 Kön 11,14–22 zwischen literarischem Kontext und Verfassergegenwart." Pages 95–109 in *Schriftauslegung in der Schrift: Festschrift für Odil Hannes Steck zu seinem 65. Geburtstag*. Edited by Reinhard G. Kratz, Thomas Krüger, and Konrad Schmid. BZAW 300. Berlin: de Gruyter, 2000.

Chun, S. Min. "Whose Cloak Did Ahijah Seize and Tear? A Note on 1 Kings xi 29–30." *VT* 56 (2006): 268–74.

Cogan, Mordechai. *1 Kings: A New Translation with Introduction and Commentary*. AB 11. New York: Doubleday, 2000.

Cohn, Robert L. "Literary Technique in the Jeroboam Narrative." *ZAW* 97 (1985): 23–35.

Debus, Jörg. *Die Sünde Jerobeams: Studien zur Darstellung Jerobeams und der Geschichte des Nordreiches in der deuteronomistischen Geschichtsschreibung*. FRLANT 93. Göttingen: Vandenhoeck & Ruprecht, 1967.

Dietrich, Walter. *Prophetie und Geschichte: Eine redaktionsgeschichtliche Untersuchung zum deuteronomistischen Geschichtswerk*. FRLANT 108. Göttingen: Vandenhoeck & Ruprecht, 1972.

Edelman, Diana. "Solomon's Adversaries Hadad, Rezon and Jeroboam: A Trio of 'Bad Guy' Characters Illustrating the Theology of Immediate Retribution." Pages 166–191 in *The Pitcher Is Broken: Memorial Essays for Gösta W. Ahlström*. Edited by Steven W. Holloway and Lowell K. Handy. JSOTSup 190. Sheffield: Sheffield Academic, 1995.

Eph'al, Israel. "Changes in Palestine during the Persian Period in Light of Epigraphic Sources." *IEJ* 48 (1998): 106–19.

Eshel, Hanan. "Israelite Names from Samaria in the Persian Period" [Hebrew]. Pages 181–89 in *These Are the Names: Studies in Jewish Onomastics*. Edited by Aaron Demsky, Y. A. Raif, Joseph Tabory, and Edwin D. Lawson. Ramat Gan: Bar Ilan University Press, 1997.

Ewald, Heinrich. *Geschichte Davids und der Königsherrschaft in Israel*. Vol. 3 of *Geschichte des Volkes Israel*. 3rd ed. Göttingen: Dieterichsche, 1866.

Finkelstein, Israel. *The Forgotten Kingdom: The Archaeology and History of Northern Israel*. ANEM 5. Atlanta: Society of Biblical Literature, 2013.

———. "A Great United Monarchy? Archaeological and Historical Perspectives." Pages 3–28 in *One God—One Cult—One Nation: Archaeological and Biblical Perspectives*. Edited by Reinhard G. Kratz and Hermann Spieckermann. BZAW 405. Berlin: de Gruyter, 2010.

———. "Saul, Benjamin and the Emergence of 'Biblical Israel': An Alternative View." *ZAW* 123 (2011): 348–67.

———. *Shiloh: The Archaeology of a Biblical Site*. SMNIA 10. Tel Aviv: Institute of Archaeology, 1993.

Finkelstein, Israel, and Eliazer Piasetzky. "The Iron I–IIA in the Highlands and Beyond: ^{14}C Anchors, Pottery Phases and the Shoshenq I Campaign." *Levant* 38 (2006): 45–61.

Finkelstein, Israel, and Lily Singer-Avitz. "Reevaluating Bethel." *ZDPV* 125 (2009): 33–48.

Finkelstein, Israel, Ze'ev Herzog, Lily Singer-Avitz, and David Ussishkin. "Has the Palace of King David in Jerusalem Been Found?" *TA* 34 (2007): 142–64.

Frevel, Christian. *Geschichte Israels*. Studienbücher Theologie 2. Stuttgart: Kohlhammer, 2015.

Frisch, Amos. "Jeroboam and the Division of the Kingdom: Mapping Contrasting Biblical Accounts." *JANES* 27 (2000): 15–29.

Galpaz, Pnina. "The Reign of Jeroboam and the Extent of Egyptian Influence." *BN* 60 (1991): 13–19.

Grabbe, Lester L. "Jeroboam I? Jeroboam II? Or Jeroboam 0? Jeroboam in History and Tradition." Pages 115–23 in *Rethinking Israel: Studies in the History and Archaeology of Ancient Israel in Honor of Israel Finkelstein*. Edited by Oded Lipschits, Yuval Gadot, and Matthew J. Adams. Winona Lake, IN: Eisenbrauns, 2017.

Gray, John. *I and II Kings: A Commentary*. 3rd ed. OTL. London: SCM, 1980.

Hentschel, Georg. *1 Könige*. NEchtB. Würzburg: Echter, 1985.

Holder, John. "The Presuppositions, Accusations, and Threats of 1 Kings 14:1–18." *JBL* 107 (1998): 27–38.

Jepsen, Alfred. *Die Quellen des Königsbuches*. Halle: Niemeyer, 1953.

Joüon, Paul. *A Grammar of Biblical Hebrew*. Translated and revised by T. Muraoka. SubBi 14. Rome: Pontifical Biblical Institute, 1991.

Knauf, Ernst Axel. *1 Könige 1–14*. HThKAT. Freiburg am Breisgau: Herder, 2016.

Knoppers, Gary N. "Revisiting the Samarian Question in the Persian Period." Pages 265–89 in *Judah and the Judeans in the Persian Period*. Edited by Oded Lipschits and Manfred Oeming. Winona Lake, IN: Eisenbrauns, 2006.

———. *The Reign of Solomon and the Rise of Jeroboam*. Vol. 1 of *Two Nations under God: The Deuteronomistic History of Solomon and the Dual Monarchies*. HSM 52. Atlanta: Scholars Press, 1993.

Kochavi, Moshe. "The Identification of Zeredah, Home of Jeroboam Son of Nebat, King of Israel" [Hebrew]. *ErIsr* 20 (1989): 198–201.

Köhlmoos, Melanie. *Bet-El—Erinnerungen an eine Stadt: Perspektiven der alttestamentlichen Bet-El-Überlieferung*. FAT 49. Tübingen: Mohr Siebeck, 2006.

Lee, Sang-Won. "Die Königsbeurteilungen und die Literargeschichte des Deuteronomistischen Geschichtswerks: Anmerkungen zu einer kontroversen Diskussion." *VT* 68 (2018): 581–605.

———. "'Den Ort, den JHWH erwählen wird…, sollt ihr aufsuchen' (Dtn 12,5): Die Forderung der Kulteinheit im Deuteronomistischen Geschichtswerk." PhD diss., Tübingen, 2015.

Leithart, Peter J. "Counterfeit Davids: Davidic Restoration and the Architecture of 1–2 Kings." *TynBul* 56 (2005): 19–33.
Leuchter, Mark. "Jeroboam the Ephratite." *JBL* 125 (2006): 51–72.
Levin, Christoph. "Das synchronistische Exzerpt aus den Annalen der Könige von Israel und Juda." *VT* 61 (2011): 616–28.
Long, Burke O. *1 Kings*. FOTL 9. Grand Rapids: Eerdmans, 1984.
Mazar, Amihai. "Archaeology and the Biblical Narrative: The Case of the United Monarchy." Pages 29–58 in *One God—One Cult—One Nation: Archaeological and Biblical Perspectives*. Edited by Reinhard G. Kratz and Hermann Spieckermann. BZAW 405. Berlin: de Gruyter, 2010.
McKenzie, Steven L. "The Source for Jeroboam's Role at Shechem (1 Kgs 11:43–12:3, 12, 20)." *JBL* 106 (1987): 297–300.
Meshorer, Yaakov, and Shraga Qedar. *The Coinage of Samaria in the Fourth Century BCE*. Los Angeles: Numismatic Fine Arts International, 1991.
Mommer, Peter. "Das Verhältnis von Situation, Tradition und Redaktion am Beispiel von 1 Kön 12." Pages 47–64 in *Altes Testament—Forschung und Wirkung: Festschrift für Henning Graf Reventlow*. Edited by Peter Mommer and Winfried Thiel. Frankfurt am Main: Lang, 1994.
Na'aman, Nadav. "Biblical and Historical Jerusalem in the Tenth and Fifth–Fourth Centuries BCE." *Bib* 93 (2012): 21–42.
———. "Five Notes on Jerusalem in the First and Second Temple Periods." *TA* 39 (2012): 93–103.
Nelson, Richard D. *First and Second Kings*. IBC. Atlanta: John Knox, 1987.
Noth, Martin. *Könige*. BKAT. Neukirchen-Vluyn: Neukirchener Verlag, 1968.
———. *Überlieferungsgeschichtliche Studien: Die sammelnden und bearbeitenden Geschichtswerke im Alten Testament*. Darmstadt: Wissenschaftliche Buchgesellschaft, 1957.
Pakkala, Juha. "Jeroboam's Sins and Bethel in 1 Kgs 12:25–33." *BN* 112 (2002): 86–94.
Plein, Ina. "Erwägungen zur Überlieferung von 1 Reg 11 26–14 20." *ZAW* 78 (1966): 8–24.
Rehm, Martin. *Das erste Buch der Könige: Ein Kommentar*. Würzburg: Echter, 1979.
Robinson, Joseph. *The First Book of Kings*. CBC. Cambridge: Cambridge University Press, 1972.
Römer, Thomas. *The So-Called Deuteronomistic History: A Sociological, Historical and Literary Introduction*. London: T&T Clark, 2005.

Rofé, Alexander. "Elders or Youngsters? Critical Remarks on 1 Kings 12." Pages 79–89 in *One God—One Cult—One Nation: Archaeological and Biblical Perspectives*. Edited by Reinhard G. Kratz and Hermann Spieckermann. BZAW 405. Berlin: de Gruyter, 2010.

———. "An Enquiry into the Betrothal of Rebekah." Pages 27–39 in *Die hebräische Bibel und ihre zweifache Nachgeschichte: Festschrift für Rolf Rendtorff zum 65. Geburtstag*. Edited by Erhard Blum, Christain Macholz, and Ekkehard W. Stegemann. Neukirchen-Vluyn: Neukirchner Verlag, 1990.

Rost, Leonard. *Die Überlieferung von der Thronnachfolge Davids*. BWANT 42. Stuttgart: Kohlhammer, 1926.

Schenker, Adrian. "Jeroboam and the Division of the Kingdom in the Ancient Septuagint: LXX 3 Kingdoms 12.24 A–Z, MT 1 Kings 11–12; 14 and the Deuteronomistic History." Pages 214–57 in *Israel Constructs Its History: Deuteronomistic Historiography in Recent Research*. Edited by Albert de Pury, Thomas Römer, and Jean-Daniel Maacchi. JSOTSup 306. Sheffield: Sheffield Academic, 2000.

Schmitz, Barbara. *Prophetie und Königtum: Eine narratologisch-historische Methodologie entwickelt an den Königsbüchern*. FAT 60. Tübingen: Mohr Siebeck, 2008.

Seebass, Horst. "Zur Königserhebung Jerobeams I." *VT* 17 (1967): 325–33.

Seeligmann, Isac L. "Menschliches Heldentum und göttliche Hilfe: Die doppelte Kausalität im alttestamentlichen Geschichtsdenken." Pages 137–59 in *Gesammelte Studien zur Hebräischen Bibel, mit einem Beitrag von Rudolf Smend*. Edited by Erhard Blum. FAT 40. Tübingen: Mohr Siebeck, 2004.

Sweeney, Marvin A. *I and II Kings: A Commentary*. OTL. Louisville: Westminster John Knox, 2007

Talshir, Zipora. *The Alternative Story of the Division of the Kingdom*. JBS 6. Jerusalem: Simor, 1993.

Thomas, Benjamin D. *Hezekiah and the Compositional History of the Book of Kings*. FAT 2/63. Tübingen: Mohr Siebeck, 2014.

Toews, Wesley I. *Monarchy and Religious Institution in Israel under Jeroboam I*. SBLMS 47. Atlanta: Scholars Press, 1993.

Trebolle-Barrera, Julio C. *Salomón y Jeroboán: Historia de la recensión de 1 Reyes 2–12;14*. Bibliotheca Salmanticensis, Dissertationes 3. Salamanca: Universidad Pontificia, 1980.

Ueberschaer, Frank. *Vom Gründungsmythos zur Untergangssymphonie: Eine text- und literargeschichtliche Untersuchung zu 1 Kön 11–14.* BZAW 481. Berlin: de Gruyter, 2015.

Weingart, Kristin. "Juda als Sachwalter Israels: Geschichtstheologie nach dem Ende des Nordreiches in Hos 13 und Ps 78." *ZAW* 127 (2015): 440–58.

———. *Stämmevolk—Staatsvolk—Gottesvolk? Studien zur Verwendung des Israel-Namens im Alten Testament.* FAT 2/68. Tübingen: Mohr Siebeck, 2014.

Weippert, Helga. "Die Ätiologie des Nordreiches und seines Königshauses (1 Reg 11 29–40)." *ZAW* 95 (1983): 344–75.

Wellhausen, Julius. *Die Composition des Hexateuchs und der historischen Bücher des Alten Testaments.* 4th ed. Berlin: de Gruyter, 1963.

Willi-Plein, Ina. "Nach deinen Zelten, Israel! Grammatik, Pragmatik und eine kritische Episode der Davidshausgeschichte." *ZAH* 17/20 (2004/2007): 218–29.

Würthwein, Ernst. *Die Bücher der Könige: 1. Kön. 17–2. Kön. 25.* ATD 11.2. Göttingen: Vandenhoeck & Ruprecht, 1984.

———. *Das erste Buch der Könige: Kapitel 1–16.* ATD 11.1. Göttingen: Vandenhoeck & Ruprecht, 1977.

Benjamin in Retrospective: Stages in the Creation of the Territory of the Benjamin Tribe

Oded Lipschits

There is a longstanding scholarly debate about the affiliation of the territory of Benjamin and its relations with the kingdom of Israel to its north and the kingdom of Judah to its south. Because the material culture of this territory in the Iron Age I–IIA cannot be used for this purpose and since Benjamin's connections to Judah in the Iron Age IIB are clear, the main debate has focused on the interpretation of the biblical text.[1] According to Nadav Na'aman and Omer Sergi, following historians and biblical scholars, Jerusalem ruled over almost all the land of Benjamin throughout the First Temple period, with the exception of the Jericho-Gilgal-Michmash area, and the line between Jericho, Bethel, Beth-horon, and Gezer served as the border between the kingdoms of Israel and Judah.[2] Israel Finkelstein,

---

1. For Iron I–IIA, see Israel Finkelstein, "Saul, Benjamin and the Emergence of Biblical Israel: An Alternative View," *ZAW* 123 (2011): 360; Omer Sergi, "The Emergence of Judah as a Political Entity between Jerusalem and Benjamin," *ZDPV* 133 (2017): 8–12, with further literature. For Iron IIB, see Nadav Na'aman, "Saul, Benjamin and the Emergence of 'Biblical Israel,'" *ZAW* 121 (2009): 216–17, with further literature; Finkelstein, "Saul, Benjamin," 350–51. On the role of Benjamin in the stamped jar administration of the late eighth and seventh centuries BCE, see Oded Lipschits, *The Age of Empires: History and Administration in Judah in Light of the Stamped Jar Handles* [Hebrew] (Jerusalem: Yad Ben-Zvi, 2018), with further literature (and see below).

2. Nadav Na'aman, "Canaanite Jerusalem and Its Central Hill Country Neighbors in the Second Millennium B.C.E.," *UF* 24 (1992): 286; Na'aman, "The Contribution of the Amarna Letters to the Debate on Jerusalem's Political Position in the Tenth Century B.C.E.," *BASOR* 304 (1996): 20; Na'aman, "Jerusalem in the Amarna Period," in *Jérusalem Antique et Médiévale: Mélanges en L'honneur d'Ernest-Marie Laperrousaz*,

on the other hand, argues that throughout the Middle and Late Bronze Ages the Benjamin plateau was affiliated with the territory of Shechem in the northern hill country, and that in the early Iron Age (eleventh–tenth centuries BCE), the area was part of a highland polity that preceded the kingdom of Israel. According to Finkelstein, it continued to be ruled by the Israelite kingdom in the ninth–eighth centuries BCE and only in the second half of the eighth century BCE, after the fall of Samaria, was it annexed to Judah.[3] Philip Davies also claimed that the district of Benjamin was part of the territory of Israel from the ninth century BCE and that Sargon II handed it over to Judah following his conquest and annexation of Samaria in 720 BCE.[4] Ernst A. Knauf has similarly suggested that the

---

ed. Caroline Arnould-Béha and André Lemaire, CREJ 52 (Paris: Peeters, 2011), 41; Naʾaman, "Saul, Benjamin," 218–19. See also Omer Sergi, "Judah's Expansion in Historical Context," *TA* 40 (2013): 226–46; Sergi, "State Formation, Religion and 'Collective Identity' in the Southern Levant," *HBAI* 4 (2015): 56–77; Sergi, "Emergence of Judah," 11–12; Sergi, "The United Monarchy and the Kingdom of Jeroboam II in the Story of Absalom and Sheba's Revolts (2 Samuel 15–20)," *HBAI* 6 (2017): 344–47; Sergi, "Rethinking Israel and the Kingdom of Saul," in *Rethinking Israel: Studies in the History and Archaeology of Ancient Israel in Honor of Israel Finkelstein*, ed. Oded Lipschits, Yuval Gadot, and Matthew J. Adams (Winona Lake, IN: Eisenbrauns, 2017), 371–88. For historians and biblical scholars, see, e.g., Klaus-Dietrich Schunck, *Benjamin: Untersuchungen zur Entstehung und Geschichte eines israelitischen Stammes*, BZAW 86 (Berlin: Töpelmann, 1963), 139–69; Otto Eissfeldt, "Der geschichtliche Hintergrund der Erzählung von Gibeas Schandtat (Richter 19–21)," in *Kleine Schriften 2* (Tübingen: Mohr Siebeck, 1963), 64–80; R. Brinker, *The Influence of Sanctuaries in Early Israel* (Manchester: Manchester University Press, 1946), 145–46.

3. Israel Finkelstein, "The Territorial-Political System of Canaan in the Late Bronze Age," *UF* 28 (1996): 234–35; Finkelstein, "The Last Labayu: King Saul and the Expansion of the First North Israelite Territorial Entity," in *Essays on Ancient Israel in Its Near Eastern Context: A Tribute to Nadav Naʾaman*, ed. Yairah Amit et al. (Winona Lake, IN: Eisenbrauns, 2006), 171–87; Finkelstein, "Saul, Benjamin," 351–52; Finkelstein, *The Forgotten Kingdom: The Archaeology and History of Northern Israel*, ANEM 5 (Atlanta: Society of Biblical Literature, 2013), 37–61.

4. Philip R. Davies, "The Origin of Biblical Israel," in Amit, *Essays on Ancient Israel*, 141–48; Davies, *The Origins of Biblical Israel*, LHBOTS 485 (London: T&T Clark, 2007), 105–26; Davies, "The Trouble with Benjamin," in *Reflection and Refraction: Studies in Biblical Historiography in Honour of A. Graeme Auld*, ed. Robert Rezetko, Timothy Limm, and W. Brian Aucker, VTSup 113 (Leiden: Brill, 2007), 93–111, esp. 103. Against this theory, see Naʾaman, "Saul, Benjamin," 339; Naʾaman, "Does Archaeology Really Deserve the Status of A 'High Court' in Biblical and Historical Research?," in *Between Evidence and Ideology: Essays on the History of Ancient*

territory of Benjamin, including the city of Bethel, was handed over to Judah during the reign of Manasseh as a reward for his longstanding loyalty to Assyria.[5]

In this paper I make the claim that the biblical territory of the tribe of Benjamin is a late and artificial aggregation of two distinct historical and geopolitical units, which throughout the second and first millennia—until the late seventh and early sixth centuries BCE—were never part of the same geopolitical region. The original territory of the Benjamin tribe was the territory of the southern tribe of the northern entity (Shechem in the Middle and Late Bronze Ages and the kingdom of Israel in the Iron Age II). The nucleus territory of this tribe included the hilly region of the southeastern Ephraim hills, the Bethel mountain and the area to its east, all the way down to the environs of Jericho.[6] This area has always been connected to the Samaria hills to its north and was geographically disconnected from the plateau to its south and southwest.

The wide plains to the north and west of Jerusalem are the immediate agricultural hinterland of the city, with Nebi Samwil and Khirbet el-Burj (biblical Beeroth) in the west, el-Jib (biblical Gibeon) and Tell en-Naṣbeh (biblical Mizpah) in the north, and the area on either side of the watershed to the east. This area was always an essential part of the polity in the central hill country (the MB and LB kingdom of Jerusalem and the Iron Age kingdom of Judah), since it is unique in its geographical characteristics, with

---

Israel Read at the Joint Meeting of the Society for Old Testament Study and the Oud Testamentisch Werkgezelschap, Lincoln, July 2009, ed. Bob Becking and Lester L. Grabbe, OTS 59 (Leiden: Brill, 2010), 165–83.

5. Ernst Axel Knauf, "Bethel: The Israelite Impact on Judean Language and Literature," in *Judah and the Judeans in the Persian Period*, ed. Oded Lipschits and Manfred Oeming (Winona Lake, IN: Eisenbrauns, 2006), 295–97, 314–16. Against this idea, see Na'aman "Saul, Benjamin," 339; Na'aman, "Does Archaeology Really Deserve."

6. In Judg 1:22–26 Bethel was assigned to Ephraim, and see, e.g., Hans-Jürgen Zobel, *Stammesspruch und Geschichte: Die Angaben der Stammessprüche von Gen 49, Dtn 33 und Jdc 5 über die politischen und kultischen Zustände im damaligen "Israel,"* BZAW 95 (Berlin: Töpelmann, 1965), 108–12, who dates this passage to the time of the judges, shortly after the composition of the Song of Deborah. See, however, Joseph Blenkinsopp, "Bethel in the Neo-Babylonian Period," in *Judah and the Judeans in the Neo-Babylonian Period*, ed. Oded Lipschits and Joseph Blenkinsopp (Winona Lake, IN: Eisenbrauns, 2003), 93–107. Bethel was in the territory of Benjamin according to Josh 18:22, and in the territory of Ephraim according to 1 Chr 7:28, and was situated on the southern boundary between Ephraim and Benjamin according to Josh 16:1–2; 18:13.

fertile land in the midst of the Judean hills.[7] The grain cultivated in these plains and the olive groves and vineyards nearby were an important source of agricultural supply and an essential part of the city's close hinterland throughout its existence.

This northern agricultural hinterland of Jerusalem could not have been united with the original territory of the Benjamin tribe to its northeast before the very late Iron Age and probably mainly during the sixth and early fifth centuries BCE (the exilic and early postexilic periods), when this area became a unified administrative region, the "district of Mizpah" (Neh 3:7, 15, 19).[8] The 720 BCE destruction of the kingdom of Israel was the historical point of departure for a long process, during which the original territory of the Benjamin tribe could be severed from the north. It was the first time in the history of the hill country that the north was weaker than the south and the first point in history when the leaders of Jerusalem could unite the northern agricultural hinterland of Jerusalem with the region between Bethel and Jericho to its north and northeast. During this period, after the loss of the Shephelah due to the post-701 BCE Assyrian arrangements, the Gibeon plain became much more important for the Judahite economy, as is evident from the stamped storage-jar handles uncovered (and see below).[9]

The unification of the agricultural hinterland of the Gibeon-Mizpah plain and the original territory of the Benjamin tribe was probably completed during the 620s, in the days of Josiah and after the Assyrian withdrawal from the Levant and the cancellation of all the Assyrian geopolitical measures, including the borders between the province of Samaria and the vassal Judahite kingdom. It was only during this period that Josiah could establish his rule over the Jericho-Bethel line and expand his northern border.[10] It was the first time in history that these

---

7. Na'aman, "Canaanite Jerusalem," 275–91. See also Sergi, "State Formation," 56–77; Sergi, "Emergence of Judah," 1–23.

8. Unless otherwise noted, all translations are mine.

9. Oded Lipschits, Omer Sergi, and Ido Koch, "Royal Judahite Jar Handles: Reconsidering the Chronology of the *lmlk* Stamp Impressions," *TA* 37 (2010): 21; Lipschits, *Age of Empires*, 124, 243–53.

10. As already claimed by Albrecht Alt, "Judas Gaue unter Josia," *PJb* 21 (1925): 106–112; see Nadav Na'aman, "The Kingdom of Judah under Josiah," *TA* 18 (1991): 33–60. See also Daniel E. Fleming, *The Legacy of Israel in Judah's Bible: History, Politics, and the Reinscribing of Tradition* (Cambridge: Cambridge University Press, 2012), 159–61.

two regions united under a single political power and one administrative unit. From the perspective of Jerusalem, however, the two regions maintained their separate identities, as portrayed in the book of Joshua: the Jericho-Bethel region was described as Canaanite territory conquered by the Israelites (Josh 6:8), while the Gibeon plain was called "Gibeonite" in the royal historiography (Josh 9) and the people living there labeled foreigners.[11] In this period the status of the area declined, along with its importance to the Judahite economy: the renewed activity of Judah in the Shephelah led to a diminished need for agricultural supply from the area of Gibeon. Na'aman associated the decline in the status of Gibeon and Benjamin with Josiah's reform (2 Kgs 23), in which he abolished the sanctuary of Gibeon.[12] It was probably the first period in the history of Jerusalem when hostile attitudes were directed against the agricultural hinterland north of the city.

The Babylonian designation of Mizpah as capital of the province of Judah following the 586 BCE destruction of Jerusalem made it, for the first time in the history of the region north of Jerusalem, of greater political and economic importance than Jerusalem.[13] During this period and probably within the framework of the new Babylonian arrangements, Jerusalem was completely isolated from its agricultural hinterland, with the establishment of the district of Beth-hakkerem to the south and southwest of Jerusalem (with Ramat Raḥel in its center) and the district of Mizpah to the north and northwest of the city. It was the first time that the entire region of greater Benjamin could be united as an administrative unit, with Jerusalem serving a marginal role on its southern border. This is the region whose borders were delineated in the tribal allotments (Josh 18:11–20; cf. Josh 15:6–10; 16:1–3, 5), a description that cannot reflect any period in the history of the region prior to 620 BCE or after the renewal of the status of Jerusalem in the early Persian period.

---

11. It is noteworthy that in Isa 10:28–32, too, all the sites mentioned lie in the region of the Jerusalemite agricultural hinterland (= the border of the kingdom of Judah).

12. Na'aman, "Saul, Benjamin," 116.

13. Oded Lipschits, *The Fall and Rise of Jerusalem: The History of Judah under Babylonian Rule* (Winona Lake, IN: Eisenbrauns, 2005), 97–126; Lipschits, "The Rural Economy of Judah during the Persian Period and the Settlement History of the District System," in *The Economy of Ancient Judah in Its Historical Context*, ed. Martin Lloyd Miller, Ehud Ben Zvi, and Gary N. Knoppers (Winona Lake, IN: Eisenbrauns, 2015), 237–64.

The conclusion to be derived from the above is that the biblical territory of the tribe of Benjamin is an artificial construct, combining the original territory of the Benjamin tribe with the agricultural hinterland of Jerusalem to the north and west of the city. This newly established unified territory gained its independent existence after the destruction of Jerusalem. Mizpah became the capital of the province under Babylonian rule, probably until the mid-fifth century BCE.[14]

1. Geopolitical Considerations: The Borders between the Geopolitical Entities in the Hill Country in the Second and First Millennia BCE

Three main geopolitical centers existed in the hill country in the second millennium BCE.[15] The historical and archaeological data points to the kingdom of Shechem as the larger and more densely populated entity, with more fertile agricultural lands and greater proximity to the rich valleys and prominent cities and roads. It controlled the northern hill country, extended north as far as the Jezreel Valley, east to the Gilead, and southwest to Gezer. These are precisely the borders of the kingdom of Israel prior to its expansion in the days of the Omride dynasty. In many ways, the kingdom of Israel of the first millennium BCE is the direct consequence and continuation of the Labaya kingdom of Shechem in the Late Bronze Age.[16] The natural southern border of the northern geopolitical units—both of Shechem of the second millennium and Israel of the first millennium—lay in the southern Ephraim hills, including the hilly region

---

14. See Oded Lipschits, "Achaemenid Imperial Policy, Settlement Processes in Palestine, and the Status of Jerusalem in the Middle of the Fifth Century B.C.E.," in Lipschits and Oeming, *Judah and the Judeans in the Persian Period*, 34–35.

15. See Na'aman, "Canaanite Jerusalem," 280–88; Oded Lipschits, Thomas Römer, and Hervé Gonzalez, "The Pre-Priestly Abraham-Narratives from Monarchic to Persian Times," *Sem* 59 (2017): 261–96; Oded Lipschits, "Abraham zwischen Mamre und Jerusalem" in *The Politics of the Ancestors: Exegetical and Historical Perspectives on Genesis 12–36*, ed. Mark G. Brett and Jakob Wöhrle, FAT 124 (Tübingen: Mohr Siebeck, 2018), 189–94.

16. Finkelstein, "Last Labayu," 171–77; Finkelstein, "The Sociopolitical Organization of the Central Hill Country in the Second Millennium B.C.E.," in *Biblical Archaeology Today, 1990: Proceedings of the Second International Congress on Biblical Archaeology; Supplement; Pre-Congress Symposium; Population, Production and Power, Jerusalem June 1990*, ed. Avraham Biran and Joseph Aviram (Jerusalem: Israel Exploration Society, 1993), 110–31; Finkelstein, "Territorial-Political System," 221–55.

of Mount Baal Hazor, the area of Bethel, and eastward as far as Jericho. It was probably also the border of the kingdom of Israel until its destruction by the Assyrians in 720 BCE.

The kingdom of Jerusalem was much smaller and less active, and the main scholarly debate concerns the territory ruled by this hilly fortress during the second millennium BCE.[17] It is difficult to accept the reconstruction of Zechariah Kallai and Haim Tadmor, followed by Finkelstein, who suggested that Jerusalem ruled the entire southern hill country, as far as the Beersheba–Arad Valley, including the Hebron hills.[18] Na'aman, following Albrecht Alt, reconstructed a very small city-state that ruled its immediate territory only, from the Gibeon plateau in the north to the Rephaim Valley and the Bethlehem area in the south.[19] Following this reconstruction, it seems quite clear that the traditional borders of the kingdom of Jerusalem were small and that Jerusalem itself was an isolated fort that controlled a sparsely populated area, probably with only a few Habiru groups and seminomadic clans roaming its territory.[20] The close hinterland around the city was its only source of agricultural supply, and indeed, the city could not exist without close ties and control over the relatively limited agricultural and human resources of these areas.

The history of Jerusalem in the tenth–ninth centuries BCE, for example, cannot be understood without considering its rule over the nearby areas to its north, west, and south.[21] In this period Jerusalem was the most developed urban center in the region, with well-built fortifications

---

17. Na'aman, "Canaanite Jerusalem," 257–91; Finkelstein, "Sociopolitical Organization," 110–31.

18. Zechariah Kallai and Haim Tadmor, "Bit-Ninurta = Beth-Horon: On the History of the Kingdom of Jerusalem in the Amarna Period" [Hebrew], ErIsr 9 (1969): 138–47; followed by Finkelstein, "Sociopolitical Organization," 110–31; Finkelstein, "Territorial-Political System," 228–29, 234–35, 255.

19. Na'aman, "Canaanite Jerusalem," 275–91; Na'aman, " Contribution of the Amarna Letters," 17–27; Na'aman, "Jerusalem in the Amarna Period," 31–48. Albrecht Alt, *Die Landnahme der Israeliten in Palästina—territorialgeschichtliche Studien* (Leipzig: Druckerei der Werkgemeinschaft, 1925); Alt, "Der Stadtstaat Samaria," in *Kleine Schriften zur Geschichte des Volkes Israel 3* (Munich: Beck, 1959), 258–302.

20. Na'aman, "Canaanite Jerusalem," 280–88; Lipschits, Römer, and Gonzalez, "Pre-Priestly Abraham-Narratives," 275–83; Lipschits, "Abraham zwischen Mamre und Jerusalem," 189–94.

21. See, e.g., Na'aman, "Saul, Benjamin," 217–18; Sergi, "State Formation," 56–77; Sergi, "Emergence of Judah," 1–23.

and structures, demonstrating that it was a well-organized political entity (even on a small scale), and the agricultural hinterland around it must have provided support in the form of necessities and manpower.[22] From this perspective, the dating of the establishment of the border between Israel and Judah as described in 1 Kgs 15:16–22 and as suggested by the conventional interpretation of the archaeological finds in Tell en-Naṣbeh (biblical Mizpah) seems to be reasonable.[23]

In the Middle Bronze Age, Hebron was the main urban center in the southern hill country. The site was destroyed at some unknown point and was probably abandoned during the Late Bronze Age, when the main urban center of the south was at Khirbet Rabûd, identified as biblical Debir. This area was the heart of local clans that later developed into the tribe of Judah.[24] According to archaeological surveys conducted in the Judean hills, during the Late Bronze Age II, the area between Jerusalem and Khirbet Rabûd (some 40 km apart) was uninhabited and the two fortified towns in the mountains were geographically set apart. Biblical traditions of the early history of Israel also consistently separated Jerusalem from the southern hill country of Judah.[25] The integration of the

---

22. E.g., Sergi, "State Formation," 56–77; Sergi, "Emergence of Judah," 1–23. It is hard to accept Israel Finkelstein's attempt to underestimate the archaeological finds in the City of David (e.g., "Jerusalem and the Benjamin Plateau in the Early Phases of the Iron Age: A Different Scenario," *ZDPV* 134 [2018]: 190–95), as part of his general conception of Judah, its material culture, history, and scribing traditions in the period before the late eighth century BCE, when "waves" of Israelite refugees came to Jerusalem with their memories and texts, high culture, traditions, skills, and wide knowledge.

23. See Jeffrey R. Zorn, "Estimating the Population Size of Ancient Settlements: Methods, Problems, Solutions and a Case Study," *BASOR* 295 (1994): 34–46; Mordechai Cogan, *1 Kings: A New Translation with Introduction and Commentary*, AB 10 (New York: Doubleday, 2001), 399–404; Sergi, "State Formation," 56–77; Sergi, "Emergence of Judah," 1–23. It is hard to see the biblical description as a simple anachronism, as claimed by Davies, *Origins*, 93–111, or to see it as an etiological story reinforced by events in the eighth century BCE, as claimed by Israel Finkelstein, "The Great Wall of Tell en-Nasbeh (Mizpah), the First Fortifications in Judah, and 1 Kgs 15:16–22," *VT* 62 (2012): 14–28. Cf. Na'aman, "Saul, Benjamin," 217–18.

24. See summary and further literature in Lipschits, Römer, and Gonzalez, "Pre-Priestly Abraham-Narratives," 275–83; Lipschits, "Abraham zwischen Mamre und Jerusalem," 189–94.

25. See also Hermann Michael Niemann, "Juda und Jerusalem: Überlegungen zum Verhältnis von Stamm und Stadt und zur Rolle Jerusalems in Juda," *UF* 47 (2016): 175–76.

southern territory into the kingdom of Jerusalem, the establishment of the kingdom of Judah, and the later integration of the lowland into that kingdom, probably in the second half of the ninth century BCE, were the most important achievements of the Davidic kings.[26]

From the establishment of the kingdom of Judah until the Babylonian exile, the city of Jerusalem was the center of a kingdom that spanned a tremendous area, stretching far beyond the Judean hills. In the kingdom's administrative framework, however, Jerusalem was the center of a small district (described as "the environs of Jerusalem" סביבי/סביבות ירושלים), while the hill country of Judah was a large separate district termed "the mountain" (ההר).[27] The former may be associated with the growth of towns, villages, hamlets, and agricultural installations to the north, west, and south of Jerusalem in the late eighth and especially the seventh century BCE.[28] It may be assumed that the "environs of Jerusalem" were divided by the Babylonians into three administrative units after the destruction of Jerusalem: the main devastation occurred in and near the city, whereas the

---

26. See Lipschits, Römer, and Gonzalez, "Pre-Priestly Abraham-Narratives," 275–83; Lipschits, "Abraham zwischen Mamre und Jerusalem," 189–94. Geographically, this unification was *not* natural to this region. Note that the unification of these two territories is described in the books of Samuel as a conquest of Jerusalem by the tribal leader of Judah from his center in Hebron, and this conquest was only part of David's long struggle against the leading families of the region around Jerusalem and to the north of the city.

27. See Na'aman, "Kingdom of Judah under Josiah," 13–16. This is probably the source for the distinction drawn by Jeremiah (17:26; 32:44; 33:13) between "the cities of Judah" and "the cities of the mountain" in the division of the areas of the kingdom into six regions.

28. See Lipschits, "Rural Economy," 242–45, with further literature. Yuval Gadot, "In the Valley of the King: Jerusalem's Rural Hinterland in the Eighth–Fourth Centuries BCE," *TA* 42 (2015): 3–26, makes it clear that the main development of this area was during the seventh century and not in the eighth century BCE, as previously assumed. Following Albrecht Alt, "Die Rolle Samarias bei der Entstehung des Judentums," in *Kleine Schriften zur Geschichte des Volkes Israel 2* (Munich: Beck, 1953), 324–28 (and also Na'aman, "Kingdom of Judah under Josiah," 15–16), the "cities of Judah" can be identified with the area to the south and west of Jerusalem, down to the Bethlehem region and should be viewed as evidence of the distinction between the area surrounding Jerusalem and the area to its south. The region known as "the environs of Jerusalem" is also described in Jer 40–42 as the area where Gedaliah the son of Ahiqam was active after the destruction of Jerusalem by the Babylonians. See Lipschits, *Fall and Rise of Jerusalem*, 152–54.

areas to its north (Benjamin, the district of Mizpah) and south (to the west and south of Ramat Raḥel, the district of Beth-hakkerem) continued to exist as before.[29] This was the historical period when the area around Jerusalem severed from it and became an independent district (the district of Jerusalem) and the area to its south became the district of Beth-hakkerem, with the Rephaim Valley at its core and Ramat Raḥel as its main administrative center.[30]

This geopolitical situation might have preserved the pre-Davidic nature of this area. In biblical traditions on the early history of Israel, Jerusalem (Jebus) is consistently disconnected from the hill country of Judah. It should be borne in mind that according to the biblical record, David's family lived within the territory of the kingdom of Jerusalem, in close proximity to the city itself—far from the tribal territory of Judah in the Hebron hills. From the stories on his early career, however, it is clear that David understood that the clans of Judah could give him the support he needed against Saul and the elite of the kingdom of Jerusalem. He continued to send them gifts and assist them (see, e.g., 1 Sam 30:26). The support of the elders of Judah led them to ask David to become their leader prior to the conquest of Jerusalem and the establishment of the Davidic kingdom.[31]

According to the biblical tradition, the territory of Saul had been in the northern agricultural hinterland of the kingdom of Jerusalem. Following his death, the areas of the kingdom of Jerusalem and that of Hebron/

---

29. See Lipschits, *Fall and Rise of Jerusalem*, 206–18, 237–58. As indicated in the list of Neh 3, and as mentioned again at the beginning of the list of "the sons of the singers" (Neh 12:28–29), the area around Jerusalem was separated and became an independent district (the district of Jerusalem).

30. On the identification of Ramat Raḥel as the biblical Beth-hakkerem, see Oded Lipschits and Nadav Na'aman, "From 'Baal Perazim' to 'Beth-Hakkerem'—On the Ancient Name of Ramat-Rahel" [Hebrew], *Beth-Miqra* 56 (2011): 65–86; Oded Lipschits et al., *What Are the Stones Whispering? Three Thousand Years of Forgotten History at Ramat Rahel* (Winona Lake, IN: Eisenbrauns, 2017), 15–18.

31. See the historical reconstruction of Nadav Na'aman, "David's Sojourn in Keilah in Light of the Amarna Letters," *VT* 60 (2010): 87–97. In this case, the stories of David as the leader of a Habiru group who became the leader of a tribal territory is similar to that of Jephtha in the book of Judges. According to this reconstruction, it is hard to accept the definition of Na'aman ("Saul, Benjamin," 342) that Saul was a Benjaminite and David was a Judahite. It is also hard to accept the understanding of the term "Israel" in these stories, as suggested by Sergi ("Emergence of Judah," 1–23), even if his reconstruction of the events is justified. On this subject, see further below.

Debir were united under the leadership of David, whose center of power was at Hebron. Jerusalem is presented in the narrative of David's rise to power as a town with a foreign population—the Jebusites—just as the agricultural hinterland to the north of the city was portrayed as foreign Hivite territory (Josh 9).[32]

The above description shows that the Davidic dynasty managed to unite the two southern regions of the hill country and to establish a single kingdom there, named after the southern part of its territory. We should assume that the agricultural land lying to the north and west of Jerusalem was also part of it. However, shortly after the destruction of Jerusalem by the Babylonians, the deportation of the Jerusalemite elite, and the removal of the Davidic kings from all their holdings, these regions became two separate geopolitical units again. The former land of the kingdom of Jerusalem now became the Babylonian-Persian province of Yehud, and the former land of the tribe of Judah became part of the province of Idumaea.

2. Benjamin as a Northern Tribe

The name Benjamin ("the son of the south") must have originated as a tribal name, when the Benjaminites were the southernmost tribe that settled in the central hill country.[33] In the biblical genealogy, Joseph (Gen 30:22–24) and Benjamin (35:16–18) are presented as sons of Jacob, maternal brothers.[34] As described in old sources originating from the Northern Kingdom, as long as the kingdom of Israel existed, it included the "core territory of Benjamin" located in the southeastern periphery of the kingdom, on its border with Judah, with Bethel in its center and Jericho as its

---

32. See Nadav Na'aman, "Jebusites and Jabeshites in the Saul and David Story-Cycles," *Bib* 95 (2014): 481–97.

33. See also Schunck, *Benjamin*, 15; Thomas L. Thompson, *The Historicity of the Patriarchal Narratives: The Quest for the Historical Abraham*, BZAW 133 (Berlin: de Gruyter, 1974), 59–60; Na'aman, "Saul, Benjamin," 337.

34. See Heinz-Dieter Neef, *Ephraim: Studien zur Geschichte des Stammes Ephraim von der Landnahme bis zur frühen Königszeit*, BZAW 238 (Berlin: de Gruyter, 1995), with further literature. It is hard to accept views such as Yigal Levin's ("Joseph, Judah and the 'Benjamin Conundrum,'" *ZAW* 116 [2004]: 223–41), who claims that the Joseph narrative in Genesis received its final form sometime after the split of the monarchy, in an effort to explain the continued inclusion of the formerly northern tribe of Benjamin within the kingdom of Judah.

southeastern border.[35] This is the territory of Benjamin as described in the story of "Ehud the son of Gera, a Benjaminite" (Judg 3:12–30).[36] It is probably also "the land of the Benjaminites" mentioned in Saul's search for the asses (1 Sam 9:4), the land of "Shimei the son of Gera, the Benjaminite who was from Bahurim" (2 Sam 19:17; cf. 16:5; 1 Kgs 2:8), and the reason that the Benjaminite Shimei ben Gera presented himself to David as "the first of all the house of Joseph" (2 Sam 19:21)—namely, belonging to Israel.[37] This is the background for the appearance of Benjamin among the northern tribes in the Song of Deborah (Judg 5:14), and as part of Ishbaal's kingdom (2 Sam 2:8–9).[38] The understanding of the location of the "original territory of the Benjamin tribe" is also key to an understanding of the story of Sheba son of Bichri (2 Sam 20). In 20:1 Sheba is described as a Benjaminite, but in 20:21 Joab describes him as one who originated from Mount Ephraim. Scholars generally describe it as two separate regions, but if the territory of Benjamin included Mount Bethel and parts of Mount Ephraim, this text could be interpreted in the same way as the description regarding Ehud, another Benjaminite, who, after killing Eglon in Jericho, escaped to Seir on Mount Ephraim (Judg 3:26–27).[39] This text may also account for Jer 4:15, which places Bethel on Mount Ephraim.[40] The

---

35. Cf. the story of the conquest of Bethel in Judg 1:22–26.

36. Naʾaman, "Saul, Benjamin," 219–20, with further literature.

37. On the identification of the region in 1 Sam 9:4, see already Zeev H. Ehrlich, "The Land of Benjamin," in *"Before Ephraim and Benjamin and Manasseh": Studies and Discoveries in Historical Geography*, ed. Z. H. Ehrlich (Jerusalem: Benjamin Regional Municipality, 1985), 50–51. For Shimei, see Naʾaman, "Saul, Benjamin," 336–37, with further literature. See also Kristin Weingart, *Stämmevolk—Staatsvolk—Gottesvolk? Studien zur Verwendung des Israel-Namens im Alten Testament*, FAT 2/68 (Tübingen: Mohr Siebeck, 2014), 186–87. It is hard, however, to accept Weingart's opinion that already in the early monarchical period, the name Israel was used for both the Northern Kingdom and for the inhabitants of the kingdom of Judah (and see below).

38. On the period of the insertion of Judg 5:14–17, see André Caquot, "Les tribus d'Israël dans le cantique de Débora (Juges 5, 13–17)," *Sem* 36 (1986): 54–55; Nadav Naʾaman, "Literary and Topographical Notes on the Battle of Kishon (Judges iv–v)," *VT* 40 (1990): 426.

39. For it as two separate regions, see Nadav Naʾaman, "Habiru and Hebrews: The Transfer of a Social Term to the Literary Sphere," *JNES* 45 (1986): 283–84; Naʾaman, "Sources and Composition in the Story of Sheba's Revolt (2 Samuel 20)," *RB* 125 (2018): 343–44.

40. In contrast to how Naʾaman ("Sources and Composition," 344, 352) understood it.

"original territory of the Benjamin tribe" also refers to the Benjamin of the pre-Priestly Jacob story (Gen 28:10–22; 35:18–20) and the territory that, according to Josh 6:8, was conquered by Joshua and the tribes of Israel (probably reflecting the actual conquest in the days of Josiah; see below).[41] This territory was essential for the Omrides and later for the Nimshides, as reflected in the description on Hiel of Bethel, who fortified the city of Jericho (1 Kgs 16:34), and this is also the region described in the northern prophetic literature as part of the kingdom of Israel (Gilgal, Jericho, and Bethel in the Elisha story in 2 Kgs 2:1–2, 4, 5, 15, 18; 4:38; Bethel and Gilgal in Amos 4:4; 5:5 and in Hosea 4:15; 9:15; 12:5).[42]

41. On the pre-Priestly Jacob story, see Erhard Blum, *Die Komposition der Vätergeschichte*, WMANT 57 (Neukirchen-Vluyn: Neukirchener Verlag, 1984), 207–8; on Gen 28:10–22 as a foundational text for Blum's work, see pp. 7–65. On Blum's "three-level model" as applied to this story, see Erhard Blum, "Noch einmal: Jakobs Traum in Bethel—Genesis 28,10–22," in *Rethinking the Foundations: Historiography in the Ancient World and in the Bible; Essays in Honour of John Van Seters*, ed. Steven L. McKenzie and Thomas Römer, BZAW 294 (Berlin: de Gruyter, 2000), 33–54. Cf. also Blum, "The Jacob Tradition," in *The Book of Genesis: Composition, Reception, and Interpretation*, ed. Craig A. Evans, Joel N. Lohr, and David L. Petersen, VTSup 152 (Leiden: Brill, 2012), 208–9; David M. Carr, *Reading the Fractures of Genesis: Historical and Literary Approaches* (Louisville: Westminster John Knox, 1996), 260–61; Carr, "Genesis 28,10–22 and Transmission-Historical Method: A Reply to John Van Seters," *ZAW* 111 (1999): 399–403. See also Koog P. Hong, "The Deceptive Pen of Scribes: Judean Reworking of the Bethel Tradition as a Program for Assuming Israelite Identity," *Bib* 92 (2011): 430–36, with further literature. See, however, the different date and origin of this story as claimed by Van Seters and Na'aman. See John Van Seters, *Prologue to History: The Yahwist as Historian in Genesis* (Louisville: Westminster John Knox), 293–94; Van Seters, "Divine Encounter at Bethel (Gen 28,10–22) in Recent Literary-Critical Study of Genesis," *ZAW* 110 (1998): 503–13; see also Nadav Na'aman, "The Jacob Story and the Formation of Biblical Israel," *TA* 41 (2014): 95–125.

42. See the scholarly attempt to describe 1 Kgs 16:34 as a redactional gloss or a later editorial interpolation, and see, e.g., Stefan Timm, *Die Dynastie Omri: Quellen und Untersuchungen zur Geschichte Israels im 9. Jahrhundert vor Christus*, FRLANT 124 (Göttingen: Vandenhoeck & Ruprecht, 1982), 55; Susanne Otto, "The Composition of the Elijah-Elisha Stories and the Deuteronomistic History," *JSOT* 27 (2003): 503; Charles Conroy, "Hiel between Ahab and Elijah-Elisha: 1 Kgs 16,34 in Its Immediate Literary Context," *Bib* 77 (1996): 217–18. For the northern prophetic literature, see, e.g., the discussion and conclusions of Na'aman ("Saul, Benjamin," 220–21) in Hos 5:8–10, with further literature. I find it difficult to accept the exilic or even postexilic date for these verses, and see, e.g., James M. Bos, *Reconsidering the Date and Provenance of the Book of Hosea: The Case for Persian-Period Yehud*, LHBOTS 580 (London: Bloomsbury T&T Clark, 2013), 53–56, 92–96; Wolfgang Schütte, *Israels Exil in Juda:*

As described above, this area belonged to the kingdom of Israel until the 720 BCE destruction and it could not be annexed by Judah before the withdrawal of the Assyrian Empire from the region "across the river," some one hundred years later. Only then could Judah establish its rule and expand to include the original nucleus of the tribe of Benjamin, conquering the territory up to the Jericho-Bethel line. This historical reconstruction was suggested by Alt, who established the dating of the town list of the four southern tribes of Judah, Benjamin, Simeon, and Dan (Josh 15:21–62; 18:21–28; 19:2–8, 40–46) to the reign of Josiah. According to Alt, in addition to the group of towns that had belonged to Judah for many years (18:25–28), another group (18:21–24) consists of towns that were previously Israelite, such as Bethel, Zemaraim, Ophrah, and Jericho, which had become part of Judah only after the conquest of the region in the reign of Josiah (and see 2 Kgs 23:15–16a).[43]

3. The History of the Core Region of Benjamin and the Agricultural Hinterland of Jerusalem after the Destruction of the Kingdom of Israel

The destruction of the kingdom of Israel marked the beginning of a new period in the hill country: for the first time, the small, hilly southern entity did not have a larger and stronger neighbor on its northern border. For this reason most scholars concur that during the seventh century BCE the land of Benjamin became part of Judah.[44]

It is reasonable to assume that the loss of the Shephelah after the 701 BCE Assyrian campaign, along with the growth of Jerusalem in the late

---

Untersuchungen zur Entstehung der Schriftprophetie, OBO 279 (Fribourg: Academic Press; Göttingen: Vandenhoeck & Ruprecht, 2016), 44–62, with further literature.

43. See Alt, "Judas Gaue," 106–12. For additional arguments for the dating of the list and for further literature, see Na'aman, "Kingdom of Judah under Josiah," 33–60; Na'aman, "Josiah and the Kingdom of Judah," in *Good Kings and Bad Kings: The Kingdom of Judah in the Seventh Century BCE*, ed. Lester L. Grabbe, JSOTSupp 393 (Sheffield: T&T Clark, 2005), 210–33; Na'aman, "The King Leading Cult Reforms in His Kingdom: Josiah and Other Kings in the Ancient Near East," *ZABR* 12 (2006): 131–42; Na'aman, "Saul, Benjamin," 338; Na'aman, "The Israelite-Judahite Struggle for the Patrimony of Ancient Israel," *Bib* 91 (2010): 5, 18–20. It is hard to accept attempts to date the lists to the sixth-fifth centuries BCE, and see, e.g., J. Cornelius de Vos, *Das Los Judas: Über Entstehung und Ziele der Landbeschreibung in Josua 15*, VTSup 95 (Leiden: Brill, 2003).

44. For literature, see above, nn. 3–5.

eighth and the seventh centuries BCE, led to a strengthening of economic relations between Jerusalem and the region around Gibeon, since greater Jerusalem would have required a regular supply of agricultural produce.[45] The grains that grew in the plain, just a few kilometers to the north of Jerusalem, and the nearby olive orchards and vineyards were an important source of this supply. The survey of this region revealed that alongside the main sites in the region, such as Tell en-Naṣbeh, el-Jib, Tell el-Fûl, Khirbet el-Burj, and Nebi Samwil, the rural settlement also demonstrated growth in the late Iron Age.[46]

In terms of the Judahite administration, almost a quarter of the eight hundred storage-jar handles stamped with late *lmlk* impressions and the handles incised with concentric circles were found in the region to the

---

45. See Oded Lipschits and Yuval Gadot, "Ramat Raḥel and the Emeq Rephaim Sites—Links and Interpretations" [Hebrew], in *New Studies in the Archaeology of Jerusalem and Its Region, Collected Papers*, ed. D. Amit and G. D. Stiebel (Jerusalem: New Studies in the Archaeology of Jerusalem and Its Region, 2008), 2:88–96; Gadot, "In the Valley of the King," 3–26.

46. For Tell en-Naṣbeh, see Jeffrey R. Zorn, "Tell en-Naṣbeh: A Re-evaluation of the Architecture and Stratigraphy of the Early Bronze Age, Iron Age and Later Periods" (PhD diss., University of California, Berkeley, 1993), 1099–1101. For el-Jib, see James B. Pritchard, *Gibeon: Where the Sun Stood Still* (Princeton: Princeton University Press, 1962), 162–63. For Tell el-Fûl, see Nancy L. Lapp, *The Third Campaign at Tell el-Ful: The Excavations of 1964*, AASOR 45 (Cambridge: American Schools of Oriental Research, 1978), 39–46; see also Israel Finkelstein, "Tell el-Ful Revisited: The Assyrian and Hellenistic Periods (with a New Identification)," *PEQ* 143 (2011): 106–18; Finkelstein, "Saul, Benjamin," 111–13. For Khirbet el-Burj, see Alon De Groot and Michal Winberger-Stern, "Wine, Oil and Gibeonites: Iron Age II–III at Kh. el-Burj, Northern Jerusalem" [Hebrew], in *New Studies on Jerusalem 19*, ed. Eyal Baruch and Avraham Faust (Ramat Gan: Bar-Ilan University Press, 2013), 95–102. For Nebi Samwil, see Yitzhak Magen and Michael Dadon, "Nebi Samwil (Montjoie)," in *One Land, Many Cultures: Archaeological Studies in Honour of Stanislao Loffreda*, ed. Giovanni C. Bottini, Leah di Segni, and Leslaw D. Chrupcala (Jerusalem: Franciscan Printing Press, 2003), 123–38. For the Neb Samwil's survey data, see Yitzhak Magen and Israel Finkelstein, eds., *Archaeological Survey of the Hill Country of Benjamin* (Jerusalem: Israel Antiquities Authority, 1993). For analyses of the survey finds, see Ianir Milevski, "Settlement Patterns in Northern Judah during the Achaemenid Period, according to the Hill Country of Benjamin and Jerusalem Surveys," *Bulletin of the Anglo-Israel Archaeological Society* 15 (1996–1997): 7–29; Oded Lipschits, "The History of the Benjaminite Region under Babylonian Rule," *TA* 26 (1999): 180–84; Lipschits, *Fall and Rise of Jerusalem*, 245–49.

north of Jerusalem, mainly at el-Jib, Tell en-Naṣbeh, and Khirbet el-Burj.[47] This vast number of early and mid-seventh-century BCE stamped handles leads to the conclusion that during this period the area of Gibeon and Mizpah became, probably for the first time, part of the Judahite administration. Furthermore, the Gibeon plateau was the third most important region of the Judahite administration (after Jerusalem and the Ramat Raḥel area) in the first half of the seventh century BCE (the reign of Manasseh) and perhaps even slightly later, during the 630s and 620s (the early regnal years of Josiah).

The importance of Benjamin in the Judahite administration was fleeting, however: the area lost its centrality in the last phase of the seventh century BCE, as is evident from the discovery of only fifteen rosette-stamped handles (about 7 percent of the corpus) in sites of Benjamin.[48] Since there was no change in the settlement history of this region at the end of the First Temple period and the demographic picture points to continued prosperity, the reason may lie elsewhere. The renewed Judahite activity in the Shephelah probably meant that there was less need for agricultural supply from the area of Gibeon. Thus, the region became less important for the administrative system, and the number of stamped handles resembled the system of early *lmlk* stamp impressions, before the Assyrian military campaign of 701 BCE and the loss of the Shephelah.

This may be the first period in the history of Jerusalem when hostile attitudes were directed against this territory. Na'aman associated the decline in the status of Gibeon and Benjamin with Josiah's reform (2 Kgs 23). In his opinion, Josiah canceled the sanctuary of Gibeon, and the local population was labeled "Gibeonite" in the royal historiography (Josh 9).[49]

---

47. Lipschits, Sergi, and Koch, "Royal Judahite Jar Handles," 21; Lipschits, *Age of Empires*, 124.

48. Ido Koch and Oded Lipschits, "The Rosette Stamped Jar Handle System and the Kingdom of Judah at the End of the First Temple Period," *ZDPV* 129 (2013): 59, 66–67; Lipschits, *Age of Empires*, 124.

49. See Na'aman, "Saul, Benjamin," 116. For scholars who supported the historicity of 2 Kgs 23 events, see, e.g., John Gray, *I and II Kings: A Commentary*, OTL (London: SCM, 1970), 663; W. Boyd Barrick, *The King and the Cemeteries: Toward a New Understanding of Josiah's Reform*, VTSup 88 (Leiden: Brill, 2002), 107–11; Marvin A. Sweeney, *I and II Kings: A Commentary*, OTL (Louisville: Westminster John Knox, 2007), 178–79; Mordechai Cogan and Hayim Tadmor, *2 Kings: A New Translation with Introduction and Commentary*, AB 11 (New York: Doubleday, 1988), 299. See, however, e.g., Juha Pakkala, "Why the Cult Reforms in Judah Probably Did Not Happen,"

The economic focus of King Manasseh on the Gibeon plateau in the early and mid-seventh century BCE was replaced with his grandson Josiah's cultic focus upon the area of Bethel and probably also the region of Jericho, areas that, as previously claimed, constituted the original core of the Israelite tribe of Benjamin. Until this point in the history of the original Benjaminite territory, it could not become part of Judah as long as the Assyrians ruled in the region. Only after their withdrawal, in the early last third of the seventh century BCE, a few years after Josiah came to power in Judah, could he transfer his administrative and economic attention from the Gibeon plateau back to the Shephelah and, at the same time, annex this territory of the original Benjamin to Judah to move the borders of his kingdom several kilometers north to include Jericho and Bethel in his kingdom.[50] By doing so, Josiah established, for the first time in history, the territory of greater Benjamin.

This annexation is reflected in the narratives of the book of Joshua, demonstrating precisely how the Deuteronomist described the conquest of the territory of Benjamin in the days of King Josiah—from Jericho to Ai, near Bethel—drawing a distinction between this area and the territory of the four cities of the Gibeonites in the western side of the plateau, the area that was always part of the kingdom of Jerusalem and became important mainly as a source of agricultural produce: Gibeon, Hakephirah, Beeroth, and Kiriath-jearim. These two areas, which were never part of the same geopolitical unit, thus became a single territory, reflecting the border of the kingdom of Judah in the days of Josiah. The description of this area as belonging to foreigners reflects the polemic attitude toward this region, an attitude that became stronger in the early Persian period (see below).

At the same time, the different fate of the area and the political features that made it distinctive on the eve of and subsequent to the destruction of Jerusalem attest to the fact that the inhabitants of this region preserved their distinctive character within the kingdom of Judah. It was perhaps for this reason that the Benjamin region became the center of the new province

---

in *One God—One Cult—One Nation: Archaeological and Biblical Perspectives*, ed. Reinhard G. Kratz and Hermann Spieckermann, BZAW 405 (Berlin: de Gruyter, 2010), 201–35; Lauren A. S. Monroe, *Josiah's Reform and the Dynamics of Defilement: Israelite Rites of Violence and the Making of a Biblical Text* (Oxford: Oxford University Press, 2011), 23–44.

50. See Alt, "Judas Gaue," 106–12; Na'aman, "Kingdom of Judah under Josiah," 33–60.

under Babylonian rule.[51] It seems that the Babylonian siege on Jerusalem and destruction of the city and—even more importantly—the return of some of the Jerusalem elite to the city in the early Persian period shaped the relations between the people of this new region with this elite, as reflected mainly in historiographical texts from the exilic and postexilic periods.

4. The History of the Core Region of Benjamin under Babylonian and Persian Rule

The core territory of Benjamin continued to differ from the agricultural hinterland of Jerusalem in its settlement pattern, demographic character, and history during and after the destruction of Jerusalem. In contrast to the demographic and settlement stability enjoyed by the region around Mizpah, Gibeon, and Nebi Samwil in the Babylonian and Persian periods and the slow decline toward the end of the Persian period (and see below on the history of the district of Mizpah), the core territory of Benjamin, which had only begun to be densely settled at the end of the Iron Age, completely disappeared from the settlement and demographic maps, probably already in the sixth century BCE.[52]

---

51. See Lipschits, *Fall and Rise of Jerusalem*, 72–112; Lipschits, "Rural Economy," 237–64.

52. For the stability of the Mizpah, Gibeon, and Nebi Samwil areas, see Lipschits, "History of the Benjaminite Region," 155–90. East of Bethel-Michmash-Gibeah-Anathoth, approximately seventy-one sites from Iron Age II were surveyed, as compared with only fourteen sites from the Persian period (a drop of about 80 percent). The major decline in number of sites is in the area between Michmash and the slope running down toward Jericho. In this area, twenty-seven sites from the Iron Age were surveyed, as compared with only one site from the Persian period, which was located in the northern part of the area. It should be noted that the existence of an isolated site in the Persian period is not certain, and its size (0.5 dunam) does not materially change the picture. See Magen and Finkelstein, *Archaeological Survey*, 279. On this archaeological picture, see Lipschits, "History of the Benjaminite Region," 155–90. This point has also been well defined by Milevski, "Settlement Patterns," 18–19. On the survey in this region, see also Amihai Mazar, David Amit, and Zvi Ilan, "The 'Border Road' between Michmash and Jericho and Excavations at Horvat Shilhah" [Hebrew], *ErIsr* 17 (1984): 236–50, with further literature. On the settlement pattern of this region at the end of the Iron Age, see also the comments of the surveyors in Magen and Finkelstein, *Archaeological Survey*, 279, 346. A marked reduction in the scope of settlement was also noted in the area of today's city of Ramallah, on the hilly region to the north

The main conclusion is that apparently by the sixth century BCE the rural settlement north of Jerusalem had withdrawn to the original agricultural hinterland of Jerusalem, while the northern and eastern zones, previously part of the Northern Kingdom and the province of Samaria, were almost entirely devoid of settlement and almost completely depopulated.[53] Most of the settlements that remained in the area north of Jerusalem were concentrated along the mountain ridge and the upper mountain slopes, around the main economic and administrative centers that continued to exist in the region.[54] The relative prosperity of the agricultural hinterland of Jerusalem must be attributed to the political centrality assigned to Mizpah and the economic importance of Gibeon and Moza; it was probably around these settlements that the agricultural hinterland was based and its settlement pattern shaped.

During the exilic and postexilic periods, the agricultural hinterland to the north of Jerusalem became the center of the province, with Mizpah as its capital. It seems that the identity of this greater Benjamin became centered around Bethel and its temple, and the change in the status of Mizpah after the destruction of Jerusalem turned the district of Mizpah into an even stronger separate administrative unit.[55] This, in turn, probably contributed to the shaping of the separate identity of Benjamin and its relations to Jerusalem.[56]

5. The Creation of the District of Mizpah and Its Borders, Function, and Status

On the basis of the archaeological data and the descriptions in 2 Kgs 25:22–26 and Jer 39–43, we may surmise that, even before the fall of Jerusalem,

---

of the plateau, where twelve Iron II sites were surveyed, most of them west of the watershed, compared to only two sites from the Persian period.

53. See Lipschits "History of the Benjaminite Region," 180–84; Lipschits, *Fall and Rise of Jerusalem*, 245–49. This assumption accords with existing information about the complete cessation of settlement that took place throughout the Jordan Valley and the western littoral of the Dead Sea. It would seem that this, too, was related to the collapse of the economic, military, and political system of the kingdom of Judah.

54. On this subject, see the description and model presented by Magen and Finkelstein, *Archaeological Survey*, 20–21.

55. On the status of Bethel in the sixth century BCE see Na'aman, "Does Archaeology Really Deserve," 165–83; Oded Lipschits, "Bethel Revisited," in Lipschits, *Rethinking Israel*, 233–46, as against the views expressed by Israel Finkelstein and Lily Singer-Avitz, "Reevaluating Bethel," *ZDPV* 125 (2009): 33–48.

56. See Lipschits, "Rural Economy of Judah," 242–47.

the Babylonians had selected Mizpah to be the capital of the Babylonian province and had appointed Gedaliah as its first governor.[57] This is the historical background for the creation of the district of Mizpah that continued to exist in the Persian period (as indicated in Neh 3). This district coincided with the Josianic region of greater Benjamin, reflecting the continuity of the region's boundaries in the seventh–fifth centuries BCE and including Jericho in the east.[58] Mizpah was the main city in the district, at least until the late fifth or even the early fourth century BCE.[59]

The historical boundary between the Benjamin region/Mizpah district and the environs of Jerusalem/Jerusalem district is probably the line formed by connecting the southern settlements of the agricultural hinterland to the north and west of Jerusalem. Moza and Kiriath-jearim are mentioned in the town list of Benjamin (Josh 18:26, 28).[60] Gibeah and Anathoth are added to the list of these towns that appears in Isa 10:28–32.[61] The line formed by these towns lies five kilometers from Jerusalem, in a northeast–northwest direction, an area bounded by Naḥal Og in the northeast and by Naḥal Soreq in the northwest. The Jerusalem district lay south of the district of Mizpah and probably included the city and its close

---

57. See Lipschits, "History of the Benjaminite Region," 155–90; Lipschits, *Fall and Rise of Jerusalem*, 68–125, 237–49.

58. This premise is opposed to the attempt of some scholars to add the Jericho district as the sixth district in the province of Yehud, or to add Gezer as another district in addition to Jericho. The attempt to include the Ono-Lod region or parts of Samaria in this area should be dismissed as well, see Lipschits, *Fall and Rise of Jerusalem*, 148–49, 157–58, 248–49, with additional bibliography.

59. On the status of the Mizpah during the Babylonian and Persian periods, see Lipschits, *Fall and Rise of Jerusalem*, 237–40.

60. On the repetitive mention of Kiriath-jearim (Josh 15:60; 18:28) in the list of cities of Judah and Benjamin, see the explanation offered by Na'aman, "Kingdom of Judah under Josiah," 8–10. The place, in any case, was considered part of Benjamin (Josh 9:17; 18:28; Ezra 2:25; Neh 7:29). On Josh 18:28, see Na'aman, "Kingdom of Judah under Josiah," 8–10; and on the part of the list that was apparently omitted from the book of Joshua, see Na'aman, *Borders and Districts in Biblical Historiography: Seven Studies in Biblical Geographical Texts*, JBS 4 (Jerusalem: Simor, 1986), 229 n. 45; Na'aman, "Kingdom of Judah under Josiah," 25–26. The affiliation of Anathoth, Jeremiah's birthplace, with the Benjamin tribal legacy is also highlighted at the height of the Babylonian siege, preceding the destruction of Jerusalem (Jer 32:7–15).

61. See Joseph Blenkinsopp, *Isaiah 1–39*, AB 19 (New York: Doubleday, 2000), 260–62.

environs.⁶² It is thus clear that Jerusalem was totally cut off from its entire agricultural hinterland. The most likely historical explanation for this state of affairs is that it was the outcome of a Babylonian decision after the 586 BCE destruction.

The relative prosperity of the Mizpah district must be attributed to the political centrality assigned to Mizpah and the economic importance of Gibeon and Moza. It was probably around these settlements that the agricultural hinterland was based and the settlement pattern was shaped. Of the forty-three storage-jar handles uncovered with *mwṣh* stamp impressions, securely dated to the sixth century BCE, thirty were found at Tell en-Naṣbeh.⁶³ These *mwṣh*-stamped jars were presumably part of the local administration of the Babylonian province of Judah and should probably be interpreted as part of the local supply to the governor of the province, whose seat was in Mizpah.⁶⁴

A concurrent system of lion stamp impressions on jar handles existed alongside the *mwṣh* stamp impressions, with seventy-three stamped jars discovered at Ramat Raḥel, twenty-nine in Jerusalem, and only nineteen in the Benjamin area (twelve in Nebi Samwil, five at Tell en-Naṣbeh, and two at Gibeon).⁶⁵ This is a clear indication that the main administrative system of stamped storage jars, which was probably connected to the imperial system of taxation, continued in the same manner as prior to the destruction of Jerusalem. As was the case with the system of rosette stamp impressions on storage jars, which operated at the end of the seventh century BCE, the area of Benjamin did not play a major role in the lion stamp-impression system of the sixth century BCE.⁶⁶

---

62. Taking into account the surrounding districts, we may surmise that the Jerusalem district extended eastward to the edge of the desert and to Mount Scopus in the north. To the south, the Jerusalem district did not extend beyond the Rephaim Valley, so its borders were very close (ca. 2–3 km) to the city itself.

63. See Jeffrey R. Zorn, Joseph Yellin, and John Hayes, "The M(W)ṢH Stamp Impressions and the Neo-Babylonian Period," *IEJ* 44 (1994): 166–68; Lipschits, *Age of Empires*, 98–104. Four more *mwṣh*-stamped handles were discovered in Gibeon, four in Jerusalem, two in Jericho, one each in Ramat Raḥel and Tsubah, and the origin of another stamped handle is unknown. See Lipschits, *Age of Empires*, 98–104, 124.

64. See Lipschits, *Age of Empires*, 287–90.

65. Lipschits, *Age of Empires*, 91–98, 124.

66. The special status of Benjamin and Mizpah in this period is likely the background to some polemical stories that were intended to reflect the right of this region

6. The Historical and Historiographical Rise and Decline of Benjamin in the Babylonian and Persian Periods

With the events of 586 BCE and the new status of Mizpah as the capital of the province of Yehud, this city became the center of the province for the first time in its history, even more important politically than Jerusalem and Judah. This new status had a great impact on the literary claims and polemics in favor of this region and its people (pro-Benjamin, pro-Mizpah, and pro-Saul stories) and against Jerusalem and its history, its status, and its leaders, especially with regard to the premonarchic and pre-Davidic period. As such, 1 Sam 7 is the most pro-Benjamin and pro-Mizpah story in the Old Testament, along with the story on the assembling of the people at Mizpah and the election there of Saul as the first king of Israel in 1 Sam 10:17–27.[67]

In the years following the Babylonian destruction, there was stability and continuity in the rural settlement and economy in the central areas of the province, which, in the absence of any dramatic external events, could apparently survive and maintain its existence. This stability was also in the interest of the ruling empires, which preserved the local system of collecting agricultural products, especially wine and oil, at a single administrative center—Ramat Raḥel, which existed throughout the period that Judah was under the hegemony of foreign empires.

Interesting changes took place during the Persian period, however: Nebi Samwil became the main administrative site, together with Mizpah, while Gibeon and Khirbet el-Burj lost the prominent role they played in the system of stamping storage jars during the seventh and probably the sixth century BCE.[68] The area between Nebi Samwil, Gibeon, and Mizpah continued to be the demographic and economic center of the province in the early Persian period. Even though the district of Mizpah was Judah's demographic center during the sixth century, at least until the mid-fifth century BCE, with around a third of all Judahite sites located there (76

---

to lead the province. These stories were added to Judges and Samuel, reflecting the pre-Monarchic/pre-Davidic period. See further below.

67. See Diana Edelman, "Did Saulite-Davidic Rivalry Resurface in Early Persian Yehud?," in *The Land That I Will Show You: Essays on the History and Archaeology of the Ancient Near East in Honour of J. Maxwell Miller*, ed. J. Andrew Dearman and M. Patrick Graham, JSOTSup 343 (Sheffield: Sheffield Academic, 2001), 69–91.

68. See Lipschits, *Age of Empires*, 243–65.

out of 238 sites), during that time Mizpah lost its status as the seat of the governor (who probably moved to Ramat Raḥel) and the settlement and its environs gradually declined in the fifth century BCE, probably after Jerusalem had established itself as the sole cultic center in Judah.[69] Consequently, there was a marked gradual demographic decline in the Benjamin region from the end of the sixth century and reaching its peak in the fifth and fourth centuries BCE, with a loss of over 50 percent of its population. This demographic decline may have been due to the strengthening of the settlement in the Modiʻin area and the northern Shephelah during the Persian period.[70] The political stability in this period, and in particular, the enhanced economic activity that developed in the coastal area, attracted many of the inhabitants of the region to settle there. The agricultural potential of the area and its proximity to the coastal trade routes and the major roads to the Benjamin region and to the Jerusalem environs served as additional incentives. In addition, one cannot rule out the possibility that the migration out of Benjamin's administrative borders was ideologically driven by animosity toward the new ruling elite in Jerusalem, which was imposing its religious and ritual practices and its social and national views upon the province.

This is the key to an understanding of the account in 1 Chr 8:12–13, which relates that the sons of Elpaal and Beriah, who hailed from Benjamin, "built Ono and Lod" and "were heads of the fathers of the inhabitants of Aijalon."[71] A note added to the account of Ishbaal's assassination by two Benjaminites informs us that the people of Beeroth, one of four Gibeonite cities, fled to Gittaim (2 Sam 4:3), a place listed as a Benjaminite settlement in Neh 11:33. If this place is synonymous with the Gath of 1 Chr 8:13, whose inhabitants were driven out by Benjaminites, this may point to Benjaminite expansion westward in the Persian period.[72]

---

69. See Lipschits, "History of the Benjaminite Region," 182–85; and see also Lipschits, *Fall and Rise of Jerusalem*, 36–126; Lipschits, "Rural Economy," 242–47.

70. Oded Lipschits, "The Origins of the Jewish Population of Modiʻin and Its Vicinity" [Hebrew], *Cathedra* 85 (1997): 7–32.

71. Lipschits, "Origins of the Jewish Population." See also Götz Schmitt, "Gat, Gittaim und Gitta," in *Drei Studien zur Archäologie und Topographie Altisraels*, ed. Rudolph Cohen and Götz Schmitt, TAVO (Wiesbaden: Reichert, 1980), 80–92.

72. On this, see already Joseph Blenkinsopp "Benjamin Traditions Read in the Early Persian Period," in Lipschits and Oeming, *Judah and the Judeans in the Persian Period*, 643–44.

Historical sources from the Persian period contain several accounts that lend support to this demographic phenomenon. Particularly striking are the Israelites' marital ties with the foreign women from among the "people of the land" (Ezra 9:1–2, 12–15; 10:2–3, 10–15; Neh 10:31). This also provides a framework for an understanding of the proposition made by Sanballat, the Horonite, and Geshem, the Arab, to meet with Nehemiah "in one of the villages in the plain of Ono" (Neh 6:2), where a Judean settlement of unclear political allegiance was located. This is apparently the source of the Jewish population that lived in this area during the Hellenistic period.[73]

7. The Rise of Anti-Benjamin Polemics in Jerusalem in the Persian Period

Already in the early Persian period, when the returnees from Babylon started to renew the status of Jerusalem, the polemic claims against Benjamin and Mizpah and in favor of Jerusalem and Judah could be written, especially in texts dealing with the premonarchic period.[74]

Throughout the Persian period, Jerusalem was no more than a small town—nothing but a temple with a few hundred priests and other temple servants living in its vicinity.[75] The isolation of Jerusalem from its agricultural hinterland and its impoverishment throughout the Persian

---

73. See Lipschits, "Origins of the Jewish Population," 10–11, 28–31.

74. I can only agree with Blenkinsopp ("Benjamin Traditions") that Judean-Benjaminite hostility had developed already during the sixth century BCE, after the destruction of Jerusalem and the deportation of the Jerusalem elite to Babylon. The question is in which texts this hostility can be located and what is the date of these texts. On this, see the discussion of Knauf, "Bethel," 326–29. On the anti-Gibeonite polemic, see already Peter J. Kearney, "The Role of the Gibeonites in the Deuteronomistic History," *CBQ* 35 (1973): 1–19; Joseph Blenkinsopp, "Did Saul Make Gibeon His Capital?" *VT* 24 (1974), 1–7. On this subject, see Edelman, "Did Saulide-Davidic Rivalry," 69–91; Edelman, "Gibeon and the Gibeonites Revisited," in Lipschits and Blenkinsopp, *Judah and the Judeans in the Neo-Babylonian Period*, 153–67.

75. See Oded Lipschits, "Persian Period Judah—A New Perspective," in *Texts, Contexts and Readings in Postexilic Literature: Explorations into Historiography and Identity Negotiation in Hebrew Bible and Related Texts*, ed. Louis Jonker, FAT 2/53 (Tübingen: Mohr Siebeck, 2011), 189–90, with additional bibliography. This is why all of the agricultural sites and their locations in the central and northern hill country are an indication that the source and reason for them were not the city or the temple but the administrative and economic system that survived in Judah, with its center at Ramat Raḥel, and with its aim to pay taxes to the ruling empire.

period are the backdrop for an understanding of many of the polemic texts that were written at this time in reaction against the status of Mizpah and Benjamin.

The economy of Jerusalem was totally dependent upon gifts, tithes, and the goodwill of the Persian governor in Mizpah (before Ramat Raḥel became the seat of the governor).[76] This is the underlying reason for the hatred toward Mizpah, Benjamin, and the people there, who were described as foreigners in the story about the Gibeonites in the book of Joshua and as a tribe that should be distinct in the story in Judg 19–21.[77]

The change in the reference of the name "Benjamin" from a very small local territory in the southern part of the kingdom of Israel to a large region in the northern part of Judah and the later change to the phrase "Judah and Benjamin," parallels the change and expansion of the original inheritance of the tribe of Judah from the area of Hebron to that of Jerusalem.[78] The latter change probably took place in the same period and in the same scribal sources as the names "Samaria" and "Israel," which underwent a long process of transformation from a separate kingdom and a hostile province to an inclusive title for the entire nation and the name

---

76. See Lipschits, "Rural Economy," 243, 248–50.

77. On Judg 19–21, see Yairah Amit, "Literature in the Service of Politics: Studies in Judges 19–21," in *Politics and Theopolitical Literature*, ed. Hermann G. Reventlow, Yair Hoffman, and Benjamin Uffenheimer, JSOTSup 171 (Sheffield: JSOT Press, 1994), 28–40; Amit, *Hidden Polemics in Biblical Narratives* (Leiden: Brill, 2000), 179–84; Amit, "Epoch and Genre: The Sixth Century and the Growth of Hidden Polemics," in Lipschits and Blenkinsopp, *Judah and the Judeans in the Neo-Babylonian Period*, 146; Cynthia Edenburg, "The Story of the Outrage at Gibeah (Jdg. 19–21): Composition, Sources, and Historical Context" [Hebrew] (PhD diss., Tel Aviv University, 2003); Blenkinsopp, "Benjamin Traditions," 638–43; Na'aman, "Saul, Benjamin," 223. For extensive literature on these chapters, see Cynthia Edenburg, *Dismembering the Whole: Composition and Purpose of Judges 19–21*, AIL 24 (Atlanta: SBL Press, 2016). On Judg 20:29–48, see Nadav Na'aman, "The Battle of Gibeah Reconsidered (Judges 20:29–48)," *VT* 68 (2018): 102–10, with further literature.

78. As clearly demonstrated by Blenkinsopp ("Benjamin Traditions," 630 and n. 3), the designation "Judah and Benjamin" appeared in the early Persian period and is otherwise restricted to Chronicles (2 Chr 11:1, 3, 10, 12, 23; 14:7; 15:2, 8–9; 25:5; 31:1; 34:9, 32). The expression in 1 Kgs 12:21, 23—"all the house of Judah and the tribe of Benjamin" and "all the house of Judah and Benjamin"—is similar but not identical. See also Lipschits, Römer, and Gonzalez, "Pre-Priestly Abraham-Narratives," 275–83; Lipschits, "Abraham zwischen Mamre und Jerusalem," 189–94.

of the past and future kingdom of both the historical kingdoms of Israel and Judah.[79]

The name Benjamin was chosen as the name of the administrative region of the district of Mizpah only at a later stage, probably not before the early Persian period, as part of the rivalry that was created between Jerusalem and the territory to its north and as part of the separation between the two units. This is also why the Benjaminites (in the territory of greater Benjamin) were pushed in the historiographical descriptions to be part of the northern kingdom, as is evident in the early Saul traditions (1 Sam 9–14; 31; and see below), in the story of the Gibeonites (Josh 9), and in the anti-Benjaminite story in Judg 19–21.[80] At the same time, the takeover of the tradition of Rachel's burial place (Gen 35:16–21; cf. 48:7) from the area north of Jerusalem (and see, e.g., 1 Sam 10:2; Jer 31:15) to the area south of Jerusalem—in Bethlehem—may be interpreted as one aspect of the process whereby Jerusalem hegemony over the Benjaminites was reflected during the early Persian period.[81]

Unlike the original region of the northern tribe of Benjamin, which, according to Josh 6 and 8, was conquered by Joshua and the people of Israel, the Benjamin plateau was not part of this conquest story, and in the polemic story against the Benjamin territory of the Gibeonites (as described in Josh 9), this territory was portrayed as an area with foreign people, whose existence in the land is as "hewers of wood and drawers of

---

79. Philip R. Davies, *In Search of Ancient Israel*, JSOTSup 148 (Sheffield: Sheffield Academic, 1992), 11–74; Davies, "Origin of Biblical Israel," 141–48; Davies, "Trouble with Benjamin," 93–111; Na'aman, "Israelite-Judahite Struggle," 1–23, with further literature. For a much earlier date of this "Israel" as the "United Monarchy," see, e.g., Erhard Blum, "Solomon and the United Monarchy: Some Textual Evidence," in Kratz and Spieckermann, *One God—One Cult—One Nation*, 59–78.

80. The Persian period date of this story is also manifest in the nature of the description: the account of military expeditions contains religious exercises, weeping, and lamenting, which are all part of a theocratic scribe who, as stated by George F. Moore, had never handled a more dangerous weapon than an imaginative pen. See George F. Moore, *Judges*, ICC (Edinburgh: T&T Clark, 1895), 431, and cf. 421–22.

81. See Benjamin D. Cox and Susan Ackerman, "Rachel's Tomb," *JBL* 128 (2009): 136. Cf. 1 Sam 17:12; Ruth 1:2; 4:11; Micah 5:1; 1 Chr 2:24, 50–52; 4:4–5. See Christine Ritter, *Rachels Klage im antiken Judentum und frühen Christentum: Eine auslegungsgeschichtliche Studie*, AGAJU 52 (Leiden: Brill, 2003), 29–32; Nadav Na'aman, "The Settlement of the Ephrathites in Bethlehem and the Location of Rachel's Grave," *RB* 121 (2014): 516–29. See, e.g., Blenkinsopp "Benjamin Traditions," 630–33. Cf. the arguments of Na'aman, "Jacob Story," 107–108, regarding the Judean origin of this story.

water." This story, which could not have been written before the Persian period, is a clear description of the unification of the two regions that had formed the territory of Benjamin—with a clear polemical attitude against the people living there, an attitude that can be well connected to other hostile descriptions of this region.[82] In this regard, the story of David and the Gibeonites, too (2 Sam 21:1–14), should be considered an anti-Benjaminite and anti-Gibeonite story from the Persian period.[83]

8. Implications of the Proposed Stages in the Creation of the Territory of the Benjamin Tribe in the Seventh–Fifth Centuries BCE for the Early History of Israel and Early Benjamin

As described above, "Benjamin" was an artificial amalgamation of the original territory of Benjamin with the agricultural hinterland of Jerusalem to the north and west of the city, which took place only after the unification of these areas in the days of Josiah, and to a greater degree after this territory obtained its independence and augmented status after the destruction of Jerusalem, with the transformation of the district of Mizpah into the tribe of Benjamin. Given these proposed stages, we should exercise caution when examining the use of this general "Benjamin" label in the historiographical descriptions.

While in the early stories that originated in the Northern Kingdom, the title *Benjaminite* referred to people and groups who did in fact hail from the original territory of Benjamin, and while it is reasonable that the borders of greater Benjamin could be delineated already in the days of Josiah, when the town list of the two Benjamins still contained two separate groups, the use of the labels Benjamin and Benjaminite (as well as other labels such as Israel, Israelite, Judah, and Judahite) in biblical historiography to refer to individuals and groups from this combined Benjaminite

---

82. On the postexilic anti-Benjaminite compositions, see Blenkinsopp, "Benjamin Traditions," 629–45; Yairah Amit, "The Saul Polemic in the Persian Period," in Lipschits and Blenkinsopp, *Judah and the Judeans in the Neo-Babylonain Period*, 647–61, with earlier literature.

83. See Jürg Hutzli, "L'exécution de sept descendants de Saül par les Gabaonites (2 S 21,1–14): Place et function du récit dans les livres de Samuel," *Transeu* 40 (2011), 83–96; Cynthia Edenburg, "II Sam 21,1–14 and II Sam 23,1–7 as Post-Chr Additions to the Samuel Scroll," in *Rereading the Relecture? The Question of (Post)chronistic Influence in the Latest Redactions of the Books of Samuel*, ed. Uwe Becker and Hannes Bezzel, FAT 2/66 (Tübingen: Mohr Siebeck, 2014), 167–82 with earlier literature.

territory, should be viewed as part of the editing process of early oral and written sources and as part of the efforts of the Deuteronomistic and later editors to be as precise as possible in their use of geographical terms. In this case, these late scribes and editors used the geographical labels as they knew them and at the same time, used them as a polemic and ideological tool that served their purposes, especially concerning the pre-Davidic periods, as described in the books of Judges and Samuel.[84]

As such, it is important to set aside duplications, exaggerations, and additional Benjaminite/Israelite/Judahite labels in the stories on early Israel, including the history of Saul's rise to power, the history of David's rise to power, the Succession Narrative, and the Saul-David narrative, and not to assign them to any theoretical early source from before the seventh century BCE and to learn from these labels about the history of Israel in these early periods.[85] With regard to Benjamin, the most prominent subject is the story cycle of Saul.[86]

---

84. On this aspect, see Oded Lipschits, "Geographical Observations on the Old Northern Israelite Tales in Judges," in *From Nomadism to Monarchy: Thirty Years After* (Tel Aviv and University Park: Penn State University Press, forthcoming).

85. In these definitions I use the terms and story cycles as defined by Leonhard Rost, *Die Überlieferung von der Thronnachfolge Davids*, BWANT 42 (Stuttgart: Kohlhammer, 1926). For recent discussions and further literature, see Walter Dietrich, "Von den ersten Königen Israels: Forschung an den Samuelbüchern im neuen Jahrtausend," *TRu* 77 (2012): 135–70, 263–316, 401–25. See, e.g., Fleming, *Legacy of Israel*, 153. Already Na'aman, however, pointed in this direction, when he argued against scholars that reconstructed Saul's kingdom on the basis of the description of Ishbaal's kingdom (2 Sam 2:8–9), and claimed that this latter system was written by the Deuteronomist on the basis of his understanding of the early reality and his concept of the Israelite borders in the premonarchical period. See Nadav Na'aman, "The Kingdom of Ishbaal," *BN* 54 (1990): 33–37. Cf. Neef, *Ephraim*, 273–77. On the late date and secondary nature of the Benjaminite episodes embedded in the narrative of David's flight and return, see François Langlamet, "David et la maison de Saül: Les épisodes 'benjaminites' des II Sam. IX; XVI, 1–14; XIX, 17–31; I Rois, II, 36–46," *RB* 86 (1979): 194–213, 385–436, 481–513; Reinhard G. Kratz, *The Composition of the Narrative Books of the Old Testament* (London: T&T Clark, 2005), 174–76. See however the date assigned to these stories by Sergi, "United Monarchy," with further literature, or the attribution of Saul's original story to Benjamin by Fleming, *Legacy of Israel*, 151.

86. Van Seters already emphasized the role of the Deuteronomistic Historian as the author of the Saul and David stories. See John Van Seters, *In Search of History: Historiography in the Ancient World and the Origins of Biblical History* (New Haven: Yale University Press, 1983), 250–64; Van Seters, *The Biblical Saga of King David* (Winona Lake, IN: Eisenbrauns, 2009), 128–29.

According to this long and complex story, Saul's activities took place in the combined Benjaminite territory and never extended northward to the central highlands, beyond the southernmost margins of Mount Ephraim.[87] It is clear, however, that, just like the attempt to connect Saul to the non-Israelite city Gibeon, the use of the label Benjaminite is dubious and is intended to place Saul in a setting far from Jerusalem, to label him as Israelite and to distance him from the Judahite house of David.[88]

In the current Deuteronomistic historiography, the use of the Benjaminite label may help to identify the pre-Deuteronomistic story cycles and identify the different use of the term Benjamin—when it has a much narrower reference, limited to the geographical borders of the original territory of the Benjamin tribe (as in 1 Sam 13; and see below). It seems to me that in many studies dealing with the date of the pre-Deuteronomistic story cycles of Saul and David, scholars identified the Deuteronomistic insertions as well as post-Deuteronomistic additions, but did not give the question of the Benjamin label sufficient consideration in their source analysis of the original narratives before drawing their conclusions on the historicity of these stories and reconstructing the historical reality and geographical background underlying them.[89]

With regard to Saul, within the supposed early material embedded in 1 Sam 9:1–10:16; 11; 13–14; 31, the Benjamin label appears only once in the editorial title depicting Saul as the hero of the story (9:1; cf. the two other cases in which Saul was presented as Benjaminite in the later additions of 9:16, 21).[90] In chapter 13 the story is mostly set within the original territory of Benjamin "in Michmash and in Mount Bethel" (1 Sam 13:2), and the location of Geba/Gibeah of Benjamin (13:2, 15, 16; 14:16) and its relation to this territory may help us situate it in modern Jebaʿ, southwest of Michmash.[91] The connection between this Gibeah and Gilgal, as set in 1 Sam 13:15, may support the geographical setting of the two places in the

---

87. See Naʾaman, "Saul, Benjamin," 346.

88. It is difficult, however, to accept views that presuppose that Saul was Israelite and David was Judahite. See, e.g., Hannes Bezzel, *Saul: Israels König in Tradition, Redaktion und früher Rezeption*, FAT 97 (Tübingen: Mohr Siebeck, 2015), 235–37.

89. Nadav Naʾaman, "The Pre-Deuteronomistic Story of King Saul and Its Historical Background," CBQ 54 (1990): 638–58. Cf. Bezzel, *Saul*, 208–28, 250–54, with earlier literature.

90. Naʾaman, "Pre-Deuteronomistic Story," 640, with further literature.

91. Naʾaman, "Pre-Deuteronomistic Story," 652.

original territory of Benjamin. On these very unclear grounds, it seems difficult to draw any clear conclusion on the original relation of Saul to Benjamin and on the original identity of his supporters and opponents.

9. Summary

In this paper I have suggested that the biblical territory of the tribe of Benjamin is a late artificial aggregation of two distinct historical and geopolitical units that were never part of the same geopolitical region: Benjamin (= "the son of the south") was a small tribe around Bethel, the southern Ephraim hills and Jericho, connected to the northern hill country, whereas the Gibeon plateau was part of the agricultural hinterland of Jerusalem. The destruction of the kingdom of Israel was the point of departure for a new period in the hill country, when, for the first time, the small, hilly southern entity did not have a larger and stronger northern neighbor. It was only in the days of Josiah, however, that Judah could conquer the area of Bethel and Jericho and extend its border up to this line. After the 586 BCE destruction of Jerusalem, the city was severed from its agricultural hinterland and the Babylonians created the district of Mizpah to the north of Jerusalem. Greater Benjamin became a unified administrative region, with Jerusalem as a marginal component at its southern border. It was the first time in the history of the region that Benjamin became central, with even greater political and economic importance than Jerusalem.

The 586 BCE events and the new status of Mizpah as the capital of the province of Yehud had an important effect on the literary claims and polemics in favor of this region and its people (pro-Benjaminite, pro-Mizpah, and pro-Saul stories) and against Jerusalem and its history, its status and its leaders, especially regarding the premonarchic and pre-Davidic period. However, it was already in the early Persian period, when the exiles began to return from Babylon and to restore the status of Jerusalem, that the anti-Benjaminite and polemic claims against Benjamin and Mizpah and in favor of Jerusalem and Judah could be written, also in this case, especially in texts dealing with the premonarchic period. This could have driven some of the inhabitants of the region around Mizpah and Gibeon to settle beyond the administrative limits of the province, close to the border, in the Ono-Lod and Modiʻin region.

This understanding of the historical process should be adopted by biblical scholars in their interpretation of historiographical texts that use this Benjamin label, probably written by late scribes and editors who used the geographical labels as a polemic and ideological tool, mainly in the pre-Davidic periods, as described in Judges and Samuel. With regard to Benjamin, the most prominent subject is the story cycle of Saul. The first monarch of the kingdom of Jerusalem, who came from the agricultural hinterland to the north of the city, was killed and his kingdom taken by David, originally from the agricultural hinterland to the south of Jerusalem. He succeeded in conquering Jerusalem and uniting it with the Judahite territory in the southern Judean hills, around Hebron. In the Jerusalemite historiography Saul was connected with the non-Israelite city of Gibeon and was pushed to the north. The late use of the label "Benjaminite" also had deceptive intentions: it was aimed at distancing Saul from Jerusalem, labeling him as "Israelite" and setting him apart from the Judahite house of David.

Bibliography

Alt, Albrecht. "Judas Gaue unter Josia." *PJb* 21 (1925): 100–116.

———. *Die Landnahme der Israeliten in Palästina—territorialgeschichtliche Studien*. Leipzig: Druckerei der Werkgemeinschaft, 1925.

———. "Die Rolle Samarias bei der Entstehung des Judentums." Pages 316–37 in *Kleine Schriften zur Geschichte des Volkes Israel 2*. Munich: Beck, 1953.

———. "Der Stadtstaat Samaria." Pages 258–302 in *Kleine Schriften zur Geschichte des Volkes Israel 3*. Munich: Beck, 1959.

Amit, Yairah. "Epoch and Genre: The Sixth Century and the Growth of Hidden Polemics." Pages 135–51 in *Judah and the Judeans in the Neo-Babylonian Period*. Edited by Oded Lipschits and Joseph Blenkinsopp. Winona Lake, IN: Eisenbrauns, 2003.

———. *Hidden Polemics in Biblical Narrative*. BibInt 25. Leiden: Brill, 2000.

———. "Literature in the Service of Politics: Studies in Judges 19–21." Pages 28–40 in *Politics and Theopolitics in the Bible and Postbiblical Literature*. Edited by Hermann G. Reventlow, Yair Hoffman, and Benjamin Uffenheimer. JSOTSup 171. Sheffield: JSOT Press, 1994.

———. "The Saul Polemic in the Persian Period." Pages 647–61 in *Judah and the Judeans in the Persian Period*. Edited by Oded Lipschits and Manfred Oeming. Winona Lake, IN: Eisenbrauns, 2006.

Barrick, W. Boyd. *The King and the Cemeteries: Toward a New Understanding of Josiah's Reform*. VTSup 88. Leiden: Brill, 2002.

Bezzel, Hannes. *Saul: Israels König in Tradition, Redaktion und früher Rezeption*. FAT 97. Tübingen: Mohr Siebeck, 2015.

Blenkinsopp, Joseph. "Benjamin Traditions Read in the Early Persian Period." Pages 629–45 in *Judah and the Judeans in the Persian Period*. Edited by Oded Lipschits and Manfred Oeming. Winona Lake, IN: Eisenbrauns, 2006.

———. "Bethel in the Neo-Babylonian Period." Pages 93–107 in *Judah and the Judeans in the Neo-Babylonian Period*. Edited by Oded Lipschits and Joseph Blenkinsopp. Winona Lake, IN: Eisenbrauns, 2003.

———. "Did Saul Make Gibeon His Capital?" *VT* 24 (1974): 1–7.

———. *Isaiah 1–39: A New Translation with Introduction and Commentary*. AB 19. New York: Doubleday, 2000.

Blum, Erhard. "The Jacob Tradition." Pages 181–211 in *The Book of Genesis: Composition, Reception, and Interpretation*. Edited by Craig A. Evans, Joel N. Lohr, and David L. Petersen. VTSup 152. Leiden: Brill, 2012.

———. *Die Komposition der Vätergeschichte*. WMANT 57. Neukirchen-Vluyn: Neukirchener Verlag, 1984.

———. "Noch einmal: Jakobs Traum in Bethel—Genesis 28,10–22." Pages 33–54 in *Rethinking the Foundations: Historiography in the Ancient World and in the Bible; Essays in Honour of John Van Seters*. Edited by Steven L. McKenzie and Thomas Römer. BZAW 294. Berlin: de Gruyter, 2000.

———. "Solomon and the United Monarchy: Some Textual Evidence." Pages 59–78 in *One God—One Cult—One Nation: Archaeological and Biblical Perspectives*. Edited by Reinhard G. Kratz and Hermann Spieckermann. BZAW 405. Berlin: de Gruyter, 2010.

Bos, James M. *Reconsidering the Date and Provenance of the Book of Hosea: The Case for Persian-Period Yehud*. LHBOTS 580. London: Bloomsbury T&T Clark, 2013.

Brinker, R. *The Influence of Sanctuaries in Early Israel*. Manchester: Manchester University Press, 1946.

Caquot, André. "Les tribus d'Israël dans le cantique de Débora (Juges 5, 13–17)." *Sem* 36 (1986): 47–70.

Carr, David M. "Genesis 28,10–22 and Transmission-Historical Method: A Reply to John Van Seters." *ZAW* 111 (1999): 399–403.

———. *Reading the Fractures of Genesis: Historical and Literary Approaches*. Louisville: Westminster John Knox, 1996.

Cogan, Mordechai. *1 Kings: A New Translation with Introduction and Commentary*. AB 10. New York: Doubleday, 2001.

Cogan, Mordechai, and Hayim Tadmor. *2 Kings: A New Translation with Introduction and Commentary*. AB 11. New York: Doubleday, 1988.

Conroy, Charles. "Hiel between Ahab and Elijah-Elisha: 1 Kgs 16,34 in Its Immediate Literary Context." *Bib* 77 (1996): 210–18.

Cox, Benjamin D., and Susan Ackerman. "Rachel's Tomb." *JBL* 128 (2009): 135–48.

Davies, Philip R. *In Search of Ancient Israel*. JSOTSup 148. Sheffield: Sheffield Academic, 1992.

———. "The Origin of Biblical Israel." Pages 141–48 in *Essays on Ancient Israel in Its Near Eastern Context: A Tribute to Nadav Na'aman*. Edited by Yairah Amit, Ehud Ben Zvi, Israel Finkelstein, and Oded Lipschits. Winona Lake, IN: Eisenbrauns, 2006.

———. *The Origins of Biblical Israel*. LHBOTS 485. London: T&T Clark, 2007.

———. "The Trouble with Benjamin." Pages 93–111 in *Reflection and Refraction: Studies in Biblical Historiography in Honour of A. Graeme Auld*. Edited by Robert Rezetko, Timothy Lim, and W. Brian Aucker. VTSup 113. Leiden: Brill, 2007.

De Groot, Alon, and Michal Wienberger-Stern. "Wine, Oil and Gibeonites: Iron Age II–III at Kh. el-Burj, Northern Jerusalem" [Hebrew]. Pages 95–102 in *New Studies on Jerusalem 19*. Edited by Eyal Baruch and Avraham Faust. Ramat-Gan: Bar-Ilan University Press, 2013.

Dietrich, Walter. "Von den ersten Königen Israels: Forschung an den Samuelbüchern im neuen Jahrtausend." *TRu* 77 (2012): 135–170, 263–316, 401–425.

Edelman, Diana. "Did Saulide-Davidic Rivalry Resurface in Early Persian Yehud?" Pages 70–92 in *The Land That I Will Show You: Essays on the History and Archaeology of the Ancient Near East in Honour of J. Maxwell Miller*. Edited by J. Andrew Dearman and M. Patrick Graham. JSOTSup 343. Sheffield: Sheffield Academic, 2001.

———. "Gibeon and the Gibeonites Revisited." Pages 153–67 in *Judah and the Judeans in the Neo-Babylonian Period*. Edited by Oded Lipschits and Joseph Blenkinsopp. Winona Lake, IN: Eisenbrauns, 2003.

Edenburg, Cynthia. *Dismembering the Whole: Composition and Purpose of Judges 19–21*. AIL 24. Atlanta: SBL Press, 2016.

———. "II Sam 21,1–14 and II Sam 23,1–7 as Post-Chr Additions to the Samuel Scroll." Pages 167–82 in *Rereading the Relecture? The Ques-*

tion of (Post)chronistic Influence in the Latest Redactions of the Books of Samuel. Edited by Uwe Becker and Hannes Bezzel. FAT 2/66. Tübingen: Mohr Siebeck, 2014.

———. "The Story of the Outrage at Gibeah (Jdg. 19–21): Composition, Sources, and Historical Context" [Hebrew]. PhD diss., Tel Aviv University, 2003.

Ehrlich, Zeev H. "The Land of Benjamin" [Hebrew]. Pages 47–53 in *"Before Ephraim and Benjamin and Manasseh": Studies and Discoveries in Historical Geography*. Edited by Z. H. Ehrlich. Jerusalem: Benjamin Regional Municipality, 1985.

Eissfeldt, Otto. "Der geschichtliche Hintergrund der Erzählung von Gibeas Schandtat (Richter 19–21)." Pages 64–80 in *Kleine Schriften 2*. Tübingen: Mohr Siebeck, 1963.

Finkelstein, Israel. *The Forgotten Kingdom: The Archaeology and History of Northern Israel*. ANEM 5. Atlanta: Society of Biblical Literature, 2013.

———. "The Great Wall of Tell en-Nasbeh (Mizpah), the First Fortifications in Judah, and 1 Kings 15:16–22." *VT* 62 (2012): 14–28.

———. "Jerusalem and the Benjamin Plateau in the Early Phases of the Iron Age: A Different Scenario." *ZDPV* 134 (2018): 190–95.

———. "The Last Labayu: King Saul and the Expansion of the First North Israelite Territorial Entity." Pages 171–87 in *Essays on Ancient Israel in Its Near Eastern Context: A Tribute to Nadav Na'aman*. Edited by Yairah Amit, Ehud Ben-Zvi, Israel Finkelstein, and Oded Lipschits. Winona Lake, IN: Eisenbrauns, 2006.

———. "Saul, Benjamin and the Emergence of 'Biblical Israel': An Alternative View." *ZAW* 123 (2011): 348–67.

———. "The Sociopolitical Organization of the Central Hill Country in the Second Millennium B.C.E." Pages 110–31 in *Biblical Archaeology Today, 1990: Proceedings of the Second International Congress on Biblical Archaeology; Supplement; Pre-Congress Symposium; Population, Production and Power, Jerusalem June 1990*. Edited by Avraham Biran and Joseph Aviram. Jerusalem: Israel Exploration Society, 1993.

———. "Tell el-Ful Revisited: The Assyrian and Hellenistic Periods (with a New Identification)." *PEQ* 143 (2011): 106–18.

———. "The Territorial-Political System of Canaan in the Late Bronze Age." *UF* 28 (1996): 221–55.

Finkelstein, Israel, and Lily Singer-Avitz. "Reevaluating Bethel." *ZDPV* 125 (2009): 33–48.

Fleming, Daniel E. *The Legacy of Israel in Judah's Bible: History, Politics, and the Reinscribing of Tradition*. Cambridge: Cambridge University Press, 2012.

Gadot, Yuval. "In the Valley of the King: Jerusalem's Rural Hinterland in the Eighth–Fourth Centuries BCE." *TA* 42 (2015): 3–26.

Gray, John. *I and II Kings: A Commentary*. 2nd ed. OTL. London: SCM, 1970.

Hong, Koog P. "The Deceptive Pen of Scribes: Judean Reworking of the Bethel Tradition as a Program for Assuming Israelite Identity." *Bib* 92 (2011): 427–41.

Hutzli, Jürg. "L'exécution de sept descendants de Saül par les Gabaonites (2 S 21,1–14): Place et function du récit dans les livres de Samuel." *Transeu* 40 (2011): 83–96.

Kallai, Zechariah, and Tadmor, Haim. "Bit-Ninurta = Beth-Horon: On the History of the Kingdom of Jerusalem in the Amarna Period" [Hebrew]. *ErIsr* 9 (1969): 138–47.

Kearney, Peter J. "The Role of the Gibeonites in the Deuteronomistic History." *CBQ* 35 (1973): 1–19.

Knauf, Ernst Axel. "Bethel: The Israelite Impact on Judean Language and Literature." Pages 291–349 in *Judah and the Judeans in the Persian Period*. Edited by Oded Lipschits and Manfred Oeming. Winona Lake, IN: Eisenbrauns, 2006.

Koch, Ido, and Oded Lipschits. "The Rosette Stamped Jar Handle System and the Kingdom of Judah at the End of the First Temple Period." *ZDPV* 129 (2013): 55–78.

Kratz, Reinhard. G. *The Composition of the Narrative Books of the Old Testament*. London: T&T Clark, 2005.

Langlamet, François. "David et la maison de Saül: Les épisodes 'benjaminites' des II Sam. IX; XVI, 1–14; XIX, 17–31; I Rois, II, 36–46." *RB* 86 (1979): 194–213, 385–436, 481–513.

Lapp, Nancy L., ed. *The Third Campaign at Tell el-Ful: The Excavations of 1964*. AASOR 45. Cambridge: American Schools of Oriental Research, 1981.

Levin, Yigal. "Joseph, Judah and the 'Benjamin Conundrum.'" *ZAW* 116 (2004): 223–41.

Lipschits, Oded. "Abraham zwischen Mamre und Jerusalem." Pages 187–209 in *The Politics of the Ancestors: Exegetical and Historical Perspectives on Genesis 12–36*. Edited by Mark G. Brett and Jakob Wöhrle. FAT 124. Tübingen: Mohr Siebeck, 2018.

———. "Achaemenid Imperial Policy, Settlement Processes in Palestine, and the Status of Jerusalem in the Middle of the Fifth Century B.C.E." Pages 19–52 in *Judah and the Judeans in the Persian Period*. Edited by Oded Lipschits and Manfred Oeming. Winona Lake, IN: Eisenbrauns, 2006.

———. *The Age of Empires: History and Administration in Judah in Light of the Stamped Jar Handles* [Hebrew]. Jerusalem: Yad Ben-Zvi, 2018.

———. "Bethel Revisited." Pages 233–46 in *Rethinking Israel: Studies in the History and Archaeology of Ancient Israel in Honor of Israel Finkelstein*. Edited by Oded Lipschits, Yuval Gadot, and Matthew J. Adams. Winona Lake, IN: Eisenbrauns, 2017.

———. *The Fall and Rise of Jerusalem: The History of Judah under Babylonian Rule*. Winona Lake, IN: Eisenbrauns, 2005.

———. "Geographical Observations on the Old Northern Israelite Tales in Judges." In *From Nomadism to Monarchy: Thirty Years Update*. Tübingen: Mohr Siebeck, forthcoming.

———. "The History of the Benjaminite Region under Babylonian Rule." *TA* 26 (1999): 155–90.

———. "The Origins of the Jewish Population of Modi'in and Its Vicinity" [Hebrew]. *Cathedra* 85 (1997): 7–32.

———. "Persian Period Judah—A New Perspective." Pages 187–212 in *Texts, Contexts and Readings in Postexilic Literature: Explorations into Historiography and Identity Negotiation in Hebrew Bible and Related Texts*. Edited by Louis Jonker. FAT 2/53. Tübingen: Mohr Siebeck, 2011.

———. "The Rural Economy of Judah during the Persian Period and the Settlement History of the District System." Pages 237–64 in *The Economy of Ancient Judah in Its Historical Context*. Edited by Martin Lloyd Miller, Ehud Ben Zvi, and Gary N. Knoppers. Winona Lake, IN: Eisenbrauns, 2015.

Lipschits, Oded, and Nadav Na'aman. "From 'Baal Perazim' to 'Beth-Hakkerem'—On the Ancient Name of Ramat-Rahel" [Hebrew]. *Beth-Miqra* 56 (2011): 65–86.

Lipschits, Oded, Omer Sergi, and Ido Koch. "Royal Judahite Jar Handles: Reconsidering the Chronology of the *lmlk* Stamp Impressions." *TA* 37 (2010): 3–32.

Lipschits, Oded, Thomas Römer, and Hervé Gonzalez. "The Pre-Priestly Abraham-Narratives from Monarchic to Persian Times." *Sem* 59 (2017): 261–96.

Lipschits, Oded, and Yuval Gadot. "Ramat Raḥel and the Emeq Rephaim Sites—Links and Interpretations" [Hebrew]. Pages 88–96 in vol. 2 of *New Studies in the Archaeology of Jerusalem and Its Region, Collected Papers*. Edited by D. Amit and G. D. Stiebel. 2 vols. Jerusalem: New Studies in the Archaeology of Jerusalem and Its Region, 2008.

Lipschits, Oded, Yuval Gadot, Benjamin Arubas, and Manfred Oeming. *What Are the Stones Whispering? Three Thousand Years of Forgotten History at Ramat Rahel*. Winona Lake, IN: Eisenbrauns, 2017.

Magen, Yitzhak, and Israel Finkelstein, eds. *Archaeological Survey of the Hill Country of Benjamin* [Hebrew and English]. Jerusalem: Israel Antiquities Authority, 1993.

Magen, Yitzhak, and Michael Dadon. "Nebi Samwil (Montjoie)." Pages 123–38 in *One Land, Many Cultures: Archaeological Studies in Honour of Stanislao Loffreda*. Edited by Giovanni C. Bottini, Leah di Segni, and Leslaw D. Chrupcala. Jerusalem: Franciscan Printing Press, 2003.

Mazar, Amihai, David Amit, and Zvi Ilan. "The 'Border Road' between Michmash and Jericho and Excavations at Horvat Shilhah" [Hebrew]. *ErIsr* 17 (1984): 236–50.

Milevski, Ianir. "Settlement Patterns in Northern Judah during the Achaemenid Period, according to the Hill Country of Benjamin and Jerusalem Surveys." *Bulletin of the Anglo-Israel Archaeological Society* 15 (1996–1997): 7–29.

Monroe, Lauren A. S. *Josiah's Reform and the Dynamics of Defilement: Israelite Rites of Violence and the Making of a Biblical Text*. Oxford: Oxford University Press, 2011.

Moore, George F. *Judges*. ICC. Edinburgh: T&T Clark, 1895.

Na'aman, Nadav. "The Battle of Gibeah Reconsidered (Judges 20:29–48)." *VT* 68 (2018): 102–10.

———. *Borders and Districts in Biblical Historiography: Seven Studies in Biblical Geographical Texts*. JBS 4. Jerusalem: Simor, 1986.

———. "Canaanite Jerusalem and Its Central Hill Country Neighbors in the Second Millennium B.C.E." *UF* 24 (1992): 257–91.

———. "The Contribution of the Amarna Letters to the Debate on Jerusalem's Political Position in the Tenth Century B.C.E." *BASOR* 304 (1996): 17–27.

———. "David's Sojourn in Keilah in Light of the Amarna Letters." *VT* 60 (2010): 87–97.

———. "Does Archaeology Really Deserve the Status of a 'High Court' in Biblical and Historical Research?" Pages 165–83 in *Between Evidence and Ideology: Essays on the History of Ancient Israel Read at the Joint Meeting of the Society for Old Testament Study and the Oud Testamentisch Werkgezelschap, Lincoln, July 2009*. Edited by Bob Becking and Lester L. Grabbe. OTS 59. Leiden: Brill, 2010.

———. "Habiru and Hebrews: The Transfer of a Social Term to the Literary Sphere." *JNES* 45 (1986): 271–88.

———. "The Israelite-Judahite Struggle for the Patrimony of Ancient Israel." *Bib* 91 (2010): 1–23.

———. "The Jacob Story and the Formation of Biblical Israel." *TA* 41 (2014): 95–125.

———. "Jebusites and Jabeshites in the Saul and David Story-Cycles." *Bib* 95 (2014): 481–97.

———. "Jerusalem in the Amarna Period." Pages 31–48 in *Jérusalem Antique et Médiévale: Mélanges en l'honneur d'Ernest-Marie Laperrousaz*. Edited by Caroline Arnould-Béha and André Lemaire. CREJ 52. Paris: Peeters, 2011.

———. "Josiah and the Kingdom of Judah." Pages 189–247 in *Good Kings and Bad Kings: The Kingdom of Judah in the Seventh Century BCE*. Edited by Lester L. Grabbe. JSOTSup 393. Sheffield: T&T Clark, 2005.

———. "The King Leading Cult Reforms in His Kingdom: Josiah and Other Kings in the Ancient Near East." *ZABR* 12 (2006): 131–68.

———. "The Kingdom of Ishbaal." *BN* 54 (1990): 33–37.

———. "The Kingdom of Judah under Josiah." *TA* 18 (1991): 3–71.

———. "Literary and Topographical Notes on the Battle of Kishon (Judges iv–v)." *VT* 40 (1990): 423–36.

———. "The Pre-Deuteronomistic Story of King Saul and Its Historical Background." *CBQ* 54 (1990): 638–58.

———. "Saul, Benjamin and the Emergence of 'Biblical Israel.'" *ZAW* 121 (2009): 211–24, 335–49.

———. "The Settlement of the Ephrathites in Bethlehem and the Location of Rachel's Grave." *RB* 121 (2014): 516–29.

———. "Sources and Composition in the Story of Sheba's Revolt (2 Samuel 20)." *RB* 125 (2018): 340–52.

Neef, Heinz-Dieter. *Ephraim: Studien zur Geschichte des Stammes Ephraim von der Landnahme bis zur frühen Königszeit*. BZAW 238. Berlin: de Gruyter, 1995.

Niemann, Hermann Michael. "Juda und Jerusalem: Überlegungen zum Verhältnis von Stamm und Stadt und zur Rolle Jerusalems in Juda." *UF* 47 (2016): 147–90.

Otto, Susanne. "The Composition of the Elijah-Elisha Stories and the Deuteronomistic History." *JSOT* 27 (2003): 487–508.

Pakkala, Juha. "Why the Cult Reforms in Judah Probably Did Not Happen." Pages 201–35 in *One God—One Cult—One Nation: Archaeological and Biblical Perspectives*. Edited by Reinhard G. Kratz and Hermann Spieckermann. BZAW 405. Berlin: de Gruyter, 2010.

Pritchard, James B. *Gibeon: Where the Sun Stood Still*. Princeton: Princeton University Press, 1962.

Ritter, Christine. *Rachels Klage im antiken Judentum und frühen Christentum: Eine auslegungsgeschichtliche Studie*. AGAJU 52. Leiden: Brill, 2003.

Rost, Leonhard. *Die Überlieferung von der Thronnachfolge Davids*. BWANT 42. Stuttgart: Kohlhammer, 1926.

Schmitt, Götz. "Gat, Gittaim und Gitta." Pages 77–138 in *Drei Studien zur Archäologie und Topographie Altisraels*. Edited by Rudolph Cohen and Götz Schmitt. TAVO. Wiesbaden: Reichert, 1980.

Schunck, Klaus-Dietrich. *Benjamin: Untersuchungen zur Entstehung und Geschichte eines israelitischen Stammes*. BZAW 86. Berlin: Töpelmann, 1963.

Schütte, Wolfgang. *Israels Exil in Juda: Untersuchungen zur Entstehung der Schriftprophetie*. OBO 279. Fribourg: Academic Press; Göttingen: Vandenhoeck & Ruprecht, 2016.

Sergi, Omer. "The Emergence of Judah as a Political Entity between Jerusalem and Benjamin." *ZDPV* 133 (2017): 1–23.

———. "Judah's Expansion in Historical Context." *TA* 40 (2013): 226–46.

———. "Rethinking Israel and the Kingdom of Saul." Pages 371–88 in *Rethinking Israel: Studies in the History and Archaeology of Ancient Israel in Honor of Israel Finkelstein*. Edited by Oded Lipschits, Yuval Gadot, and Matthew J. Adams. Winona Lake, IN: Eisenbrauns, 2017.

———. "State Formation, Religion and 'Collective Identity' in the Southern Levant." *HBAI* 4 (2015): 56–77.

———. "The United Monarchy and the Kingdom of Jeroboam II in the Story of Absalom and Sheba's Revolts (2 Samuel 15–20)." *HBAI* 6 (2017): 329–53.

Sweeney, Marvin A. *I and II Kings: A Commentary*. OTL. Louisville: Westminster John Knox, 2007.

Thompson, Thomas L. *The Historicity of the Patriarchal Narratives: The Quest for the Historical Abraham*. BZAW 133. Berlin: de Gruyter, 1974.
Timm, Stefan. *Die Dynastie Omri: Quellen und Untersuchungen zur Geschichte Israels im 9. Jahrhundert vor Christus*. FRLANT 124. Göttingen: Vandenhoeck & Ruprecht, 1982.
Van Seters, John. *The Biblical Saga of King David*. Winona Lake, IN: Eisenbrauns, 2009.
———. "Divine Encounter at Bethel (Gen 28,10–22) in Recent Literary-Critical Study of Genesis." *ZAW* 110 (1998): 503–13.
———. *In Search of History: Historiography in the Ancient World and the Origins of Biblical History*. New Haven: Yale University Press, 1983.
———. *Prologue to History: The Yahwist as Historian in Genesis*. Louisville: Westminster John Knox, 1992.
Vos, Jacobus Cornelius de. *Das Los Judas: Über Entstehung und Ziele der Landbeschreibung in Josua 15*. VTSup 95. Leiden: Brill, 2003.
Weingart, Kristin. *Stämmevolk—Staatsvolk—Gottesvolk? Studien zur Verwendung des Israel-Namens im Alten Testament*. FAT 2/68. Tübingen: Mohr Siebeck, 2014.
Zobel, Hans-Jürgen. *Stammesspruch und Geschichte: Die Angaben der Stammessprüche von Gen 49, Dtn 33 und Jdc 5 über die politischen und kultischen Zustände im damaligen "Israel."* BZAW 95. Berlin: Töpelmann, 1965.
Zorn, Jeffrey R. "Estimating the Population Size of Ancient Settlements: Methods, Problems, Solutions and a Case Study." *BASOR* 295 (1994): 31–48.
———. "Tell en-Naṣbeh: A Re-evaluation of the Architecture and Stratigraphy of the Early Bronze Age, Iron Age and Later Periods." PhD diss., University of California, Berkeley, 1993.
Zorn, Jeffrey. R., Joseph Yellin, and John Hayes. "The M(W)ṢH Stamp Impressions and the Neo-Babylonian Period." *IEJ* 44 (1994): 161–83.

The Israelite Tribal System: Literary Fiction or Social Reality?

Erhard Blum

In this paper I will discuss some issues concerning the nature and history of tribal structures of ancient Israel as reflected in the traditions of the Hebrew Bible and possible historical implications of these traditions. My observations will draw on important insights expounded by Kristin Weingart in her dissertation about the concept of Israel in the pre- and postexilic literature.[1] At the same time, I will draw in some respects on my own dissertation, which was written over thirty-five years ago.[2]

1. The Basic Alternative: Two Paradigmatic Examples

Martin Noth built one of the most influential hypotheses in twentieth century's exegetical research upon the well-known biblical notion of the twelve tribes of Israel.[3] His ingenious theory of an archaic Israelite amphictyony, that is, a sacral tribal union around a common sanctuary, seemed to provide a reasonable historical reformulation of biblical traditions—supported by old Greek and Italian analogies—and a convincing answer to the question of how the institutional unity of Israel could be thought of in its early history, preceding the constitution of state and monarchy. Especially the remarkable consistency of the number twelve in the different tribal lists of the Old Testament found an elegant explanation in Noth's theory: it was not a phenomenon of literary tradition but of institutional and social reality. Relying on Greek analogy, Noth supposed that

---

1. Kristin Weingart, *Stämmevolk—Staatsvolk—Gottesvolk? Studien zur Verwendung des Israel-Namens im Alten Testament*, FAT 2/68 (Tübingen: Mohr Siebeck, 2014).
2. Erhard Blum, *Die Komposition der Vätergeschichte*, WMANT 57 (Neukirchen-Vluyn: Neukirchener Verlag, 1984), esp. 479–91.
3. Martin Noth, *Das System der zwölf Stämme Israels*, BWANT 52 (Stuttgart: Kohlhammer, 1930).

originally every member of the tribal league had the task of maintaining the common sanctuary for one month. Although the amphictyony gained worldwide recognition for several decades, eventually it did not stand up to exegetical scrutiny.[4] In the early seventies, at the latest, the beautiful amphictyony was gone.

Again, some twenty years later, Christoph Levin, then *Privatdozent* at Göttingen, gave a lecture at the International Organization for the Study of the Old Testament Congress in Paris (1992) about "Das System der zwölf Stämme Israels," which was exactly the title of Noth's classical study from 1930.[5] Levin, however, was not concerned with the amphictyony anymore but with the Israelite tribal system as we find it in the Hebrew Bible. In terms of literary diachrony, Levin's understanding implied an almost complete reversal of Noth's position: The concept of Israel as a community of twelve tribes did not exist in premonarchical times but was of late postexilic origin. According to Noth, the tribal lists transmitted in Num 26, Num 1, and Gen 49 (Jacob's blessing) represented an older tradition than the birth story of Jacob's children in Gen 29–30 (J/E from the tenth or ninth centuries BCE). According to Levin, the former texts were late post-Priestly material, whereas the earlier birth story in Gen 29–30 referred to Israelite tribes since a Yahwistic redaction in exilic times reconstructed by Levin. This Yahwistic layer comprised only six sons of Jacob: "Drei fanden sich in den Vorlagen: Ruben, Simeon, Josef; drei sind hinzugefügt: Levi, Juda und Benjamin."[6] That means Reuben, Simeon, and Joseph belonged to older source material, whereas the exilic Yahwistic redactor introduced Levi, Judah, and Benjamin. Moreover, through this redaction, the very nature of the narrative material was changed: according to Levin, the preexilic Jacob-Esau-Laban story was a fairy tale (*Märchen*), and only the Yahwistic redactor transformed it into a story about Israel's origins, inter

---

4. See, e.g., Andrew D. H. Mayes, "The Period of the Judges and the Rise of the Monarchy," in *Israelite and Judean History*, ed. John H. Hayes and J. Maxwell Miller (London: SCM, 1977), §2B, pointing out that there is no central sanctuary in the traditions of premonarchic Israel, no common festivals of all tribes, no regular maintenance of the sanctuary, etc.

5. Christoph Levin, "Das System der zwölf Stämme Israels," in *Congress Volume Paris 1992*, ed. J. A. Emerton, VTSup 61 (Leiden: Brill, 1995).

6. Levin, "System der zwölf Stämme," 174. See also Levin, *Der Jahwist*, FRLANT 157 (Göttingen: Vandenhoeck & Ruprecht, 1993), 221–31.

alia by identifying Jacob with Israel in Gen 32. In short, the Israelite tribal system was conceived in redactional supplements.

Since it would be difficult to deny that preexilic Israelites or Judahites understood themselves in some form or other as ethnic entities with diverse lineage groups, namely tribes, clans, and so on, the reconstruction of tribal tradition history just mentioned cannot but raise some obvious questions:[7] Is it plausible that preexilic Israel had tribes and clans but no certain idea of how these tribes were related to each other? that preexilic Israelites had fairy tales about different brothers like Jacob, Esau, Joseph and his brothers but no etiological stories about their own origin (*Ursprungssagen*)? Or did such *Sagen* exist once in preexilic Israel without leaving any trace, because they were supplanted by redactional innovations after 587 BCE? What is the historical plausibility of a single scribe reinventing the collective identity of a mostly illiterate society? – It seems only a bit of an exaggeration to say that the underlying paradigm presumes *the literature*, more exactly, the canonical literature we have, as the origin of the cultural world of the ancient Judeans (since the exile); the motto could be: "Literature as the father of all things." We will later come back to the literary-genetic approach, but first we shall move to some fundamental data of empirically based research concerning kinship-based societies.

2. Genealogy in Tribal Societies

The most elaborate descriptions and documentation of tribal societies have been provided by the fieldwork of British and American social anthropologists after World War I who studied Asian and African peoples. Such scholars were, for instance, Edward E. Evans-Pritchard, Meyer Fortes, and Laura and Paul Bohannan. A helpful introduction providing important insights with regard to our field had been presented by Robert R. Wilson

---

7. Aside from the objections to the implied massive literary-critical operations in Gen 29–30 that show a serious disregard of the pericope's narrative logic. See esp. Weingart, *Stämmevolk*, 236–44, with a detailed critical examination of Levin's analysis (Levin, "System der zwölf Stämme"; Levin, *Jahwist*, 221–31); as well as of those by Reinhard G. Kratz, *Die Komposition der erzählenden Bücher des Alten Testaments: Grundwissen der Bibelkritik*, UTB 2157 (Göttingen: Vandenhoeck & Ruprecht, 2000), 270–71; and Daniel Fleming, *The Legacy of Israel in Judah's Bible: History, Politics, and the Reinscribing of Tradition* (Cambridge: Cambridge University Press, 2012), 77–81.

(of Yale University) already in 1977.[8] In most of these societies, *kinship* plays a fundamental role: "A person receives his status, his rights and obligations, by virtue of the kinship ties that link him to the other people with whom he comes in contact."[9] The social identity of an individual and their interactions with other people depend mainly on their position in a lineage, that is, a line of descent, be it through males or females. This holds true mutatis mutandis for greater lineage groups as well, even for clans or tribes and their relationship to other groups. In this respect, genealogy structures and regulates the social world of individuals and groups. Most importantly, however, the opposite holds true as well: if a kin group realizes substantial alterations or discrepancies between the ruling genealogy and the actual social constellations, there will be a process of genealogical adjustment—for instance, by moving persons or lineage groups to another position in the genealogy or by introducing new branches into the stock of descent: "Genealogical changes are put forth, either by individuals or by groups, and when the majority of the society accepts these changes, then the new version of the genealogy may be regarded as established."[10] After some time, the alignment will be forgotten, because we are talking about oral traditions in almost completely oral societies. Wilson gives an illuminating example concerning the Humr tribe of the Baggara Arabs in Sudan, whose genealogy was recorded in 1905 by government officials and studied again by the anthropologist Ian Cunnison fifty years later.[11] Surprise, surprise: in 1955 the tribe presented a substantially extended and restructured genealogy (see the figures below, p. 222).[12]

In general, there is a characteristic fluidity of oral genealogies with an interesting additional aspect: Lineage groups may synchronically cite variant genealogies in different social functions. The Humr, for instance, can use one lineage configuration while discussing issues in the *political* sphere and another one in the *domestic* context.[13]

---

8. Robert R. Wilson, *Genealogy and History in the Biblical World*, YNER 7 (New Haven: Yale University Press, 1977).

9. Wilson, *Genealogy and History*, 18.

10. Wilson, *Genealogy and History*, 29.

11. Wilson, *Genealogy and History*, 48–53. Ian Cunnison, *Baggara Arabs: Power and the Lineage in a Sudanese Nomad Tribe* (Oxford: Clarendon, 1966).

12. The figures are modified from Wilson, *Genealogy and History*, 49, 50, through additional highlighting of added or shifted segments; the corresponding changes in the tribal political structure are explained by Wilson, *Genealogy and History*, 51–54.

13. Wilson, *Genealogy and History*, 52–53 with figs. 1.2 and 1.3. See his illumi-

The empirical material provides additional data that call into question fundamental premises of some literary-historical reconstructions. One of the more important examples is the popular assumption that several stories in the biblical ancestor tradition are based on fairy tales (*Märchen*), which were only secondarily transformed into primordial *Sagen*. In general, there is one basic reason: the name(s) of main actor(s) is not eponymous as, for instance, Esau (versus Edom), Jacob (versus Israel), Laban (versus Aram), and so on. Of course, the alleged founders of clans, tribes, peoples are quite often "eponyms" in the genealogies, but this is by no means necessary, especially not in the case of founders of greater segments (like those of tribes or people). Accidently, the Humr provide a fine example: according to their tradition, the founder of the tribe was a man named Ḥeymir, and according to some Humr the ancestor's name was Ḥamid el Aḥmar.[14] Another erroneous presupposition is that names of real tribes, clans, and so on, cannot be personal names, which justifies the conclusion that tribes with such names are fictitious. There is not only plenty of counterevidence (see again the Humr genealogies given below, p. 222), such a rule would also be inconsistent with the basic genealogical logic that presumes an individual founder at the beginning of every segment. In short: in this context, scholarly a priori presuppositions run the risk of overlooking the factual aspects of traditions in terms of social reality.[15]

In conclusion, especially two basic aspects deserve emphasis in our context:

First, kinship relations apparently have an influence on social behavior, but above all, social reality determines genealogy. Since reality changes and sometimes seems contradictory, genealogies change and might even appear in divergent versions.

---

nating comment: "It should be stressed that the Humr see no contradiction between the domestic version of the genealogy, which gives 'Ajar two or three sons, and the political version, which assigns 'Ajar five sons. Each is considered accurate in its own context, and each may therefore be regarded as 'true'" (54).

14. Cunnison, *Baggara Arabs*, 8 with n. 24, 112.

15. Another set of questionable presuppositions concerns the diachronic relations between genealogies and narrative traditions. I restrict myself to one quote from Wilson: "there is no evidence that the genealogies are ever used to relate narrative complexes if the persons mentioned in the genealogies were not already related by the narratives themselves. Genealogies at the oral level are apparently not created for the purpose of linking preexistent narratives" (Wilson, *Genealogy and History*, 55).

Second, this nature of genealogies in tribal societies implies a plain fact that is of immense importance for historical research: kin relations as the basis of tribal or ethnic identities are not biological but social phenomena; they are not a question of DNA but of collective recognition and consciousness. In the realm of social sciences, such an understanding might be a matter of course, but in biblical studies, this is not yet the case, unfortunately.[16]

3. Tribal Structures in Preexilic Times: Biblical and External Evidence

Coming back to ancient Israel, it is quite obvious that the features of African or Arab tribal societies cannot be transferred one-to-one to Israelite or Judean/Judahite societies, at least in the periods of kingdoms and state structures (with respect to prestate conditions, it might look different). Nevertheless, it seems just as obvious that kinship relations played a crucial role in ancient Israel at any period, for the Israelite individual as well as for the collective identity. With regard to the latter, suffice it to refer to

---

16. Besides the cautious considerations in Fleming, *Legacy of Israel*, esp. 252–54, the monograph of Weingart, *Stämmevolk*, appears to be the first investigation treating the issue comprehensively. Since the traditional biological understanding functions mainly as tacit presupposition, it might be useful to give a prominent example. Dealing with the time of Nehemiah and Ezra, Herbert Donner summarizes a quite common conception of postexilic Judah: At this time, he states, "vollzog sich eine Neubestimmung der schon längst undeutlich und unübersichtlich gewordenen Größe 'Israel'. Wir sind im Zeitalter der heiligen Schriften, in dem sich 'Israel' als theokratische Gemeinde unter dem Gesetz formierte. Diese Gemeinde verstand sich als eine Blutsgemeinschaft, obwohl sie das faktisch schon lange nicht mehr war und genau genommen weder je gewesen war noch hatte sein können" (Herbert Donner, *Geschichte des Volkes Israel und seiner Nachbarn in Grundzügen*, GAT 4 [Göttingen: Vandenhoeck & Ruprecht, 1987], 431 [= 3rd ed., 2001, 465]). Besides the question of how Donner could judge on the DNA of the Judeans in the Persian period, the basic problem in terms of method is the search for "factual," i.e., biological kinship as such. The only thing that matters is, in actual fact, how the community understood itself. In this respect, one should recall that nowhere in the Hebrew Bible do we find more genealogies und lineage registers than in the Priestly layer of the Pentateuch, in Chronicles, and in Ezra–Nehemiah; see also Erhard Blum, "Volk oder Kultgemeinde? Zum Bild des Judentums in der alttestamentlichen Wissenschaft" (1995) in *Grundfragen der historischen Exegese: Methodologische, philologische und hermeneutische Beiträge zum Alten Testament*, ed. Wolfgang Oswald and Kristin Weingart, FAT 95 (Tübingen: Mohr Siebeck, 2015), 195–214.

the kinship relations claimed with Aram, Moab, Ammon, Edom, or the Ishmaelites, but not with the Philistines, the Phoenicians, and so on.

Fine examples of linear as well as segmented lineages occur, inter alia, in our Saul tradition. At the very beginning, we find a solemn linear lineage with Saul through six (!) generations (1 Sam 9:1–2):

> There was a man of Benjamin, whose name was Kish, the son of Abiel, the son of Zeror, the son of Bechorath, the son of Aphiah, a Benjaminite, a mighty man of power. He had a son whose name was Saul.[17]

In contrast, the procedure of taking Saul by lot in 1 Sam 10:19–21 presupposes a classically segmented lineage:

> And now present yourselves before the Lord by your tribes and by your thousands [אלף]."
> Then Samuel brought all the tribes of Israel near,
> and the tribe [שבט] of Benjamin was taken by lot.
> He brought the tribe of Benjamin near by its clans,
> and the clan [משפחה] of the Matrites was taken by lot.
> Finally, he brought the clan of the Matrites near,
> and Saul the son of Kish was taken by lot.

The passage was possibly reworked by the main Deuteronomistic composer, but at this point there is no need to enter either literary- or tradition-historical debates or the sometimes annoyingly simplifying discussion about "secondary, tertiary," etc. biblical sources. Instead, I will focus on two examples of external evidence.

The first example, however, shall be introduced through the beginning of the Gideon-story in Judg 6:11:

> ויבא מלאך יהוה וישב תחת האלה
> אשר בעפרה
> אשר ליואש אבי העזרי
> וגדעון בנו חבט חטים בגת להניס מפני מדין

Gideon is identified through his father Joash, who belonged to Abiezer, which represents the clan to which Joash's family belonged. This informa-

---

17. The biblical quotations in this article represent an eclectic use of KJV, NIV, and NRSV including individual modifications.

tion prepares Gideon's objection against the commission by the angel of YHWH, still unrecognized by Gideon, to deliver Israel from the hand of Midian (Judg 6:15):

> And he said unto him,
> Oh my Lord, wherewith shall I save Israel?
> behold, my clan (thousand) is poor in Manasseh,
> and I am the least in my father's house.

The objection as such represents a stock motif of call narratives that aim to legitimize political and/or prophetical leaders, such as Saul, Gideon, Jeremiah, and Moses. In the case of Gideon, we have the reference to the whole range of genealogical segments: *bet ab* = extended family, *eleph* = clan, the tribe *Manasseh* and the whole people of *Israel*. In terms of diachrony, we are talking about a quite clearly preexilic and pre-Deuteronomistic tradition.[18]

More or less by chance, we have an allegedly complete set of the clans of the tribe of Manasseh or of their respective founders in several pericopes: Num 26:29–34 (27:1); Josh 17:1–3; 1 Chr 7:14–19, partially also in Num 36. The literary connections between these texts prove to be complicated as a result of mutual interpretations and corrections, as well as textual corruptions (especially in Chronicles). Probably, Josh 17:1–3 is based on Num 26, but not in its current form. Concerning the Cisjordan, Josh 17:1–2.3 LXX presents the following genealogical segments in Manasseh:

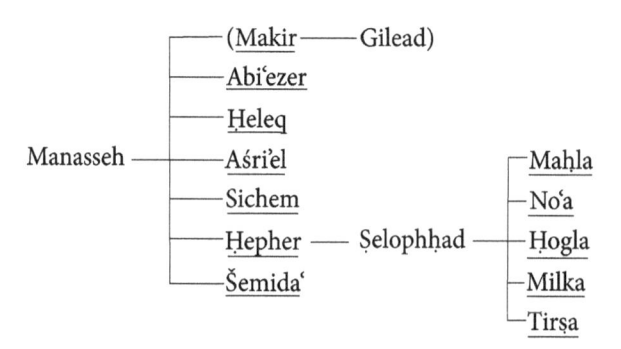

```
                  ┌── (Makir ── Gilead)
                  ├── Abiʿezer
                  ├── Heleq
Manasseh ─────────┼── Aśriʾel                    ┌── Mahla
                  ├── Sichem                     ├── Noʿa
                  ├── Hepher ── Ṣelophḥad ───────┼── Hogla
                  └── Šemidaʿ                    ├── Milka
                                                 └── Tirṣa
```

---

18. See the latest thorough analysis in Walter Gross, *Richter*, HThKAT (Freiburg im Breisgau: Herder, 2009), 365–73, 388–89.

The underlined names are characterized in Num 26 as "clans." These are destined to get a נחלה, that is, to inherit a portion of land. The inheritance of land is the main issue of both texts in Num 26 and Josh 17, indeed. There is, however, a major peculiarity in this case: we have in one lineage five clans with *female* "founders." The reason is that Zelophehad, the son of Hepher, had no sons but five daughters. Their right to inherit land is approved (implicitly) in Num 26 and (explicitly) in Num 27.

The diachronic position of all these passages seems clear in a broader perspective: they are postexilic, late priestly *Einschreibungen* into the Pentateuch, as well as into Joshua, several generations after the exilic Deuteronomistic History. Given these analytical data, one has good reasons to assume postexilic inventions of fictitious tribal genealogies—with the exception of the Abiezer clan that was given in the Gideon narrative. In fact, however, most of these names represent historical clans or clan districts, respectively, in the traditional region of the tribe of Manasseh. The evidence is epigraphical, the so-called Samaria ostraca that were found in 1910 as filling in floors of the royal palace in Samaria. The about one hundred ostraca are dated to the first half of the eighth century. Except for Hepher[19] and Transjordan Machir, all male clan-names of Josh 17 and two of the female names (Noa, Hogla[20]) are mentioned as areas from which certain quantities of wine or oil were delivered to the capital and registered there.[21]

```
                    ┌── (Makir ────── Gilead)
                    ├── Abi'ezer      (2x)
                    ├── Ḥeleq         (6x)
  Manasseh ─────────┼── Aśri'el       (2x) שראל   ┌── Maḥla
                    ├── Sichem        (1x)        ├── No'a (3x)
                    ├── Hepher ─── Ṣelophḥad ─────┼── Hogla (3x)
                    └── Šemida'       (18x) שמידע ├── Milka
                                                  └── Tirṣa
```

---

19. Hepher might be missing by pure chance. Nevertheless, it is interesting because Hepher as a clan is in some tension with his role as lineage founder of the five female clans Mahla, etc. (see above).

20. The appearance of Noa and Hogla shows the historicity of those Manassite clans in the period of the kingdom; the etiological explanation of the female names in Num 26–27 might be much later.

21. For the interpretation of the names as areas, see already Martin Noth, "Das Krongut der israelitischen Könige und seine Verwaltung" (1927), in *Archäologische,*

All in all, the clans of Manasseh constitute a very interesting case (1) regarding the reality of kinship categories in preexilic Israel, (2) regarding the high contingency of archaeological evidence of social data concerning the Israelite *Lebenswelt*, and (3) regarding the potential weakness of historical conclusions founded exclusively on literary-historical data, no matter how reliable the exegetical dating might be.

My second example for external evidence of the basically tribal character of Israelite society refers to the Mesha Stela. Elusive reality like the consciousness of ethnic identity or—correspondingly—of otherness does exist as long as it is perceived, whether from within or from without. In this respect, the well-known proposition of the Moabite king Mesha that "the men of Gad [איש גד] lived in the country of Atarot from very long times [מעלם]" is of major historical interest. Its usual interpretation as a reference to an *Israelite* tribe Gad is, however, strongly contested in recent German-speaking scholarship. Especially Manfred Weippert advocates the understanding that Mesha is talking about a *Moabite* tribe. The most prominent presentation of this theory is to be found in Weippert's monumental *Historisches Textbuch zum Alten Testament*.[22] Although Weippert's Gad theory would have important implications, there has not been any controversial debate about it, as far as I know. Therefore, its presentation in some detail appears appropriate. The crucial passage is found in lines 10–14 of the inscription (*KAI* 181), here presented in sentences (with my numbering):

22 ואש. גד. ישב. בארץ. עטרת. מעלם.
23 (11) ויבן. לה. מלך. ישראל. את. עטרת |
24 ואלתחם. בקר.
25 ואחזה |
26 ואהרג. את. כל. העׄםׄ.
27 (12) הקר. הית. לכמש. ולמאב |

---

exegetische und topographische Untersuchungen zur Geschichte Israels, vol. 1 of *Aufsätze zur biblischen Landes- und Altertumskunde*, ed. Hans Walter Wolff (Neukirchen-Vluyn: Neukirchener Verlag, 1971), 159–82, esp. 167, 173–80. Regarding the interpretation as deliveries to the capital, see, e.g., Volkmar Fritz, *Das Buch Josua*, HAT 1/7 (Tübingen: Mohr Siebeck, 1994), 174 with literature.

22. Manfred Weippert, *Historisches Textbuch zum Alten Testament*, GAT 10 (Göttingen: Vandenhoeck & Ruprecht, 2010), 242–48. Since its publication, the book has been reckoned as the standard handbook in German for nonbiblical textual sources pertaining to Israelite history.

The Israelite Tribal System

28 ואשב. משם. את. אראל. דודה.
29 וא̊[ס](13)חבה. לפני. כמש. בקרית |
30 ואשב. בה. את. אש. שרן. ואת. אש̊ (14) מ̊חרת |

Weippert reads as follows:

22 Und die Leute von Gadd hatten seit jeher im Land ʿAṭarōt gewohnt.
23 Aber der König von Israel baute sich ʿAṭarōt aus.
24 Da kämpfte ich mit der Stadt,
25 nahm sie ein
26 und tötete alles Volk,
27 [und] die Stadt gehörte Kamōš und Moab.
28 Da brachte ich von dort das Bratbecken des Altarherds weg
29 und sch[l]eppte es vor Kamōš in Qarīyōt.
30 Da siedelte ich darin die Leute von Šarōn und von *Mḥrt* an.

The main arguments go as follows: (1) The biblical geography of the tribes in Transjordan is not always historically reliable. (2) Since Dibon, Mesha's own city, is called Dibon-Gad in Num 33:45–46, Mesha himself was most probably a Gadite. (3) Mesha's statement that the people of Gad always lived in Atarot arguably matches the view of the Gadites themselves, a view inconsistent with the Israelite tradition of the conquest. (4) Mesha makes a distinction in his stela: the conquest of cities that "did not originally belong to Moab" "had to be legitimized by an explicit order by Kamōš [Chemosh], Moab's 'national' god"; this is the case for Nebo and Ḥoronaim but not for Atarot.[23]

Statement (1) is reasonable. The weight of argument (2) depends on the question whether Num 33:45–46 would be suitable evidence for a *Moabite* point of view. Statement (3) builds on several uncertain presuppositions,[24] and the textual interpretation supposed in the last argument (4) cannot

---

23. Argument (4) is expounded in Manfred Weippert, "Mōšiʿs Moab," *Transeu* 46 (2014): 133–51. The quotation is taken from the English summary.

24. One presupposition is that the hypothetical Gadite tradition was concurrent with the biblical conquest tradition(s), another concerns the meaning of מעלם in an absolute ("without beginning") or a relative sense ("ever since Moabites and Israelites settled in this region" or words to that effect). Regarding a third presupposition, which concerns Mesha's impulse to say something like this, see below, p. 213 with n. 28.

stand on its own (see hereafter) but depends on the reading's overall conclusiveness.

Weippert himself has seen that his reading might be difficult with regard to sentence 26 (ואהרג את כל העם). Therefore, he postulates that עם in sentence 26 means "military force" ("Kriegsvolk") and refers to Israelite occupation troops assumed to be there. Nevertheless, this issue remains a weak point because in line 24 we have ואמר לכל העם referring simply to the people of the city. In sentence 26, in contrast, Mesha could easily avoid any ambiguity by speaking about עם ישראל or something to that effect. Moreover, apart from this difficulty, sentence 30 also does not fit the proposed understanding because Mesha explains here that he settled Moabite people in conquered Atarot, an action that arguably presupposes the massacre of the original population.[25]

Last, but not least, this interpretation seems irreconcilable with sentence 27 (הקר הית לכמש ולמאב). This cannot mean that Atarot *had* belonged to Moab all the time, because first, that would be said already in sentence 22, according to Weippert, and second, the statement would come too late in this place (in biblical texts this would be undoubtedly a case for *Literarkritik*). Therefore, היה ל in sentence 27 must have the (inchoative) meaning "to pass into somebody's possession." If sentence 27 was asyndetic (i.e., without the conjunctive "*waw*"), we have a special syntax marking the sentence as a kind of résumé: "Chemosh and Moab came in possession of the city!," which is immediately explicated, first concerning Chemosh by the sentences "and I carried away from there the altar of its beloved[26] and I dragged it to Chemosh at Qariyot" and eventually concerning Moab by the sentence "and I settled in [Atarot] the people of Sharon and the people of *Mḥrt*."[27] Given this understanding, the passage might be translated as follows:

---

25. In Weippert, "Mōšiʿs Moab," 148–49, he explains additionally that the "people" killed by Mesha were not "die einheimische Bevölkerung," "die wohl bereits von den israelitischen Truppen vertrieben oder umgebracht worden war," adding, however, again information that is missing in Mesha's text, though sentences 22–23 would have provided a unique opportunity in this regard.

26. Given *dwd* as designation of the Israelite God (see *KAI* 2 ad loc.), possibly in a mocking distortion by the Moabite (*dwd* instead of *dd* [incl. a pun alluding to "Dawid"?]), the suffix in *dwdh* can refer only to *hqr* (sentence 27) = Atarot. If so, sentence 28 implies final evidence against Gad as a Moabite tribe.

27. The assumption that Mesha exclusively legitimizes attacks on cities that originally were not thought Moabite (Nebo, Ḥoronaim) with an oracle of his god Che-

22	And the men of Gad lived in the land of Ataroth from ancient times.
23	(11) And the king of Israel built Ataroth for himself.
24	And I fought against the city,
25	captured it,
26	and killed all the people.
27	(12) Chemosh and Moab came in possession of the city.
28	I carried away from there the fire-hearth of its beloved
29	and hauled (13) it before Chemosh in Qariyot.
30	And I settled in it the men of Sharon und the men of (14) *Mḫrt*.

So, if "Gad" referring to a Moabite tribe proves incompatible with the context of the stela, a last question remains: Why on earth would Mesha emphasize Gad's autochthony in the region of Atarot in sentence 22? The resuming sentences in the final part of the stela (lines 28 and 29) provide the answer revealing his motivation: "And I became king of hundreds of cities that I annexed to the land!" That is to say, conquering non-Moabite area is Mesha's proud boast.[28]

In sum, the interesting fact remains that the ninth-century Moabite Stela confirms the existence of one of the most peripheral tribes of the Israelite tradition. Remarkably enough, this tribe does not appear in the ancient song of Deborah (Judg 5; see below). In addition, this evidence shows the natural significance of *tribal* affiliation, mirrored in an outsider's perception.

4. The Twelve Tribes System: No Postexilic Invention. The Case of Benjamin and Judah

If our demonstration that tribal structures constituted some social reality in ancient Israel and Judah proves convincing, then the idea that the Israelite twelve-tribe system was invented by postexilic redactors proves to be impossible.[29] Suffice it to refer to one crucial point, the position of Benjamin in the lineage. As is well known, the Persian province Yehud

---

mosh appears unfounded as well. First, it is improbable that Mesha would not rate Ḥoronaim as Moabite (as the statement "and Chemosh brought it back in my days" [line 33] confirms; *pace* Weippert, *Textbuch*, 248 n. 51). Second, in the case of Nebo, the high military risk could just as well be the reason for the divine confirmation.

28. For a probable additional aspect, see below, p. 217 n. 38.
29. See already Weingart, *Stämmevolk*, 293–96.

comprised a significantly reduced territory of earlier Judah—and all Benjamin. The idea that Judean scribes would construct a genealogy in which Benjamin would not belong to the lineage group of Judah but to Joseph (of all brothers) and that this tradition would be unanimously accepted without even a sign of competing concepts seems abstruse. On the contrary, the Joseph-Benjamin connection obviously constituted in Persian times a frozen genealogical scheme given by a strong tradition that could be touched no more. Reality conflicted with genealogy in a similar way already in the days of King Josiah after the collapse of the Assyrian Empire.[30]

In the times of the Northern Kingdom and of the Assyrian province of Samaria, the constellation was a bit more complicated because the eastern part of Benjamin in the Jordan Rift valley belonged to the kingdom of Israel, whereas the Benjamin plateau on the mountain was part of "Bet-David." That means Judah controlled by far the main part of Benjaminite population, whereas the Joseph-dominated kingdom of Israel included only a small part, but at least Gilgal and Jericho. Nevertheless, the northern tribes in this way kept some share of Benjamin. On the other way around, there is no need to explain the vital interest of Judah in keeping the border with the Northern Kingdom at a distance from Jerusalem. Given the clear superiority of Israel over Judah in terms of resources and military force, it was a remarkable achievement of Judah to succeed in this respect. According to our textual sources, it appears that this achievement was mainly due to contingent historical constellations.[31] Concerning the primordial brotherhood of Joseph and Benjamin, the overall picture suggests that the origins of that kinship lie some time before the ninth century BCE. If one looks for a political constellation that perfectly fits this Joseph-Benjamin connection, I would primarily point to the kingdom of Saul and Ishbaal (see below). That means somewhere around 1000 BCE.

Finally, a last point: Judah as part of Israel.[32] The main question is, of course, at what point was Judah genealogically integrated into "Israel." As

---

30. Probably, this holds true also regarding the northern expansion of Benjaminite territory into the region of Bethel, as reflected in postexilic biblical sources.

31. Important examples are Judah's vassalage to Shoshenq (1 Kgs 12:25–26) and Bar Hadad's (1 Kgs 15:17–21), Tiglath-pileser III's (2 Kgs 16:7–9), and Hazael's massive weakening of the Northern Kingdom.

32. This, again, constitutes a central issue of Weingart's work (Weingart, *Stämmevolk*, 235–87, 340–73). I take up several arguments of hers; some of my conclusions, however, might go beyond her own position.

already mentioned, the kingdom of Israel included, so to speak, a portion of Benjamin, whereas its lion's share was part of Judah. Seen the other way around, this implies that the kingdom of Judah always included a quite substantial portion of Israel, since Benjamin was hard-core Israel in origin (see the Saul tradition). This fact should suffice to question the widespread opinion nowadays that Judah could have adopted the name "Israel" only after 720 BCE (i.e., after the Northern Kingdom's pitiful disaster). Besides the undisputable close cultural ties[33] that implied that the two kingdoms did not see each other as foreign countries in the same sense as, for instance, Aram or Egypt, there is literary evidence of primordial kinship relations in elaborated northern narrative traditions[34] from the eighth century: the Jacob story with his twelve sons including Judah and Simeon.[35]

---

33. Cf., especially, the realm of religion, but also the uniform scribal culture (see Johannes Renz, *Schrift und Schreibertradition: Eine paläographische Studie zum kulturgeschichtlichen Verhältnis von israelitischem Nordreich und Südreich*, ADPV 23 [Wiesbaden: Harrassowitz, 1997]) or the close ties between the royal houses, not least in the period of the Omrides.

34. In addition to the prose traditions, the so-called blessing of Moses (Deut 33) should be mentioned, at least. Isac L. Seeligmann, "A Psalm from Pre-Regal Times," in *Gesammelte Studien zur Hebräischen Bibel*, ed. Erhard Blum, FAT 41 (Tübingen: Mohr Siebeck, 2004), 50, rightly saw "the northern character of the Blessing of Moses established by vv. 7 and 16," with regard to the basic substance of the poem. In 33:16, I accept the reading by Ernst A. Knauf, *Midian: Untersuchungen zur Geschichte Palästinas und Nordarabiens am Ende des 2. Jahrtausends v. Chr.*, ADPV 10 (Wiesbaden: Harrassowitz, 1988), 50 with n. 248: *škny Sinā*, i.e., "Who dwells on Sinai" giving expression to the north-Israelite Sinai tradition (see Erhard Blum, "Der historische Mose und die Frühgeschichte Israels," *HBAI* 1 [2012]: 58–62).

35. For the Jacob story, see Erhard Blum, "The Jacob Tradition," in *The Book of Genesis: Composition, Reception, and Interpretation*, ed. Craig A. Evans, Joel N. Lohr, and David L. Petersen, VTSup 152 (Leiden: Brill, 2012), 181–211, reckoning with two editions of the Jacob story, the first in the ninth century, the second (including the Bethel etiology, a *Fortschreibung*-layer in Gen *29–31 and Gen *32–33) in the eighth century. This etiological *Ursprungsgeschichte* of Israel has to be distinguished from broader compositions of the ancestor stories including the divine *promises* of land, offspring, and blessing that presuppose an exilic context (*pace* Nadav Na'aman, "The Jacob Story and the Formation of Biblical Israel," *TA* 41 [2014]: 95–125). The obviously northern setting of the narrative plot (including the Isaac- and Edom-connections, see Blum, "Jacob Tradition," 208–9) determines the etiological reference of Gen *28:11–22 to the royal Israelite sanctuary at Bethel. A Bethel sanctuary flourishing in the seventh to sixth centuries (see already Fritz Dumermuth, "Zur deuteronomischen Kulttheologie und ihren Voraussetzungen," *ZAW* 70 [1958]: 96–97 with n. 180), for

Further evidence is provided by the northern Joseph story with a prominent triangular relationship between Joseph, Benjamin, and Judah and by the use of "Israel" in early David narratives.³⁶

On the other hand, there are two significant traditions of tribal constellations without Judah and Simeon: The Song of Deborah and a note about Ishbaal's kingdom. Judges 5* represents probably the oldest epic poetry in the Hebrew Bible and one of its oldest texts in general. The song differentiates in 5:6–18 between two groups in Israel.³⁷ On the one side are the tribes that are praised for their brave and willing participation in the

---

which there is allegedly archaeological evidence, has appeared as a popular idea in recent research (see, e.g., Joseph Blenkinsopp, "Bethel in the Neo-Babylonian Period," in *Judah and the Judeans in the Neo-Babylonian Period*, ed. Oded Lipschits and Joseph Blenkinsopp [Winona Lake, IN: Eisenbrauns, 2010]; Ernst A. Knauf, "Die Adressatenkreise von Josua," in *The Book of Joshua*, ed. Ed Noort, BETL 250 [Leuven: Peeters, 2012], 203–2, "Anhang I: Der Tempel von Betel im 6. Jh. v.Chr"). But in fact, we are talking about a scholarly phantom (see already Klaus Koenen, *Bethel: Geschichte, Kult und Theologie*, OBO 192 [Fribourg: Universitätsverlag; Göttingen: Vandenhoeck & Ruprecht, 2003], 59–64): Neither is there any archaeological evidence, at present, esp. concerning the sanctuary (Israel Finkelstein and Lily Singer-Avitz, "Reevaluating Bethel," *ZDPV* 125 [2009]: 33–48; Oded Lipschits, "Bethel Revisited," in *Rethinking Israel: Studies in the History and Archaeology of Ancient Israel in Honor of Israel Finkelstein*, ed. Oded Lipschits, Yuval Gadot, and Matthew J. Adams [Winona Lake, IN: Eisenbrauns, 2017], 233–46), nor does the common ancient Near Eastern concept of sanctuaries being the *axis mundi* place Gen 28 in the Neo-Babylonian period (*pace* Victor A. Hurowitz, "Babylon in Bethel—New Light on Jacob's Dream," in *Orientalism, Assyriology and the Bible*, ed. Steven W. Holloway, Hebrew Bible Monographs 10 [Sheffield: Sheffield Phoenix, 2007], 436–48), nor does there exist any biblical hint to a sixth century Bethel sanctuary (Zech 7:1–6 is to be ruled out because Bethel in verse 2 belongs to the well-known personal name Bethel-Sar-Eṣer [see Robert Hanhart, *Sacharja*, BKAT 14.7 (Neukirchen-Vluyn: Neukirchener Verlag, 1998), ad loc., drawing on Julius Wellhausen], and *bet YHWH* in Jer 41:5 referring to Bethel makes no sense in terms of geography and plot). Regarding the birth episode in Gen 29–30, see above, n. 7.

36. For the triangle, see, in detail, Erhard Blum and Kristin Weingart, "The Joseph Story: Diaspora Novella or North-Israelite Narrative?," *ZAW* 129 (2017): 501–21. For Israel in the early David narratives, see Weingart, *Stämmevolk*, 171–90.

37. According to Fleming, *Legacy of Israel*, 66, "Judg. 5:14–18 is all the more striking for the absence of the name 'Israel'" (see also pp. 68–69). But it is not clear what exactly should be striking. After all, changing from an imposing introduction, including the general praise of ישראל חוקקי, עם יהוה, and צדקות יהוה, etc. to praise or rebuke of single tribes and their behavior is part of the song's lively movement, which goes on with even more dramatic cuts—until the closing vantage point of the women in

war against the kings of Canaan. These are Ephraim and Benjamin (5:14a), Machir and Zebulun (5:14b), Issachar (Barak!) (5:15) and Naphtali (5:18). On the other side, we have the idle tribes Reuben, Gilead, Dan, and Asher, which are rebuked by the singer (5:16–17). Several names of the canonical tribes are missing. In the case of Manasseh, his lineage rank was possibly (still) occupied by Machir. A similar case might have been Gad being included in Gilead; alternatively, and in my view more probably, this tribe might still have been independent between Israel and nascent Moab.[38] The last option provides the only reasonable explanation for the complete silence about the southern tribes Judah and Simeon, at any rate, which means that these tribes were not thought to be part of Israel (as has been a broad scholarly consensus for long).[39] As a consequence, scholarly theories that promote a postexilic dating of Judg 5 should have an answer to the simple, but decisive question of what a Jewish author or redactor tried to say to his alleged addressees in Persian or Hellenistic times by excluding Judah from Israel.[40]

The other quite early evidence for a concept of Israel that does not include Judah is the description of Ishbaal's kingdom in 2 Sam 2:8–9:

8 ואבנר בן־נר שר־צבא אשר לשאול לקח את־איש בשת בן־שאול ויעברהו מחנים:
9 וימלכהו אל־הגלעד ואל־האשורי ואל־יזרעאל ועל־אפרים ועל־בנימן ועל־ישראל כלה:

8 Meanwhile, Abner son of Ner, the commander of Saul's army, had taken Ishbosheth [= Ishbaal] son of Saul and brought him over to Mahanaim. 9 He made him king over the Gilead, the Ashurite(s), Jezreel, Ephraim, and Benjamin, that means, over all Israel.

Sisera's palace. After all, there is no reason for repeating already explicated matters throughout the poem.

38. If there still was in Mesha's time some memory of Gad's earlier independence (until David? until Omri?), this might have been an additional motivation for his remark about Gad in line 10. Cf. a similar consideration by Fleming, *Legacy of Israel*, 245.

39. Differently Weingart, *Stämmevolk*, 372 n. 331.

40. See Levin, "System der zwölf Stämme," 178 n. 39: "Das Debora-Lied Jdc. v … ist eines der spätesten Stücke der vorderen Propheten." With more detail, Levin, "Das Alter des Deboralieds," in *Fortschreibungen: Gesammelte Studien zum Alten Testament*, BZAW 316 (Berlin: de Gruyter, 2003), 124–41 (with literature). Regarding the popular "linguistic dating" of Judg 5—whether very early or very late—see the prudent discussion in Gross, *Richter*, 295–97.

Reading the opaque הָאֲשׁוּרִי according to the mostly preferred conjecture as *the Asherites*, the description starts with the eastern (Gilead) and northern (Asher, Jezreel) periphery and moves through Ephraim finally to Saul's own tribe Benjamin.[41] Defining a dominion, the list can combine clear regional (*hglʿd, yzrʿl*) with tribal designations (*hʾšry* cj., *ʾprym* [?], *bnymn*). Since "Jezreel" might include the territories of the tribes adjacent to the northern valley (Issachar, Naphtali, Zebulun) and since "Ephraim" can also refer to the central mountain to the south of Jezreel, it seems possible that Ishbaal's territory is shown here in a way that matches almost the tribal constellation of Judg 5 (apart from the remote enclave of the Danites, of course).[42] The wording of וְעַל־יִשְׂרָאֵל כֻּלֹּה is per se ambiguous, meaning either "that is to say: all Israel" or "and what else belonged to Israel"; the context, however, supports the first option, making clear that "the house of Judah" (2 Sam 2:4, 10) did not belong to the reign of the Saulides.[43] Since it is about political dominion, the tradition about Ishbaal—unlike the Song of Deborah—does not have direct implications on the alleged kinship relations between Judah and the Israelite tribes.

However, the question remains still open, when was Judah (+ Simeon) eventually incorporated into the primordial lineage of Israel. One could, perhaps, imagine constellations of rapprochement between the Northern Kingdom and Judah that induced the Israelites to adopt the Judeans into the Jacob/Israel genealogy. Such a rapprochement is attested especially in the Omride era (e.g., the political marriage of Joram with Athaliah), which in my view is too late, however, because of, inter alia, the court history of David with its notion of an Israel comprising both northern Israel and Judah.[44] At any rate, the most natural context for the formation of such an enlarged concept of Israel is provided by the biblical tradition of a

---

41. For the conjecture, see the latest detailed discussion in Walter Dietrich, *Samuel*, BKAT 8/3.5 (Neukirchen-Vluyn: Neukirchener Verlag, 2017), ad loc.

42. For Jezreel, see Yohanan Aharoni, *The Land of the Bible: A Historical Geography*, trans. and ed. Anson F. Rainey, 2nd ed. (London: Burns & Oates, 1979), 222, map 16. For Ephraim, see Aharoni, *Land of the Bible*, 288 map 20, and 289.

43. Siegfried Herrmann, building upon insights of Alt (see Albrecht Alt, "Die Landnahme der Israeliten in Palästina," in *Kleine Schriften zur Geschichte des Volkes Israels 1* [Munich: Beck, 1953], 89–125, esp. 116–19), has shown that this holds also for Saul's kingdom in general; see Siegfried Herrmann, *Geschichte Israels in alttestamentlicher Zeit* (Munich: Kaiser, 1973), 181–82.

44. For the court history of David, see Erhard Blum, "Solomon and the United Monarchy: Some Textual Evidence," in *One God—One Cult—One Nation: Archaeo-*

temporary Davidic personal union comprising the southern and northern kingships in the tenth century BCE. It is true that so far, we do not have any extrabiblical evidence for such a union, as is the case for many other aspects of Levantine history in the first millennium BCE. But at the same time, I do not see any striking external evidence against such an early patrimonial "united kingdom" either.

Bibliography

Aharoni, Yohanan. *The Land of the Bible: A Historical Geography*. Translated and edited by Anson F. Rainey. 2nd ed. London: Burns & Oates, 1979.

Alt, Albrecht. "Die Landnahme der Israeliten in Palästina." Pages 89–125 in *Kleine Schriften zur Geschichte des Volkes Israels 1*. Munich: Beck, 1953.

Blenkinsopp, Joseph. "Bethel in the Neo-Babylonian Period." Pages 93–107 in *Judah and the Judeans in the Neo-Babylonian Period*. Edited by Oded Lipschits and Joseph Blenkinsopp. Winona Lake, IN: Eisenbrauns, 2010.

Blum, Erhard. "Der historische Mose und die Frühgeschichte Israels." *HBAI* 1 (2012): 37–63.

———. "The Jacob Tradition." Pages 181–211 in *The Book of Genesis: Composition, Reception, and Interpretation*. Edited by Craig A. Evans, Joel N. Lohr, and David L. Petersen. VTSup 152. Leiden: Brill, 2012.

———. *Die Komposition der Vätergeschichte*. WMANT 57. Neukirchen-Vluyn: Neukirchener Verlag, 1984.

———. "Solomon and the United Monarchy: Some Textual Evidence." Pages 59–78 in *One God—One Cult—One Nation: Archaeological and Biblical Perspectives*. Edited by Hermann Spieckermann and Reinhard G. Kratz. BZAW 405. Berlin: de Gruyter, 2010.

———. "Volk oder Kultgemeinde? Zum Bild des nachexilischen Judentums in der alttestamentlichen Wissenschaft." Pages 195–214 in *Grundfragen der historischen Exegese: Methodologische, philologische und hermeneutische Beiträge zum Alten Testament*. Edited by Wolfgang Oswald and Kristin Weingart. FAT 95. Tübingen: Mohr Siebeck, 2015.

Blum, Erhard, and Kristin Weingart. "The Joseph Story: Diaspora Novella or North-Israelite Narrative?" *ZAW* 129 (2017): 501–21.
Cunnison, Ian. *Baggara Arabs: Power and the Lineage in a Sudanese Nomad Tribe*. Oxford: Clarendon, 1966.
Dietrich, Walter. *Samuel*. BKAT 8/3.5. Neukirchen-Vluyn: Neukirchener Verlag, 2017.
Donner, Herbert. *Geschichte des Volkes Israel und seiner Nachbarn in Grundzügen*. GAT 4. Göttingen: Vandenhoeck & Ruprecht, 1987.
Dumermuth, Fritz. "Zur deuteronomischen Kulttheologie und ihren Voraussetzungen." *ZAW* 70 (1958): 59–98.
Finkelstein, Israel, and Lily Singer-Avitz. "Reevaluating Bethel." *ZDPV* 125 (2009): 33–48.
Fleming, Daniel. *The Legacy of Israel in Judah's Bible: History, Politics, and the Reinscribing of Tradition*. Cambridge: Cambridge University Press, 2012.
Fritz, Volkmar. *Das Buch Josua*. HAT 1/7. Tübingen: Mohr Siebeck, 1994.
Gross, Walter. *Richter*. HThKAT. Freiburg im Breisgau: Herder, 2009.
Hanhart, Robert. *Sacharja*. BKAT 14.7. Neukirchen-Vluyn: Neukirchener Verlag, 1998.
Herrmann, Siegfried. *Geschichte Israels in alttestamentlicher Zeit*. Munich: Kaiser, 1973.
Hurowitz, Victor A. "Babylon in Bethel—New Light on Jacob's Dream." Pages 436–48 in *Orientalism, Assyriology and the Bible*. Edited by Steven W. Holloway. Hebrew Bible Monographs 10. Sheffield: Sheffield Phoenix, 2007.
Knauf, Ernst A. "Die Adressatenkreise von Josua." Pages 183–210 in *The Book of Joshua*. Edited by Ed Noort. BETL 250. Leuven: Peeters, 2012.
———. *Midian: Untersuchungen zur Geschichte Palästinas und Nordarabiens am Ende des 2. Jahrtausends v. Chr*. ADPV 10. Wiesbaden: Harrassowitz, 1988.
Koenen, Klaus. *Bethel: Geschichte, Kult und Theologie*. OBO 192. Fribourg: Universitätsverlag; Göttingen: Vandenhoeck & Ruprecht, 2003.
Kratz, Reinhard G. *Die Komposition der erzählenden Bücher des Alten Testaments: Grundwissen der Bibelkritik*. UTB 2157. Göttingen: Vandenhoeck & Ruprecht, 2000.
Levin, Christoph. "Das Alter des Deboralieds." Pages 124–41 in *Fortschreibungen: Gesammelte Studien zum Alten Testament*. BZAW 316. Berlin: de Gruyter, 2003.

———. *Der Jahwist*. FRLANT 157. Göttingen: Vandenhoeck & Ruprecht, 1993.

———. "Das System der zwölf Stämme Israels." Pages 163–78 in *Congress Volume Paris 1992*. Edited by J. A. Emerton. VTSup 61. Leiden: Brill, 1995.

Lipschits, Oded. "Bethel Revisited." Pages 233–46 in *Rethinking Israel: Studies in the History and Archaeology of Ancient Israel in Honor of Israel Finkelstein*. Edited by Oded Lipschits, Yuval Gadot, and Matthew J. Adams. Winona Lake, IN: Eisenbrauns, 2017.

Mayes, Andrew D. H. "The Period of the Judges and the Rise of the Monarchy." Pages 285–331 in *Israelite and Judean History*. Edited by John H. Hayes and J. Maxwell Miller. London: SCM, 1977.

Na'aman, Nadav. "The Jacob Story and the Formation of Biblical Israel." *TA* 41 (2014): 95–125.

Noth, Martin. "Das Krongut der israelitischen Könige und seine Verwaltung." Pages 159–82 in *Archäologische, exegetische und topographische Untersuchungen zur Geschichte Israels*. Vol. 1 of *Aufsätze zur biblischen Landes- und Altertumskunde*. Edited by Hans Walter Wolff. Neukirchen-Vluyn: Neukirchener Verlag, 1971.

———. *Das System der zwölf Stämme Israels*. BWANT 52. Stuttgart: Kohlhammer, 1930.

Renz, Johannes. *Schrift und Schreibertradition: Eine paläographische Studie zum kulturgeschichtlichen Verhältnis von israelitischem Nordreich und Südreich*. ADPV 23. Wiesbaden: Harrassowitz, 1997.

Seeligmann, Isac L. "A Psalm from Pre-Regal Times." Pages 349–64 in *Gesammelte Studien zur Hebräischen Bibel*. Edited by Erhard Blum. FAT 41. Tübingen: Mohr Siebeck, 2004.

Weingart, Kristin. *Stämmevolk—Staatsvolk—Gottesvolk? Studien zur Verwendung des Israel-Namens im Alten Testament*. FAT 2/68. Tübingen: Mohr Siebeck, 2014.

Weippert, Manfred. *Historisches Textbuch zum Alten Testament*. GAT 10. Göttingen: Vandenhoeck & Ruprecht, 2010.

———. "Mōšiʿs Moab." *Transeu* 46 (2014): 133–51.

Wilson, Robert R. *Genealogy and History in the Biblical World*. YNER 7. New Haven: Yale University Press, 1977.

Erhard Blum

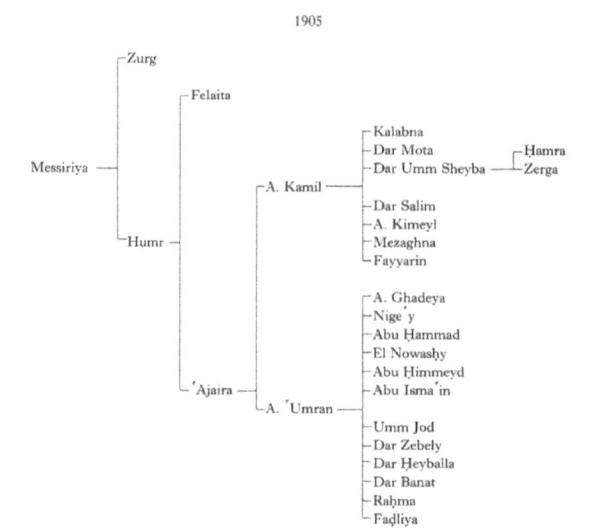

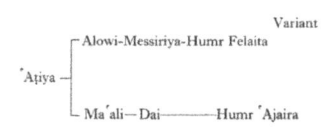

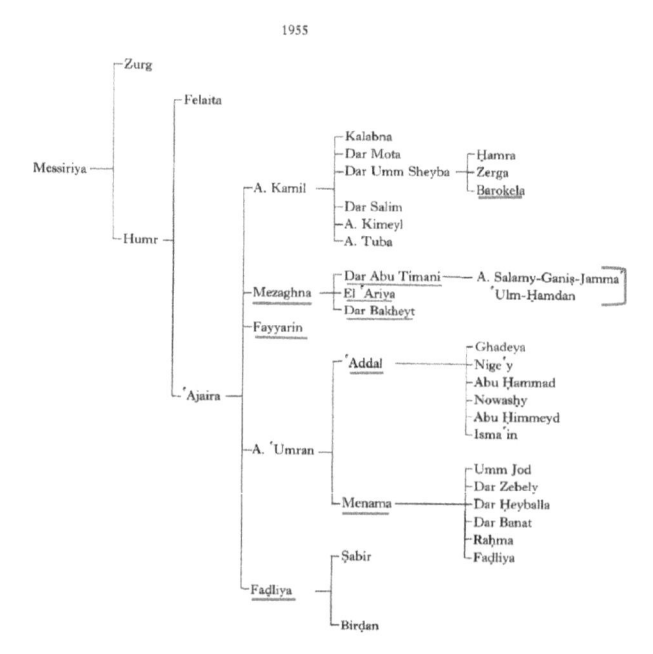

1905

- Messiriya
  - Humr
    - Felaita
      - Zurg
    - Ajaira
      - A. Kamil
        - Kalabna
        - Dar Mota
        - Dar Umm Sheyba
          - Ḥamra
          - Zerga
        - Dar Salim
        - A. Kimeyl
        - Mezaghna
        - Fayyarin
      - A. ʿUmran
        - A. Ghadeya
        - Nigeʿy
        - Abu Ḥammad
        - El Nowashy
        - Abu Ḥimmeyd
        - Abu Ismaʿin
        - Umm Jod
        - Dar Zebely
        - Dar Ḥeyballa
        - Dar Banat
        - Raḥma
        - Faḍliya

Variant

- ʿAṭiya
  - Alowi-Messiriya-Humr Felaita
  - Maʿali — Dai — Humr ʿAjaira

1955

- Messiriya
  - Humr
    - Felaita
      - Zurg
    - ʿAjaira
      - A. Kamil
        - Kalabna
        - Dar Mota
        - Dar Umm Sheyba
          - Ḥamra
          - Zerga
          - Barokela
        - Dar Salim
        - A. Kimeyl
        - A. Tuba
      - Mezaghna
        - Dar Abu Timani — A. Salamy-Ganiṣ-Jamma
        - El ʿAriya   ʿUlm-Ḥamdan
        - Dar Bakheyt
      - Fayyarin
      - A. ʿUmran
        - ʿAddal
          - Ghadeya
          - Nigeʿy
          - Abu Ḥammad
          - Nowashy
          - Abu Ḥimmeyd
          - Ismaʿin
        - Menama
          - Umm Jod
          - Dar Zebely
          - Dar Ḥeyballa
          - Dar Banat
          - Raḥma
          - Faḍliya
      - Faḍliya
        - Ṣabir
        - Birḍan

Charts from Wilson, *Genealogy and History*, see above, p. 204 n. 12.

Contributors

Erhard Blum, University of Tübingen

Israel Finkelstein, Tel Aviv University

Ido Koch, Tel Aviv University

Joachim J. Krause, University of Tübingen

Oded Lipschits, Tel Aviv University

Wolfgang Oswald, University of Tübingen

Omer Sergi, Tel Aviv University

Kristin Weingart, University of Munich

Ancient Sources Index

Hebrew Bible

Genesis
Reference	Page
24	143
27	143
28	216
28:10–22	173
28:11–22	215
29–30	202–3
29–31	215
30:22–24	102, 171
32	203
32–33	215
35:16–18	102, 171
35:16–21	186
35:18–20	173
43:16	103
43:30	103
45:14	103
45:22	103
48:7	186
49	202

Exodus
Reference	Page
15:14	22

Numbers
Reference	Page
1	202
26	202, 208–9
26:29–34	208
27	209
27:1	208
33:45–46	211
36	208

Deuteronomy
Reference	Page
27	105
33	215

Joshua
Reference	Page
6	186
6:8	165, 173
8	186
9	165, 171, 176, 185–86
9:17	180
13:3	20
15:6–10	165
15:21–62	174
15:60	180
16:1–2	163
16:1–3	165
16:5	165
17	209
17:1–3	208
18:11–20	165
18:13	163
18:19	100
18:21–28	174
18:22	163
18:25–28	174
18:26	180
18:28	180
19:2–8	174
19:40–46	174
19:50	44
21:21	44
22:24	148
24	105

Ancient Sources Index

Judges
- 1–21   170
- 1:22–26   163, 172
- 3:3   20
- 3:12–30   95, 172
- 3:15   99
- 3:26–27   172
- 3:31   9
- 4   95
- 4–5   72
- 4:5   44, 99
- 5   213, 216
- 5:6–18   216
- 5:14   172, 217
- 5:14–17   172
- 5:14–18   216–17
- 6:11   207
- 6:15   208
- 7   95
- 8:4–21   70
- 10:1   44
- 11:12   148
- 12:5   136
- 13–16   9
- 14:3   17
- 15:18   17
- 16:5   21
- 16:8   21
- 16:18   21
- 16:23   21
- 16:27   21
- 16:30   21
- 19–21   106, 185–86
- 21   71

1 Samuel
- 1–14   69
- 1:1   44, 136
- 4–2 Sam 8   7
- 5:8   21
- 5:11   21
- 6:1   18
- 6:4   21
- 6:12   21
- 6:16   21
- 6:17   21
- 7   182
- 7:7   21
- 7:14   141
- 8:16–18   78, 93
- 9–14   2, 57, 66–75, 78 186
- 9–2 Sam 5   3, 57, 59, 82
- 9–2 Sam 8   3
- 9:1   189
- 9:1–2   95, 207
- 9:1–10:16   66–67, 75, 93, 189
- 9:2   75
- 9:3   75
- 9:4   172
- 9:4–5   44
- 9:5–10   76
- 9:16   189
- 9:21   189
- 10:2   186
- 10:5   39, 67, 77
- 10:17–27   67, 93, 182
- 10:19–21   207
- 11   66, 189
- 11:1   71, 103
- 11:1–13   94
- 11:1–15   67–68
- 11:3   71
- 11:5   71
- 11:8   47
- 11:9–11   71
- 11:15   67, 78
- 12   93
- 13   189
- 13–14   17, 66–69, 71, 76–79, 94, 189
- 13:2   189
- 13:3   17, 39, 49, 77
- 13:4–6   78
- 13:5–6   71
- 13:7–15   68
- 13:15–16   189
- 13:17–18   17, 71
- 13:17   44
- 13:19–22   71
- 13:20   71, 78
- 14   71

14:1–13	77	20:30–34	76
14:3	144	20:35–42	76
14:6	17	21:11	74
14:16	189	21:11–16	20
14:21–22	17	21:13	74
14:22–24	78	22:3–4	103
14:24–30	76	22:7	95
14:29	76	23–26	74
14:31	71	23:1–5	17–19
14:36–45	76	23:2	81
14:46–52	69	23:4	81
14:47	78, 96	23:19	38
15	93	24:1–2	38
15:27–28	137	24:20–21	94
15:28	138	24:21	96
16–19	76	25:28	94
16–2 Sam 5	57–58, 73–78, 82	26	93
16:1	95	27	18, 74
16:1–13	93	27–2 Sam 1	73
16:14–23	73	27:1	18
16:14	93	27:2–4	74
17	17, 93	27:2–28:2	20
17–19	73	27:3	18
17:1–3	46	27:7	18
17:2	78	27:11	18, 74
17:4	74	27:12	81
17:12	81, 136, 186	28	93
17:14	141	28:17	138
17:23	74	29	20
17:52	74	29–30	74
17:58	81	29:1–11	20
18–19	80	29:2	21
18:1–4	76	29:6–7	21
18:2	81	29:9	21
18:14 30	17	29:11	18
18:17	81	30	18
18:18	81	30:8	81
18:25	17	30:16	18
18:27	17	30:26	81, 170
18:30	21	31	66–73, 75, 77–78, 186, 189
19:1–7	76	31:1	72
20–26	73	31:1–13	68–69, 76–77
20:1	141	31:4	17
20:1–17	76	31:9	18
20:16	94	31:10	72

228   Ancient Sources Index

1 Samuel (cont.)
31:12	71

2 Samuel
1:1–16	93
1:20	17
2:1–4	73, 81–82
2:4	218
2:8–9	172, 188, 217
2:9	36, 47, 50
2:10	95, 218
2:15	95
2:18	136
2:25	95
2:31	95
3:1	94
3:8	69
3:10	96
3:14	17
3:19	95
4:2	95
4:3	183
5	74
5:1–2	80–82
5:1–3	73, 77, 81
5:5	96
5:6	82
5:17–25	77
5:19	81
5:23–24	81
7	93, 146
8:1	77
8:1–15	93
9	77
9–20	95
10:1–2	103
16:5	95, 172
16:7–8	95
19:17	172
19:21	95, 172
20	172
20:1	95, 148, 172
20:2	95
20:21	172
21:1–14	187
21:15	19
21:15–22	17, 39
21:19	46
23:8–39	19
23:8–21	39
23:9–17	17
23:14	17, 39, 49

1 Kings
1 Kgs–2 Kgs	74
1–2	95
1:33	67
1:39	67
2:8	172
2:39–40	20
5:1	18
9:16	119, 125
11	117, 136
11–12	5
11–14	134
11:1	118
11:5	118
11:11–13	137–38
11:14	137
11:23	137
11:26	136, 140
11:26–27	140
11:26–28	136, 147
11:26–39	116
11:26–40	4–5, 133, 135–36, 143
11:27	136, 140, 145
11:29	144
11:29–30	137
11:29–40	135, 137
11:31	137–38, 152
11:32	147
11:32–34	138
11:32–35	140, 152–53
11:35	138
11:36	138, 140, 147, 150
11:37	139, 146
11:38–39	139–40, 146, 149
11:40	123
11:43	117
12:1–20	4, 133, 135, 140, 143

12:1–24	115–17	21:20–22	139
12:2–3	140–41	21:24	139
12:15	141		
12:16	141, 146, 148, 152	2 Kings	
12:17	140–41	2:1–2	173
12:17–18	104	2:4–5	173
12:19	140	2:15	173
12:20	112, 116, 140–41, 150–52	2:18	173
12:21	112, 185	3:4	62
12:21–24	103, 112, 116–18, 152	4:38	173
12:23	185	8:2–3	18
12:25	44, 70	12:18	18
12:25–26	214	12:19	99
12:25–33	133, 145	14:11–13	47
12:32	151	14:11–14	99
13	134	14:25	99
14	118, 122–23, 125	16:7–9	214
14:7–16	147	17	134
14:8	139	23	165, 176
14:21–24	118	23:15–16	174
14:21–31	117–21	25:22–26	179
14:22–24	142		
14:25	115	Isaiah	
14:25–26	121, 124–26	10:28–32	165, 180
14:25–28	119–20	14:29	22
14:26	121	14:31	22
14:26–28	121		
14:29–31	118	Jeremiah	
14:30	117–18, 152	7:12	144
15	127	7:14	144
15:4	139	17:26	169
15:6	118, 152	25:20	21
15:15	7	26:6	144
15:16	119, 126	26:9	144
15:16–22	95, 99, 103, 168	31:15	186
15:17	126	32:7–15	180
15:17–21	214	32:44	169
15:17–22	126–27	33:13	169
15:27	7	39–43	179
16:1–4	139	40–42	169
16:24	61	41:5	216
16:34	173	41:9	126
17:18	148		
21:11	143	Hosea	
21:17	139	4:15	173

Hosea (cont.)
- 5 — 143
- 5:8–10 — 173
- 9:15 — 173
- 12:5 — 173

Joel
- 4:4 — 22

Amos
- 4:4 — 173
- 5:5 — 173
- 6:2 — 18

Micah
- 5:1 — 186

Zechariah
- 7:1–6 — 216

Psalms
- 60:10 — 22
- 78:60 — 144
- 83:8 — 22
- 87:4 — 22
- 108:10 — 22

Ruth
- 1:2 — 136, 186
- 4:11 — 186

Esther
- 2:5 — 106
- 3:1 — 106

Ezra
- 2:25 — 180
- 9:1–2 — 184
- 9:12–15 — 184
- 10:2–3 — 184
- 10:10–15 — 184

Nehemiah
- 3 — 170, 180
- 3:7 — 164
- 3:15 — 164
- 3:19 — 164
- 6:2 — 184
- 7:29 — 180
- 10:31 — 184
- 11:33 — 183
- 12:28–29 — 170

1 Chronicles
- 1:10 — 3
- 2:24 — 186
- 2:50–52 — 186
- 4:4–5 — 186
- 7:14–19 — 208
- 7:28 — 163
- 8:12–13 — 183
- 10:13–14 — 105–6

2 Chronicles
- 9:31 — 113
- 10–11 — 113
- 10:2 — 140
- 10:12 — 71
- 11 — 134
- 11:1 — 185
- 11:1–4 — 113
- 11:3 — 185
- 11:5–12 — 113–14
- 11:10 — 114, 185
- 11:12 — 114
- 11:13–17 — 113, 115
- 11:17 — 115
- 11:18–23 — 114
- 11:23 — 185
- 12:1 — 115
- 12:2–9 — 114–15
- 13 — 134
- 14:7 — 185
- 15:2 — 185
- 15:8–9 — 185
- 25:5 — 185
- 31:1 — 185
- 34:9 — 185
- 34:32 — 185

Ancient Sources Index

Ancient Near Eastern Texts

Amarna correspondence	60
EA 279	19
EA 280	19
EA 287	19
EA 289	19
Karnak Inscription	4, 98, 121–25
Samaria ostraca	6
Mesha Stela	6, 79–80, 210
Merenptah Stela	9, 79
Dan Inscription	79
Kurkh Monolith	79

Septuagint

Joshua
  17:1–3   208

3 Kingdoms
  11:24   136
  11:32   151
  11:36   151
  12:20   150
  12:24   134, 141–42, 150

1 Maccabees
  11:34   44

Josephus

Jewish Antiquities   8

New Testament

Matthew
  27:57   44

John
  19:38   44

Place Names Index

Acco	45, 47
Adullam	37
Ai (et-Tell)	38, 44, 48, 177
Ajalon	23, 98, 183
Ammon	45, 103–4
Amurru	11, 45
Anatoth	178, 180
Arad	18, 167
Aram-Damascus	70, 103, 215
Arimathea	44
Arnon	45
Ashdod	20
Ashkelon	14, 20
Atarot	210–13
Babylon	5, 184
Bahurim	172
Beeroth (Khirbet el-Burj)	163, 175–77, 182–83
Beersheba	18, 65, 167
Beth-hakkerem	165, 170
Beth-horon	23–24, 98, 161
Beth-shean	36, 68, 72
Beth-shemesh	99
Beth-zur	64
Bethel	5, 33, 35, 42–44, 60, 64–65, 69, 78, 83, 98–99, 133, 161, 163–65, 167, 171–74, 177–79, 189–90
Bethlehem	17, 23, 39, 42, 46, 49, 64, 78, 81, 167, 169, 186
Bezeq	46
City of David	39–42, 63, 168
Crete	8
Cyprus	14
Dan	145
Dead Sea	99
Debir (Khirbet Rabûd)	168, 171
Dibon	211
Ebla	79
Edom	103
Egypt	48–50, 215
Ekron (Tel Miqne)	14–15, 20, 22–23, 39
el-Jib. *See* Gibeon	
Elah Valley	23–24, 36–38, 46
et-Tell. *See* Ai	
Gath (Tell es-Ṣafi)	14, 18–20, 22–23, 38–39, 45–46, 49, 71–72, 74, 104, 183
Gaza	20, 22
Geba (Jaba)	17, 35–36, 39, 43, 49, 99, 126, 189
Gibeah (Tell el-Full)	35, 39, 43–44, 71, 78, 98–99, 101–2, 107, 175, 178, 180, 189
Gezer	14, 98, 161, 166, 180
Gibeon (el-Jib)	5–6, 23, 35, 37–39, 43–44, 46, 48–49, 98, 100–102, 107, 122, 163–65, 167, 175–82, 189–91
Gihon Spring	40
Gilead	35–37, 48, 69–71, 96, 166
Gilgal	67–68, 161, 173, 189, 214
Gittaim	183
Greece	9
Hakephirah	177
Hazor	62
Hebron	6, 23, 38, 45, 96, 167–71, 185, 191
Heleq	209
Ḥoronaim	211–12
Idumaea	171
Jaba. *See* Geba	
Jabbok River	35, 48, 70

Place Names Index

Jabesh-gilead 47, 67–68, 71
Jericho 5, 161, 163–164, 167, 171–74, 177–78, 180, 190, 214
Jerusalem 1–6, 19, 33, 37–42, 44–51, 58, 60, 62–66, 69, 71–72, 80–83, 96, 98–100, 103–4, 107, 112, 114–15, 119, 122–23, 127, 139, 161, 163–71, 174–76, 178–87, 189–91
Jezreel 62, 96, 218
Jezreel Valley 47, 49, 60, 62, 64, 72, 166
Jordan River 35
Judah 18, 94, 96, 97, 99–101, 103–7, 214–15
Keilah 18–19
Khirbet ed-Dawwara 44, 48
Khirbet el-Burj. *See* Beeroth
Khirbet Qeiyafa 35, 37, 45–46, 48–49
Khirbet Rabûd. *See* Debir
Kiriath-jearim 177, 180
Kuntillet 'Ajrud 47
Lebanon 45
Lebo-Hamat 99
Lod 180, 183, 190
Mahanaim 70
Manasseh 209
Mari 79
Megiddo 14, 49, 62
Michmash 36, 161, 178, 189
Millo 145
Mizpah (Tell en-Nasbeh) 5, 21, 44, 65, 99–100, 126, 163–66, 168, 170, 175–76, 178–87, 190
Moab 45, 62, 80, 162, 103–4, 211–12
Modi'in 183, 190
Motza 100, 179–81
Mount Baal Hazor 167
Mount Gilboa 21, 36, 46, 68
Mount Scopus 181
Nahal Og 180
Nahal Soreq 180
Nebi Samwil 163, 175, 178, 181–82
Nebo 211, 12
Negev 123
Ono Valley 180, 183–84, 190
Ophrah 44, 174

P(e)nuel 69–70, 122, 124, 141
Philistia 9, 12, 22–23
Rama 44, 99
Ramat Raḥel 101, 165, 170, 176, 181–85
Ramathaim 44
Rantis 44
Ras Karkar 44
Rephaim Valley 167, 170, 181
Samaria 1, 3, 57, 59–62, 64–65, 69, 77–78, 80, 100–101, 104–5, 134, 162–64, 179–80, 214
Seir 172
Sha'alim 44
Shalishah 44
Shechem 1, 3, 37–38, 42–44, 46–50, 60–62, 64–65, 69–70, 78, 105, 162–63, 166, 209
Shephelah 18, 23, 36, 38, 45, 49, 71, 74, 164–65, 174, 176–77, 183
Shiloh 42, 60, 64–65, 144
Succoth 70
Sudan 204
Tel Masos 46
Tel Miqne. *See* Ekron
Tell Beit-Mirsim 9
Tell el-Far'ah (N). *See* Tirzah
Tell el-Far'ah (S) 23
Tell el-Full. *See* Gibeah
Tell en-Nasbeh. *See* Mizpah
Tell es-Ṣafi. *See* Gath
Tirzah (Tell el-Far'ah [N]) 1, 61–62, 64, 69, 98–99, 101–2
Tsubah 181
Yehud 105, 171, 180, 182, 190, 213
Yenoam 14
Zemarajim 98, 174
Zeredah 44, 136
Zuph 44

Ingram Content Group UK Ltd.
Milton Keynes UK
UKHW040637190323
418778UK00003B/43